THE CONSTITUTION
That Delicate Balance

BOOKS BY FRED W. FRIENDLY

See It Now (with Edward R. Murrow)
Due to Circumstances Beyond Our Control . . .
The Good Guys, the Bad Guys and the First Amendment
Minnesota Rag

THE CONSTITUTION
That Delicate Balance

Fred W. Friendly
Martha J. H. Elliott

Random House New York

98765

Copyright © 1984 by Random House, Inc.

Library of Congress Cataloging in Publication Data

Friendly, Fred W.
  The Constitution—that delicate balance.

  Bibliography: p.
  Includes index.
  1. United States—Constitutional law. 2. United States. Supreme Court. I. Elliott, Martha J. H. II. Title.
KF4550.F73   1984   342.73   84-42656
ISBN 0-394-54074-3   347.302
ISBN 0-394-33943-6 (pbk.)

Cover and interior design: Barbara A. Grodsky
Manufactured in the United States of America

Cover Photo: Robert Glander/Shostal Associates

To Potter Stewart, who has taught us
". . . what the British Crown had feared—
and what the American Founders decided to risk."

Prologue

WHOSE TRIAL IS THIS ANYWAY?

It was an unusually long oral argument—two hours when most are only one. At noon on March 29, 1961, the nine members of the United States Supreme Court began listening to oral arguments in *Mapp* v. *Ohio,* a case that seemed to be challenging the constitutionality of Ohio's obscenity laws. Then, late in the arguments, Chief Justice Earl Warren leaned forward and asked Ohio's advocate the whereabouts of Dollree Mapp, the woman who had been sentenced to 1 to 7 years in the state penitentiary for possession of obscene materials. The prosecutor, Gertrude Bauer Mahon, answered, "She's never served time. She's out on bail."

Actually, Dollree Mapp was sitting in the spectators' section of the courtroom. She had traveled all the way from Cleveland to hear the arguments that would decide whether she would go to prison. But to prosecutor Mahon and the justices, she was a nonperson, just another spectator in that majestic setting. Dollree Mapp's thought was "whose trial is this anyway?"

Miss Mapp is one of the very few who have witnessed her own Bill of Rights case being decided by the highest tribunal in the land. But all the cases that have shaped our Constitution have names attached—from Barron to Near to Mapp to Francis to DeJonge to Doe and Roe. They are seemingly faceless names in a pageant, names known to constitutional scholars and lawyers as citations rather than as human beings testing their rights.

Constitutional law and interpretation meanders like an ancient river, winding its way through valleys, continuously cutting new channels. The chapters in this book chart some of these channels. What follows is a series of essays that reach beyond the scholarly casebooks and bring to life some of the human dramas which have helped determine what our Constitution means, reminding us that all landmark cases begin with people.

Justice Felix Frankfurter once observed that "the safeguards of liberty have frequently been forged in controversies involving not very nice people." Some were; some were not. The names of the people involved in these landmark cases appear on no hallowed honor roll; the facts of how they reached the high court are often forgotten, but these cases can teach us all something about how that delicate balance between individual rights and the rights of society works. They also help explain how our Constitution adapts to changing times and how one Supreme Court corrects errors of past courts. These cases are what shaped the Constitution into the living document that Chief Justice John Marshall said it must become.

On September 17, 1787, the framers signed the Constitution, but that did not end the writing of that document. As the delegates left Philadelphia and the ratification process began, one Philadelphia pamphleteer asked that future generations not consider it error-proof. Tench Coxe wrote: "There is no spirit of arrogance in the new federal Constitution. When experience has taught us its mistakes, the people whom it preserves, absolutes all powerful, can reform and amend them." Two years later the 462 words of the Bill of Rights were added; since then 16 other amendments have updated the Constitution, addressing the issues of slavery, women's suffrage, prohibition, income tax, and presidential succession. Yet the amendments are only a part of the updating. The Constitution has also been shaped by the 104 justices of the Supreme Court—from John Jay to Sandra Day O'Connor—as they applied that eighteenth-century document to a constantly shifting spectrum of disputes. The cases involved issues ranging from one man's wharf and the silt in Baltimore harbor to one woman's right to have an abortion to the rights of children of illegal aliens. These "petty cases," as Justice Frankfurter called them, which caused the Constitution to review itself, frequently began in such humdrum places as gloomy police stations or high school classrooms or bank branches.

It turns out that the 1787 version of the Constitution was only the first draft of what we now call the law of the land. A parade of disparate claims brought by citizens and noncitizens demanding their day in court has made all the difference. These heroes and scoundrels, winners and losers, may have had as much to do with the writing of the Constitution as the drafters. They fought the system and proved that the written Constitution was worth more than the parchment it was written on—if only by showing that it could adapt as the nation grew and changed in the centuries that followed. It is these cases and the justices of the Supreme Court that have insured that our basic charter was not a prolix legal code but a human document. As Chief Justice Marshall wrote, the Constitution was "intended to endure for the ages . . . and consequently to be adapted to the various crises of human affairs."

The Constitution has to do with our law, but it also has to do with how we live our lives and the anguishing choices that confront us and our society every day. "A free government is a complicated piece of machinery," wrote John Adams, "the nice and exact adjustment of whose springs, wheels, and weights is not yet well comprehended by the artists of this age and still less by the people." From that contraption of springs, wheels, and weights, constructed in Philadelphia, has come a living Constitution. Those who have relied on it, from John Barron to Estelle Griswold to Dollree Mapp, may not have comprehended all its complexities and ambiguities, but in pleading for their rights they laid out a schematic plan for all of us who want to learn how it works.

This book does not attempt to cover all the parts of our Constitution. It is intended to provide a background and understanding of those pivotal issues that are raised in the television series "The Constitution: That Delicate Balance." The aim of the book, as of the series, is not to change but to open minds, to provide insights into how Supreme Court justices, presidents, journalists, and others have faced up to complex, but crucial decisions. To quote John Marshall again, "the Constitution is meant to be understood by the public." We hope this book, along with the television series, will provide a way for all citizens—not just lawyers and judges—to take part in the great constitutional debates of our time.

Contents

The Constitution of the United States is not a self-executing document.

Where, ladies and gentlemen [of the press], do you think these great constitutional rights that you were so vehemently asserting, and in which you were so conspicuously wallowing yesterday, where do you think they came from? The stork didn't bring them. These came from the judges of this country, from these villains here sitting at the table. That's where they came from. They came because the courts of this country at some time or place when some other agency of government was trying to push the press around or, indeed, may be trying to do you in, it's the courts that protected you. And that's where all these constitutional rights came from. . . . It's not that it was done for you or that it was done for ourselves. It happened because it is our understanding that that's what the Constitution provides and protects. But let me point out that the Constitution of the United States is not a self-executing document. . . .

If you look at the literal language in the First Amendment of the Constitution of the United States, it says, "Congress shall pass no law abridging the freedom of the press." That's all it says on this subject, absolutely all. It doesn't say a word about what a state can or can't do. It doesn't say a word about a reporter's privilege before a grand jury. . . . The very fact that these protections are available is attributable to the creative work of the judiciary over the last 190 years.

If you say it's self-evident, that this was always clear, let me tell you that it wasn't always so clear. If you went back to the original understanding of our ancestors, back in the early years of the nineteenth century, you would find that their understanding of this clause and the Constitution in their judgment allowed them to enact the Alien and Sedition law. And if those laws were still on the books, Richard Nixon would still be President of the United States and Spiro Agnew would still be Vice President of the United States, and all of you people would probably be in prison.

Justice Potter Stewart
Washington Post/Ford Foundation
Seminar on Media and the Law,
March 9, 1975[1]

Baltimore harbor, c. 1830. *The Bettmann Archive*

John Barron's profitable wharf in Baltimore Harbor was being ruined because of excavation and street grading by the city of Baltimore. Barron and his partner felt the city should pay for the damage because the Fifth Amendment protected citizens from having their property taken away without just compensation. But the Supreme Court said the Bill of Rights did not apply to the states or local government. This chapter explains how the Court came to that conclusion, as well as the history of the framing of the Bill of Rights. It also explains important judicial powers such as judicial review and shows how Chief Justice John Marshall turned the Supreme Court from a weak tribunal into the ultimate arbiter of constitutional conflicts.

BARRON'S WHARF
The First Test
of the Bill of Rights

For within one year last past, many parts of Our
Wharves have been filled up with sand and dirt from
four to six feet. We apprehend, and fear, that if the City
Commissioners continue digging diteches to alter the
Water Course ... that Our Wharves will be useless to us,
and intirely ruinned.

Letter of **Hezekiah Waters,** April 2, 1817

America at the dawn of the nineteenth century was an awakening economic power. The continental nation, unexplored and unexploited, offered limitless possibilities for young men with courage and foresight.

Such a hardy soul was John Barron. Scion of an old and established Baltimore family, Barron in 1815 joined with John Craig to purchase a dock and warehouse on the Fell's Point harbor front of Baltimore. Until 1800, Annapolis had been the major city of Maryland and the surrounding area, but as shipping had grown, its harbor had lacked the depth to accommodate the ever greater clipper ships and trade carriers. A valuable prize was to be had by the person or persons who could find safe harbor for the traders of the central states.

Fell's Point on the east side of the Baltimore harbor seemed to be an ideal site. It was deep and well protected on the Patapsco River, sheltered behind the promontory of Fort McHenry from both storm and hostile invaders—an important consideration, as the burning of Washington, D.C., in the War of 1812 was still a vivid memory. Moreover, Fell's Point had a long and successful maritime history of its own. The first cruisers of the navy of the "Thirteen United Colonies" had been fitted out there in 1775. On January 24, 1777, the Fell's Point shipyard of George Wells, at Thames and Bond streets, had delivered the *Virginia,* a frigate of 28 guns and the first ship built for the Continental navy.[1]

It is not surprising, then, that Craig and Barron had been attracted to the fistlike peninsula of Fell's Point. There, each day, tall sailing ships, their cargo holds swollen with coffee from South American plantations, would tie up to wooden wharves jutting out from the land. The coffee would be off-loaded into adjoining four-story warehouses, warehouses that also held cotton which the ships would carry away to northern mills to be spun into cloth. This was a profitable and highly competitive business, with only one indisputable requirement: a deep-water location and serviceable dock. Craig and Barron's dock was one of the few in Baltimore that could accommodate vessels of four and five hundred tons "drawing upwards of seventeen feet of water."[2]

Today, Craig and Barron's warehouse is, of course, gone, but its location can still be seen on the aged maps that decorate the entrance to the Baltimore Historical Society. And from those maps the problem becomes evident. Craig and Barron had decided to locate their shipping operation at the foot of Aliceanna Street on the point. This location gave them access to the markets and placed them on the eastern extremity of the point. It also placed them closest to the mainland—probably out of the sweep of the more powerful currents of the Patapsco River, but, unfortunately, in the way of runoff from the city itself.

The boom that allowed Fell's Point to expand so quickly also had its impact on the city of Baltimore. Building went on continually and construction meant excavation; the excavation combined with the rain and the swollen streams of Baltimore County meant vast amounts of silt-laden runoff pouring into the Patapsco River, and settling, as it turned out, beneath the docks of traders like Craig and Barron. Just two years after the purchase, the wharf was under siege from silt and mud. Fearing for their business, the owners decided to fight city hall—a decision that led ultimately to the first real test of the Bill of Rights. The question was whether Baltimore could deprive Craig and Barron of their property without due process and without just compensation.

THE LEGAL BATTLE BEGINS

In 1817 Hezekiah Waters and ten other enraged wharf owners, including Barron and Craig, wrote to the city charging that "Our Wharves are likely to be filled upe and ruinned by reason of the large torrent or collection of rain Water which descends from Washington Street directly to the front of Our Wharves. . . . [F]or within one year last past, many parts of Our Wharves have been filled up with sand and dirt from four to six feet. We apprehend, and fear, that if the City Commissioners continue digging ditches to alter the Water Course . . . that Our Wharves will be useless to us, and intirely ruinned."[3] The wharf owners then requested that the sand and dirt be dredged at the expense of the city.

But the city of Baltimore turned a deaf ear to the businessmen, and the paving of streets, dam building, and regrading continued. By 1822 Barron and Craig had endured all they could and hired a lawyer, Charles

F. Mayer. They wanted to take legal steps to force the city to pay for the damages, but it would be a slow, painstaking process. Although the parties first appeared in court on March 28, 1822, it was only after three years and six postponements that Mayer's formal plea was made.

The strongly worded document charged that the "mayor and city council of Baltimore, well knowing the premises, but wrongfully and injuriously contriving and intending to injure the said Craig and Barron . . . wrongfully and injuriously turned and diverted certain streams of water, and graded and paved streets, and cut down certain grounds, and erected and made certain dams and ditches and embankments,"[4] all of which resulted in the harbor being filled in with sand, dirt, and clay. Mayer assessed the damages to his clients at $20,000. He was proposing that as the city had taken away Barron and Craig's property, they deserved just compensation.

The case dragged on, with delay after delay, for three more years. It wasn't until March 1828—six years after the complaint was first presented in court—that a jury was finally called. By this time Barron's partner, Craig, had died. But Barron decided to continue his fight against city hall. As the trial progressed, the jury heard extensive evidence. Witnesses testified as to the depth of the harbor at various times in the past and its present depth and condition. The twelve men listened as the history of Baltimore's street paving and grading was presented by both sides.

The positions were clear. On behalf of his client, Mayer was trying to prove that the city fathers had made the short-sighted error of diverting all the streams and runoff into one area. The result of this error was the silting of the East Bay. The solution, Mayer argued, was simple: pay Barron for the damages done to his dock.

The city council and the mayor's position, argued by their attorney John Scott, was that they had acted in their official capacity and under laws passed by the state legislature and city. Their motive in acting was the welfare and benefit of the city. They also introduced evidence that "there is a great tendency in every part of Baltimore Harbor to become shallower from the washings from the surrounding hills."[5] It was often necessary, they claimed, to dredge out the harbor with "the mud machines," but this was done at the dock owners' expense.

When the trial judge charged the jury on May 14, 1828, it was clear where his sentiments lay. He told the twelve men that if they believed that Craig and Barron's property had been injured by the runoff, the owners were "entitled to damages." Although the judge did not mention the federal Constitution's Fifth Amendment guarantee that property shall not "be taken for public use without just compensation," the spirit of the amendment can certainly be felt in his words that "it would be unjust [that Barron should be] deprived of his property without remuneration."[6] The jury, apparently sympathetic to Barron's predicament, ruled in his favor, but was willing to award only $4,500 in compensation.

By the end of July, the city of Baltimore had requested an appeal. In his arguments at the state court, Mayer now charged specifically that his client's Fifth Amendment rights had been abridged. But the wheels of justice turned as slowly in Maryland's high court as they had in the trial court. It wasn't until December 6, 1830, that the court of appeals reversed the jury verdict. Six months later the decision was appealed on a writ of error to the United States Supreme Court "on the ground of it [the judgment] being repugnant to the Constitution of the United States." Barron's decision to fight the city fathers was about to present Chief Justice John Marshall with what turned out to be his first Bill of Rights case and his last monumental constitutional issue.

THE MARSHALL COURT

At the time Barron's case was finally argued before the Supreme Court, John Marshall had been molding the Court in his own image for more than 30 years. In the wake of a Federalist defeat in the election of 1800, Secretary of State Marshall had been nominated to the Court by outgoing President John Adams. In fact, in the waning moments of the Adams administration, Marshall had held both the chief justiceship and the office of secretary of state. Marshall then spent his 35 years on the Court with three driving goals in mind: strengthening the Union, which he saw as a "well regulated democracy";[7] strengthening the United States Constitution; and strengthening the federal judiciary, especially the Supreme Court, which he felt should be on an equal plane with the Congress and the presidency.

Marshall's strong Federalist sentiments supporting the Union and the Constitution should have been no surprise. In 1788 at the Virginia Ratifying Convention, he had voiced his firm support for the new Constitution and especially for the judiciary. He had been picked to champion the Federalist position and specifically to counter the eloquent rhetoric of Patrick Henry, who, as an Antifederalist opposing the Constitution, severely attacked the judicial system.[8] In his eloquent defense, Marshall asked, "To what quarter will you look for protection from an infringement on the Constitution if you will not give the power to the judiciary? There is no other body that can afford such protection."[9]

But in 1801 this branch of government, which lacked both "the sword [and] the purse,"[10] was far from being the defender of rights that Marshall had earlier envisioned. Before nominating Marshall, John Adams had offered the chief justice's post to John Jay, who had served as the nation's first chief justice.[11] In rejecting the offer, Jay wrote: "I left the bench perfectly convinced that under a system so defective it would not obtain the energy, weight and dignity which was essential to its affording due support to the national government; not acquire the public confidence and respect which, as the last resort of the justice of the nation, it should possess."[12] So it was the new chief justice's challenge to breathe life into that still-fledgling institution. "Marshall . . . moved into a judicial vacuum and in thirty-five years converted the Supreme Court from an object of derision, even contempt, to a major coordinate agency of the national government."[13]

One of Marshall's first strengthening measures was to institute the practice of having a single justice—often the chief justice—issue an opinion for the entire Court. Prior to that, the justices had simply given their opinions *seriatim,* or individually.[14] The repercussions of this change were enormous. As Marshall's biographer Leonard Baker points out, under Marshall the Supreme Court spoke "as an institution and in so doing it sought and achieved a moral force as great as that obtained by the presidency and the Congress."[15] Moreover, Marshall was able to use this change in molding the Court. Of the 1106 opinions issued by the Marshall Court, the chief justice wrote 519, and he delivered 36 of the 62 decisions involving major constitutional questions.[16]

Thomas Jefferson, Marshall's cousin and relentless enemy, was one of the first to comment on this new practice. "Another most condemnable practice of the supreme court to be corrected is that of cooking up a decision in Caucus & delivering it by one of their members as the opinion of the court, without the possibility of our knowing how many, who, and for what reasons each member concurred,"[17] wrote Jefferson. "An opinion is huddled up in conclave perhaps by a majority of one, delivered as if unanimous, and with the silent acquiescence of lazy or timid associates, by a crafty chief judge, who sophisticates the law to his own mind."[18]

Even Marshall had made it "his custom" to acquiesce silently when he had "the misfortune to differ from th[e] Court."[19] Historian William Crosskey has suggested that his reason may have been that "he wished to disguise from the country at large that the Constitution had, in fact, been flouted."[20]

Giving Constitutional Force to Judicial Review

In order to consider a case like Barron's, the Court had to claim a power not explicitly granted to it by the federal Constitution—judicial review. This refers to the power to look at the acts of Congress or state legislatures and the actions of the executive branch in light of the Constitution and, if an action is found to go beyond constitutional limits, to declare it unconstitutional and therefore void. Judicial review has been described as "a terrestrial forum for the peaceful resolution of conflicts, thus institutionalizing revolution"[21] and as "the substitution of a court of law for the battlefield to determine the correctness of a governmental act."[22]

It had been practiced by some courts in the colonial period and some of the delegates at the Constitutional Convention had suggested that the Supreme Court should have a "negative" on the legislature. Nevertheless, judicial review was not specifically written into the Constitution. But where explicit language failed, interpretation stepped in. In *The Federalist,* No. 78, Alexander Hamilton discussed the concept of judicial review. "There is no position which depends on a clearer principle than that every act of a delegated authority, contrary to the tenor of the commission under which it is exercised is void," he wrote. "No legislative act, therefore, contrary to the Constitution, can be valid. To deny this would be to affirm that the deputy is greater than his principle; that the servant is above his master; that the representatives of the people are superior to the people themselves." Hamilton explained that the legislature could not be the judge of the constitutionality of its own acts. It was necessary, he argued, to interpose the courts between the people and the legislature "to keep the latter within the limits assigned to their authority. The interpretation of the laws is the proper and peculiar province of the courts."

Marshall too had made his position clear very early on. As a 33-year-old lawyer arguing for the adoption of the Constitution at the Virginia Ratifying Convention of 1788, he had spelled out the doctrine of judicial review. "If Congress makes a law not warranted by any of the powers enumerated, it would be considered by the judges as an infringement of the Constitution which they are to guard. They would not consider such a law coming within their jurisdiction. They would declare it void." Fifteen years later, in 1803, Marshall would have the chance to solidify that sentiment in his first opinion of constitutional magnitude, *Marbury* v. *Madison.*

The case of the midnight judges might have gone down in the annals of history as the sloppiness of lame duck Secretary of State John Marshall had it not been for that same man's ability "to turn a dilemma into a victory."[23]

What appeared to be at stake in the *Marbury* case was the appointment of William Marbury to the prosaic office of a justice of the peace for the District of Columbia.[24] The appointment had been signed by outgoing President John Adams late in the evening on March 3, 1801, the night before Thomas Jefferson's inauguration. However, the formal appointment documents had never been delivered to Marbury and some other appointees; ironically, that oversight was largely the fault of then Secretary of State John Marshall. Almost 10 months after Jefferson took office, Marbury asked the Supreme Court to order James Madison, Jefferson's secretary of state, to deliver the documents so that he could be sworn in to his new post.[25]

One wonders why Chief Justice Marshall even participated in the arguments and decision, since the case dealt with his own responsibilities as secretary of state. A justice today would have recused himself, but in 1803 Marshall apparently saw no conflict of interest or perhaps simply could not resist the opportunities he saw in writing the opinion.

What was startling at the time about the thundering opinion was that Marshall scolded President Jefferson and Secretary of State Madison for denying poor Marbury the job. What lives on for future generations is that Marshall decided that the Supreme Court did not have the power to give Marbury his appointment but that it did have the constitutional power to strike down acts of Congress. In the end, Marbury didn't get the lowly job of justice of the peace that he wanted, but Marshall got what he wanted: a firmly established system of judicial review that gave the Supreme Court enormous power. He was also able to spell out the theory of the supremacy of a written Constitution over acts of a legislature.

Specifically, Marbury had asked the Court to issue a writ of man· damus* to Madison. That writ would have forced Madison to deliver the commission. Marbury had taken his case directly to the Supreme Court, in accordance with Section 13 of the Judiciary Act of 1789, which had given the Supreme Court original jurisdiction (i.e., the power hear a case the first time it is tried) to issue this type of writ to government officials. Marshall now said that that section of the act was unconstitutional. He reasoned that since the Constitution had not given the Supreme Court that particular power of original jurisdiction, the Congress could not give it that power either. So, in his own crafty way, Marshall had denied the Court a miniscule power while setting in concrete a monumental one—judicial review. For although judicial review had been a practice in several states in the colonial era, this was the first time that an act of Congress had been overturned.[26]

It was also the first time that the constitutional principle had been so didactically and forcefully stated. If an annotated copy of the Constitution had but one "hidden amendment," it would be this "commandment" by Marshall:

The question, whether an act, repugnant to the constitution, can become the law of the land, is a question deeply interesting to the United States; but, happily, not of an intricacy proportioned to its interest. . . .

The powers of the legislature are defined and limited; and that those limits may not be mistaken, or forgotten, the constitution is written. To what purpose are powers limited, and to what purpose is that limitation committed to writing, if these limits may, at any time, be passed by those intended to be restrained? The distinction between a government with limited and unlimited powers, is abolished, if those limits do not confine

*A writ of mandamus is an order by a court ordering another court, a government official, or in some cases an individual to perform an act. The purpose of the order is to restore the rights or privileges being denied to the complainant.

the persons on whom they are imposed, and if acts prohibited and acts allowed, are of equal obligation. It is a proposition too plain to be contested, that the constitution controls any legislative act repugnant to it; or, that the legislature may alter the constitution by an ordinary act.

Between these alternatives there is no middle ground. The constitution is either a superior paramount law, unchangeable by ordinary means, or it is on a level with ordinary legislative acts, and like other acts, is alterable when the legislature shall please to alter it.

If the former part of the alternative be true, then a legislative act contrary to the constitution is not law: if the latter part be true, then written constitutions are absurd attempts, on the part of the people, to limit a power, in its own nature illimitable.

Certainly all those who have framed written constitutions contemplate them as forming the fundamental and paramount law of the nation, and consequently the theory of every such government must be that an act of the legislature, repugnant to the constitution, is void.

This theory is essentially attached to a written constitution. . . .

It is emphatically the province and duty of the judicial department to say what the law is.[27]

Marbury v. *Madison* was Marshall's first major constitutional decision. *Barron* v. *Baltimore* would be his last. In between Marshall spent his career always remembering that "it is a constitution we are expounding."[28] As Leonard Baker points out, "His genius was that he could develop these principles in such a coherent way, make them appear to be so much a part of the case as he did in *Marbury,* that they seemed irrefutable at least to future generations of judges. [Legal historian] Edwin S. Corwin quotes John Randolph [the Virginia attorney and ardent Antifederalist] crying in despair at a Marshall decision: 'All wrong, all wrong, but no man in the United States can tell why or wherein.' "[29] His opinions gave new sinew to a Constitution and a Court that had been little more than ideas in the minds of men.

BARRON GOES TO THE SUPREME COURT— TESTING THE BILL OF RIGHTS

When Charles Mayer, Barron's lawyer, went to Washington in 1833, he found a dusty, muddy "city of magnificent intentions with broad avenues that begin in nothing and lead nowhere," as Charles Dickens had described it. Hogs, cows, and geese roamed the undrained swamp that was desperately trying to become a city and a capital.

The original Supreme Court chamber, where Barron's case would be argued, was in the same primitive condition as the city. Because the Court had no permanent home, Congress had given it a crypt beneath the old Senate—a dank, cold basement space only 24 feet wide and 30 feet

long. The room was described by the *New York Tribune* as "a potato hole
of a place . . . a queer room of small dimensions and shaped overhead like
a quarter section of a pumpkin shell."[30] Others viewed it more kindly. A
visitor in the late 1820s was "impressed by the Court's simplicity." The
justices sat at a long table and the lawyers sat on cushioned chairs;
spectators were given comfortable sofas. Opposite the justices was a rep-
lica of the Goddess of Justice.[31]

To argue the case, the State of Maryland sent one of its own legal
giants, Roger Brooke Taney. Taney would soon become attorney general*
under President Andrew Jackson and would eventually succeed Marshall
as chief justice. In 1857 Taney would write the shattering *Dred Scott*
decision, which triggered the Civil War (see Chapter 2). But in 1833 Roger
Taney was in Annapolis as Maryland's attorney general. One of his assist-
ants, John Scott, had been primarily responsible for arguing the case at
the trial court, with Taney making an occasional appearance. However,
Taney did not miss the chance to travel to Washington to argue for states'
rights versus the Fifth Amendment and, in particular, for Baltimore's
right not to be obliged to pay Barron any damages.

Taney and Mayer sat facing the seven justices, with Chief Justice
Marshall in the middle; one ancient Federalist surrounded by Republicans. Marshall, now 75, was frail and greying, his body still weak from
a bladder operation the year before. The golden age of the Marshall Court
was ending. The chief justice had suffered two major defeats. The more
severe blow was an emotional one—the death of his wife, Polly, on December 26, 1831.[32] The second defeat had come in 1832, when President
Andrew Jackson refused to enforce Marshall's decision in *Worcester* v.
Georgia.[33] In that case the Court had ruled that Georgia had no legislative
authority over Cherokee Nation lands and ordered the release of a missionary prosecuted under an unconstitutional Georgia statute which forbade white people from being on Indian lands. On hearing Marshall's
opinion, President Andrew Jackson is reported to have said, "John Marshall made his decision, now let him enforce it." Whether the story is
apocryphal or not, Jackson never moved to enforce the court order, and
Georgia did not release missionary Worcester, though he was later pardoned by the governor.

Attorney Mayer, speaking for dock owner Barron, was the first to
address the Court. He never got to talk about the wharf and the silt. He
was immediately directed by the justices to confine "the argument to the
question whether, under the amendment to the constitution the court had
jurisdiction of the case." According to the court reporter, Mayer argued
that the city's "exercise of authority was repugnant to the Constitution

---

*In the time that elapsed between the argument of *Barron* and the decision, Taney was elevated
from attorney general of Maryland to attorney general of the United States.

of the United States, contravening the fifth article of the Amendments to the Constitution, which declares that 'private property shall not be taken for public use without just compensation,' the plaintiff contending that this article declares principles which regulate the legislation of the States, for the protection of the people in each and all of the states regarded as citizens of the United States or as inhabitants subject to the laws of the Union."[34] In plain language, Mayer was trying to convince the Court that the Fifth Amendment required Baltimore to compensate Barron for having destroyed the value of his wharf.

It was then Taney and Scott's turn to address the Court, but the armed-for-battle Taney was barely able to open his mouth. The chief justice stopped him short. He said he needed no pleadings by the state of Maryland; apparently the Court had already made up its mind.

WHY A WRITTEN BILL OF RIGHTS?

To understand Barron's case and the issue before the Court, one has to go back to the birth of the Bill of Rights, to what it was intended to achieve and what was said in the debates in Congress. Marshall was well aware of the debates over the passage of the Bill of Rights. Indeed, as mentioned earlier, he had been part of the Virginia Ratifying Convention which, like the conventions in many other states, had urged the passage of written constitutional guarantees of liberty.

The Bill of Rights was not part of the original U.S. Constitution written in 1787 and ratified in 1789, but had been drafted in 1789 and ratified in 1791. It was motivated by the conviction of men such as Thomas Jefferson, James Madison, and George Mason that a written constitution would be a hollow document without specific measures to protect minorities from the tyranny of the majority. Jefferson, earlier the chief architect of the Declaration of Independence, had not been a member of the Constitutional Convention.[35] Although enthusiastic about the Constitution as drafted, Jefferson nonetheless felt, as he wrote to Madison from Paris, that "there is also for me a bitter pill or two." He continued, "The Bill of Rights is what the people are entitled to against every government on earth, general or particular [i.e., federal or state] and what no just government should refuse or rest on interferences."[36]

Others, such as Alexander Hamilton, scoffed at the idea of a written bill of rights. In *The Federalist* papers, he described the existing bills of rights in the states as "aphorisms . . . which would sound much better in a treatise of ethics than in a constitution of government."[37] Such protections, Hamilton wrote, are redundancies. To him, the Constitution enumerated the powers of the federal government. As the Constitution did not give the new government the power to abridge fundamental freedoms, there was no danger. In fact, to Hamilton, the danger lay in trying to list all the rights to be protected, because some might be inadvertently overlooked. "I go no further," he wrote in *The Federalist,* "and affirm that bills of rights . . . are not only unnecessary in the proposed Constitution but would even be dangerous. They would contain various exceptions of powers which are not granted; and, in this very account, would afford a colorable pretext to claim more than they were granted. For why declare that things shall be done for which there is no power to do?"[38]

Much of that sentiment was present when James Madison's proposed amendments finally were put before the House of Representatives at the first Congress:

> Mr. Sedgewick [of Massachusetts] replied that if the committee were governed by that general principle, they might have gone into a very lengthy enumeration of rights; they might have declared that a man should have a right to wear his hat if he pleased; that he might get up when he pleased and go to bed when he thought proper; but he would ask the gentleman whether he thought it necessary to enter these trifles in a declaration of rights, in a Government where none of them were intended to be infringed.[39]

Many of the congressmen felt that there was "more pressing business" to be taken up, such as the methods for raising money or the setting up of the federal judiciary. Others simply thought that it was not a wise idea to trifle with the new document. As Representative Jackson of Georgia so eloquently argued:

> Our Constitution, sir, is like a vessel just launched and lying at the wharf; she is untried. You can hardly discover any one of her properties. It is not known how she will answer her helm, or lay her course, whether she will bear with safety the precious freight to be deposited in her hold. But, in this state, will the prudent merchant attempt alterations? Will he employ workmen to tear off the planking and take asunder the frame? He certainly will not. Let us, gentlemen, fit out our vessel, set up her masts and expand her sails, and be guided by the experiment in our alterations. If she sails upon an uneven keel, let us right her by adding weight when it is wanting. In this way, we may remedy her defects to the satisfaction of all concerned; but if we proceed now to make alterations, we may deface a beauty, or deform a well proportioned piece of workmanship. In short, Mr. Speaker, I am not for amendments at this time.[40]

Yet, despite the resistance, James Madison was relentless because he knew that the Congress must "extinguish from the bosom of every member of the community any apprehension that there are those among his countrymen who wish to deprive them of the liberty for which they valiantly fought and honorably bled."[41]

Throughout that summer of 1789 Madison and a congressional committee of ten others hammered out the provisions that would become the Bill of Rights. If one wonders whether Madison intended for those provisions to apply to the states, and therefore Barron's wharf, one need only look at a draft of one of his amendments: "No state shall violate the equal right of conscience, freedom of press, or trial by jury in criminal cases; because it is proper that every government should be disarmed of powers which treat upon those particular rights."[42] In proposing this amendment, Madison said that he realized that some of the state constitutions provided for these protections but he thought the "double security" wise because state governments were "as liable to attack these invaluable privileges as the General Government is and therefore ought to be as cautiously guarded against."[43] Obviously, then, Madison thought that the other proposed amendments that became the Bill of Rights did *not* apply to the states, because he spelled out a portion of their contents again in a separate amendment for the states.

Late in the day on August 17, 1789, Madison's amendment giving protections against states was put before the 11-member committee. Only one member, Representative Tucker, spoke against it, arguing that it was wiser "to leave the State Governments to themselves, and not to interfere with them more than we already do; and that is thought by many to be rather too much."[44] Tucker's sentiments did not convince his fellow committeemen; the amendment passed the committee and then the entire House of Representatives as well. It was in the Senate and the Conference Committee that the measure regarding the states was dropped.[45]

MARSHALL'S DECISION ON BARRON'S WHARF

All this constitutional history was relevant to Barron's case, the first test of whether those amendments applied to the states. So it was with "great importance, but with not much difficulty"[46] that Chief Justice Marshall announced that the Fifth Amendment was not binding on the states. Barron and his wharf could get no help from the Bill of Rights. His voice often growing feeble, Marshall explained his reasoning:

> The constitution was ordained and established by the people of the United States for themselves, for their own government, and not for the government of the individual states. Each state established a constitution for itself, and, in that constitution, provided such limitations and restrictions on the powers of its particular government as its judgment dictated. ... [The Bill of Rights and the provisions of the Constitution] are limitations of power granted in the instrument itself; not of distinct governments, framed by different persons and for different purposes.

If these propositions be correct, the fifth amendment must be understood as restraining the power of the general [federal] government, not as applicable to the states.[47]

Thus, the Court asserted that the Bill of Rights placed restrictions only on the federal government, not on the states.[48]

Marshall believed that if "the framers of these amendments intended them to be limitations on the powers of the state governments, they would have . . . expressed that intention." He recalled the extensive opposition to the proposed constitution and the public outcry for a bill of rights that would provide "security against the apprehended encroachments of the general government—not against those of the local governments." In short, the amendments passed in 1789 contained no indication that they applied to the state governments and hence, Marshall stated, "This court cannot so apply them."[49] He concluded, "We are therefore of opinion that there is no repugnancy between the several acts of the general assembly of Maryland, given in evidence by the defendants at the trial of this cause, in the court of that state, and the constitution of the United States. This court, therefore, has no jurisdiction of the cause; and it is dismissed."[50]

And so, barely a half century after the Bill of Rights had been drafted, the Supreme Court made it clear in the case of Barron's dock that those guarantees were only protections against the central government; the states were not obliged to follow the same rules. It would take a civil war and another century of judicial theorizing to change that interpretation.

Dred Scott and Harriet Scott. *The Bettman Archive*

Barron is no longer the law of the land. But it took a hundred years and a civil war to change that. It all started with the suit of a slave who wanted his freedom, Dred Scott. After the Court's disastrous opinion in that case, it was not long before the Union was in tatters. In the wake of the Civil War, Congress passed the Fourteenth Amendment, which dramatically changed the relationship between the federal government and the states.

SEVENTEEN WORDS
The Quiet Revolution of the Fourteenth Amendment

Before the Civil War and the Fourteenth Amendment, the United States were. After the Fourteenth Amendment the United States is.

Carl Sandburg

It took 44 years for the Supreme Court even to consider the question of whether the Bill of Rights applied to the states, and Marshall answered the question in the negative. If *Barron* were still the ruling opinion, then the individual states might be free to censor newspapers or inflict cruel and unusual punishments or deny a person the right to a jury trial.* Not only is this not the case, but the Supreme Court today spends more than half its time wrestling with questions related to the fundamental liberties guaranteed by the Bill of Rights. How, then, did the situation change so dramatically? The answer is a complicated combination of the Civil War, the Fourteenth Amendment, and the Supreme Court itself.

John Marshall never lived to see the Civil War or the subsequent passage of the Fourteenth Amendment and the gradual chiseling away of his *Barron* decision by the use of 17 words in that amendment: "nor shall any State deprive any person of life, liberty, or property, without due process of law."

The Fourteenth Amendment was a direct result of the Civil War, a war many statesmen had tried to avoid. Men such as Marshall on the Court and Daniel Webster and Henry Clay in the Senate had devoted their energies to preserving the Union. However, economics, free trade versus protectionism, states' rights, party politics, and especially that "peculiar institution" of slavery created a vortex of irreconcilable differences. Slavery was the "constitutional cancer"[1] that could not be checked, and it was the spreading of slavery into the territories that posed the

---

*Of course, some state constitutions also prohibit these encroachments of liberty. However, under *Barron*, if a state constitution did not guarantee these protections, the federal government was powerless to enforce them.

greatest threat to the Union. For each time a territory was organized or a new state wanted to be admitted, the balance of slave states versus free states was threatened. In 1820, the Northern states, where slavery was prohibited, had a clear majority in the House of Representatives with, on the basis of census, 105 members compared to 81 for the Southern states. However, an equilibrium existed in the Senate because there were 11 free and 11 slave states. The Southern states feared that if they lost their equal representation in the Senate, slavery might be outlawed by Congress. In 1820 Missouri, a territory situated north of the Mason-Dixon line of demarcation between free and slave states, applied for admission to the Union as a *slave* state. After heated debates, Missouri was admitted as a slave state with the compromise that in the future slavery was to be prohibited above the latitude of 36°30'. At the same time, Maine was admitted as a free state, keeping the Senate balance at 12 and 12. Yet the growing boundaries of the nation and the impetus to admit new states continually threatened that balance.

DRED SCOTT'S FIGHT FOR FREEDOM

It might all have happened if there had been no slave called Dred Scott. It might have been any of the other two million descendants of Africans who had been dragged in chains to a new world to be sold and traded like mules, cows, or cotton gins. But Dred Scott is the name coupled with that of John F. A. Sanford (which the Court records mistakenly spelled as "Sandford") on that decision of 1857 which the later Chief Justice Charles Evans Hughes described as the Court's first "self-inflicted wound . . . a public calamity." Historian James MacGregor Burns described more specifically the decision's effect: "As a political decision it upset the delicate position between North and South, exacerbated antagonism between proslavery and antislavery, and destroyed that superb device of compromise."[2]

No one knows the real facts behind the Dred Scott case. Its history is so tangled in conjecture and myth that the facts are almost impossible to unravel. It's not even clear that Dred Scott was the slave's real name; some historians are convinced that for his first 30 years he was called "Sam." What is known is that Scott was probably born in Virginia around the turn of the nineteenth century and had been the property of Peter Blow. When the Blow family moved to St. Louis in 1830, Scott was taken along with five other slaves. Blow died two years later, and either just before or just after his death, Scott was sold to Dr. John Emerson. What happened after that was most significant: Dred Scott was taken to out of a slave state to free soil. In December 1833, Dr. Emerson reported for duty at Fort Armstrong in Illinois, a free state, and took his slave with him. In 1836, when the army vacated Fort Armstrong, Dr. Emerson was transferred to Fort Snelling, near what is now St. Paul, Minnesota. The "Wisconsin territory," as it was then called, was an area where slavery had been forbidden by the Missouri Compromise.

The cold, harsh Minnesota winters were too much for Dr. Emerson, who was continually complaining of ill health; he requested a transfer and was sent to Fort Jesup in Louisiana. Dred Scott and his wife, Harriett, remained in Fort Snelling as rented servants until February 1838, when Dr. Emerson married and apparently sent for his two slaves. But Emerson was not happy with the damp Louisiana climate either and requested yet another transfer. In his letter to the army requesting the change he listed some of the other difficulties he was having, including the fact that "even one of my negroes . . . has sued me for his freedom."[3] As Don E. Fehrenbacker points out in his masterful study of the case, "No record of this suit has been found and . . . it is not impossible that the slave in question was Dred, making an early abortive attempt to secure his freedom."[4] Certainly, even if the suit had been initiated by another slave, the process might have given Dred ideas about his own chances for freedom.

The Emersons and Scotts eventually returned to St. Louis via a brief stint in Fort Snelling. Dr. Emerson died in 1843, only one month after the birth of his daughter Henrietta. Mrs. Emerson then hired out Dred, first to her brother-in-law and in 1846 to a man named Samuel Russell. A few weeks later after being hired out to Russell, Dred and his family sued for their freedom on the basis that since they had resided in free territory, they were no longer slaves.

How the suit got started is the biggest mystery of all. Some historians have suggested that Taylor Blow, the son of Scott's original owners and still in St. Louis, financed the suit in order to help Scott. Others have suggested that Blow's primary motive was to win a big "test case" victory against slavery. Another theory is that the lawyers handling the case were looking for profit from a large settlement in back wages due to the Scotts. The Scotts might have gotten the idea from their extensive travels to free soil or from discussions with old friends such as the Blows. Each of the suggestions has merit; each also has some flaw due to a detail of fact. One hundred twenty-five years later, it seems unlikely that the answer will ever be completely clear.

Dred Scott spent 11 years on an odyssey toward emancipation. It was a complex judicial process with a series of cruel dead ends, a process characterized by legal maneuvers that frustrated Scott's attempts at freedom and now frustrate scholars who try to sort it all out. For Dred Scott and his family there were many defeats with only one small victory that was quickly reversed. Finally, in March 1852, Missouri's highest court ruled against Scott.

At about this time, the Scotts were sold to Mrs. Emerson's brother, John F. A. Sanford. Many historical accounts have characterized this as a contrived sale. Since *Dred Scott* v. *Emerson* had been decided by the state's highest court, it could have gone directly to the United States

Supreme Court for review. However, the suit Scott now instituted against Sanford was a new case against a "new master." Moreover, because Sanford was a resident of New York and Scott claimed Missouri residency, the case would this time wind its way through the federal system, as suits between citizens of different states fall into federal jurisdiction.

Meanwhile, during all this legal maneuvering the Supreme Court had issued a decision in 1851 that would be an important precedent for the Scotts' case. It involved three Kentucky slaves who were taken into the free state of Ohio by their master. They later escaped to Canada with the help of a man named Strader, and their former master sued Strader for damages. Chief Justice Roger Taney dismissed the case for lack of jurisdiction (there was no federal question involved), but he could not resist giving his opinion on the matter despite the Court's refusal to decide the case. His "non-decision decision" confirmed the doctrine of "reversion." In other words, no matter what effect the laws of Ohio might have had on the slaves while they were in the state, the slaves were reverted back to their former status when they returned to Kentucky, a slave state.

Taney, born to a Maryland plantation-owning family, had manumitted (legally granted freedom to) his own slaves, but remained a Southerner at heart. To Taney it was not slavery that was at issue, but the right of the states to regulate themselves. He had made this sentiment clear in his draft of Andrew Jackson's 1836 farewell address, which proclaimed that "each state has the unquestionable right to regulate its own internal concerns according to its own pleasure." This was a way of saying that slavery was an internal concern of the states and that the federal government should keep out. The speech continued, "all efforts on the part of people of other states to cast odium on their institutions [i.e., slavery] and . . . to disturb their rights of property . . . are in direct opposition to the spirit in which the Union was formed. . . ."[5] It seems incredible that Taney wrote a speech for President Jackson after he had assumed the chief justiceship. Today, that sort of collusion between the executive and judicial branch would be viewed as a serious breach of ethics.

When the case finally reached the nation's highest court, it took two hearings and pressure applied by President James Buchanan, following his election in 1856, to get a decision in the tortuous case of Dred Scott. As president-elect, Buchanan wrote to some of the justices, pleading for a speedy and forceful answer in the case. Buchanan wanted the Court to decide that slavery could be extended to all United States territory and two justices did assure him that the Court would go along with his wishes. Then, in his inaugural address, Buchanan spoke of the impending decision and his intention to "cheerfully submit, whatever [the decision] might be."[6] And on March 6, 1857, just two days after the inauguration, Chief Justice Taney, once a towering figure, now at 80 bent with pain and palsied, read, his voice failing at times, the opinion that denied one man's freedom while protecting another man's property.

The Supreme Court could have avoided the large slavery question simply by asserting that it lacked jurisdiction, that since slaves were not citizens, they could not sue in federal court. Indeed, the chief justice began with that issue, "The question is simply this: Can a negro, whose ancestors were imported into this country, and sold as slaves, become a member of the political community formed and brought into existence by the Constitution of the United States, and as such become entitled to all the rights and privileges, and immunites, guaranteed by that instrument to the citizen?"[7] The Court's answer was a resounding "no."

Taney reasoned that when the Constitution was drafted, the Negro race "had for more than a century before been regarded as being of an inferior order; and altogether unfit to associate with the white race, either in social or political relations; and so far inferior, that they had no rights which the white man was bound to respect; and that the negro might justly and lawfully be reduced to slavery for his benefit."[8] Because of this attitude, the Court now ruled that Negroes, emancipated or not, were not citizens of the United States and could not sue in federal court.

In addition, following the *Strader* case, the Court said that Dred Scott and his family were not citizens of Missouri. Under the doctrine of reversion once they had returned to Missouri, a slave state, its laws—not those of Illinois, a free state—were controlling. In Missouri no Negro slave could be a citizen.

However, the pressure from the White House and the loyalties of the five Southern justices led them to a further ruling, and it was this final conclusion of the Court that was most intolerable to the abolitionists and free soilers (those who wished to keep slavery out of certain areas of the nation). The Court ruled that the Missouri Compromise of 1820, which prohibited slavery north of the 36°30′ line, was unconstitutional. Declaring that the rights of a United States citizen were the same in a territory as in a state, Taney reasoned:

> No one, we presume, will contend that Congress can make any law in a Territory respecting the establishment of religion, or the free exercise thereof, or abridging the freedom of speech or the press . . . thus the rights of property are united with the rights of person and placed on the same ground by the fifth amendment. . . . And if the Constitution recognizes the right of property of the master in a slave, and makes no distinction between that description of property and other property owned by a citizen . . . no tribunal acting under the authority of the United States . . . has a right to . . . deny to it the benefit of the provisions and guarantees which have been provided for the protection of private property against the encroachment of the Government.[9]

Thus, Taney stated, the Missouri Compromise, "which prohibited a citizen from holding and owning property of this kind in the territory of the United States north of the line therein mentioned, is not warranted by the Constitution, and is therefore void."[10]

Despite the practice of judicial review, never before had the Court overturned a major act of Congress. And never before had there been such a "deep and widespread revulsion against a finding of the nation's highest judicial tribunal. . . . [The later Supreme Court] Justice Felix Frankfurter once remarked that after the Civil War justices of the Supreme Court never mentioned the Dred Scott case, any more than a family in which a son had been hanged mentioned ropes and scaffolds."[11]

For Dred Scott the decision meant that he remained a slave. However, a few weeks afterwards, he was manumitted by his owners. He died less than a year later.

For the nation the decision was another factor that would lead to a bloody civil war. Instead of settling the question of slavery, as President Buchanan had hoped, the decision had heightened antagonisms. His Democratic party—with Northern and Southern factions—was in splinters; soon the nation would be. Four years later, in March 1861, with the nation on the brink of war, Abraham Lincoln was sworn into office as the sixteenth president. It was Chief Justice Taney who administered the oath. "Did the lonely and frustrated Chief Justice standing there on that bleak Tuesday in March on the eve of war, recall the tragic part that he, more than any other, had played in starting that march to war?"[12] The words are those of Justice Robert Jackson, written almost a century after the *Dred Scott* decision.

THE POSTWAR "REVOLUTION"

When the military battles ended in 1865, the political battles continued in Congress, as the blueprints for reconstructing the Union were drawn up. The cessation of war and the passage of the Thirteenth Amendment had ended slavery but had not settled many of the complex and controversial questions that faced the nation. Under what conditions would the Confederate states be readmitted to the Union? How would the rights of the emancipated slaves be protected? What, if any, punishments would be meted out to the rebel leaders? It was an uneasy time, a time filled with hatred and with hope.

The radical Republicans—most notably Representative Thaddeus Stevens of Pennsylvania—did not approve of the provisional governments set up by Presidents Lincoln and Johnson and, in December 1865, they blocked the seating of the newly elected Southern senators and representatives.* Congress set up a special joint committee on Reconstruction to handle the thorny question of how to deal with the postwar situation.

One special concern was the treatment of the emancipated slaves. The provisional Southern legislatures had drawn up "black codes," special laws "so harsh as to constitute thinly veiled attempts to reinstitute slavery."[13] Although the codes varied from state to state, "they specifed that blacks might not purchase or carry firearms, that they might not assemble after sunset, and that those who were idle or unemployed should be 'liable to imprisonment or hard labor, one or both . . . not exceeding twelve months.' . . . South Carolina forbade blacks from practicing 'the art, trade or business of an artisan, mechanic or shopkeeper, or any other trade, employment or business.' "[14]

In reaction to these laws, Congress passed the Civil Rights Act of 1866,[15] which stated that "all persons born in the United States . . . excluding Indians not taxed, are hereby declared to be citizens of the United States." The act provided further that "such citizens, of every race and color, without regard to any previous condition of slavery or involuntary servitude . . . shall have the same right, in every State and Territory in the United States, to make and enforce contracts, to sue, be parties, and give evidence, to inherit, purchase, lease, sell, hold, and convey real and personal property, and to full and equal benefit of all laws and proceedings for the security of person and property, as is enjoyed by white citizens."[16]

Doubtful of the constitutionality of the act and at odds with the Republican leadership, President Andrew Johnson vetoed the law, but his veto was overridden. Even radicals such as Representative John A. Bingham of Ohio, himself a member of the joint committee on Reconstruction, had doubts about the new law's constitutionality because it would force the states to uphold liberties which under *Barron* they were not obliged to respect. Many feared that the legislation could later easily be repealed. (The readmission of the Southern states would give the South about 15 more representatives than before the war, as now the freedmen would be counted. Prior to the war only three-fifths of the slave population was counted for purposes of determining number of representatives.) The Republicans wanted to add constitutional strength to the legal safeguards for blacks, that is, to completely nullify what the *Dred Scott* decision stood for. What emerged from this effort was the Fourteenth Amendment of 1866, which stated that "All persons born or naturalized in the United

---

*Lincoln and Johnson had appointed provisional governors in each state to reorganize the state governments, repeal the acts of secession, and amend the state constitutions. The Radical Republicans feared that if the Confederate states were allowed to take their seats, there would be a Democratic majority which would repeal legislation aiding the newly freed slaves.

States, and subject to the jurisdiction thereof, are citizens of the United States and of the State wherein they reside." The part of the Amendment that would eventually lead to the overturning of *Barron* was at the end of Section 1:

> No State shall make or enforce any law which shall abridge the privileges or immunities of citizens of the United States; *nor shall any State deprive any person of life, liberty, or property, without due process of law;* nor deny to any person within its jurisdiction the equal protection of the laws. (Emphasis added.)

It is impossible now to look back and conclusively prove what exactly the framers of the Fourteenth Amendment had in mind when they wrote those words. What did they mean by "privileges or immunities" or "due process of law" or "equal protection"? Twentieth-century legal scholars and historians have debated the intention of the authors, of the Congress, and of the states that eventually ratified the measure. On one side of the debate is the position of Justice Hugo Black, who wrote "[m]y study of the historical events that culminated in the Fourteenth Amendment, and the expressions of those who sponsored and favored, as well as those who opposed its submission and passage, persuades me that one of the chief objects that the provisions of the Amendment's first section . . . were intended to accomplish was to make the Bill of Rights applicable to the states."[17] He argues that the framers' express intention was to overturn the constitutional rule set in *Barron*. Justice Black felt that the due process clause "incorporated" or took in the entire Bill of Rights, making those rights a national standard enforceable on the states.

Professor Raoul Berger of Harvard Law School has a decidedly different point of view: "[T]he framers were content to bar discrimination, to assure blacks that they would have judicial protection on the same terms as whites, no more, no less. . . . [T]he due process clause was not meant to create a new, general criterion of justice. Like state laws at which 'equal protection' was aimed, state justice had to be nondiscriminatory. It was 'equal justice to all men and equal protection under the shield of law.' "[18] Berger sees no justification for Black's incorporation theory.

In between Black and Berger is the view of constitutional scholar Charles Fairman, who reminds us that the framers were not "concentered upon our nice constitutional question" but on burning political questions: "Whether the freedman should be given suffrage, what should be the new basis of representation in Congress and . . . how could the Confederate leaders best be excluded from the councils of the nation."[19] Fairman's detailed analysis of the debates in the Congress, the state legislatures, and the newspapers convinces him that Congress wished to "establish a federal standard below which state action must not fall." He concludes,

"Brooding over the matter in the writing of this articles has, however slowly, brought the conclusion that Justice Cardozo's gloss on the due process clause [written in an opinion in 1937]—what is 'implicit in the concept of ordered liberty'—comes as close as one can to catching the vague aspirations that were hung upon the privileges and immunities clause."[20]

Whatever their intent, the framers of the amendment could not have foreseen the impact that those 17 words of the due process clause would have on the Bill of Rights and the future balance of power between the federal and state governments. It was as if the Congress had held a second constitutional convention, and created a federal government of vastly expanded proportions. The concern of the framers in 1787 had been to protect the people and the states from intrusion by the central government, and the Bill of Rights had been drafted to insure protection of those fundamental liberties. The Fourteenth Amendment and its later interpretation by the Supreme Court changed that balance; now the federal government—and especially the judiciary—would protect the people from arbitrary action by state governments. It was the beginning of a new era in constitutional development, in which the federal government would play a much larger role.

Of course, this new era did not spring into being overnight. The changes took place over the next hundred years and involved hundreds of cases and tens of thousands of pages of constitutional opinions, many of them first written by dissenters.

GIVING MEANING TO
THE FOURTEENTH AMENDMENT

In 1871, three years after the Fourteenth Amendment was ratified, Congressman Bingham, its primary architect, had an opportunity to explain what the amendment's framers had intended. In a debate on a bill designed to enforce the amendment, Bingham attempted to convince his fellow congressmen that the amendment had been designed to "vest in Congress a power to protect the rights of citizens against the States, and individuals in States, never before granted." Bingham said that he had written the first section with the counsel of John Marshall "who, though departed this life still lives among us is his immortal spirit, and still speaks to us from the reports of the highest judicial tribunal on earth." He explained that in February of 1866 he had reread Marshall's decision in *Barron* and "apprehended as I never did before certain words in the opinion." Bingham told his colleagues that Marshall had been powerless to enforce the Bill of Rights in the state of Maryland. As Marshall had said, if the framers of the Bill of Rights "intended them to be limitations on the State governments, they would have . . . expressed that intention."[21] In other words, since the Bill of Rights amendments did not specify that their guarantees of rights applied against the states, Marshall felt he could not read that interpretation into them.

Bingham explained that he considered that problem seriously when writing the language of the Fourteenth Amendment. He wanted to make sure that his intention to grant those protections against the states was absolutely clear. Although he did not mention the due process clause in his oration to his colleagues, Bingham did assert that the privileges and immunities of a citizen were defined in the first eight amendments.* He had, he claimed, tried to give the Supreme Court the power it didn't have at the time of *Barron:* the power to apply the Bill of Rights to the states.

Whatever Bingham had intended when he drafted the amendment, his explanation was planting a new idea—that the Constitution as now amended went beyond setting up the federal government and protecting citizens from the potential abuses of the central government. It was the beginning of an era in which, ever so slowly, the federal government would begin scrutinizing the activities of state governments—although initially in areas involving property, not individual rights.

Bingham's sentiments were echoed in 1873 by the plaintiffs' attorneys in the *Slaughterhouse Cases*.[22] That litigation began when the carpetbag Louisiana state legislature passed laws that gave the exclusive privilege to operate slaughterhouses to one butcher firm. The adversely affected butchers sued, alleging that their "privileges and immunities" as citizens—specifically the right to operate a business—had been violated. In a 5 to 4 vote, the Supreme Court disagreed, and with that decision the "privileges and immunities" clause of the Fourteenth Amendment was all but nullified.

However, Justice Field's dissent[23] argued for the absolute right of a man to be engaged in a given business or profession. Field insisted that the Fourteenth Amendment protects "the citizens of the United States against the deprivation of their common rights by state legislation." He explained that the amendment had been enacted "to place the common rights of American citizens under the protection of the national government." Those rights, he stated, were "inalienable rights, rights which are the gift of the creator; which the law does not confer, but only recognizes."[24]

Thus, although the Court had reaffirmed the notion put forth in *Barron* that the Bill of Rights did not apply to the states, Justice Field's dissent was the beginning of the concept that liberty had, with the Four-

---

*The Ninth and Tenth Amendments were not relevant. The Ninth Amendment says that "The enumeration in the Constitution, of certain rights, shall not be construed to deny or disparage others retained by the people." The Tenth reads "The powers not delegated to the United States by the Constitution, nor prohibited by it to the States, are reserved to the States, respectively, or to the people."

teenth Amendment, taken on a new constitutional and national meaning. Under that broader definition, states must meet a national standard in their legislation and administration of justice, and the federal government had the duty to see that the standard was enforced.

Field's view of the Fourteenth Amendment would not be the prevailing sentiment of the Supreme Court for some time. However, it lived on in dissenting opinions. In 1884, Justice John Marshall Harlan took a slightly different tack, advocating the incorporation of the entire Bill of Rights via the due process clause of the Fourteenth Amendment. In his dissent in *Hurtado* v. *California*[25] Harlan argued that Joseph Hurtado's murder conviction was unconstitutional because he had been indicted by "information" rather than by a grand jury. Harlan felt that the lack of a grand jury proceeding was a violation of the due process guarantees in the Fifth and Fourteenth Amendments. Subsequently, Harlan never failed "in appropriate cases—of which there really were not very many —to write impassioned opinions in dissent, urging his associates to accept the principle of the nationalization of the Bill of Rights."[26]

While Harlan argued for personal liberties, a majority of the Court developed this broader concept of liberty into a legal framework designed to protect property. It was an outgrowth of an era of laissez-faire economics in which business and industry resisted the efforts of government to regulate the economy. Known as "substantive due process," the theory held that the Fourteenth Amendment's due process clause incorporated the protections of property vested in the Fifth Amendment's guarantee that no person shall "be deprived of life, liberty, or property without due process of law." Due process came to mean more than a procedural guarantee—that a person would have his day in court. It came to mean that the substance of an act of a legislature could in and of itself be a violation of rights. Thus legislation was now scrutinized not just in terms of *how* it was administered, but *what* it was controlling. Out of the substantive due process theory came the notion of "liberty of contract" or "Lochnerizing," as it was called, through which the Court overturned progressive economic legislation enacted by the states. The Lochner case of 1905 is an example of this process.

Lochner, a bakery owner, was convicted of violating a New York State law that limited the hours of bakery workers to 10 hours a day and 60 hours a week. He appealed, and the Supreme Court overturned his conviction and voided the statute because the state of New York had engaged in "meddlesome interferences with the rights of the individual." The Court explained, "The general rights to make a contract in relation to his business is part of the liberty of the individual protected by the Fourteenth Amendment of the Federal Constitution."[27] If bakery workers wanted to work more hours—or perhaps if their employers demanded it —the state could not interfere. Child labor was another area which the Supreme Court, in 1905, felt could not be regulated.[28]

However, it was also in the Lochner case that Justice Holmes first blasted the notion of a constitutionally guaranteed "liberty of contract": "This case is decided upon an economic theory which a large part of the country does not entertain. . . . But a constitution is not intended to embody a particular economic theory, whether of paternalism . . . or of *laissez faire.*"[29]

The principle of substantive due process prevailed throughout the first quarter of the twentieth century, but it slowly fell into discredit when economic conditions, worsened by the Depression, called for more experimentation by the states in economic legislation.

FROM CONTRACTS TO FUNDAMENTAL LIBERTIES

First in dissents, Justices Holmes and Brandeis maintained a steadfast and pervasive pressure against the concept of substantive due process, viewing it as a subversion of the original purpose of the Fourteenth Amendment by the very institution charged with its preservation, the Supreme Court. At the same time these justices were willing to use the Amendment as a vehicle to nullify state laws that they believed fettered essential individual rights of political expression. In this way, the Court began to give closer scrutiny to those liberties which were written into the Bill of Rights. And as the membership of the Court gradually changed, its view of what the Fourteenth Amendment meant shifted.

Starting, in 1925, with the free speech guarantee of the First Amendment,[30] the Court began to accept the Harlan–Brandeis–Holmes theory that many of the fundamental liberties written into the Bill of Rights were enforceable on the states. In a piecemeal fashion began another phase of constitutional interpretation, in which certain personal liberties were taken under the protective umbrella of the Constitution. From freedom of speech to freedom of press to the right to counsel, the list grew.

Finally, in 1937, Justice Benjamin Cardozo spelled the Court's position on the relationship between the Bill of Rights and the states in *Palko* v. *Connecticut.*[31] Frank Palko had been tried for killing two policemen and convicted of second-degree murder with a sentence of life imprisonment. The state of Connecticut had appealed the verdict and sentence, and after a new trial, Palko was convicted of first-degree murder and sentenced to death. He appealed on the ground that his second trial was an instance of double jeopardy, prohibited by the Fifth Amendment.

Although Cardozo rejected Palko's claim that his Fifth Amendment rights against double jeopardy could not be violated by the state, the Justice did set up an "Honor Roll" of rights. In Cardozo's view there were certain rights enumerated in the Bill of Rights which were "the very essence of a scheme of ordered liberty" and must be protected from state infringement. Others were not ranked as being fundamental; "justice would not perish" without them. Double jeopardy, the right to trial by jury, the right of indictment by grand jury were not part of "the concept of ordered liberty." Freedom of speech and press and religion, in contrast, did fall within that framework.

Thus by the time of *Palko,* the role of the federal government through the judiciary had undergone another metamorphosis; it was now to protect actively certain fundamental civil liberties of the citizens of the states against state action. This mandate was expressed a year later in a famous footnote written in an otherwise insignificant case, *United States v. Carolene Products Company.* [32] While first asserting that economic legislation would be given less constitutional scrutiny (and thus signaling the end of "liberty of contract"), Justice Harlan Fiske Stone announced a new double standard of what legislation the court would give close review. Laws that threatened basic liberties were to receive a close scrutiny by the Court; economic legislation would not.*

For much of the last half century, the Court has been spending the majority of its time on questions concerning the Fourteenth Amendment and its relationship to the Bill of Rights. Some justices have relied on the Cardozo concept; others, such as Justice Hugo Black, have insisted that the entire Bill of Rights must be incorporated. Another judicial interpretation of the Fourteenth Amendment, known as "selective incorporation plus," would guarantee that states must not violate most of the rights specified in the first eight amendments as well as certain other fundamental rights. Under this interpretation, the Court has recognized a "right of privacy" and other "natural" and "fundamental" rights. It was this theory that led to the Court's ruling on abortion (see Chapter 12).

Thus, in this century the Supreme Court has given new meaning to the Bill of Rights, a meaning probably never imagined by John Marshall or James Madison or Thomas Jefferson. This new meaning traces back to a slave called Dred Scott and a case that caused first a bloody war and then a quiet revolution of constitutional proportions.

---

*1. There may be narrower scope for operation of the presumption of constitutionality when legislation appears on its face to be within a specific prohibition of the Constitution, such as those of the first ten Amendments, which are deemed equally specific when held to be embraced within the Fourteenth. . . . 2. It is unnecessary to consider now whether legislation which restricts those political processes which can ordinarily be expected to bring about repeal of undesirable legislation, is to be subjected to more exacting judicial scrutiny under the general prohibitions of the Fourteenth Amendment than are most other types of legislation.[33]

The only photograph of Jay M. Near, from his obituary in the *Minneapolis Tribune. Minnesota Historical Society*

Jay M. Near and Howard Guilford ran a scandal sheet in Minneapolis during the 1920s. It was an anti-Semitic, anti-black, anti-establishment rag, in which attacks were launched against everyone—gangsters, police commissioners, and even the mayor. Minnesota had its own weapon—a law that could silence "public nuisances" such as Near and Guilford's *Saturday Press.* When County Prosecutor Floyd Olson decided to put a prior restraint on the paper, Jay Near fought him all the way to the Supreme Court. That case was a landmark in the establishment of freedom of the press.

MINNESOTA RAG
The Newspaper That Gave New Meaning to Freedom of the Press

Some degree of abuse is inseparable from the proper use of everything, and in no instance is this more true than in that of the press. It has accordingly been decided by the practice of the States, that it is better to leave a few of its noxious branches to their luxuriant growth, than, by pruning them away, to injure the vigour of those yielding proper fruits.

Chief Justice Charles Evans Hughes,
quoting James Madison in *Near* v. *Minnesota*

In the 1920s throughout America there were literally hundreds of weekly rags, scandal sheets filled with the lurid and the profane, some of the scions of the Hearst brand of yellow journalism.* Some survived for years; others vanished as quickly as they had appeared, surviving only long enough to fleece some well-heeled sucker and skip town.

When Lincoln Steffens wrote *The Shame of the Cities* in 1904, Minneapolis was one of his examples of "a boodle town," where "the people who were left to govern the city hated above all things, strict laws. They were loafers, saloon keepers, gamblers, criminals and the thriftless poor of all nationalities."[1] In the next two decades little changed in Minneapolis except the players and the magnitude of the corruption. The city's strategic location provided gangsters with a bonanza. It was the crossroads in the Canadian whiskey trade; from there the hooch was shipped to Chicago and St. Louis.

Ed Ryan, who was a cop on the beat in the 1920s and who as chief of police under Mayor Hubert H. Humphrey was later credited with cleaning up Minneapolis, recently described the city of that era as a "wide open town with gambling joints, slot machines, houses of prostitution. . . . You name it, we had it. . . . If you can't buy off the mayor, if you can't

---

*This chapter is a condensation of the book of the same name by Friendly, which was originally published by Random House in 1981.

buy off the chief, then you can't operate a racket . . . no matter what community you're in. . . . When you see slot machines and gambling all over the place, there has to be a payoff."[2]

The respectable newspapers permitted themselves to squint at the link between those who broke the law and those charged with its enforcement; moreover, many reporters were on the take. In the void created by the big newspapers' failure to fight city hall, scandal sheets flourished. The twin city thus provided a happy hunting ground for Jay M. Near, who had come east from Fort Atkinson, Iowa, and Howard A. Guilford, who had come west from Northampton, Massachusetts. Together, they practiced a brand of journalism that teetered on the edge of legality and often toppled over the limits of propriety.

Howard Guilford always had one foot in jail. All 200 pounds of him managed to offend a lot of people, many of them law enforcement officials. In his checkered Minneapolis career he was indicted 19 times but never convicted of anything—with the exception of a parking violation, for which he was fined $1. In his memoirs Guilford tells of diabolical plots to arrest him, cooked up by corrupt politicians and bribe-taking policemen. He claimed his only crime was trying to expose the corruption "with its tentacles in pulpit, brothels and public life,"[3] but many remember him still as a shrewd con man, who was not above blackmail and extortion.

Guilford's bludgeon was the *Reporter,* a St. Paul weekly that he had founded in 1913, which became the *Twin City Reporter* in 1914 when it moved to Minneapolis. It was a sensationalist paper with scant socially redeeming value. To Guilford, a journalist was "a reporter out of a job." The grist for the *Reporter* was gambling, prostitution, and the sexual adventures of the Twin Cities' upper crust. A vice president of one of the largest wholesale grocery chains and a member of the exclusive Minneapolis Club was branded as "leaning toward children of ten to twelve years of age rather than the mature old hens of fifteen and sixteen." This was the paper's staple kind of story and tone.

In 1916 Guilford hired Jay M. Near, a reporter of equal reputation but with a different flair. Without an ounce of flab on his tall, gaunt frame, Near dressed beyond his means in slick, showy suits and elevator shoes. He had the look of a handsome leading man in a traveling stock company. Near was anti-Catholic, anti-Semitic, anti-black, and anti-labor, and his pen and typewriter were weapons for hire, allowing him to scratch out his living as a sort of scavenger of the sins and political vulnerability of others. He had basic writing skills and a quick-on-the-draw sense of outrage.

Under Near and Guilford, the headlines of the *Twin City Reporter* provided a steady diet of gossip. Typical banners read: "Smooth Minneapolis Doctor with Woman in St. Paul Hotel" and "White Slavery Trade: Well-Known Local Man Is Ruining Women and Living Off Their Earnings." The *Reporter's* labeling of minority groups was usually pejorative—yids, bohunks, spades, etc.—and it showed a deep-seated hostility for most institutions, from the Salvation Army right down to the "Communist" labor unions.

"It was a shakedown completely," remembers Orlin Folwick, a longtime reporter for the *Minneapolis Morning Tribune.* "Guilford was hanging around the police department all the time, and for a five or ten spot, a cop would give him a tip-off about some prominent citizen who had been found in the back seat of a car in a procreative position. Near and Guilford had access to more adjectives than you and I would ever want to use in a lifetime, and they used them. This is what sold the sheets."[4]

The political corruption in Minneapolis and St. Paul and the truce between bootleggers, gamblers, and prostitution merchants and the police and city fathers provided endless material for Near and Guilford. The negative image that the paper gave the Twin Cities was matched by the bad name it gave to all reporters; yet much that the two men published was true or at least more true than false. Mingled with the exposés of the exploits of Minneapolis's well-to-do were reports of crime and of the corruption of elected officials.

In 1917 Guilford, "weary of turning down thousands of dollars" to act as a go-between for corrupt officials, had decided to sell out his interests in the *Reporter* to Near and Jack Bevans, another associate, for $30,000. None of the parties had any cash, so there was no down payment; Near and Bevans simply agreed to pay 40 percent of the net profits against the purchase price. Guilford later claimed he had warned Near about taking Bevans as a partner because he "was a mighty uncertain individual and dangerous to trust." In any event, Near quickly discovered that Bevans had been blackmailing choice victims without his knowledge. He also learned that the paper wasn't very profitable, and he sold his interest and migrated to California for occupations unknown.

Almost 10 years later, in August 1927, Guilford, down on his luck, ran into Jay Near, who had returned from California. According to Guilford, Near suggested that "we enter the weekly newspaper game together again" and though he was wary because of the kind of extortionist rag Near had permitted the *Twin City Reporter* to become he finally consented. He told Near he "would join him with one understanding—that never a word of a sex nature appear in the columns of our paper." The *Twin City Reporter* was still in existence, now owned by Bevans and a partner, Edward J. Morgan. Near and Guilford's avowed primary goal was to run that paper out of business forever because, they charged, its current owners were hoods, who used it exclusively for blackmailing and extortion.

Indeed, the first issue of the *Saturday Press,* Near and Guilford's new venture, was to report on alliances that made possible a Bevans gambling establishment. This establishment was owned by Bevans in conjunction with Mose Barnett, a local hood. Rumor had it that Barnett had promised Chief of Police Frank Brunskill that there would be no bank robberies as long as the gambling house was left alone. In addition, Brunskill got a piece of the action. It was an ideal relationship: the gambling house got police protection, the chief of police got a moratorium on bank robberies, and they all got rich.

Word traveled fast. Before the first issue of the *Saturday Press*[5] was even written, Chief of Police Brunskill had given his men an unofficial but clear message: Get the *Saturday Press* off the newsstands. His authority for this command was the sheer power of his office.

The first issue of the *Saturday Press* didn't mention Brunskill's unofficial ban but did report a threat from the underworld to bump off Near and Guilford if they persisted in their exposé of conditions in the city. The editors warned, "Just a moment, boys, before you start something you won't be able to finish."

The next Monday afternoon, September 26, 1927, Howard Guilford and his sister-in-law Esther Seide, were driving from his home to his office. At the corner of West Broadway and Lowery Avenue a touring car overtook them, and before Guilford could pull his own gun, two assailants pumped four bullets into his car. The last one struck Guilford in the abdomen as his car careened to a stop. He was rushed to the hospital in critical condition.

"I headed into the city on September 26, ran across three Jews in a Chevrolet; stopped a lot of lead and won a bed for myself in St. Barnabas Hospital for six weeks," Guilford later reported in his paper. "Wherefore, I have withdrawn all allegiance to anything with a hook nose that eats herring."[6]

Guilford always insisted that "Big Mose" had ordered the shooting. Word had been leaked to Barnett about the first issue of the *Saturday Press,* and Guilford assumed that Barnett was trying to settle the score.

While Guilford was in the hospital, Near published one of the *Saturday Press*'s biggest scoops, concerning an incident involving Barnett which had occurred earlier in the year. The incident was as follows.[7] One morning in July 1927, young Irving Shapiro stood behind the partition separating the front of his father's dry-cleaning store on East Franklin Avenue from the work area. His father had stationed him there when he realized that Big Mose Barnett was about to pay him a not-so-social visit.

Barnett, 6 feet tall and 240 pounds, swaggered into Sam Shapiro's shop. A fancy dresser sporting a small dark mustache, Barnett looked the part of a strong-armed hoodlum. He was there as an enforcer for the Twin Cities Cleaners and Dyers Association, a syndicate whose purpose was to fix prices and control the market by keeping small entrepreneurs like Sam Shapiro from doing their own dry cleaning. Shapiro and his partner, Yale Morovitz, had recently added their own dry-cleaning plant at the rear of their shop, despite the threats of Philip Moses, head of the local dry-cleaners protection association. For three years the two men had sent out their cleaning to a member of the association; now they were determined to do their own. A tough, stubborn Lithuanian who had started in the business as a pants presser, Shapiro believed he had the right to his American dream.

Now, terrified, Shapiro stood behind his counter as Mose made his demands: "Sam, cut out your dry-cleaning plant or else there'll be trouble." But Sam was adamant, and in his blunt way told Mose Barnett that the dry-cleaning operation would continue. His bravado was despite the fact that earlier that month, thugs had broken in, ripped the locks off the naphtha tanks, and poured sulfuric acid into his cleaning fluid. (After that incident the police had stationed a man there, but this guard had soon been pulled off.)

On August 19 Barnett followed up his visit with a phone call, advising Shapiro to "stop operating the dry-cleaning plant or else . . ." But Shapiro, the self-schooled immigrant who kept a shelf of constitutional law books, knew his rights and refused to be shaken down. The next morning the mob, acting for the dry-cleaning association, struck again. Four men, three of whom Shapiro later identified, entered the shop, "lined me and three employees up against the wall and began to spray my customers' clothing with sulfuric acid."[8]

Shapiro told the police, "When I turned my head, I was struck on it with the butt end of a pistol and I was injured so badly that I was under a doctor's care."[9] At least $8,000 worth of his customers' clothing was destroyed. When Irving came home from school, he found his father with his head swathed in bandages, the shop in disarray, and his mother, Freda, hysterical. For two years afterward, Shapiro and Morovitz took turns sleeping in the store with a loaded pistol beside them—though, as Irving recounts, "neither of them really know how to fire a gun." The assault was reported in the newspapers (the *Saturday Press* was not yet being published), without a mention of Barnett or his boys.

Sam Shapiro gave up seeking help from the police, because of their links with Barnett and organized crime. He went to the county attorney and the grand jury, but still no action was taken. In desperation, Shapiro finally told his story to Jay Near, who had heard about the incident from a mutual acquaintance, and Near then began writing the story for the *Saturday Press.* Although Near was no doubt an anti-Semite, he and Shapiro eventually became friendly. Irving remembers that his father had a soft spot in his heart for Near, and "occasionally would give him a bag of groceries or a ten-dollar bill to keep him going. . . . Near was a smooth-talking operator who had my father coming on pretty good."

The third issue of the *Saturday Press,* published on October 8, carried as its lead the Shapiro story. It appeared under a seven-line, two-column head, which read "Police 'Baffled' in Their Attempts to Identify Acid-Throwing Thugs Who Assaulted Sam Shapiro AFTER He Had Been Threatened by Mose Barnett. Guilford Shot Down in Cold Blood by

Gangsters AFTER He Had Been Threatened by Mose Barnett. Will The Present Grand Jury Act?"

Near depicted Shapiro as a martyr: "And right here I ask you as man to man IF SAM SHAPIRO HAD NOT THE RIGHT UNDER OUR CONSTITUTION TO LAUNCH HIS TINY SHIP IN OUR COMMERCIAL SEA?" The editor's account of the threats on the Shapiro dry-cleaning shop, though spiked with his own brand of bias, had most of the facts straight. He chided the major dailies for their lack of courage and veracity. "Journalism today isn't prostituted so much as it is disgustingly flabby," Near wrote, and he added, revealing his true character, "I'd rather be a louse in the cotton shirt of a nigger than be a journalistic prostitute." His constant theme was that the *Minneapolis Tribune* and the other papers were "afraid to mention the name of Mose Barnett, gambler, gangster, gunman."

Years later, Sam Shapiro got the justice he sought. Seventy-five members of the Twin Cities Cleaners and Dyers Association were charged with illegal restraint of trade in attempting to fix prices in the St. Paul and Minneapolis area. Although many of the defendants bargained for nominal fines in exchange for a guilty plea, the Minnesota Supreme Court later disbarred the association's leader, Attorney Philip Moses, for his criminal activity. Mose Barnett was eventually convicted of the criminal assault and spent four years in Stillwater State Prison.*

GAGGING A "MALICIOUS, SCANDALOUS AND DEFAMATORY" NEWSPAPER

With each issue Near's broadsides became more vehement. He accused Mayor George Leach, Charles G. Davis, head of the Law Enforcement League, and County Attorney Floyd Olson of being either blind or party to the illegal gambling dens run by Mose Barnett and Jack Bevans. His attacks on individuals were combined increasingly with his anti-Semitism.

In the November 19th issue Near and the partially recovered Guilford seemed to be summoning up every ounce of their anger, bitterness, and hate. This was an attack that would reverberate far beyond the newsstands in Minneapolis:

Facts Not Theories

"I am a bosom friend of Mr. Olson," snorted a gentleman of Yiddish blood, "and I want to protest against your article," and blah, blah, blah, ad infinitum, ad nauseam.

---

*One of the key witnesses in the Barnett trial was Irving Shapiro—11 at the time of the shakedown and 18 at the time of the trial. His testimony was so precise that an elderly spectator congratulated him. "Young man," she said, "you make an excellent witness. Someday you may be governor of Minnesota." Shapiro never made it to the governor's mansion in Minnesota, but in 1974 became Chairman of the Board and Chief Executive Officer of E. I. du Pont de Nemours & Co.

I am not taking orders from men of Barnett's faith, at least right now. There have been too many men in this city and especially those in official life, who HAVE been taking orders and suggestions from JEW GANGSTERS, therefore we HAVE Jew Gangsters, practically ruling Minneapolis.

It was buzzards of the Barnett stripe who shot down my buddy. It was Barnett gunmen who staged the assault on Samuel Shapiro. It is Jew thugs who have "pulled" practically every robbery in this city. . . . It was a gang of Jew gunmen who boasted that for five hundred dollars they would kill any man in the city. It was Mose Barnett, a Jew, who boasted that he held the chief of police of Minneapolis in his hand—had bought and paid for him. . . .

Practically every vendor of vile hooch, every owner of a moonshine still, every snake-faced gangster and embryonic yegg in the Twin Cities is a JEW.

Having these examples before me, I feel that I am justified in my refusal to take orders from a Jew who boasts that he is a "bosom friend" of Mr. Olson. . . .

I simply state a fact when I say that ninety per cent of the crimes committed against society in this city are committed by Jew gangsters. . . .

It is Jew, Jew, Jew as long as one cares to comb over the records.

I am launching no attack against the Jewish people AS A RACE. I am merely calling attention to a FACT. And if the people of that race and faith wish to rid themselves of the odium and stigma THE RODENTS OF THEIR OWN RACE HAVE BROUGHT UPON THEM, they need only to step to the front and help the decent citizens of Minneapolis rid the city of these criminal Jews.

Either Mr. Guilford or myself stand ready to do battle for a MAN, regardless of his race, color or creed, but neither of us will step one inch out of our chosen path to avoid a fight IF the Jews want to battle.

Both of us have some mighty loyal friends among the Jewish people but not one of them comes whining to ask that we "lay off" criticism of Jewish gangsters and none of them who comes carping to us of their "bosom friendship" for any public official now under our journalistic guns.

Floyd B. Olson, the county attorney who was accused in the same issue of dragging his feet in the investigation of the shooting, was a rising star on the political scene. He was a Viking-like figure, over 6 feet tall and with wavy reddish-brown hair which accented his sharp Scandinavian features and penetrating blue eyes. Olson had grown up in the poor, predominantly Jewish north side of Minneapolis. His father was a laborer who drank too much; his mother was a dominating personality who wanted her son to be a white-collar worker. This heritage, combined with his exposure to Jewish families with a Talmudic obsession for learning, had produced an ambitious leader. Olson, who had begun by selling newspapers on the street corner, was eventually to build the Farmer-Laborer party into a vital force of political reform in Minnesota and serve three terms as governor. He had already been amply tested by his 10 years in his first political job, the county attorneyship.

Following the November 19th issue, Olson promised to wage war on the yellow press and "put out of business forever the *Saturday Press* and other sensational weeklies."[10] His legal justification was a public nuisance law pushed through the Minnesota legislature in 1925 by state legislators with their own axes to grind:

> Any person who . . . shall be engaged in the business of regularly or customarily producing, publishing or circulating, having in possession, selling or giving away, (a) an obscene, lewd and lascivious newspaper, magazine, or other periodical, or (b) a malicious, scandalous and defamatory newspaper . . . is guilty of nuisance, and all persons guilty of such nuisance may be enjoined, as hereinafter provided. . . . In actions brought under above, there shall be available the defense that the truth was published with good motives and for justifiable ends.

On November 21, 1927, Olson filed a complaint with Hennepin County District Judge Mathias Baldwin, alleging that the *Saturday Press* in its short lifetime had managed to defame Charles Davis, Chief Brunskill, Mayor Leach, the *Minneapolis Tribune,* the *Minneapolis Journal,* the Hennepin County grand jury, Olson himself, and the entire Jewish community. Olson described the *Saturday Press* as "a malicious, scandalous, and defamatory publication" and asked that "said nuisance be abated." He wanted the court to issue a restraining order barring Near and Guilford or anyone else from "conducting or maintaining said nuisance under the name of the *Saturday Press,* or any other name."[11] Aware that the court would not act until there had been a hearing, he asked that a temporary restraining order be issued until the matter could be settled.

Judge Baldwin did not hesitate to issue the order which prohibited Near, Guilford, or anyone else "from producing, publishing, editing, circulating, having in their possession, selling and giving away" a publication known as the *Saturday Press.* This order applied to issues already printed as well as future issues. But Baldwin went even further by forbidding them "to produce, edit, publish, circulate, have in their possession, see, give away any publication known by any other name whatsoever containing matter of the kind alleged in the plaintiff's complaint."[12] In other words, they were forbidden to publish any paper which included attacks on public officials.

In response, Near and Guilford demurred to the temporary restraining order six days after it was issued, arguing that even if the allegations made in the complaint were true, the Public Nuisance Law of 1925 was unconstitutional. This was a procedural tactic—a legal way of saying "So what?" Thomas Latimer, their attorney, also advised his clients to obey the injunction while challenging the law.

When Near and Guilford got their day in court on December 1, Latimer argued that the law was "a subterfuge voted by the 1925 Legislature to get away from the state's constitution and libel laws"[13] in an effort to silence the *Ripsaw*, a sheet published in Duluth by a God-fearing, teetotaling crusader named John L. Morrison. Some of Morrison's "targets" had been state representatives and senators, and the politicians' retaliation, claimed Latimer, had been the gag law.

To Judge Baldwin, the *Saturday Press* was a "nuisance" in a "class of things that are harmful to the community at large."[14] However, although he rejected the demurrer, the judge was sensitive to the section of the Minnesota constitution which declared that "the liberty of the press shall forever remain inviolate, and all persons may freely speak, write and publish their sentiments on all subjects." As a result, he certified* the case to the Minnesota Supreme Court. Of course, by extending the temporary restraining order, the court also kept the *Saturday Press* off the streets of Minneapolis indefinitely.

In January, Latimer petitioned the state high court for an expedited hearing; one hundred days later the Minnesota Supreme Court convened to hear arguments on whether the state legislature had violated the Minnesota constitution when it voted for the public nuisance bill. In his argument, Latimer stressed that the publishers of the *Saturday Press* had been denied a jury trial guaranteed by the Sixth Amendment and that the entire concept of freedom of the press guaranteed by the First Amendment had been breached. Five weeks later, Chief Justice Samuel Bailey Wilson, speaking for a unanimous court, upheld the 1925 Public Nuisance Law. "In Minnesota no agency can hush the sincere and honest voice of the press," the Chief Justice wrote, "but our constitution was never intended to protect malice, scandal and defamation when untrue or published with bad motives or without justifiable ends."[15] He said it was the liberty of the press that was guaranteed—not the licentiousness. Now the tactic of demurrer no longer prevented Judge Baldwin from making the injunction permanent, as Olson had requested. But it would take four and a half months before the judge had both sides back in his courtroom.

In the meantime, Near had heard about a new organization in New York that championed lost causes and had written its founder, Roger Baldwin. His desperate appeal must have touched some responsive chord at the American Civil Liberties Union because Baldwin committed $150

---

*Unlike the rule in some other states, if the lower court judge in Minnesota does not so certify a case involving an injunction, there is no way the case can be appealed. However, the tactic of demurrer made an appeal possible. State law stipulated that if a demurrer to a temporary restraining order was overruled and if the question was certified by a judge, the order could be appealed to the Minnesota Supreme Court.

for the legal defense. Calling the Public Nuisance Law a "menace to the freedom of the country," the ACLU introduced a phrase that would become central to a series of landmark decisions: "prior restraint." In a press release announcing its decision to take the case, the ACLU stated its objection as follows: "Heretofore the only control of the press has been by prosecution for criminal or libelous matter after the offence. We see in this new device for previous restraint of publication a menace to the whole principle of freedom of the press."[16]

THE DADDY WARBUCKS OF THE FIRST AMENDMENT

Perhaps Near didn't feel completely comfortable with his new ally, Roger Baldwin, a brotherhood-of-man evangelist and a conscientious objector during World War I. Perhaps he didn't feel comfortable being defended by a group whose board included the likes of Clarence Darrow, Felix Frankfurter, and Norman Thomas. Or perhaps he didn't think that $150 was very much and wanted to make sure he had all the help he could get. For whatever reason, Jay Near decided to send out another SOS—this one to Robert Rutherford McCormick, publisher of the *Chicago Tribune*.

Six feet four inches tall, "Bertie" McCormick was a scrappy, swashbuckling, right-wing isolationist. Also known as the "Colonel" because of his commission (which originated in the Illinois militia), the jingoist publisher was reported to appear occasionally in the city room of the *Tribune* in the military attire of his beloved 1st Division, flourishing a polo mallet in one hand and reining in his German shepherd guard dogs with the other. He had waged pitched battles against mayors, presidents, and giants of industry. His many detractors described him as the most dangerous newspaper publisher in the world and as "one of the finest minds of the fourteenth century." But a veteran *Tribune* reporter was more temperate in his assessment: "He had his megalomaniac side, but that only made his reign one of grandeur."[17]

More than anything, the Colonel treasured the First Amendment, and it was his incorrigible zeal for freedom of the press—something most Americans had never thought of—that kept him from tossing Near's appeal for help into the trash basket. Near's request was simple: He needed financial and legal aid; would the Colonel help?

The penniless publisher from Minneapolis and the millionaire publisher from Chicago had much in common. Like Near, Colonel McCormick had a reputation as a bigot. "If the Ku Klux Klan had a brief life in Illinois, it undoubtedly prospered while it lived because of the *Tribune*'s aid,"[18] wrote Oswald Garrison Villard, editor and publisher of the *Nation*. The colonel had been known to make fun of Jews in public. "In one instance he went so far as to mock the accent and forms of speech of an earlier speaker at the same luncheon table," reporter Frank Waldrop wrote in his biography of McCormick. McCormick and Near were also both anti-communists, convinced that the "Red Menace" was more than a scare.

McCormick felt that Near's charges were true and assessed the articles in the *Saturday Press* as "fairly temperate and possessed of some literary merit."[19] However, he was not about to join Near's campaign before consulting a few advisors like Weymouth Kirkland, an old law partner and one of his few lifelong friends. Kirkland could not wait to get his hands on the case. After studying the files of the *Saturday Press,* Kirkland wrote McCormick: "Bert, the mere statement of the case makes my blood boil. Whether the articles are true or not, for a judge without a jury to suppress a newspaper by writ of injunction, is unthinkable." He urged the Colonel to act and warned: "If this decision is sustained in the Supreme Court, how easy it would be for a 'small' administration, through control of the legislature, to pass a like statute in Illinois or some other State." Concerned that the ACLU might be in over its head, Kirkland suggested that "we . . . get in touch with the people appealing to see that their briefs are properly prepared."[20] It was not long before the ACLU was nudged out of the case.

In October, when Judge Baldwin called his court to order, Latimer was not the only attorney seated at Near's table; the *Chicago Tribune*'s lawyers William H. Symes and Charles Rathbun sat beside him. The hearing was what Judge Baldwin described as "a mere formality," and so, after 26 months, the temporary injunction became permanent.

One person conspicuously absent was Howard Guilford. Having grown impatient with the tedious litigation and no longer interested in tilting at constitutional windmills, he had sold his interest in the paper to Near for an unknown sum of money (some say no cash changed hands). As Near and McCormick had no objections, the state supreme court complied with Guilford's request to be severed from the case, which would be eventually known as *Near* v. *Minnesota.*

Although McCormick's attorneys were anxious to bring the case to the United States Supreme Court, Baldwin's second opinion had first to be appealed to the state's highest court. That December 2, 1929, hearing was little more than a procedural ceremony. This time it took the state high court only 18 days to issue a single-page rejection of Near's final appeal.

It had become apparent to Near that McCormick's attorneys had no serious intentions of winning this round in the Minnesota court, but were aiming for the high court in Washington. Near was enraged with the members of McCormick's law firm as well as the Minnesota judges. To him, the latter were corrupt and the former inept stuffed shirts from Chicago. Near was not interested in far-off constitutional victories, but in getting his paper back on the streets as soon as possible. He could not have known that the "procrastination" would be to his benefit.

ATH HOLDS TWO WILD-CARD SEATS ON THE SUPREME COURT

On March 8, 1930, the justices of the Supreme Court of the United States began their weekly conference. It was to be a festive day, marking the 89th birthday of Oliver Wendell Holmes, Jr. Painfully stooped, his thick snowy hair glittering, his blue-grey eyes flashing, Holmes had been an associate justice since President Theodore Roosevelt appointed him in 1902.

That afternoon the Court was just getting down to cases when a page interrupted to announce that Associate Justice Edward T. Sanford had died suddenly. They later learned that the 65-year-old justice from Tennessee had collapsed in his dentist's office while having a tooth extracted. The justices adjourned immediately, only to be jolted five hours later by the news that William Howard Taft, the only former president in history to serve as chief justice, had also died, after slipping into a coma. The 72-year-old Taft had resigned from the Court a month earlier, broken in health and spirit by a stroke and arteriosclerosis.

The resignation and death left a large hole in the conservative Court that Taft had carefully molded. Five of the associate justices had been Taft's stalwart supporters: Edward T. Sanford, Pierce Butler, Willis Van Devanter, James C. McReynolds, and George Sutherland. With Taft's vote, they provided a consistent conservative majority of 6 to 3, with Justices Louis Brandeis, Oliver Wendell Holmes, and often Harlan Fiske Stone dissenting. Taft was frequently irked by the three dissenters. "I think we can hold our six to steady the court," he had written in 1929. "Brandeis is of course hopeless, as Holmes is, and Stone is. . . . The only hope we have at keeping a consistent declaration of constitutional law is for us to live as long as we can."[21]

Sanford's voting had in fact been so in tandem with Taft's that it had been eclipsed by the chief justice's 340-pound shadow, just as now Sanford's demise was obscured by obituaries about Taft. Yet among the opinions Sanford wrote was one that would be of crucial relevance to *Near* v. *Minnesota*. In 1925 Sanford had written the majority opinion upholding the conviction of Benjamin Gitlow, an avowed radical socialist and publisher of a socialist paper. In that 7-to-2 decision the majority had upheld the constitutionality of New York State's Criminal Anarchy law, under which Gitlow had been sent to prison for 5 to 10 years for advocating in his paper rule by the proletariat. Nestled in Sanford's sweeping denunciation of inflammatory language was one sentence that even the dissenters Holmes and Brandeis treasured. For the first time a majority opinion of the Supreme Court hinted that the First Amendment could be applied to the states: "For present purposes we may and do assume that freedom of speech and press—which are protected by the First Amendment from abridgment by Congress—are among the fundamental personal rights and liberties protected by the due process clause of the Fourteenth Amendment from impairment by the States."[22]

The role of the Fourteenth Amendment was at the heart of what divided the Court factions. It was a question of how to interpret the term "liberty." Holmes, Brandeis, and Stone looked to the Bill of Rights for guidance in defining the concept. The result was that they would incorporate the fundamental principles guaranteed in the Bill of Rights into the Fourteenth Amendment and make them applicable to the states. But to Taft's majority, the Fourteenth Amendment and the judicial theory of substantive due process* was a means of preserving a way of life, a way of organizing society by which the establishment retained control of the institutions of business and government. Thus, they defined "liberty" to mean "liberty of contract," a term not expressly stated in the Constitution.

Because this difference was such a basic one and the Court factions were so solid, had *Near* v. *Minnesota* been argued and decided while Taft and Sanford were still alive, the two justices' interpretation of the First and Fourteenth Amendments would have almost certainly decided *Near,* and conceivably stood as a precedent in press-freedom cases for the next half century. And, indeed, at the time there was no reason to believe that the outcome would be any different, as it was expected that President Hoover would appoint two more conservatives.

Hoover, the thirty-first President of the United States, appointed the eleventh chief justice. His choice was New York Republican Charles Evans Hughes. The 68-year-old chief justice designate, with his Jove-like beard, long, flowing grey-white mustache, and luxuriant eyebrows, was a sculptural vision of a chief justice. "He looked more like God than any other man I ever knew,"[23] former solicitor general Erwin Griswold recently observed.

Although Hughes was perceived by many as a corporate-loving conservative, this image was far from accurate. It is true that of the 54 cases he argued before the Supreme Court from 1925 to 1930, most were on behalf of large corporations, but during his legal career he also fought for the United Mine Workers, Socialist legislators in New York, and the Legal Aid Society. During his earlier tenure on the Supreme Court as an associate justice from 1910 to 1916, Hughes had voted to uphold minimum wage laws and to restrict working hours for women. Hughes considered himself less of a conservative than the "four horsemen" of the old guard (Van Devanter, McReynolds, Sutherland, and Butler), less the crusading liberal than Holmes and Brandeis. "It is well to be liberal, but not messy,"[24] Hughes was to write of himself.

*See Chapter 2, p. 27.

Sanford's seat was taken by Owen J. Roberts, often referred to as the most powerful member of the Court in the 1930s because he was, as it turned out, the roving, swing vote between conservatives and liberals. As a Philadelphia lawyer, Roberts had had an impressive list of clients, ranging from J. P. Morgan and Company to the Pennsylvania Railroad, and his annual income was reported to be $150,000. (In those days, a supreme court justice was paid $20,000.) He had also been a determined prosecutor of the Teapot Dome oil scandals, which had sent several members of the Harding administration to prison. Roberts' views on the First Amendment were not known. The Fourteenth Amendment Roberts viewed as having worked revolutionary changes on the United States Constitution—greater, he believed, than those embodied in any other amendment before or since. Those who had known him in Pennsylvania classified Roberts as being conservative, but not in the style of McReynolds and Butler.

ARGUMENT DAY

Near's case was docketed on April 26, 1930, but oral arguments were not scheduled until Friday, January 30, 1931. At the stroke of noon, the old marble clock above the golden eagle summoned the nine justices in their silk robes. It was the same eagle beneath which Daniel Webster, John C. Calhoun, and Henry Clay had dueled in their classic debates, culminating in the Compromise of 1850. But the U.S. Senate had moved in 1859 to a more spacious chamber in the new north wing of the Capitol. The focal point of the tiny room was the long mahogany bench, decorated with spooled balustrades, from which the nine justices ruled. Around the arc of the semicircular chamber were the busts of men who had served before them—John Jay, John Marshall, and Roger Taney among them. The courtroom's intimate size did not detract from the majesty of "this unique and hallowed spot";[25] its coffered ceilings, marbled Ionic columns, and red wool carpet gave it a quality that caused visitors to whisper in hushed awe.

"The Honorable, the Chief Justice and the Associate Justices of the Supreme Court," trumpeted the Court crier. "Oyez! Oyez! Oyez!" As Justices Van Devanter and McReynolds were absent, Hughes leaned forward and said in his bass voice, "I presume Justices Van Devanter and McReynolds are vouched in,"[26] meaning that even though they would miss the oral arguments, they could participate in the decision. No one objected, and the Court proceeded. (The practice has since been changed. Those who don't hear oral arguments don't vote.)

Each side was allotted an hour to argue its position. Hughes was known for his timekeeping. The moment an advocate opened his mouth he was being timed, and the Chief Justice was meticulously strict about informing counsel when time was up—even in the middle of a word.

Weymouth Kirkland, as appellant's counsel, was the first to address the Court. The arguments were not much different from those presented at the two previous hearings in the Minnesota Supreme Court—that the injunction was a prior restraint, which violated the First and Fourteenth Amendments.[27]

Kirkland admitted that the articles were defamatory, but added "So long as men do evil, so long will newspapers publish defamation." He told the Court that "every legitimate newspaper in the country regularly and customarily publishes defamation, as it has a right to in criticizing government agencies."

But Kirkland's arguments went even further He contended that every person has a constitutional right to publish "malicious, scandalous and defamatory matter, though untrue and for unjustifiable ends." Kirkland added that a person publishing such material might be subject to punishment *afterwards*. Thus Kirkland touched on the central issue of the conflict: Was the injunction a prior restraint against future publications or was it merely punishment?

Arguing for the state of Minnesota was Deputy Attorney General James E. Markham, along with William C. Larsen and Arthur Markve, representing Hennepin County's prosecutor's office which had brought the original injunction in 1927. (Olson was now governor.)

Markham, who did most of the argument, denied that the Minnesota action against Near amounted to a previous restraint or censorship. He pointed out that no injunction had been issued until after the *Saturday Press* had defamed public officials and had become a nuisance.

THE BAREST OF MARGINS

Now the Supreme Court's hardest work would begin in a hot, stale room on the ground floor of the Capitol. Every Saturday at noon the nine justices assembled, and closeted behind two double doors, with windows bolted to prevent leaks, they conducted the vital business of listening to and debating one another's views on cases, and then voting.

It was up to the chief justice to set the agenda and, subsequently, if he voted with the majority, to assign the writing of opinions. As usual, there were many items on the afternoon's agenda—items as diverse as double jeopardy in a tax case and patents for the "false rabbit" at a dog track.

After each justice had a chance to comment, Hughes called for the vote. Voting order reversed the order of comment, with the most junior member voting first, the chief justice last. And so, late that afternoon, the roll call was finally taken on what was in effect the fate of the nation's press and reading public. Was the Minnesota statute constitutional? Roberts: No. Stone: No. Butler: Yes. Brandeis: No. McReynolds: Yes. Van Devanter: Yes. Holmes: No. It was up to the chief justice to cast the deciding vote. Hughes: No. By the barest of margins, 5 to 4, previous restraints were ruled to be unconstitutional.[28]

No one was more acutely aware of how precarious the decision had been than the Chief Justice himself. At about 5:30, after the other justices left for home, Hughes sat down with his law clerk and began working out the assignment of opinions. He realized that the opinion in *Near* v. *Minnesota* would have to include the absolutist views of Brandeis and the far-from-absolute ones of Roberts. It would have to be a temperate opinion that would carry political weight; next to *Near* he wrote the name "Hughes."

It took four months of circulating drafts and redrafts to iron out the intricacies and subtleties of the opinion. The opinion came June 1, 1931, the last day of the 1930 term, and was the sixth and last opinion of the day. Although Hughes usually summarized opinions, he chose to read the *Near* opinion word for word.

After reading the 15 paragraphs summarizing the facts, Hughes raised his voice and eyes as he recited his opinion. "It is no longer open to doubt that the liberty of the press, and of speech, is within the liberty safeguarded by the due process clause of the Fourteenth Amendment from invasion by state action."[29] Until this point spectators might not have detected any signals of what the judgment was to be, but now it was clear. Hughes' voice echoed across the chamber as he summed up his view of the Minnesota law, "This is of the essence of censorship."

"Chief Justice Hughes threw all his ardor" into delivery, the *Chicago Tribune* correspondent Arthur Sears Henning wrote. "In a loud voice into which he injected considerable feeling at times, the head of the judicial branch of government, who in a long public career has been subjected to a vast amount of bitter denunciation in the press, argued for the liberty of the press to criticize public officials as an outstanding safeguard of the people from the imposition of tyranny."[30]

Hughes's majority opinion had borrowed richly from the great English legal scholar William Blackstone, adamantly insisting that libel laws, not suppression, were the proper solution to false accusations and defamation. Quoting James Madison, who he said was a leading spirit in the preparation of the First Amendment, the Chief Justice stated:

> Some degree of abuse is inseparable from the proper use of everything, and in no instance is this more true than in that of the press. It has accordingly been decided by the practice of the States, that it is better to leave a few of its noxious branches to their luxuriant growth, than, by pruning them away, to injure the vigour of those yielding proper fruits.

Hughes was buttressing the position that the right to criticize public officials was one of the bulwarks of the nation:

The fact that for approximately one hundred and fifty years there has been almost an entire absence of attempts to impose previous restraints upon publications relating to the malfeasance of public officers is significant of the deep-seated conviction that such restraints would violate constitutional right. Public officers, whose character and conduct remain open to debate and free discussion in the press, find their remedies for false accusations in actions under libel laws providing for redress and punishment, and not in proceedings to restrain the publication of newspapers and periodicals. The general principle that the constitutional guaranty of the liberty of the press gives immunity from previous restraints has been approved in many decisions under the provisions of state constitutions.

As one reporter wrote, "The Chief Justice fairly thundered as he came to the meat of the coconut," emphasizing that the importance of the immunity had not lessened and that the problems of abuses of the press had not increased. Hughes noted that "the administration of government has become more complex, the opportunities for malfeasance and corruption have multiplied, crime has grown to most serious proportions, and the danger of its protection by unfaithful officials and of the impairment of the fundamental security of life and property by criminal alliances and official neglect, emphasizes the primary need of a vigilant and courageous press. . . ." The occurrence of abuses, perpetrated by "miscreant purveyors of scandal does not make any the less necessary the immunity of the press from previous restraint in dealing with official misconduct." The proper way of dealing with those abuses was by subsequent punishment, for example, for libel, rather than by unconstitutional prior restraints.

Yet Hughes' views were not absolute. One carefully drawn paragraph in the majority opinion, which few newspapers highlighted, acknowledged that there could be limitations. Borrowing from Holmes in the 1919 free speech case of *Schenck* v. *United States** to make his point, the Chief Justice wrote that even the protection against prior restraint is not "absolutely unlimited":

When a nation is at war many things that might be said in time of peace are such a hindrance to its effort that their utterance will not be endured so long as men fight and that no Court could regard them as protected by any constitutional right. . . . No one would question but that a government might prevent actual obstruction to its recruiting service or the publication of sailing dates of transports or the number and location of troops. On similar grounds, the primary requirements of decency may be enforced against obscene publications. The security of the community life may be protected against incitements to acts of violence and the overthrow by force of orderly government.

*See Chapter 5.

But, Hughes concluded, "These limitations are not applicable here."

Now it was the four dissenters' turn to be heard. Pierce Butler read the dissent. He complained that the Hughes opinion "declares Minnesota and every other State powerless to restrain by injunction . . . malicious, scandalous and defamatory periodicals." He denounced the court judgment: "It gives to freedom of the press a meaning and a scope not heretofore recognized and construes 'liberty' in the due process clause of the Fourteenth Amendment to put upon the State a Federal restriction that is without precedent."

Further, Butler and the minority commented that the Minnesota Public Nuisance Law "does not operate as a *previous* restraint on publication within the proper meaning of that phrase." To Butler, a previous restraint was "administrative control in advance such as was formerly exercised by the licensers and censors." In this case the minority of four, including the two who had not heard the oral arguments, argued that there was previous publication—in fact, nine malicious, scandalous, and defamatory editions. Butler included a lengthy footnote quoting from the *Saturday Press* to support his characterization. "The business and publications unquestionably constitute an abuse of the right of free press," Butler wrote. "There is no question of the power of the State to denounce such transgressions." The restraint on publication, Butler continued, "is only in respect of continuing to do what had been duly adjudged to constitute a nuisance."

Butler struck hard at a weak point in the majority opinion. "The opinion seems to concede that . . . the business of regularly publishing and circulating an obscene periodical may be enjoined as a nuisance." If "lewd publications constitutionally may be enjoined it is hard to understand why the [nuisance] resulting from a regular business of malicious defamation may not."

Butler ended his dissenting opinion by denying the majority's view that existing laws could effectively eradicate the evils resulting from such publications as the *Saturday Press.* As Butler, Van Devanter, Sutherland, and McReynolds put it, in the name of freedom of the press the Supreme Court of the United States "exposes the peace and good order of every community" to "malicious assaults of any insolvent publisher who may have . . . sufficient capacity to contrive and put into effect a scheme or program for oppression, blackmail or extortion."

THE FORGOTTEN CHAMPION

Jay M. Near was gloatingly triumphant when he heard the news, but none of the national, state, or even local newspapers bothered to report his reaction; indeed, most of the papers did not even mention his name when they spoke of the decision, referring to it as "the gag law case." The *Minneapolis Tribune* falsely reported that Guilford had been the one to take the case to the Supreme Court. Near, the unorthodox champion of the First Amendment, was all but forgotten.

In October 1932, bearing the caption "The Paper That Refused to Stay Gagged," the *Saturday Press,* edited by Jay M. Near, reappeared. The slightly exaggerated slogan under the flag of the paper contained Near's version of the decision: "The only paper in the United States with a United States Supreme Court record of being right; the only paper that dared fight for freedom of the press—fought and won."

That distinction would eventually not belong solely to the *Saturday Press.* Other newspapers would challenge the government's right to issue a prior restraint or a judge's right to limit pretrial coverage. And in each case the constitutional foundation on which they would rely was Jay Near's case, *Near* v. *Minnesota.* The case's ultimate legacy was finally realized 40 years later, almost to the day, in the clash between the President of the United States and two powerful newspapers, the *New York Times* and the *Washington Post,* in a case known as the Pentagon Papers.

American newsmen inspect the wreckage of an American-made B-26 bomber near Ciron, Cuba, shortly after the Bay of Pigs invasion, April, 1961. *AP/Wide World Photos*

Tad Szulc had the story of the century, the imminent invasion of Cuba by Cuban exiles trained and equipped by the United States. But significant parts of the story didn't make the front page of the *New York Times* because the editors were worried about the national security of the United States. When should the press put national security before the public's need to know? Who should decide?

THE MYTH ABOUT THE BAY OF PIGS
Freedom of the Press and National Security

In times of clear and present danger, the courts have held that even the privileged rights of the First Amendment must yield to the public's need for national security.

John F. Kennedy, April 27, 1961,
10 days after the Bay of Pigs invasion[1]

Maybe if you had printed more about the [Bay of Pigs] operation, you would have saved us from a colossal mistake.

John F. Kennedy, in private conversation with *New York Times* Managing Editor Turner Catledge, April 1961[2]

On the last day in March 1961, *New York Times* reporter Tad Szulc stopped over in Miami en route from an assignment in Brazil to a new post in Washington. Szulc, who had earned a reputation as an investigative reporter with a knack for stumbling on big stories, hoped simply to spend some time with friends and a few Miami sources. He joined a friend at the Mac Bar in the MacAllister Hotel for a drink and some conversation, little knowing that one of the biggest stories of the decade was about to land in his lap.[3]

Szulc's friend was telling him that rumors in the Cuban community about an American-backed invasion of Cuba were now being taken seriously by the press. Although Cuba's routine wails in the United Nations about an imminent invasion were met by America's routine denials, the evidence indicated that Cuba had been speaking the truth. Szulc pondered these remarks but was really more interested in moving on to Washington. He had served his stint as Latin American affairs reporter. It was no longer his beat. But then an old source from the Cuban exile community wandered into the bar. He corroborated the rumors for Szulc, proudly admitting that American government officials were backing and sponsoring the invasion. Coincidentally, a few minutes later, a U.S. naval officer whom Szulc recognized as an old hand from the pre-Castro days in Cuba, sauntered ominously by and bid Szulc a nervous good evening.

Too many things were adding up. Despite Szulc's desire to move on to Washington, he couldn't resist a little more nosing around. Donning his characteristic trench coat, Szulc ducked into the Latin Quarter of Miami. He soon learned that a hospital ship was anchored off the Florida coast, awaiting orders to sail. Young women from the Cuban exile community were volunteering to be trained as nurses. Blood was being collected. Groups of young Cuban exiles were saying goodbye to their families and leaving on trucks for an abandoned airstrip. From his CIA sources in Miami, Szulc then learned that not only was the agency training these men for the invasion, but the invasion was soon to be launched.

What was developing here—what Szulc was uncovering—was, of course, the last stage of preparations for the ill-fated Bay of Pigs invasion, launched on the morning of April 17, 1961, only 18 days after Szulc had his drink in the bar. It was a covert operation, planned by the United States government, to overthrow Castro's Communist regime in Cuba. The mission was to be carried out by Cuban exiles who would land at the Bay of Pigs. The exiles had been encouraged by the CIA to think that the landing would have "umbrella" support from American air and sea forces in the area, but Kennedy finally decided against such direct American involvement. For this reason, among others, the invasion was a ludicrous failure.

The Bay of Pigs fiasco stands as one of the major embarrassments not only to the presidency and the Central Intelligence Agency, but to the press as well. Szulc was in fact not the first to come across the story, and when the Cuban exiles pushed off that baleful morning, there were possibly more members of the press in on this presidential secret than any other in recent history. Many editors didn't dare publish the story they had. Some had been asked not to by the CIA or by the White House itself; others made the decision on their own. And those editors who did publish cleansed their stories of enough detail to mollify even the strictest of censors. Hence the press's failure to publish involved not legal intervention, but self-censorship. Curiously, it wasn't only the government and the press that knew about the invasion, but also the enemy. Only the American public was left out of the secret.

Thus, the Bay of Pigs raised complex issues, showing that the press's constitutional claim to inform and the government's claim to national security are not easily squared. Every reporter and editor must wonder what they would have done had they been, for example, Tad Szulc, who unraveled the story, or the *Times* managing editor, Turner Catledge, who received it. Obviously, the decision could not have been a simple one. This was no story of a greedy politician who embezzled a few dollars or of a little corruption at city hall. This was an invasion of a foreign country. People might die if you printed this story. That thought clearly hung in the minds of the editors and writers who were asked directly by the government not to publish. What do you do when you have the story and the White House or the CIA asks you not to print? After all, an entire intelligence community planned this invasion. Don't they know much more than you? And yet our Constitution makes no mention of "national security," only that Congress should have the power "to make all laws which shall be necessary and proper" in order to carry out their other explicit powers. The government's position has been that if Congress is to have the power to declare war and if the president is to have the power to wage war, they must also have the power to keep military secrets. The Constitution, however, does speak explicitly of freedom of the press. The rationale was that we should have government in the sunshine, open and well-aired, responsive to an informed electorate.

THE CONSTITUTIONAL CONVENTION

Both of these issues—national security and a free press—trace back to the Constitutional Convention of 1787. On August 11, James Madison of Virginia and John Rutledge of South Carolina proposed that each house of Congress keep a journal of its proceedings "except such part of the proceedings of the Senate when acting not in its Legislative Capacity as may be judged by that House to require secrecy." Elbridge Gerry of Massachusetts and Roger Sherman of Connecticut agreed with the proposal but wanted to narrow it to read "except such [proceedings] as relate to treaties and military operations." But others objected to the exclusions. James Wilson of Pennsylvania argued, "The people have a right to know what their agents are doing or have done, and it should not be in the option of the Legislature to conceal their proceedings."[4] So the secrecy clause was voted down. A guarantee of freedom of the press was also introduced during the debates, but also voted down as not necessary. Of course, when the Bill of Rights was drafted two years later, freedom of the press—which Madison called one of the most essential liberties— was guaranteed by the First Amendment.

One of the earliest clashes of national security and press freedom involved a firebrand named Benjamin Franklin Bache, a grandson of Benjamin Franklin and a Republican, who mounted a tireless attack on Adams and the Federalists. Bache had inherited his grandfather's love of press liberty but—as he showed on numerous occasions—not his tact. For example, when George Washington, a Federalist, stepped down after two terms as President, Bache wrote in his *Philadelphia Aurora,* "If ever a man has debauched a nation, George Washington has debauched the

United States."[5] For this particular instance of free expression, incidentally, Bache paid dearly. Although the government did nothing to abridge his press freedom, the general public, who revered Washington, stormed Bache's office, pommeled him, and destroyed his press.

In 1798, the second year of John Adams' term, Bache printed one of the first national security leaks in our history. It was a secret missive from the French foreign minister Charles Talleyrand to Adams. Since it intimated that war between the two nations could be prevented, Bache ran it in his paper before Adams had a chance to read it, seriously embarrassing the President. An enraged chief executive had Bache arrested on common law charges of seditious libel. But Bache's arrest was only the beginning. A few weeks later, at the goading of President Adams, Congress passed the Sedition Act, which provided for prosecution of editors critical of the government. To the Federalists, who were in power, the fate of the new nation was far more important than the freedom of a few Republican newspapers. To them, the national security depended on suppression of "factions" threatening to tear the country apart over the issue of our foreign relations with England and France.

The issue of national security versus freedom of the press was not addressed by the Court until 1931 in *Near* v. *Minnesota.* Chief Justice Hughes, in asserting that prior restraints were unconstitutional, noted that there might be exceptions. "No one would question," he wrote, "but that a government [at war] might prevent . . . the publication of sailing dates of transports."[6] He seemed to be indicating that there were certain areas in national security where that prohibition against prior restraint would not apply.

ANOTHER ERA

It may seem difficult to believe—given today's adversarial relationship between press and president—that journalists acquiesced so readily to a White House or CIA request. Yet more unbelievable, perhaps, is the fact that others quashed the story in the absence of any request. But the times were different; the CIA, and the OSS (Office of Strategic Services) before that, were greatly respected by the public, and a friendly trust existed between the press and the White House, built up by affable presidents like Roosevelt, Truman, and Eisenhower. In fact, in tracing the decline of that trust, many historians and journalists perceive the Bay of Pigs incident as the rite of passage that set the press free of presidential influence. For example, in the 1970s *New York Times* correspondent Max Frankel, now editor of the *Times* editorial page, looked back at the Bay of Pigs as the beginning of the end of a trust that was finally "lost somewhere between Dallas and Tonkin."[7]

Thus, the Bay of Pigs changed journalists' attitude toward the presidency from professional awe to back-alley suspicion. Consider Tad

Szulc. After the fiasco ended, he was stunned to hear Arthur Schlesinger, Jr., President Kennedy's special assistant, reason away his own denials with the remark, "I, at least, had the excuse that I was working for the government."[8] Outraged, Szulc wrote that Schlesinger, in effect, was suggesting that "we should have assumed from the outset that we are dealing with a bunch of liars."[9] Today many reporters begin with precisely that assumption. I. F. Stone, the intrepid investigative journalist, regularly cautions young journalists with the cynical admonition, "Every government is run by liars. Nothing they say should be believed. That's a prima facie assumption unless proven to the contrary."[10]

As Szulc recently summed up the situation: "It was a different time. This was before Vietnam and the Dominican Republic [invasion of 1965], it was an age of innocence."[11]

THE PRESS AND THE BAY OF PIGS

In order to fully understand the behavior of the press in the Bay of Pigs incident, it is also necessary to return to the events in late 1960 just a few days before John Kennedy was to win his election. Under President Eisenhower's order, Cuban exiles in Miami and New York were being quietly recruited by the CIA for the purpose of invading Cuba. A remote camp in Guatemala was being used to train the young soldiers, in accordance with CIA plans.* No one outside knew a thing.

The *Miami Herald* was probably the first publication to learn anything about the Bay of Pigs invasion. Its information dated back to August 1960 and was acquired unexpectedly. Some kids had thrown firecrackers into a CIA training camp near Homestead, Florida, about 25 miles south of Miami, where the agency was training exiles for the mission. The exiles, fearing they were being attacked by pro-Castro spies, rushed out shooting. One of their bullets wounded a youngster. When the subsequent investigation was quashed by federal authorities, *Herald* editors ordered their Washington correspondent, David Kraslow, to investigate.

In short order, Kraslow uncovered the story and turned over a 1,500-word account to his editors. The implications of such a story were obvious, and the editors' anxiety led to an audience with CIA director Allen Dulles. In that meeting, reporter Kraslow and Washington Bureau Chief Ed Lahey were told that publication "would be most harmful to the national interest."[12] The story was spiked.†

---

*One of the top CIA planners was Howard Hunt. Eleven years later, White House consultant Hunt's phone number would be discovered in a petty burglar's jacket. That connection would lead to another American humiliation called "Watergate."

†The *Miami Herald* did eventually publish some of its information before the invasion, but only after the *New York Times* had "broken" the story in its own tepid fashion. When the *Herald* eventually did publish, its editors ran a disclaimer, explaining that they were lifting their self-

Just a few weeks after the *Miami Herald* had uncovered and then covered up the story, an article appeared on the front page of a Guatemalan daily called *La Hora*. Written by journalist Clemente Marroquin Rojas, who would later become the country's vice president, the first sentence informed Guatemalans that "there is little doubt that an invasion of Cuba is being prepared in Guatemala."[13] By coincidence, Ronald Hilton, a Stanford professor and specialist in Latin American affairs, was passing though Guatemala at the time. He took Rojas' story and its full details of a CIA training camp in a small Guatemalan town called Retalheleu and published the information in his scholarly journal, *American Hispanic Report*. But there it had little impact.

So, knowing that what he had was important, Hilton took it to Carey McWilliams, editor of the *Nation*. In its November 19, 1960, edition, the *Nation* editorialized:

> The United States Central Intelligence Agency has acquired a large tract of land in Guatemala, at an outlay in excess of $1,000,000, which is stoutly fenced and heavily guarded. Dr. Hilton was informed that it is "common knowledge" in Guatemala that the tract is being used as a training ground for Cuban counter-revolutionaries who are preparing for an eventual landing in Cuba. It was also said that U.S. personnel and equipment are being used at the base. The camp is said to be located in Retalheleu, between Guatemala City and the coast. . . . We ourselves, of course, pretend to no first-hand knowledge of the facts; nevertheless, we feel an obligation to bring the subject to public attention. If Washington is ignorant of the existence of the base, or, knowing that it exists, is nevertheless innocent of any involvement in it, then surely the appropriate authorities will want to scotch all invidious rumors and issue a full statement of the real facts. On the other hand, if the reports as heard by Dr. Hilton are true, then public pressure should be brought to bear upon the Administration to abandon this dangerous and hair-brained [sic] project.
>
> There is a second reason why we believe the reports merit publication: they can, and should, be checked immediately by all U.S. news media with correspondents in Guatemala.[14]

Only one daily newspaper immediately took up the *Nation*'s plea for exposure, the *Gazette and Daily* in York, Pennsylvania. This lone crusading voice, which is now, unfortunately, gone, reprinted the *Nation*'s editorial and tried to goad a reluctant Associated Press into an investiga-

---

imposed embargo because the information had been already revealed: "Publication of the accompanying story on the Miami–Guatemala airlift was withheld . . . by the Herald. Its release was decided upon only after U.S. aid to anti-Castro fighters in Guatemala was first revealed elsewhere." See Victor Bernstein and Jesse Gordon, "The Press and the Bay of Pigs," *Columbia University Forum*, Fall 1967, p. 12.

tion. The AP lethargically pursued the story, reporting only the government's version of the facts. In a November 25, 1960, editorial, the *Gazette and Daily* chastised the AP: "So, the Gazette and Daily asked the Associated Press, which has correspondents all over the world, to check this report. The AP said The Nation article seemed "thin"—an adjective which, we think, fairly describes any story as it begins to develop from hearsay or secondhand sources—and did not justify retelling on the AP wire."[15]

At the end of the editorial the *Gazette and Daily* reported an incident which, had it been pursued, could have opened up the story. The incident had taken place in San Francisco and reached the *Gazette and Daily* via Dr. Hilton. The inspector general of the CIA, Lyman B. Kirkpatrick, had made a speech before the Commonwealth Club. After finishing, he was asked about the reports of an invasion. He paused thoughtfully and then said, "It will be a black day if we are found out." Even with this high-ranking confirmation, the story languished on. In ending its editorial, the *Gazette and Daily* wrote wistfully about "the facts," intimating —accurately, as it turned out—that the press would not act fast enough to inform the people about an issue they should, but never would, be able to decide:

> Well, do we yet have the facts? The answer is no. Some, maybe. Or the leads to facts. But not the simple truth itself. And yet it is there. And the distance between the people and the facts on this story is a measure of how far we have to go to secure, really, government of, by and for the people.[16]

Even after several more papers pressed for coverage, the wire services responded with nothing more than silence and inertia. A clue to their inaction emerged two years later. At his retirement party in 1963, AP boss Alan J. Gould, remarking on the issue of unofficial censorship by the government, said that "when the President of the United States calls you in and says this is a matter vital to security, you accept the injunction."[17]

Meanwhile, the *Nation* continued its attempt to publicize the story, sending the galley proofs of its editorial to the major publications. The story was universally ignored. At the *New York Times,* it was unpursued for two months until a reader wrote to the *Times* asking why the charges hadn't been either corroborated or denounced. Clifton Daniel, the assistant managing editor, then told the foreign news editor to have the story investigated. Reporter Paul Kennedy was then sent to Guatemala and on January 10, 1961, the story received its first exposure in a major newspaper. But Kennedy's article was a disappointment. Short on answers and long on the official line, it elucidated nothing. Kennedy merely interviewed Guatemalan President Ydigoras. Given the well-known fact that the president had been installed in a 1954 coup d'état that was masterminded by the CIA, it is no surprise that his version of things closely paralleled Washington's.

But as preparations for the invasion accelerated, more reporters uncovered the story, and some of them began to consider the national security implications. One such reporter was Howard Handleman, who worked for *U.S. News & World Report.* On March 31, the day of Tad Szulc's arrival in Miami, Handleman, who had already uncovered similar facts, went to Arthur Schlesinger, Jr., and told him what he had learned. As Handleman recalls, Schlesinger, although shocked at his accuracy and details, did not ask him to hold the story. But Handleman was already aware of the national security implications. "I was conditioned by the Korean War," Handleman says. "When you sat down to write a story in those days, you always thought of three things—what is the story, what are the national security implications, and what is that SOB down the hall going to write. So the guy who took the most lax view, got the play." Handleman admits that he had the whole story before the invasion. "But I didn't feel privileged to tell any of it," he says. In fact, he was stunned at what others were printing. "When I called my office," he says today, "and told them what the Miami papers were printing, my deputy editor's reaction was, 'My God, are these guys Americans?'"[18]

At about the same time in early April, Karl Meyer, a specialist in Latin American affairs for the *Washington Post,* submitted a lengthy exposé on CIA activities among the Cuban refugees to the *New Republic.* Meyer had rejected the idea of publishing the article for his employer. "Frankly I just didn't think they'd print it," he says today.[19] Philip Graham, the *Post*'s dynamic and flamboyant publisher, was a close friend of and advisor to President Kennedy. Besides, Meyer doubted that the climate was right for such a story at the *Post,* which was still a decade away from its Watergate-era investigative reporting. Meyer admired the style of the *New Republic* and its editor Gilbert Harrison. He sent Harrison the story but, curiously, requested that it be run under a pseudonym. Meyer has difficulty in explaining his request. "Mostly I guess I had no desire to embarrass the *Post,*" he says.

Harrison reluctantly agreed to the pseudonym but decided that "so stunning" a story required some kind of checking. "And then," Harrison recalls, "I did something I later regretted, something I'd never done before and which I'd never do again." He sent the manuscript to his friend Arthur Schlesinger at the White House. "My original reaction was that I didn't want to run it unless Meyer put his name on it. So I called Arthur, whose response was, 'Will you let me see it?'"[20] Schlesinger mentions the incident in his book *One Thousand Days* and says he found the article "a careful, accurate and devastating account of CIA activities among the refugees."[21] Schlesinger called Harrision back immediately, told him that he had shown the article to one other person, and then said, "I must ask you on the highest authority of the government not to publish it."[22] Schlesinger has since confirmed in a private interview that the other person was President Kennedy himself, who had indicated that he hoped the story could be stopped. Harrison notified Meyer, who also expressed reservations about the appropriateness of publishing his story. The story was pulled.

In the weeks before the invasion, only one member of the press— the *New York Times*—really struggled with the clash of national security and press freedom. The other media either dropped coverage of the story or waited it out. The press knew that no president had ever taken legal measures to restrain the press—any more than Kennedy was doing now. Freedom of the press was understood, and still is, as a nearly inviolable right. For the American press in 1961 it was not a question of whether they *had the right* to publish the information, it was a question of whether publishing it *was right*.

After Tad Szulc had spent twenty-four hours investigating the story in Miami, he too wondered about that. Hesitant to simply file the story over the phone, he requested a meeting with his editors in New York and flew up at once. His editors agreed that the story posed problems, but they wanted the facts first. So they directed Szulc to return to Miami and assigned him to the story fulltime. On the way back, Szulc briefed James Reston, who was the *Times*'s bureau chief in Washington. Reston took Szulc's report to CIA director Allen Dulles for confirmation. Dulles would not deny the story to Reston, cryptically suggesting that there was an invasion in progress. He did not make any request for suppression.

In Florida, meanwhile, Szulc quickly dug up enough facts to write the story. On April 6, he filed a dispatch to New York, leaving the dilemma of publication in the hands of the *Times*'s editors. The story was scheduled to lead the front page of the April 7 edition. In those days, the two men who presided over the front page were Theodore Bernstein, an assistant managing editor, and Lewis Jordon, the news editor. They put the story in column eight, the location of the day's most important news, and topped it with a dramatic four-column headline. During this time, Reston was in contact with both the managing editor, Turner Catledge, and the publisher, Orvil Dryfoos. Reston argued that with a story such as this, the editors should consider the national security implications.

It has been charged—most notably by Pultizer-Prize-winning author David Halberstam in his book *The Powers That Be*—that Reston was acting in response to pressure from President Kennedy or his aides:

> When word leaked out in Washington that the *Times* planned to run the Szulc story, President Kennedy called Scotty Reston, the *Times*'s Washington bureau chief, and tried to get him to kill the story. Kennedy argued strongly and passionately about what the Szulc story would do to his policy

and he spoke darkly of what the *Times*'s responsibilities should be. Reston, somewhat shaken, called Orvil Dryfoos, the publisher, and passed on Kennedy's arguments, They were quite chilling—the blood of dead men in the expeditionary force might be on the hands of the *Times*'s editors.[23]

Reston, however, maintains that he was arguing solely from his own conscience, not from pressure from the White House. "I don't remember any request from the White House to me about the Tad Szulc story," he says.[24] And although many journalists still believe the Kennedy intervention story, no one interviewed for this book could corroborate it. Harrison Salisbury, the unofficial historian of the *Times*, wrote in his *Without Fear or Favor,* "Dramatic stuff but it never happened."[25] Pressed for his sources in a recent interview, Halberstam said, "The story was generally known in the newsroom."[26] When pressed further, Halberstam, curiously enough, offered up Harrison Salisbury as a confirming source.

According to Reston, he argued to his editors about the dilemma of running a story about an "imminent" invasion. His views apparently affected the recently appointed publisher, Orvil Dryfoos, who—for the only time in his career—interfered with the news judgment of his editors. Dryfoos ordered that the four-column head be reduced to one column and that references to the invasion's "imminence" be killed and mentions of the CIA deleted. Although toned down, however, the story *did* run on April 7, 1961, only 10 days before the invasion. Dryfoos, the most conscientious of publishers, made the changes because he felt that they balanced the *Times*'s obvious responsibility to report the story with the publisher's responsibility to ensure that the paper didn't run roughshod over national security.

Those substantive changes nevertheless infuriated Bernstein and Jordon, who felt that their editorial territory had been infringed. They demanded from their managing editor, Catledge, that Dryfoos tell them to their faces why he was meddling in their work. According to Clifton Daniel, the assistant managing editor, when Dryfoos came to see Jordon, he insisted that the changes had to be made for reasons of "national security, national interest, and above all, concern for the safety of the men who were preparing to offer their lives on the beaches of Cuba."[27] Ten days later, on April 17, the invasion took place; 1,189 Cuban exiles were captured by Castro and 114 died.

Theodore Bernstein remained furious over the headline change. The other details didn't bother him so. "A multi-column head in this paper means so much,"[28] Jordon later explained to Daniel. The impact of the size of the *Times*'s headline has been debated ever since the story was published. Nevertheless, it is doubtful that a larger headline in the *Times* would have affected the course of events. While interesting, the problem of the size of a *Times* headline is ultimately trivial and internal to the

Times. In this it differs utterly from the questions of journalistic standards and national security that were raised by the Bay of Pigs incident —questions of vital concern to all the news media.

In the aftermath of the Bay of Pigs, President Kennedy issued two conflicting signals about how he felt about the press and national security. In a private conversation with *New York Times* Managing Editor Turner Catledge, he said, "Maybe if you had printed more about the operation, you would have saved us from a colossal mistake." Most journalists who have reflected on that remark point out that if the press had published and the administration had gone ahead with the invasion, the press would have been a convenient scapegoat for its failure. This supposition seems to be borne out by Kennedy's remarks of April 27, 1961, ten days after the invasion. Speaking to the American Newspaper Publishers Association, he warned, "In times of clear and present danger, the courts have held that even the privileged rights of the First Amendment must yield to the public's need for national security."

THE CUBAN MISSILE CRISIS

Less than a year later, the issue of national security considerations returned to haunt the newsrooms of both the *New York Times* and the *Washington Post.* An air of crisis had developed in U.S.–Soviet relations, centering on two hot spots: Berlin, where the superpowers were still at loggerheads over the construction of the Berlin Wall in August, 1961, and Cuba, a Soviet-controlled Communist country that was apparently becoming a Soviet military base. Rumors of a strategic problem in Cuba surfaced first in Congress. In September and October 1962, New York Republican Senator Kenneth Keating took the floor ten times to charge that the Soviets were placing offensive nuclear missiles in Cuba. The administration denied the allegations, dismissing them as the political rhetoric of an election year. As late as October 14, only eight days before Kennedy would confront Khrushchev with undeniable proof of such missiles in Cuba, National Security Advisor McGeorge Bundy stated in a television interview that "there is no present likelihood" of missiles in Cuba.[29]

However, despite the administration's denials, it was clear to Washington reporters that something serious was up. Confirmation of the existence of Soviet missiles in Cuba finally came on Saturday, October 20, when *New York Times* Washington bureau chief James Reston managed to trap Bundy into a confirmation by feigning to know more than he did. Realizing that the *Times* might print the information about the missiles, Bundy called Kennedy.[30] The President recalled the Bay of Pigs and remembered that Dryfoos had invited him to call him personally during the next such crisis. Kennedy then asked Dryfoos to hold the story—which was scheduled for Sunday morning—until he could "break" it himself. He planned to address the nation that Monday. If the story were printed prematurely, he told Dryfoos, Khrushchev would score a publicity coup by issuing an ultimatum before Kennedy could implement his strategy and inform the country about the missiles. Kennedy wanted the extra time so he could put Khrushchev on the defensive. Dryfoos accepted the President's arguments and Sunday morning, the *Times* ran a story with the vague lead, "There was an air of crisis in the capital tonight."

Just as the Bay of Pigs coverage at the *New York Times* has been distorted by elaboration and hearsay, so has the story about the *Washington Post*'s performance during the missile crisis. The distortion is along the same lines; that is, legend holds that the *Post* bowed to Kennedy's wishes. But in fact, before Kennedy had a chance to call, the *Post* ran a story on Sunday morning which began, "Large-scale movements of United States Marines were reported yesterday in Florida Keys and at Marine bases in the South. The movements were believed to be in connection with the Cuban situation."[31]

After the first edition of the paper hit the streets, Kennedy realized that the *Post* was also closing in on the story. He called his friend, publisher Phil Graham, and made the same plea he had made to Dryfoos— to hold the story for a day. Graham, like Dryfoos, accepted Kennedy's arguments. But Graham also had to contend with the *Post* reporter on the story, Murrey Marder, known for his crusading efforts in the 1950s against Senator Joseph McCarthy.

Marder recalls being called into the office of Managing Editor Alfred Friendly. Graham was also there. Graham knew of Marder's rebellious spirit and played devil's advocate. He asked Marder whether he was certain of his sources and whether he thought there was really enough information to justify a story.

In effect, what he did, Marder says today, "was act like he, Phil Graham, the publisher, was just questioning the degree of information I had."[32]

Although Graham didn't directly order Marder not to write the story, his intent was clear. As a result, Marder left Friendly's office furious and determined to write the story. He knew if he could just link the crisis to Cuba, he would be getting the story out. "Just putting the word 'Cuba' in had its own political symbolism at that time," Marder explains. "It was a flashword." But he also knew that even to do this, he would have to work around Graham. Employing a bit of cunning, he tacked onto his story a false lead, which read: "Official Washington yesterday wrapped itself in one of the tightest cloaks of secrecy ever seen in peace-time, while key policymakers worked out a major international decision they were forbidden to discuss." The second sentence, which Graham apparently did not read before publication, confirmed the Cuban connection in a classic instance of a double negative, the form that would become the stock in trade of Watergate reporting 10 years later: "At the White House and

State and Defense departments, officials refused to confirm or deny reports published in the *Washington Post* yesterday that Cuba is the focus of the extraordinary operation."[33]

While Marder was writing his story, Tad Szulc, who was now working in the *Times*'s Washington office, was flying back from Mexico to help out on the story at the urgent request of James Reston. Szulc says that although he "never stayed awake nights or drank myself to death over the national security issues" in his Bay of Pigs coverage, he thinks the *Times* was right in its missile crisis decision. "It was a counseled decision," he says. "The missile crisis endangered the United States in a nuclear context. It's not at all similar to the Cuban invasion."

Murrey Marder disagrees. "I don't think it was credible at the time," he says of Kennedy's rationale, "and I don't think it's credible now. Silence on an issue only gives an administration time to get its ducks in a row." Although he has never seen a "cause-and-effect" relationship between the publication of a story and any threat to national security, he admits that if there were a "discernable immediate consequence" from publishing, an argument might be made for censorship.

"But once you accept their logic, you find yourself bargaining for every story," he says. "We [at the *Post*] have been told that announcing the appointment of an ambassador to Venezuela threatens national security. The government said it would make the appointment embarrassing. You're going to get the national security argument on the story of a dogcatcher. So where do you draw a line?" Marder is not swayed by the current arguments that in a nuclear age national security should weigh more heavily on editors. He feels, on the contrary, that "when we are that much closer to such a situation, then the obligation is that much more critical to report."

Those who have read Robert Kennedy's account of the Cuban missile crisis, *Thirteen Days,* may have come to realize that Marder's attitude may have been somewhat cavalier. What the press didn't know was that it wasn't until that Saturday afternoon that Kennedy himself had decided to go with a blockade of Cuba as an alternative to military intervention. While the *Times* and the *Post* were trying to get the story, the White House was trying to decide what to do. Once that decision was made late Saturday afternoon, it was necessary to work through diplomatic channels to be assured that the United States had the support of its allies in Europe and Latin America. In the meantime, the military was making the necessary preparations for the blockade. Perhaps, in times of crisis, it is necessary for the administration "to get its ducks in a row" before it is backed into a corner. In the case of the missile crisis, early revelation by the press of the existence of the missiles could have escalated the situation into a military confrontation. By printing the story about the missiles in Cuba, the press might have foreclosed some of Kennedy's options.

THE PENTAGON PAPERS

Ten years after the Bay of Pigs invasion, the issue of national security versus freedom of the press was addressed not just by journalists but by the Supreme Court. The official name of the case was *New York Times Co.* v. *United States,* but it is remembered as the Pentagon Papers case.

It began when the *New York Times* obtained a 47-volume classified history of the Vietnam war from Daniel Ellsberg, a former analyst of the Rand Corporation. After a time-consuming review of the documents, the *Times's* editors were convinced that the nation—bitterly embroiled in controversy over the war—should be apprised of the information in the report. On June 13, 1971, the *Times* began publishing its own synopsis and analysis of the secret documents; two days later the Nixon administration, convinced that the publication would endanger the United States' position in Vietnam, began legal efforts to stop any further publication. Later that week the government also sought to enjoin the *Washington Post* from publishing the same material.

The case flew through the court system in a "frenzied train of events," as Justice Harlan later put it.[34] The Supreme Court met hastily on Saturday morning, June 25, and five days later announced its 6-to-3 decision. The Court held that the heavy burden of justifying the imposition of a prior restraint had not been met by the government. The administration had not been able to prove to six of the justices that publication of the Pentagon Papers would cause irreparable harm to the national security. The intensity of conviction on this issue is evidenced by separate passionate opinions from each of the nine justices.

In his much quoted concurring opinion, Justice Hugo Black vigorously condemned the government's attempt to obtain a temporary restraining order. "I believe that every moment's continuance of the injunctions against these newspapers amounts to a flagrant, indefensible, and continuing violation of the First Amendment. . . . I can imagine no greater perversion of history." Black added, "In my view, far from deserving condemnation for their courageous reporting, the *New York Times,* the *Washington Post,* and the other newspapers should be commended for serving the purpose that the Founding Fathers saw so clearly. In revealing the workings of government that led to the Vietnam war, the newspapers nobly did precisely that which the Founders hoped and trusted they would do."[35]

Three members of the Court, Chief Justice Warren Burger and Associate Justices John Harlan and Harry Blackmun, balanced the two competing interests in the opposite direction—in favor of national security. Burger dismissed the arguments of six of his colleagues: "Of course, the First Amendment right itself is not an absolute." Later he suggested, "Would it have been unreasonable, since the newspaper could anticipate the Government's objections to release of secret material, to give the Government an opportunity to review the entire collection and determine whether agreement could be reached on publication?"[36]

The newest arrival on the bench, Justice Blackmun, summed up the problem most succinctly: "What is needed here is a weighing, upon properly developed standards, of the broad right of the press to print and of the very narrow right of the Government to prevent. Such standards are not yet developed."[37]

It is worth noting that *Near* v. *Minnesota* (see Chapter 3) was dominant in the opinions of both the majority and the minority. In their rejection of the prior restraint, Justices Black and Douglas quoted extensively from Chief Justice Hughes' opinion in *Near*. On the other hand, Burger, Harlan, and Blackmun, the dissenters, also cited the case and pointed to Hughes' exceptions to the prohibitions against prior restraint, such as interfering with recruiting during wartime and publishing troopship sailing dates.

Perhaps more important, the Court was weighing freedom of the press against national security interests in a historical document—not a crisis such as the Bay of Pigs when an invasion was imminent. The Court's judgment in the Pentagon Papers case did not establish the absolutism of the First Amendment (as some journalists contend) against *all* prior restraints. As Justice Byron White wrote: "I do not say that in no circumstances would the First Amendment permit an injunction against publishing information about government plans and operations."[38]

THE PENDULUM SWINGS

What the government and the press learned from the Pentagon Papers case is that prior restraints are not easily obtained. Except in extreme circumstances—and those circumstances have not yet been clearly defined—the Court is reluctant to bar the press from publishing.

Perhaps as a result of this heavy burden, the government has recently attacked the problem of publication of classified information from the other end—at the source of information to the press. On March 11, 1981, President Reagan issued an executive order, subject to congressional approval, requiring *all* government officials with access to classified documents to sign a contract agreeing to submit for governmental review any material which they intend to publish. Simultaneously, the administration drastically broadened the standard of what is considered classified. The number of pages of paper now ranked as "classified" in Washington is quickly approaching one billion.

However, this is not to imply that plugging the leaks in the ship of state has resolved the national security issue with respect to the press. Indeed, the 23-year-old hostilities between the presidency and the press, which had simmered since the Bay of Pigs, enjoyed an uneasy truce during the Cuban missile crisis, and erupted during the Vietnam war, culminated in October 1983, when the United States invaded the Caribbean island of Grenada. To its shock, the journalistic community was not forewarned of the invasion and was not allowed on the island for two days. The message that the news media heard from the administration was that if the press can't be trusted, it won't be informed.

The storm that arose over the communications quarantine, the collision between the media and the Defense Department and White House, will probably be remembered longer than the invasion itself. In any event, the trust and cooperation that had characterized the military–press relationship during World War II and the Korean War had ended. The press learned that the public's right to know was perceived by the Pentagon as a "shrill, over-used slogan of a highly vocal trade union," as one military official phrased it.

Ultimately, in an open society undelayed and comprehensive war coverage may be inherently unworkable. General William Westmoreland, commander of the United States joint forces during the Vietnam war, wrote in his book *A Soldier Reports:* "If the nation is to wage war —declared or undeclared—a policy should be set to protect the interests of both the press and government and avoid the ambiguity that characterized relationships in South Vietnam."[39] The haunting question is whether a democracy can successfully wage war against a totalitarian, closed society, where secrets remain secret. When the government controls the news media, the press becomes just another piece of artillery. In the United States during Vietnam, the government fought a two-front war: one on the battlefield and the other in American living rooms, as each night Americans watched the fighting on the news.

When the framers drafted the Constitution, they discussed the question of when Congress should meet. Some suggested May because the European governments would make decisions in winter and reports would reach the United States in spring. The Battle of New Orleans was fought after the peace treaty was signed ending the War of 1812 because word had not reached General Andrew Jackson that the war had ended. High-speed communications in a thermonuclear age has changed all that and compounded the hard choices. The questions asked after the Bay of Pigs and Grenada force us to examine the indelicate balance where a war could be fought in minutes and reported with the speed of light.

Dirk DeJonge, c. 1937. *The Oregonian*

Dirk DeJonge was a Communist in Portland, Oregon, in the 1930s. He wanted to get his message across to the citizens of Portland. But an Oregon law made any meeting held under the auspices of the Communist party a crime. DeJonge's case would give new meaning to the First Amendment freedoms of speech and assembly. Forty years later that precedent would test the First Amendment to its limits in Skokie, Illinois.

PROTECTING "THE THOUGHT THAT WE HATE"
Freedom of Speech and the Right of Peaceable Assembly

[I]f there is any principle of the Constitution that more imperatively calls for attachment than any other it is the principle of free thought—not free thought for those who agree with us but freedom for the thought that we hate.

Justice Oliver Wendell Holmes,
United States v. *Schwimmer[1]*

DEJONGE: A TERRIBLE PRICE TO PAY FOR WARPED IDEAS

Dirk DeJonge was a 42-year-old, balding, broken-toothed laborer, who had immigrated from Holland and now worked for the Portland Street Car Company. He was also a dues-paying member of the Communist party. On July 17, 1934, he was picked up for distributing Communist literature and sentenced by a local magistrate. He received a $10 fine.

The next day DeJonge was arrested again, and this time he didn't get off so easily. Portland police made a surprise raid on Communist headquarters, rooms 18 and 19 on the second floor of the Mulkey Building on Morrison Street. There they found Don Cluster, 22, who "refused to make a statement," and two others. Not satisfied with their "catch," the police contingent waited until 32 others had drifted in. Among them was DeJonge, who was then charged with "advocating criminal syndicalism"[2] and released on bail set at $2,000 and put up by his attorneys.

But these arrests did not stop DeJonge, a one-time candidate for mayor of Portland and the Oregon legislature on the Communist ticket. He and the other 260 Communists were determined to continue their work.[3] They felt they had a right to spread the ideas of their party. Their persistence would ultimately give new significance to the First Amendment rights of free speech and of peaceable assembly.

THE LONGSHOREMEN'S STRIKE

At the time of DeJonge's arrest, Portland was in the midst of a bitter, volatile strike by the International Longshoremen's Association (ILA). When Dirk DeJonge had joined the Communist Party, his motive had been "to protest the actions of ship owners whom he considered 'tools of capitalism' and the 'enemies of the working class.' "[4] Now he and his fellow Communists in Portland were dedicated to helping the longshoremen win their right to bargain collectively.

The longshoremen had been attempting to organize on the West Coast for more than a decade. For the ship owners, unionism was unthinkable—a gigantic Marxist plot to contaminate the masses of toilers. As Justice Oliver Wendell Holmes, Jr., had remarked in a speech in 1913, "Twenty years ago a vague terror went over the earth and the word 'socialism' began to be heard. I thought and still think that fear was translated into doctrines that had no proper place in the Constitution or the common law."[5]

In the twenties the ship owners had been able to defeat the efforts to organize the dock workers, but the conditions of the Depression had "rekindled the fires of unionism."[6] In 1933, "it was estimated that in Portland and elsewhere three-fourths of [the longshoremen] were averaging no more than $10 to $12 a week with the balance always on the brink of starvation."[7] They sometimes worked 36-hour shifts. Workers were hired in the morning for ships to be unloaded at night but, as one longshoreman remembers, "[workers] didn't dare leave. . . . You were hired but you weren't getting paid. . . . It got so bad. . . . They didn't care whether you went to eat or not."[8]

When Congress passed the National Industrial Recovery Act in June 1933, there seemed some hope for the unions, because the act gave workers the "right to organize and bargain collectively through representatives of their own choosing."

In the year following the act, union elections were held all over the West Coast, with the ILA gaining overwhelming support. Portland's election had been set for May 11, 1934, but earlier that week, the ship owners had made it clear that they would not honor the results of the vote and would appeal the election all the way to the United States Supreme Court if necessary. Realizing that an appeal could take years, the longshoremen called a general strike for May 9. It was "an action that created the most devastating work stoppage in Oregon's history." The strike, which was to last 82 days, stopped all shipping in the port and meant the loss of jobs of "at least 50,000 other workers in Oregon. . . . Practically all lumber mills ceased export production and the export grain business all but dried up."[9]

The strikers were involved in a number of confrontations, not only with the police, but also with the newly created Citizens Emergency

League, led by General Ulysses G. McAlexander. The CEL, funded by local businessmen through the Chamber of Commerce, was designed to give more police protection to the strikebreakers and to show the businessmen's united stand against what they saw as a Communist plot. Coincidentally, many of the men who were being arrested by General McAlexander's "red squad" had served under him in World War I. B. A. Green, a noted Portland labor attorney, pointed out this and other ironies in his radio address of July 5, 1934:

> [M]ore than 65% of these men are ex-servicemen. More than 95% are married men . . . and a great majority have children. . . . Until they went on strike, they had the stamp of approval of the employers, and were fine and upright citizens. The minute they caught the Spirit of President Roosevelt when he said that American rights henceforth should be prior to property rights and began to assert their rights under the National Recovery Act, they became and have at all times since been reds.

The strike was an embarrassment to the White House; President Roosevelt wanted it ended. The same day that the Communist party headquarters were raided—July 18—Senator Robert F. Wagner, Chairman of the National Labor Relations Board, arrived in Portland as the special envoy of the President. He was sent to inspect the situation, but he also was determined to initiate a settlement. Roosevelt was scheduled to cruise into Portland Harbor on the U.S.S. *Houston* in early August to dedicate the Bonneville Dam site, a project that local leaders hoped would bring industrial prosperity to the area. The President was worried that the strike would not end before his arrival.

B. A. Green, the labor attorney, was Wagner's escort on the scheduled inspection of the docks at Terminal 4, where there had been trouble. Two cars set out for the site. Green recounts the incident: "We had proceeded probably three or four blocks when we heard bullets shizzing [sic] over the car. Senator Wagner said, 'This can't be true.' We drove on to the top of the hill where many pickets were stationed, and there found that [the other car] had been shot through the trunk."[10] After initial denials by the mayor, it was admitted that the shots had been fired by special guards hired to help protect the docks. Three guards were arrested, but none was ever tried.

The following day the National Guard was called out. At first the employers interpreted this as a sign that the strike would be broken forcibly, but they were soon disappointed when they tried to move cargo: the National Guard stayed encamped. Then, on July 20 the Waterfront Employers Association agreed to accept arbitration with the union. Governor Julius Meier announced that he would open all docks on July 30 and that the longshoremen were to report back to work on July 31.

THE MEETING ON ALDER STREET

The strikers had won a victory, but Dirk DeJonge's activities continued on other fronts. He began passing out handbills announcing a meeting for Friday evening, July 27. The purpose was to protest police brutality and conditions in the county jail.

Somewhere between 150 and 300 people attended the rally at Unity Center on 68 Alder Street. Few of them were Communists. The first speaker was 22-year-old Don Cluster, who "really didn't say much. I just asked them to buy some of the papers I was selling."[11]

DeJonge was the second to speak. "The reason for these attacks on the working class," he charged in his slight Dutch accent, "is a stepping stone on the part of the steamship companies and stevedore companies to break the strike by pitting the longshoremen against the Communist workers." Later, when questioned as to whether he was peddling Communist literature, DeJonge wryly commented, "I usually do at such meetings. Every Communist is a literature salesman as well as an organizer."[12]

None of the speakers advocated violence. There had been rumors that the CEL would attempt to cordon off the area and stop the meeting. But after two more speeches, it was not the CEL but the Portland police who arrived to break up the meeting. Although there was a stirring at the back as the officers arrived, there was no resistance. The four speakers—DeJonge, Don Cluster, Earl Stewart, and Edward R. Denny—were arrested and charged with violating the Oregon Criminal Syndicalism Act.

Criminal syndicalism, according to the Oregon statute, was the doctrine "which advocates crime, physical violence, arson, destruction of property, sabotage, or other unlawful acts or methods as means of accomplishing or effecting industrial or political ends, or as a means of effecting industrial or political revolution or for profit."[13] The Oregon statute made it a felony to advocate or teach by word of mouth or writing the doctrine of criminal syndicalism. It was also a felony to become a member of an organization that advocated the doctrine or even to "voluntarily assemble with any society or assemblage of persons which teaches, advocates or affirmatively suggests the doctrine."[14] The purpose of the legislation was to outlaw communism without actually doing so.

DeJonge insisted on being tried separately. Don Cluster was the first to go to court. He received a one-year sentence but was immediately paroled. "Afterwards, I went up to the judge to see what I could do," Cluster recalls. "He said I should get the law repealed and that he had done all he could."[15]

DeJonge's judge was not so sympathetic. As E. Kimball MacColl notes in *The Growth of the City,* "DeJonge experienced judicial treatment tantamount to a kangaroo court. Judge Jacob Kanzler was a much decorated veteran officer of World War I, an active member of both the American Legion and the Veterans of Foreign Wars, a loyal Republican and a member of Portland's Americanization Committee." Although Judge Kanzler would later claim that he had done all he could to protect De Jonge's constitutional rights, most observers thought otherwise. In fact, it was disclosed that during the trial the prosecutor had put pressure on a witness to change his testimony.[16]

Stanley Doyle, as special prosecutor, based his case on hundreds of pages of Communist literature, including copies of the *Daily Worker* and the *Young Communist,* seized at the meeting. He even went so far as to read from the *Communist Manifesto* as evidence that DeJonge was a vital part of "the conquest of power by the proletariat, . . . the overthrow of bourgeois power, [and] the destruction of the capitalist state apparatus."[17]

In his final charge to the jury, Doyle lashed out at the defendant, implying that if it were war time, the mob would have taken matters into their own hands: "I will tell you the type of man this DeJonge is. And I will tell you further than that, each and every one of this jury, if these were war times, there wouldn't be a trial here at all; I wouldn't be able to hold down the sentiment that has accumulated as a result of this man's dangerous activities."[18]

DeJonge's lawyers, Irwin Goodman and Harry Gross, claimed there was no evidence that criminal syndicalism had been taught or advocated at the meeting at Unity Center. They also asked the judge to acquit DeJonge on the grounds that the portion of the syndicalism statute under which he was charged was "a violation of the due process clause of the 14th Amendment because it demands that the defendant comply with a standard of conduct which he could not know in advance."[19] They also argued that the other portion of the Oregon law violated the First Amendment, that DeJonge was disobeying an unconstitutional law which limited his right to peaceable assembly.

The 12-man jury, after considerable deliberation, told the judge that they were deadlocked 6-to-6. Under some pressure and after being given assurances that DeJonge would receive a lenient sentence, the jury came in with a 10-to-2 vote for conviction. (Oregon criminal law allowed for conviction without unanimity of the jury.)

Judge Kanzler then meted out his "lenient" sentence: seven years in the state penitentiary. There were gasps in the courtroom, which was filled with DeJonge supporters clad in red armbands. The *Oregonian* of November 28, 1934, castigated the decision and the syndicalism law:

> Communist candidates for office regularly are entered on the ballot in state of Oregon elections, yet now Dirk DeJonge is convicted of violation of the criminal syndicalism law and sentenced to seven years' imprisonment, primarily because he is a communist and advocates the principles of his party.

If it is possible to find a more barefaced paradox, we do not know where to look for it. . . . It is one more evidence of the folly to which the criminal syndicalism law leads the community. . . . The law itself is a mistake.

The conviction was appealed to the Oregon Supreme Court, but the majority of the court, in an opinion written by Justice J. O. Bailey, declined to overturn the sentence. The judges said it was not necessary to show that criminal syndicalism had been advocated at the meeting. The court asserted that the evidence "shows, as may be noted in excerpts from the Communist literature . . . that the Communist Party was at that time, as well as prior thereto, teaching and advocating the doctrine of criminal syndicalism and sabotage."[20] As the meeting was under the auspices of the Communist party, and DeJonge was a member of that party, he was guilty under the Oregon law.

Only Justice Harry Belt's dissent challenged the conviction. "It is, indeed, a terrible price to pay for warped ideas," he wrote. "With all deference to the conscientious judge who imposed such sentence . . . it seems to me that the sentence has no reasonable relation to the offense alleged to have been committed." Belt was shocked by the prosecutor's final charge to the jury, in which he had suggested that in war times he "wouldn't be able to hold down the sentiment" resulting from DeJonge's activities. Justice Belt saw it as an "appeal to passion and prejudice."[21]

DeJonge's lawyers appealed to the governor for clemency, but the newly elected chief executive turned a deaf ear. His advice to police on handling labor "goons" was to "beat the hell out of 'em." DeJonge was to stay behind bars in Salem for eight months as the appeal to the United States Supreme Court was launched.

Actually there might not have been an appeal to the Supreme Court at all if a young Oregonian had not been attending Columbia University in 1927, when a protest rally was called for the Massachusetts anarchists Sacco and Vanzetti. Gus Solomon was spellbound by the oration of Arthur Garfield Hayes, a New York lawyer and civil rights activist. As a result, he became involved in the Civil Liberties Union and, after completing his legal education at Stanford, went on to found its Oregon chapter.

When he heard about DeJonge's case, Gus Solomon was a young Portland attorney. The Communists gave him scant encouragement about the Supreme Court appeal. "Some people do their best work in jail,"[22] one of DeJonge's attorneys quipped. A martyred DeJonge in jail would be an effective propaganda symbol. But Gus Solomon preferred to have DeJonge freed as proof of the effectiveness of American due process guarantees, rather than as a symbol of American capitalism shackling communism.* So he contacted the national headquarters of the ACLU in New York; Roger Baldwin, one of the ACLU founders and leaders, put Solomon in touch with Osmond K. Fraenkel, a New York attorney who had argued many unpopular causes before the Supreme Court.

THE CONSTITUTIONAL BACKGROUND

DeJonge's chances in the 1936 Supreme Court had to be measured not just in terms of where the Court might be headed, but also in terms of where it had been. In making decisions, judges are guided not only by how they interpret a particular statute or section of the Constitution, but also by their ideas regarding the intent of the framers of the Constitution and Bill of Rights and by the way previous courts have decided similar issues.

The right of peaceable assembly was considered so fundamental a liberty that a member of the First Congress thought it was a waste of time to be discussing such a provision in the Bill of Rights: "If people converse together they must assemble for that purpose. It is a self-evident, inalienable right which the people possess. It is derogatory to the dignity of the House to descend to such minutiae."[23]

The right had originated in England, where any assembly was permitted up to the point where positive (i.e., written) law forbade a gathering because it would endanger the public, and had been carried over to the colonies. As the United States Supreme Court said in 1876, "The right of the people peaceably to assemble existed long before the adoption of the Constitution. . . . In fact, it is, and always has been one of the attributes of citizenship under a free government. . . . It is found wherever civilization exists."[24] Had it not been for that right, the Constitution might not have been drafted since it was "written by a little group of willful men who took it upon themselves to assemble semi-secretly."[25] Eventually, the First Congress produced a Bill of Rights, which included a written guarantee that the federal government would not interfere with public gatherings as long as they were peaceable.

Later the word "peaceable" began to be interpreted as "legal," and courts narrowed the freedom by extending the police power "to meet what were conceived of as the new dangers arising from the complicated machinery of urban life, speedy communication through instant newspaper publicity, and the immediate reaction of the public to suggestions that might affect their morale."[26] Thus by the early twentieth century assemblies that might have "a bad tendency" were considered dangerous and therefore punishable.

---

*Years later Solomon's foes would use his defense of DeJonge as ammunition in an unsuccessful attempt to block his appointment to the judiciary. For more than three decades he has served with distinction as a federal district judge in the ninth circuit.

What the founding fathers meant by free speech has been contested by many scholars. Professor Zechariah Chafee, Jr., has argued that the First Amendment went beyond the mere Blackstonian concept of no prior restraint (see Chapter 3). He writes that the framers "intended to wipe out the common law of sedition, and make further prosecutions for criticism of government without any incitement to law-breaking forever impossible in the United States of America."[27]

However, Professor Leonard W. Levy contends that the framers were "hardly libertarians." He concludes that they "did not intend to give free rein to criticism of government that might be deemed seditious libel."[28] In fact, in the 1790s, in the newly created United States, there were local and national laws that limited speech: laws punishing defamations against individuals, laws punishing "seditious libels" against the government or its head, laws punishing blasphemy and obscenity.

Whether the framers of the Bill of Rights were libertarian in their ideals remains in dispute. However, the actions of the Congress in passing the Alien and Sedition Acts in 1798 shows that its members were willing to sacrifice some fundamental liberties in exchange for what they saw as a necessary protection of the nation. Criticism of government, they thought, could threaten the constitutional government itself and must be suppressed and punished.

It was under the suppression of the Alien and Sedition Acts that the minority faction of Jeffersonian Republicans espoused a broad libertarian theory of freedom of speech and press. After Jefferson was elected president, he pardoned those convicted under the Alien and Sedition Acts and the laws were allowed to expire. However, the Republicans were not much more tolerant than their Federalist predecessors. Although Jefferson felt that the federal government did not have the power to prosecute seditious libel, he thought the states did have that power.[29] That sentiment prevailed for more than a century.

THE EARLY SPEECH CASES

It is important to remember that for the first quarter of the twentieth century, the Supreme Court upheld the right of Congress and the states to use their police power to punish "dangerous" or "subversive" speech. The initial rhapsodic First Amendment proclamations in the 1920s were in dissents, not majority opinions. Yet First Amendment law at that time was going through an evolution. The ideas propounded by the "prophets of dissent," as Chief Justice Charles Evans Hughes later termed such opinion writers as Holmes and Brandeis, were slowly being accepted by the majorities.

During the First World War, many Americans regarded the concept of free speech as wrong-headed and dangerous. Even Justice Holmes, "the great dissenter," saw limits to the speech protections provided by the First Amendment. In 1917, while American troops were fighting in

France, the general secretary of the Socialist party, Charles T. Schenck, and his fellow party members mailed some 15,000 leaflets to draftees, urging them to resist conscription and describing a draftee as "little more than a convict." Resistance of the draft, the leaflets argued, was an American's right and duty.

In upholding Schenck's sedition conviction, Justice Holmes wrote for a unanimous Court that "in many places and in ordinary times the defendants in saying all that was said in the circular would have been within their constitutional rights." However, he continued, any act depended on the circumstances in which it was done. "The most stringent protection of free speech," he wrote, "would not protect a man in falsely shouting fire in a crowded theatre and causing a panic. It does not even protect a man from an injunction against uttering words that may have all the effect of force." For the Court the question was whether the speech was used in circumstances that would "create a clear and present danger" that "Congress has a right to prevent. . . . When a nation is at war many things that might be said in time of peace are such a hindrance to its effort that their utterance will not be endured so long as men fight and that no Court could regard them as protected by any constitutional right."[30]

Eight months later, Holmes wrote for a minority of two—himself and Justice Louis D. Brandeis—in another case. His opinion in the *Abrams* case was the first indication of a change that would alter the course of First Amendment law.

Just eight months before the armistice, Jacob Abrams, 29, and four fellow anarchists (all were born in Russia and none had applied for naturalization) had been indicted for dumping Yiddish and English pamphlets from tenement windows on New York's Lower East Side. The pamphlets were critical of President Wilson, whom they characterized as a "coward" and a "hypocrite," for sending troops to Russia. One of the articles declared: "The Russian Revolution cries: Workers of the World! Awake! Rise! Put down your enemy and mine! Yes! friends, there is only one enemy of the workers of the world and that is CAPITALISM." Another article urged all to throw away their confidence in the United States government and to "spit in the face the false, hypocritic, military propaganda which has fooled you so relentlessly, calling forth your sympathy, your help, to the prosecution of war."[31] It also called for a general strike of workers.

The majority opinion, written by Justice John H. Clark, concluded that the purpose of the pamphlets "was to excite, at the supreme crisis of the war, disaffection, sedition, riots, and . . . [defeat] the military plans of the Government."[32] Citing *Schenck,* the majority upheld the five defendants' sentences of a maximum of 20 years in a federal penitentiary.

To Holmes, the intent to hinder the American war efforts had not been proven. Although he still stood by his *Schenck* opinion, he qualified it. In his dissent, which Brandeis joined, he said, "only the present danger of immediate evil or intent to bring it" gives Congress the power to set a limit on opinion. Congress, he wrote, "certainly cannot forbid all efforts to change the mind of the country. Now nobody can suppose that the surreptitious publishing of a silly leaflet by an unknown man, without more, would present any immediate danger."[33]

Holmes argued further that "the ultimate good desired is better reached by free trade in ideas . . . the best test of truth is the power of the thought to get itself accepted in the competition of the market. . . . That at any rate is the theory of our Constitution. It is an experiment." He continued, "While that experiment is part of our system I think we should be eternally vigilant against attempts to check the expression of opinions that we loathe . . . unless they so imminently threaten immediate interference with the lawful and pressing purposes of the law that an immediate check is required to save the country."[34] Thus Holmes's criterion of punishable speech had moved from that which creates a "clear and present" danger to that which poses "imminent danger." The First Amendment's "sweeping command, 'Congress shall make no law . . . abridging the freedom of speech' " could only be infringed in cases of imminent danger.

Six years later, in *Gitlow* v. *New York* (1925), Brandeis and Holmes were still in the minority, but there was an important change in the majority view, and a seldom-quoted conservative justice led the way, albeit not in the main thrust of his opinion. Benjamin Gitlow, a member of the left-wing faction of the Socialist Party, was arrested and convicted of criminal anarchy under a New York State statute. The indictment charged that he had "advocated, advised and taught the duty, necessity and propriety of overthrowing and overturning organized government by force, violence and unlawful means, by certain writings . . . entitled 'The Left Wing Manifesto' and 'The Revolutionary Age.'"[35] Gitlow was sentenced to 5 to 10 years.

Justice William T. Sanford, writing for the majority, allowed that "[t]here was no evidence of any effect resulting from publication and circulation of the Manifesto." Nonetheless, the Court, moving away from Holmes's "clear and present danger" test, said that Gitlow's writings produced "a bad tendency" to corrupt public morals and to incite crime. "This is not the expression of philosophical abstraction . . ." Sanford wrote, "it is the language of direct incitement." Sanford continued by asserting that a state has the "right of self preservation," and that this right was essential because "[a] single revolutionary spark may kindle a fire that, smoldering for a time, may burst into a sweeping and destructive conflagration." Thus the state could "extinguish the spark without waiting until it has enkindled the flame or blazed into the conflagration."[36] So Benjamin Gitlow would go to jail because what he wrote might produce a "bad tendency" at some future time.

But in Gitlow's defeat there was a major breakthrough. Nestled in the majority opinion was the ground-breaking assumption that the First

Amendment applied to the states—that the Fourteenth Amendment, in effect, nationalized the First Amendment. "For present purposes," Sanford wrote, "we may and do assume that freedom of speech and of the press—which are protected by the First Amendment from abridgment by Congress—are among the fundamental personal rights and 'liberties' protected by the due process clause of the Fourteenth Amendment from impairment by the States."[37]

Holmes and Brandeis felt that Gitlow's sentence should be voided. "[T]here was no present danger of an attempt to overthrow the government by force on the part of the admittedly small minority who shared the defendant's views," Holmes wrote in dissent. "It is said that this manifesto was more than a theory, that it was an incitement. Every idea is an incitement. It offers itself for belief and if believed it is acted on unless some other belief outweighs it or some failure of energy stifles the movement at its birth. . . . Eloquence may set fire to reason. But whatever may be thought of the redundant discourse before us it had no chance of starting a present conflagration."[38]

Gitlow served three years of his sentence and was eventually pardoned by New York Governor Alfred E. Smith. Ironically, the dangerous inciter of the twenties became a passionate anti-Communist informer, who from the 1940s until his death in 1965 supported himself as a government informant at $50 a day.[39] Justice Sanford died in 1930, never knowing the seminal role that his dictum would play in First Amendment law.

DEJONGE GOES TO THE SUPREME COURT

So the course of the Constitution begins with the framers and then either evolves ever so slightly from decision to decision or progresses in great leaps, depending on how the justices make their decisions. When *DeJonge* was argued on December 9, 1936, although the First Amendment had been given new strength with *Near* v. *Minnesota* and the Hughes Court, freedom of speech and assembly still stood on less than firm ground.

Osmond Fraenkel, DeJonge's attorney, remembered the oral arguments in *DeJonge* as being quite brief. There were two surprising exchanges between two conservative justices and Morris Tarshis, one of the lawyers for the state of Oregon. Justice James C. McReynolds asked:

McReynolds:	Was Mr. DeJonge convicted on the theory that his mere attendance at the meeting was a violation of the law?
Tarshis:	Yes, that is all.
Van Devanter:	How would DeJonge have been charged had the meeting at Unity Hall been called for the simple purpose of adopting resolutions regarding deceased members?
Tarshis:	It still would have been a crime, sir.[40]

What Van Devanter seemed to be getting at was that the Oregon statute was so broad that peaceable assembly could never be held if it were under Communist auspices.

Indeed, the entire Court, including the justices who had voted against Jay M. Near, saw the flaw in the Oregon law. For the first time, the Supreme Court of the United States held that state laws that prohibited the Communist party from discussing public issues were "repugnant to the due process clause of the Fourteenth Amendment."[41]

Chief Justice Hughes, writing for himself and seven other justices (Harlan Fiske Stone was absent), declared that DeJonge should be set free because he was "entitled to discuss the public issues of the day and thus in a lawful manner, without incitement to violence or crime, to seek redress of alleged grievances." His opinion provided new strength to the freedom of speech and the right to assemble peaceably:

> The greater the importance of safeguarding the community from incitement to the overthrow of our institutions by force and violence, the more imperative is the need to preserve inviolate the constitutional rights of free speech, free press and free assembly in order to maintain the opportunity for free political discussion, to the end that government may be responsive to the will of the people and that changes, if desired, may be obtained by peaceful means. Therein lies the security of the Republic, the very foundation of constitutional government. . . . The holding of meetings for peaceable political action cannot be proscribed. . . . The question, if the rights of free speech and peaceable assembly are to be preserved, is not as to the auspices under which the meeting is held but as to its purpose; not as to the relations of the speakers, but whether their utterances transcend the bounds of the freedom of speech which the Constitution protects.[42]

So Dirk DeJonge spent eight months in the penitentiary but won his constitutional victory. Since that day in 1937 the court has wrestled with the question of what expression is permissible under our Constitution. It has decided that it is not acceptable to call somone a "damned fascist,"* but it is permissible to wear a jacket into a courthouse with "Fuck the draft" written on the back.[43] The Court has said school boards cannot prohibit students from wearing black armbands in protest of the Vietnam war,[44] but they apparently can limit the length of hair.[45] Some questions have seemed easy; others excruciatingly difficult. The balancing is a task which never ends.

*See page 86.

THE BATTLE OF SKOKIE:
THE FIRST AMENDMENT ÜBER ALLES

In 1978, 40 years after DeJonge's victory in the Supreme Court, there was another hysterical, but historical confrontation over the "views we hate." The ACLU was again being denounced, as had occurred so many times in its history, but these denunciations did not come from the usual sources. Rather, they came from the Anti-Defamation League of B'nai B'rith, from liberal priests and rabbis, and from thousands of dues-paying members of the ACLU itself. One angry ACLU member proposed that the new slogan of the Civil Liberties Union be "The First Amendment Über Alles."[46] The case the ACLU was arguing was *Village of Skokie* v. *National Socialist Party of America*[47]—a case that tested to the limits the protections of free speech and the right of assembly. It involved the right of an American Nazi group to stage a rally in Skokie, Illinois.

The existence of neo-Nazis worshipping Hitler's memory remains a shock, as well as an insult to the 100,000 survivors of the Holocaust scattered throughout the world. But in 1977, the American Nazi party could hardly be classified as "an imminent danger." The party was more of a patchwork of anti-Jew, anti-black hatemongers professing a lofty devotion to *Mein Kampf.* Among its splinter groups was the National Socialist Party of America. This Chicago-based storefront "bund" contained no more than 50 members, who goose-stepped about, more often than not in the safety of their own headquarters, dressed in brown-shirted uniforms with swastika armbands and Hitler-style black boots. Their leader, Frank Collin, lived over the headquarters with his German shepherd police dog and two full-time lieutenants. The fact that Frank Collin was the son of Max Cohen, a Jewish survivor of Dachau, only made his crusade more of a tragic farce.[48]

The American Jewish Committee keeps track of the Frank Collins of America and their extremist followers. There may be as many as 1,000 to 1,500, mostly in Chicago, Cincinnati, San Francisco, and Los Angeles, but the American Nazi movement is more a myth than a genuine menace. The Anti-Defamation League, a Jewish watchdog agency, in 1978 characterized the movement as "politically impotent, capable and noteworthy only in the production of vicious hate propaganda, occasional street violence and trouble making on the local level."[49] One Nazi publication admitted that its American members included "all manner of dead-beats, police informers, regalia freaks, dilettantes and dabblers, right-wing kooks, religious nuts, anarchists and nihilists."[50]

But in Skokie, Illinois, in 1978, the American Nazis seemed much more real. If the Chicago suburb were to change its name, the "Village of Refuge" would be appropriate. Some 600 residents are survivors of concentration camps; together with their children and grandchildren, they *are* Skokie, which is about 40 percent Jewish. The stench of burned flesh and the vision of corpses stacked like cordwood are as much a part of them as the serial numbers tattooed on their arms at places like Auschwitz, Bergen-Belsen, and Buchenwald. No Nazi would ever march, no swastika would ever appear in Skokie. Never.

So it is ironic that in fact it was not so much Collin who selected Skokie as a proving ground, but, in a way, Skokie which selected itself.

Collin and his small band of followers really wanted to demonstrate in the Chicago neighborhood of Marquette Park. That neighborhood is dominated by sharply divided white ethnic groups, mostly Eastern Europeans, who are united only in a bitter struggle to preserve their culture as inner-city blacks move in, looking for refuge from the ghettos. Shouting the message "Nigger beware," Collin's group had staged demonstrations in the park from which the area takes its name. The demonstrations had been uneventful for years. But now the plan was to hold a parade that would start in Marquette Park and continue into a neighboring black community. The odds for violence seemed high. The Chicago Park District then cracked down and required permits.

City lawyers had made the process of obtaining a permit a labyrinthian one, with a high premium for the right to assemble. The Nazis were required to purchase $350,000 worth of insurance to reimburse the city for any damages. With ACLU assistance, Collin challenged the Marquette Park requirement; while the litigation languished in the federal courts, Collin, as a tactical ploy, wrote some ten letters to suburban park districts, asking permission to demonstrate in their public parks. Most of the communities ignored Collin's query; the rest waited a long time before replying with a vaguely worded refusal—except for Skokie.

Moving with what turned out to be unfortunate speed, Skokie Park District officials fired off a response, telling Collin in no uncertain terms he was not wanted. Following the Marquette Park lead, Skokie's park officials said Collin would have to obtain an unobtainable $350,000 insurance bond if he wanted to rally. Some Skokie officials had opened the door, and Collin quickly stuck his foot in. He announced that his Nazis would hold a quiet assembly in front of the Skokie Village Hall to protest the insurance requirement. The demonstrators would be dressed in full Nazi regalia, swastikas and all; they would carry signs with such slogans as "Free Speech for White People." Collin said they would make no speeches and hand out no literature. He contended that his group wanted only to protest the park district's infringement of the group's right to free speech and assembly.

Now, the Skokie Village Council had two choices: It could seek an injunction and try to put a legal halt to the protest rally, or it could allow Collin and his scraggly group their march, avoiding a battle with First Amendment forces. At first, the council tried to take the latter route. Council members hoped that by letting the Nazis come and ignoring them, Skokie would deny them the media attention they so coveted, and the episode would thereby be ended. But that plan never had a chance of being pulled off—not in Skokie. As soon as the council brought its idea to leaders of the Skokie Jewish community, the response, a scream from the heart, was a loud, "Never again!"

Erna Gans, a concentration camp survivor, made a point of going to the special town meeting to discuss the Nazi rally and was horrified at the mere association of Nazism and free speech. "I felt like a nightmare living over again. . . . In Germany they also started with a bunch of crazies." Mrs. Gans, an active leader in the Skokie B'nai B'rith, believes there is something wrong with the First Amendment if it offers "protection for hatred and killing. . . . Anybody who advocates killing should not be allowed to rally." Although she understands Holmes's idea that the First Amendment is based on the marketplace of ideas, she argues that certain ideas should never be put up for sale. "What do you want to sell in the marketplace? What idea? The idea of murder?" To Erna Gans that is a perversion of the First Amendment, because the "freedom of speech will not be about freedom, but about death."[51]

The cry of protest voiced by Mrs. Gans and hundred of others changed the council's plans. Furthermore, it changed the legal mind of Skokie Village Attorney Harvey Schwartz, who began to believe that the Nazi rally was not a form of free expression protected by the Constitution. In Schwartz's mind the idea that people, faced with many different ideas, will grab the good ideas and toss out the bad is generally acceptable, but not when Holocaust survivors are faced with a Nazi rally. "There is not really a free exchange of ideas at all," he argues. Schwartz is a 54-year-old lawyer who has spent his life "interpreting the Constitution as it applies to localities and . . . affects individual rights and freedoms." He says, "What the swastika meant to [the survivors], very simply, was death. That's what they faced. It wasn't an arguable position. It wasn't an exchange of ideas. It wasn't a difference of opinion. These weren't ideas being discussed. These were Nazis, who said we are going to display a symbol that to you means death. What it really came down to . . . was that the symbol of the swastika was not an expression of protected free speech. It amounted to an assault just as much as a physical assault, just as much as a battery or beating."[52]

THE AMERICAN CIVIL LIBERTIES UNION TAKES THE CASE

When Schwartz filed a lawsuit asking the Circuit Court of Cook County to enjoin the Nazi rally, Frank Collin turned to the ACLU for help. It was not the first time the civil liberties group had defended Collin and his band's right to free expression, but it was certainly the most tormenting. Throughout the year-long battle, David Hamlin, the executive director of the Illinois ACLU, and David Goldberger, the young staff attorney who did most of the work on the case, were cursed, spat at, and pelted with tomatoes by those who usually would have been sympathetic to civil liberties. Their lives were threatened in phone calls and anonymous notes. Aryeh Neier, national executive director of the ACLU and himself a Jewish refugee who escaped from Berlin in 1939, was also a target of criticism. His grandparents and much of his family had perished in Hitler's death camps. It was to be Neier's destiny to take part in the legal battle defending his enemies. He now bears the pain of a letter from a citizen of Boston written during the heat of Skokie: "My only hope is that if we are both forced into a march someday to some crematorium, you will be at the head of the parade, at which time you will in your rapture have an opportunity to sing hosannas in praise of freedom of speech for your tormentors."[53]

To this day Erna Gans is almost as bitter about the ACLU and especially Goldberger, who is also Jewish, as she is about the Nazis themselves. "He should have been quartered," Mrs. Gans says of Goldberger, "hung up in small pieces on hooks." Her voice trembles, "A louse like that who has no pride of his own roots and heritage." In contrast, she speaks with pride of the 600,000 Americans who signed the petition to ban a Nazi rally in Skokie.

David Goldberger now teaches constitutional law at the University of Ohio Law School. He argues that his position was quite in keeping with pride in his "roots and heritage": if the Nazis could be stopped from assembling so could anyone else, even, conceivably, a Jewish group. Goldberger concedes he is not a constitutional absolutist: "You'd have heard me object if it had been [Collin] picketing a religious service on a High Holiday; or if there were ten million of them instead of fifty. . . . I had to say that my position would be different. I don't think I'd have been defending the son of a bitch." In Skokie, however, "because Collin was basically employing symbols and not political power, it seemed to be a comparatively easy case." Still, as much as Goldberger reveres the First Amendment, the Skokie case tore up his insides like none of the countless other civil liberties cases he has worked on. "I had usually represented the good guys against the bad guys," Goldberger says, but "here the bad guy was my client and the good guy was on the other side. . . . I could really understand what was going on on the other side." Goldberger, in fact, empathized with the people of Skokie and doesn't resent their anger. What infuriated him was the news media; "journalistic mooning" is how he described the coverage of the case. "The whole thing was portrayed as basically a three-cornered fight between a bunch of fanatical Jewish war survivors, a rigid and bizarre Jewish lawyer from the ACLU, and a twisted Nazi."[54]

COLLIN GOES TO COURT

Skokie won the first round of the fight. This round took place at an emotionally charged hearing in the Municipal Court of Chicago, at which Holocaust survivors were seated just feet from Collin, the person whom they saw as the reincarnation of their most horrible nightmares. After hearing testimony from the community that a Nazi rally might incite them to violence, Judge Joseph Wosik enjoined any demonstration on May 1, 1977, by persons wearing Nazi uniforms or displaying the swastika. But Collin, always the opportunist, took advantage of the fact that the order was limited to May 1 and declared that his group would move up the protest to April 30. Then, without notice to Collin, Skokie sought and obtained a second injunction, which extended the ban indefinitely.

Meanwhile, the Skokie Village Council, a bit tentative about the legal grounds for the absolute injunction, adopted a set of three new ordinances designed to put the ban on firm legal footing. The first ordinance, #994, made the $350,000 insurance requirement official. It also gave the council the power to censor public gatherings, requiring that the village manager issue a permit only if he found that "the conduct of the parade, public assembly, or similar activity will not portray criminality, depravity, or lack of virtue in, or incite violence, hatred, abuse or hostility toward a person or group of persons by reason of reference to religious, racial, ethnic, national or regional affiliation." Ordinance #995 made it a crime to distribute in Skokie any material "which promotes and incites hatred against persons by reason of their race, national origin or religion." And ordinance #996 prohibited any public demonstration by a person wearing a "military-style uniform." A fine of up to $500 and six months in prison awaited those who broke the new rules.

Collin was, of course, denied a permit as soon as he applied for one, and once this happened, Goldberger and the ACLU rushed off to federal court to challenge the ordinances. As both cases climbed the appeals ladder—the ordinance suit in federal court and the injunction blocking the demonstration in state court—almost every legal argument and remedy open to the Village of Skokie and to the neo-Nazis and their defenders, the ACLU, was mobilized and tested. The court record, from a half-dozen courts in all, and two compassionate and riveting books—*Defending My Enemy* by Aryeh Neier and *The Nazi/Skokie Conflict* by David Hamlin—document the legal and human history.

At first the courts seemed to bow to the shouts of outrage heard around the country. Then in June 1977, the United States Supreme Court told the Illinois Supreme Court to shake off its sluggishness. In a 5-to-4 per curiam (unsigned) decision, the high court told the Illinois court to expedite the appeal of the Cook County injunction or grant a stay of that injunction and permit the Nazis to rally. "If a state seeks to impose a restraint of this kind, it must provide strict procedural safeguards . . . including immediate appellate review."[55] Finally, when the Illinois Supreme Court demanded that the Illinois Appellate Court decide the case, the appellate court responded with a half-hearted attempt to tiptoe through the battleground. It ruled that the Nazis could march, but only in clothing stripped of the swastika. Swastikas, the court said, would be banned under the "fighting word" doctrine established in *Chaplinsky* v. *New Hampshire.*[56] In that case, the United States Supreme Court upheld the conviction of a Jehovah's Witness who said to a police officer, "You are a goddamned racketeer . . . a damned fascist and the whole government of Rochester are fascists or agents of fascists."[57] The appellate court decision stated, "The swastika is a symbol [which] is inherently likely to provoke reaction among those of the Jewish persuasion or ancestry. ...The swastika is a personal affront to every member of the Jewish faith in remembering the nearly consummated genocide of their people."

Ultimately, the Illinois Supreme Court overruled this decision and declared the ban on the demonstration as originally planned to be unconstitutional. Judge Bernard Decker of the federal district court and the Seventh Circuit Court then invalidated the ordinances. Later, on October 16, 1978, after 18 months of battle which only intensified with time, the United States Supreme Court declined to review the decision of the United States Court of Appeals for the Seventh Circuit. In effect, that meant that Judge Decker's overruling of the Skokie ordinances was upheld. Decker's opinion expresses an awareness of the very grave dangers posed by the Nazis' demonstration of hate in so sensitive a public place as Skokie, but says, in effect, that these dangers are outweighed by the evils of banning the march:

> In this case, a small group of zealots, openly professing to be followers of Nazism, have succeeded in exacerbating the emotions of a large segment of the citizens of the Village of Skokie who are bitterly opposed to their views and revolted by the prospect of their public appearance.
>
> When feeling and tensions are at their highest peak, it is a temptation to reach for the exception to the rule announced by Mr. Justice Holmes, "If there is any principle of the Constitution that more imperatively calls for attachment than any other it is the principle of free thought —not free thought for those who agree with us but freedom for the thought we hate."
>
> Freedom of thought carries with it the freedom to speak and to publicly assemble to express one's thoughts.
>
> The long list of cases reviewed in this opinion agrees that when a choice must be made, it is better to allow those who preach racial hate to expend their venom in rhetoric rather than to be panicked into embarking on a dangerous course of permitting the government to decide what its citizens must say and hear.[58]

Judge Decker found the insurance requirement to be "a virtually insuperable obstacle to the free exercise of First Amendment rights."[59] The racial slur ordinances, he said, were "unconstitutionally vague" and "overbroad," and the prohibition against parading in uniform was "patently and flagrantly unconstitutional on its face."[60]

In the period before the march, Collin and his handful of neo-Nazis dominated the local news and frequently attracted network coverage. Schwartz realized that the fight to keep Collin out had provided the Nazi the attention he wanted. "We gave him publicity," the village attorney admits. "And many people argue we were wrong in doing that because we were only promoting him. As it turned out they were wrong. What happened is that all of the publicity didn't help him a bit."[61]

THE NAZIS MARCH

As the scheduled day approached, plans for massive counterdemonstrations were announced. The police became concerned that the violence of the two emotionally charged rallies could not be contained, and the Chicago political establishment was frantically looking for a way out.

David Goldberger was still pushing for a ruling to permit the Nazis to have their demonstration in Marquette Park, their original target. Because the courts had declared the $350,000 bond unconstitutional, the Chicago Park District had employed the strategy of reducing the insurance required to $60,000. But that was not sufficient for District Judge George N. Leighton, who ruled that because no insurance was available in the marketplace, the requirement was unconstitutional as applied to Collin. No bond was valid; Collin and his platoon could parade in Marquette Park without meeting the insurance requirement.

At this point, Collin himself was not averse to avoiding a confrontation in Skokie, while saving face. He announced plans to march in Marquette Park and canceled his march in Skokie. "My overall goal was to speak in Marquette Park to my own white people," Collin boasted, "rather than a mob of howling creatures." Collin also announced that first he would lead a Nazi rally at the Federal Plaza in downtown Chicago on June 24, 1978.

So it was, after all the hate and counter-hate, that a small band of professed Nazis demonstrated at Federal Plaza on a warm Saturday afternoon in June. There were 25 Nazi demonstrators, 2,000 police, and far more counterdemonstrators than police. With all the heckling and screaming, Collin's flat, dull speech could not be heard. In any event, the entire spectacle was over in less than 20 minutes.

The sanitation department quickly cleaned up all that remained— a few beer cans, some rocks, and splattered rotten eggs. The next day, a quiet Sunday in Skokie, some 200 people of various religious denominations assembled on the steps of the Village Hall to attend a memorial service for the martyrs of the Holocaust. The pain was still present, but as Schwartz points out, "the survivor group who lived in Skokie felt that they had won a great battle . . . in their mind they felt that now finally they had stood up to a symbol and that they had defeated it."[62]

The second Nazi rally, in Marquette Park on July 9, was even more anticlimactic. Collin, this time with a few hundred sympathizers, was again upstaged and overwhelmed by 2,000 hecklers and counterdemonstrators. The police provided the same professional—but considerably more extensive—protection that they presumably would have given 14 months earlier had Frank Collin's original permit to march not been denied. The expense to the city of Chicago to clean up after the Nazi demonstrators was $10,000; the bill for police overtime was $90,000. Freedom had its risks and its price tag. One cannot resist wondering what the tab would have come to had the march taken place without all the legal entanglements.

Gus Solomon, who defended Dirk DeJonge's right to assemble in Portland, Oregon, and who was almost kept off the federal bench because he had defended a Communist, can identify with the trauma that Goldberger and Neier experienced. Yet those who feared a Communist pamphleteer in 1934 and a neo-Nazi provocateur in 1978 were neither fools nor knaves. They simply saw limits to the First Amendment protections of free speech. It is a close call for some, a delicate balance for all. No plaque exists to commemorate the battle of Skokie, but its name—as that of DeJonge—endures as a crucible of the First Amendment freedoms of speech and peaceable assembly.

Former U.S. Senator James Buckley whistlestopping during his reelection campaign of 1976. *AP/Wide World Photos*

In 1974 Congress decided that campaign practices and spending had to be cleaned up, so it passed legislation limiting the amounts that individuals could contribute and that candidates could spend. Senator James Buckley felt the law violated his First Amendment right to get his political message across. He challenged the law. The Supreme Court responded in a decision that has been described as the "worst of both worlds."

DOES MONEY TALK?
Elections, Contributions, and Speech

We are talking about speech; money is speech and speech is money, whether it be buying television or radio time or newspaper advertising, or even buying pencils and paper and microphones.

Justice Potter Stewart[1]

We know that money talks; but that is the problem, not the answer.

Paul Freund to Anthony Lewis[2]

In the beginning there were no political parties, no primaries, no nominating conventions, and virtually no campaign spending. A political campaign consisted of providing some "good cheer" in the form of grog just prior to—or even on—election day. When George Washington ran for the Virginia House of Burgesses in 1757, "he provided his friends with the 'customary means of winning votes': namely 28 gallons of rum, 50 gallons of rum punch, 34 gallons of wine, 46 gallons of beer, and 2 gallons of cider royal."[3] Washington didn't even "run" for president in 1789. Yet, despite the fact that he didn't make any speeches or actively seek office, he received the unanimous vote of the electors.[4]

But over the next two centuries, the method of obtaining the presidency—or any elected office—changed dramatically. It metamorphosed as the country expanded, as the number of eligible voters grew, as parties developed, and as politicians and big business realized the tremendous power of the federal government. Whereas early candidates had paid their "stomping" expenses out of their own pockets, by the mid nineteenth century politicians needed organization and money to make their way into elective office. Money had become, as Jesse Unruh of California once remarked, "the mother's milk of politics."

In the Kennedy-Nixon election of 1960, $25 million was spent in the race for the Oval Office. (A total of $175 million was spent for all campaigns that year.) It has been estimated that the Kennedy family personally spent $4 million. By 1972, the spending had escalated dramatically, to $105 million in the Nixon-McGovern race and $250 million nationally.

As spending grew, so did the public's concern—particularly with regard to the influence that might be wielded by contributors of large amounts of cash. That concern intensified during the revelations of the Watergate scandal, when it emerged that Nixon's top ten contributors had given him almost $3 million and that $1.7 million in contributions had come from people who received ambassadorial appointments. Even more jarring was the fact that shortly after the dairy industry had pledged $2 million to his campaign, President Nixon had decided to increase milk price supports (reversing a decision of his secretary of agriculture).

Spurred by the outcry of concerned citizens, the Congress decided to act. In 1974 it passed reforms intended to close up the "loopholes" of earlier and weaker efforts at curbing corruption in the election process, particularly a 1971 act. The new legislation limited both the amounts that individuals could contribute and the amounts of their personal fortunes that candidates could spend. It also set up detailed reporting procedures for election committees. The constitutionality of that legislation would be weighed by the Supreme Court in a case known as *Buckley* v. *Valeo*. The major issue the Court would grapple with was whether the campaign law violated the First Amendment rights of politicians and campaign contributors. In plain language, was spending in elections the equivalent of political speech?

POLITICS IN 1787

Although James Wilson and other delegates to the Constitutional Convention were keenly aware that they were "providing a Constitution for future generations, and not merely for the peculiar circumstances of the moment,"[5] it is clear that in their wildest dreams they could not have imagined—or intended—the political process that has evolved since 1787. The delegates loathed the idea of parties, or "factions" as they were called. In 1789 Thomas Jefferson wrote, "If I could not go to heaven but with a party, I would not go there at all." Far from having a conception of hard-fought, extensively financed campaigns, they even envisioned the situation in which a person elected might not want to serve. But even if campaign finances were not foreseen, the possibility of political intrigue was. In an effort to prevent such practices, some, including Benjamin Franklin, proposed that the representatives, senators, and president all serve without pay. The rationale was that if there was no monetary gain in officeholding, only the ablest and most honest men would accept the positions.

The aim of avoiding political intrigue was apparent in the discussion of how the president was to be elected. The ideal the framers strove for was that the man best suited for the job of chief executive would be chosen because of his "distinguished character or services." He should have a "continental reputation."[6]

But how was this to be accomplished? Some delegates wanted the state legislatures to choose the president. Others wanted the Senate to elect him. Another group, headed by James Madison, wanted a direct election by the people. Many delegates objected to a popular election. Roger Sherman of Connecticut argued that the people "will never be sufficiently informed of characters, and besides they will never give a majority to any one man." George Mason of Virginia remarked that "it would be as unnatural to refer the choice of proper character for chief Magistrate to the people, as it would to refer a trial of colors to a blind man. The extent of the Country renders it impossible that the people can have the requisite capacity to judge the respective pretentions of Candidates."[7]

Madison opposed the election by the Senate as contrary to the principle of checks and balances expressed in the Constitution. If the national legislature were to choose the executive, Madison argued, he would be the pawn of that body.

The major objection to the election by the state legislatures was that they would be subject to "cabal and corruption" and would merely opt for a favorite son.

In the end, the Committee of Detail came up with a compromise, what has become the electoral college. Each state would choose electors —the number chosen was to equal the number of senators and representatives from the state—in whatever manner the state legislature prescribed. (Initially very few prescribed direct election; it was not until 1828 that 22 out of the 24 states chose electors by popular vote.) Electors would meet in their own state and vote by ballot for two persons, one of whom could not be from their state. The ballots from the states were to be sent to the Senate, where the vote would be counted. The person with the greatest number of votes—if it were a majority—would become president. If two people had a majority, the House of Representatives would choose between them. If no one had a majority, then the House would select a president from among the five candidates with the most votes.*

The rationale for this method of electing the president was to guard against corruption or undue influence by any sitting legislative body. It also provided a compromise in what seemed to be a deadlock, because it gave a role to the states, the people (in states that prescribed direct elections), and the Congress.

The first presidential election had, needless to say, no campaign, no party nominations, no waiting for late-night returns. The electors voted

---

*This system was changed in 1804 by the Twelfth Amendment, which was passed to avoid ties between the president and vice president.

on February 4, 1790, and the votes were counted by the Senate on April 6. (They could not be counted earlier because the Senate had not been organized on March 1, as scheduled, for want of a quorum.) George Washington, whom some say did not want the office, was informed on April 14 that he had been the unanimous choice of the electors. His reply was that the overwhelming vote "scarcely leaves me the alternative for an option."[8]

THE EMERGENCE OF PARTIES

The framers of the Constitution had sought to avoid "factions." "The solution, then," historian Richard Hofstadter writes, "lay in a nicely balanced constitutional system, a well-designed state which would hold in check a variety of evils, among which the divisive effects of parties ranked high."

The framers "hoped to create not a system of party government under a constitution but rather a constitutional government that would check and control parties."[9] Yet, ironically, it was the Constitution itself which helped create the first American political parties. In the state conventions held to ratify the Constitution, two groups emerged—the Federalists, who supported the Constitution, and the Antifederalists, who opposed it. The Federalists never considered themselves a "party," but rather a coalition that sought to promote and preserve the new central government. The Antifederalists, who later became known as "Jeffersonians" or "Republicans," advocated state sovereignty and a weak national government.*

This early schism was more of ideological groupings than organized parties. As Hofstadter points out, "The Federalists and Republicans did not think of each other as alternating parties in a two-party system. Each side hoped instead to eliminate party conflict by persuading and absorbing the more acceptable and 'innocent' members of the other," and to put the other "out of business as a party."[10]

Nevertheless, as early as the election of 1792, distinct parties had emerged. Although there was no attempt to displace Washington as president, the Republicans did mount a challenge to Vice President Adams. In October, 1792, party leaders met in Philadelphia and selected New York Governor George Clinton as their vice presidential candidate. Although Clinton was defeated, his candidacy marked the beginning of the presidential nominating process. From 1796 until 1824, each party of significant size held a secret congressional caucus to choose candidates for presi-

---

*It is important to note that many historians refer to this group as "Democratic-Republicans." However that nomenclature was not used at the time. The label was adopted to prevent confusion with the modern Republican party established in 1854.

dent and vice president. Thus, from early on the electoral college was meeting to consider the nominees of parties rather than to choose from all possible candidates.

In 1816 the Federalist party had all but disappeared and did not nominate any presidential candidate. By 1824 there was so much dissension in the Republican party that the caucus system no longer worked. Many candidates refused to yield to the choice of the party caucus. That year a number of candidates were nominated by state legislatures. After considerable political maneuvering, some dropped out, but there were still four candidates for the electoral college to consider. With no candidate receiving a majority, the election was thrown into the House of Representatives and John Quincy Adams was elected.

A satisfactory alternative to the caucus system finally emerged in 1831, when the Anti-Masonic party held the first American national party convention. By 1840, national conventions were used to nominate the candidates of the two major parties: William Henry Harrison, Whig, and Martin Van Buren, Democrat. With the convention, which took the nomination process out of the hands of the few, came the modern, organized political party. What had begun as an ideological label had become the framework of the American political system.

MONEY BEGINS TO TALK

At the time of the first election in 1789, there were only 800,000 eligible voters* in the 13 states. As the country grew in population and more states dropped property qualifications for voting, the task of getting elected to any office became more expensive. Campaigns became not only a factor, but a growing expense, which candidates could no longer afford to pay out of their own pockets. They needed money to pay for pamphlets, travel, and other means of getting their messages out to the public. In the early elections candidates' views were primarily heard at partisan rallies and public meetings. By the 1830s, with one million voters, the candidates needed money and organization. Party organization had become almost a necessity.

The need for ever-larger amounts of campaign money led also to corruption, which was often tied to party organization. Corruption crept in slowly in the early nineteenth century and was at first not widespread. One way of getting votes and money was to hand out patronage jobs. Those who contributed received a "prize" and were expected to kickback a percentage of their salary into the party coffers. Another vote-getting scheme was to bribe the voters. Party bosses encouraged voters to "vote

---

*Each state determined the eligibility of voters; the qualifications for voting had to be the same as the "Qualifications requisite for Electors of the Most numerous Branch of the State Legislature."

early and often." In the 1838 New York mayoral race, the Whigs offered $22 for the first vote and $18 for each additional one a voter could get away with.[11] Later, the corrupt party bosses realized that it was much more efficient to pay off election officials to rig votes than to entice voters, and so this became a common practice.

With parties, too, came many of the features characteristic of modern campaigns. In 1840, Whig William Henry Harrison defeated incumbent Democrat Martin Van Buren with all sorts of campaign paraphernalia—handkerchiefs, log cabins, banners, and the first presidential campaign slogan, "Tippecanoe and Tyler, too."

Again, the costs of winning an election climbed, and candidates began to look to men of wealth and big business for contributions. That a relationship between politicians and businessmen developed at this point was natural. Candidates realized that they needed money to win, and businessmen realized that politicians were making decisions that could greatly affect their profits.

Corruption, which before 1860 had been minimal, grew rapidly after the Civil War. The fifty years following the war have been described by George Thayer as "the golden age of boodle."[12] Senate seats could be purchased by the highest bidder.* It was during this period, too, that ties between politicians and the underworld were established—a connection that was later reinforced during the Prohibition era. The gangsters provided the campaign money; the politicians provided protection. Thus, scarcely more than a century after the Constitution was ratified, the political process had become the antithesis of what the framers had striven to establish.

ATTEMPTS AT REFORM

In the early part of this century Congress made some efforts to clean up corruption, but the legislation was fraught with loopholes. One of these early efforts was the Corrupt Practices Act of 1925, which limited campaign expenditures to $5,000 for House candidates and $25,000 for senatorial candidates. It also reinforced an earlier ban against contributions from corporations and banks. But the lack of audits and the fact that money could be spent without the candidate's knowledge made the act little more than a joke.

It was not until 1971 that Congress tried to close some of the loopholes with two bills regulating campaign finance: the Federal Election Campaign Act (FECA) and the Presidential Election Campaign Fund Act (Fund Act).

---

*Originally, senators were chosen by the state legislatures. The practice of "buying" seats led in 1913 to the passage of Seventeenth Amendment, which provided for direct election by the people.

FECA required detailed, regularly scheduled reporting of campaign contributions and expenditures by all federal candidates. The legislation also set limits on the amounts of money candidates could spend for communications media—the extensive use of television, radio, newspapers, magazines, and even billboards for advertising political messages. The rise of television in particular had transformed campaigns; whistle-stops had been to a great extent replaced by the electronic platform. The money spent on media advertising had become astronomical. The price tag included not only airtime, but the additional expense of media consultants, image-makers, as image had become a crucial factor.

The Fund Act set up a system of public financing of presidential elections. Taxpayers could check off a box on their federal income-tax return, designating $1 to be paid into a treasury fund. Starting in 1976, major-party presidential nominees would have the option of financing their elections with public money or of raising funds from private sources. Those candidates who opted for public financing could not spend more than they were entitled to receive from the public fund nor could they accept private contributions. Candidates who chose to rely on private contributions could raise as much as they wished; there was no ceiling on the amount that such candidates could spend.* Congress wanted to remove the burden of fund raising from presidential aspirants and at the same time tackle the problem of influence. During the debates, Senator Russell Long described the act as a "major change that would be a tremendous improvement toward lifting the office of President above the power of private money to control it."[13] Senator Edward Kennedy remarked that the Fund Act would "end the most flagrant abuse in our democracy, the unconscionable power of money."[14]

But there was at least one gaping hole in FECA; it didn't go into effect until April 7, 1972, at which time the 1972 campaigns were well under way. This delayed implementation permitted a vast amount of last-minute contributions, contributions without disclosure. During the Watergate hearings, Hugh W. Sloan, Jr., testified that the Committee to Reelect the President had received more than $20 million in contributions before the cutoff, including $6 million in the last two days. Additionally, the law did not set any limits on contributions and thus had not really addressed the problem of influence. The law was also unpopular with the media because of the limits set on advertising.† Congress would have to act again.

---

*Minor-party candidates who received more than 5 percent of the vote would be reimbursed after the election on a percentage basis. In other words, they would receive a portion of what the major-party candidates received based on how many votes they had. Also, once a minor party was established, it was automatically eligible for some funding in subsequent elections.

†This provision was challenged in a lawsuit. However, before it reached the Supreme Court the case became moot because Congress repealed the provision in 1974.

"A GOOD DAY FOR 213 MILLION AMERICANS"?

On October 15, 1974, only two months after President Nixon's forced resignation, President Gerald R. Ford signed into law amendments to the FECA and Fund Act. "By removing whatever influence big money and special interests may have on our federal election process, this bill should stand as a landmark of campaign reform legislation," Ford said of the amendments. "This is a good day for 213 million Americans."[15]

One intention of the amendments was to curb the influence of "fat cat" contributors. The annual ceiling for an individual's contributions to any given candidate was set at $1,000 per election and per primary. No individual could contribute more than $25,000 to all federal candidates and political action committees (PACs) supporting federal candidates. The PACs themselves could not give any candidate more than $5,000 per election.

The amendments also provided for limitations on candidates' use of their own money, which was defined as including money from members of their immediate family. This ceiling was set at $25,000 for races for the House, $35,000 for Senate races, and $50,000 for presidential and vice presidential races. The "Kennedy-Rockefeller provision," as it was called, was intended to insure that wealthy candidates did not have an inherent political advantage.

Under a complicated formula, the 1974 amendments established a ceiling for all campaign spending for federal office. The limits applied separately to primaries and general elections. Under the overall spending limitations, House candidates were limited to $70,000 per election—in other words, to $70,000 for a primary and another $70,000 for the general election. In addition, a House candidate was allowed to spend $14,000 for fund-raising costs and could receive $10,000 from both the national and state party committees during the general election. All told, this meant that a House candidate could spend up to $84,000 in a primary and another $104,000 in the general election.

In primaries Senate candidates were limited to $100,000 or 8 cents per voter, whichever was higher, plus an additional 20 percent of that limit for fund raising. In general elections, they could spend no more than $150,000 or 12 cents per voter, whichever was higher, plus an additional 20 percent for fund raising. Individuals or groups (such as PACs) independent of the candidates could spend no more than $1,000 per calendar year on behalf of or in opposition to a "clearly identified candidate" for federal office.

To insure that these various ceilings were not exceeded, the amendments required strict reporting and disclosure. Each candidate was to designate one campaign committee which would file reports of all contributions and expenditures on the candidate's behalf. The committee was to keep on file the names and addresses of contributors of more than $10 and report the occupation and place of business of contributors of more than $100. Additionally, the committee had to account for every expenditure over $10. These reports were due 10 days before and 30 days after each election and within 10 days of the close of each quarter (April 10, July 10, October 10, and January 10).

The 1974 amendments to the Fund Act were along similar lines. During the primary season, candidates for their party's presidential nomination were eligible to match private contributions of up to $250 with equal amounts in federal funds. In order to qualify for these matching funds, a presidential candidate had to raise $100,000. That $100,000 had to come from 20 different states in which the candidate had received a minimum of $5,000. The $5,000 had to consist of contributions of no more than $250 per contributor.

Funds were also provided for nominating conventions. Major parties were eligible for up to $2 million to cover their convention expenses. Minor or new parties could receive a percentage of the $2 million based on their past vote or could be reimbursed based on the vote they received in the upcoming general election. The provision for full public financing of presidential campaigns after the convention was not amended.

Finally, the 1974 amendments established the Federal Election Commission (FEC). It was with this commission that candidates' campaign committee reports were to be filed. The commission was to consist of eight members. Two of these—the secretary of the Senate and the clerk of the House—were ex officio members and didn't have the right to vote. Of the remaining members, two were to be appointed by the president, two by the president pro tempore of the Senate, and two by the Speaker of the House. All six appointments were subject to confirmation by the full Congress. The FEC's job was to make sure that the candidates and the public complied with the law.

SENATOR BUCKLEY OPPOSES THE AMENDMENTS

Although the 1974 amendments passed by a wide margin, they did not do so without a fight. In the Senate the fight was led by James Buckley, the junior senator from New York and the brother of journalist and novelist William F. Buckley. Buckley's six years as a senator from New York may not occupy a major space in history books, but his fight on the issue of campaign spending would soon have constitutional impact. He argued on the Senate floor that the amendments were unconstitutional: limits on the amount that candidates could spend violated their First Amendment right to convey their political message to the public. Buckley told the Senate during the debates that "the importance of the First Amendment in all its aspects, especially in its political aspects, is so essential to a free society that I urge this body not to be swept into enacting legislation that we will all live to regret, legislation that will almost assuredly be found unconstitutional once its key provisions are tested."[16]

In addition, Buckley had another reason for opposing the amendments—his own experience. He now explains that when he decided to run for the Senate as a Conservative party candidate, he needed about $15,000 just to take a poll to find out whether his candidacy would be viable. "One family came up with $15,000 to finance this," Buckley says. "People that I'd never met before." He explains that he needed an additional $50,000 to get his campaign rolling, which was spent for security deposits of $25,000 to New York Telephone and $20,000 to a landlord. "A friend of mine put up securities with which we borrowed $50,000. He was going to get paid out of the first proceeds from mass mailings." Buckley explains that since he was a third-party candidate, the "institutional sources of money simply were not available. That is terribly relevant to this whole reform of campaign law because the ground rules that exist today would have made it impossible for me to get into politics. I wouldn't have the $15,000. I couldn't have gotten that $50,000."[17]

Buckley's critics have charged that the reason he was opposed to the legislation was that he would be up for reelection in 1976 and wanted to be free to spend as much of his ample personal fortune as he needed. Buckley sees this as a ridiculous charge in view of his personal conviction that he should not spend his own money to be elected. Pointing out that in his 1970 race against Richard Ottinger and Charles Goodell, "I didn't spend a nickel," Buckley explains, "I didn't believe in it. I was going to take a substantial cut in pay, and if I succeeded there would be all kinds of expenses such as a second home. My feeling was that if I was going to win, it was because I was going to be able to attract support. . . . I could have dug into personal assets, but as a matter of principle, I felt that I shouldn't." Buckley also points to the fact that his situation in the 1976 campaign would be different. "Once you're a sitting Senator, you don't worry about these things. The money would come in," he explains. His opposition, then, was based on principle supported by experience:

> I was gagging at the proposition that the size of the contribution is per se corrupting. My own experience is that I attracted money . . . some in large chunks, because I represented a set of beliefs and other people were betting on me as a horse, not in order to corrupt me. They thought I represented a public interest, as they understood the public interest, and in my opinion all that is required to protect the public from corruption is that the debt be published. I'm not saying that money never counts, but in my own experience, it sure as hell didn't. I think I'm probably the average experience.

Buckley adds that total strangers gave him large sums of money with no strings attached. "I never heard from but one of those people. He asked if I would mind taking his grandson to the Senate dining room."

In addition to viewing the legislation as unnecessary, Buckley was concerned about its potential effects on the political system. He explains: "It was a way of freezing out new movements in politics. I am a strong believer in the two-party system, but I also believe you have to have a place for the third man." He said that the rules made it difficult to launch a campaign—made it hard for a candidate to get started without party funds. Moreover, "if you manage to get on the ballot, you get no money that year when you represent a cause." On the other hand, because once a third party is established it is automatically entitled under the amended Fund Act to money for future elections, "you perpetuate something that ought to be the oddball rather than the regular."

Buckley adds that the "part that bothered me most was that this was something that was going to distort the political system in pursuit of things described as the public interest where, I think, the public interest would not be enjoyed at all. You made it impossible for someone like me or [George] McGovern to have launched a campaign." He said that another impact was to "freeze out spontaneity. Once you established the kind of reporting required, you had to centralize a campaign. That meant that a group of citizens in Elmira, New York, couldn't on their own pass around a hat, have a little store front on behalf of a candidate they believed in. It all had to be cleared from central headquarters."

Buckley recognized during the congressional debates that his constitutional objections to the amendments would not prevent their passage. His only way to challenge the legislation was to go through the federal courts. Yet he knew that it might take several years before such a challenge would wind its way through the system to the Supreme Court. Buckley wanted a quick answer, and to insure this, he introduced an extraordinary amendment to the 1974 act. This amendment provided that certain designated parties "may institute such actions in the appropriate district courts of the United States . . . to construe the constitutionality of any provision of this act." The federal district court was then to certify the constitutional questions to the court of appeals. The court of appeals was required to hear the case *en banc* (that is, the entire membership must decide, rather than the customary three-judge panel). The decision of the court of appeals could be taken to the Supreme Court "no later than 20 days after the decision of the Court of Appeals." Finally, the amendment made it the duty of the court of appeals and the Supreme Court to expedite the case as much as possible.

Buckley explained his amendment on the Senate floor. "I am sure that we will all agree that if, in fact, there is a serious question as to the constitutionality of this legislation, it is in the interest of everyone to have this question determined by the Supreme Court at the earliest possible time."[18] Apparently, the Congress agreed; the Buckley provision was made part of the amendments. In a sense, the provision gave Congress a way of having its cake and eating it, too. Congress could go on record as voting for the campaign reform, while providing a method through which it could be overturned.

BUCKLEY GOES TO COURT

Although Jim Buckley had fought for the judicial review provision, he had not decided to fight the amendments himself. In fact, following his principle of not using his own money, he made it clear from the beginning that he was not going to finance the suit. "It was suggested to me that this was something that ought to be litigated and litigated fast. I was willing to bring the suit, but I wasn't willing to put my own money into it."[19] He said that the Washington law firm of Covington and Burling was willing to take the case *pro bono*, or without fee, but there was still the problem of paying for the the the printing of briefs and other such expenses. So a coalition—candidates, citizens, and political organizations—was patched together to raise the necessary money.

What resulted was a prime example of the old saw that "politics makes strange bedfellows." Besides Buckley, the challengers of the 1974 legislation included Eugene McCarthy, a former senator and an announced Liberal candidate for president; McCarthy's campaign committee; William Steiger of Wisconsin, a member of the House; Stewart Mott, an heir to the General Motors fortune and a substantial contributor to left-wing candidates for federal offices; the Conservative party of the state of New York; the New York chapter of the American Civil Liberties Union; the American Conservative Union, a political action committee; and Human Events, Inc., a publication.

The suit, filed on January 2, 1975, challenged virtually every major provision of the campaign law. Buckley and his broad spectrum of coplaintiffs alleged that the limitations on spending by individual and group contributors and by candidates violated the First Amendment by limiting political speech. They contended that in campaigns, spending was the equivalent of speech because it was the means by which a candidate got his or her message to the public. The provision requiring disclosure of all contributions over $100 violated contributors' rights of privacy.

In addition, the plaintiffs charged that the spending ceiling violated the Fifth Amendment by discriminating against candidates who were challenging incumbents, as in theory challengers needed to spend more money to get elected because they were less well known. Moreover, the public financing of presidential elections was discriminatory to third- and minor-party candidates.

With regard to the provision establishing the FEC, the suit argued that the method of selecting members violated the separation of powers. The Congress was usurping the president's appointment power.

After a factual record was developed and the constitutional questions were certified by a district court, the case was sent to the United

States Court of Appeals for the District of Columbia. At this point, more groups were allowed to join in the suit. Common Cause, the League of Women Voters, and the Center for Public Financing of Elections joined the government as defendants. Buckley's group added the Mississippi Republican party, the Libertarian party, and the Conservative Victory Fund, a PAC.

The Court of Appeals issued a *per curiam* opinion (one by the court as a whole rather than by a specific judge) which upheld the 1974 campaign law on the key issues. However, the opinion did concede that the law "imposed restraints on first amendment" rights of free speech, and it overturned the provision requiring disclosure of contributions by any group (i.e., a PAC) that has a "design to influence" the outcome of a federal election. Two judges, Edward Tamm and Malcom Wilkey, would have overturned all of the contribution and expenditure limits.

Buckley's group immediately appealed the case to the Supreme Court.

THE SUPREME COURT HEARS BUCKLEY'S CASE

The oral arguments in *Buckley* v. *Valeo,* * as the case was known, were heard on November 10, 1975. In a rare move, occasioned by both the number of issues and the number of parties, the Supreme Court allowed the arguments to continue for almost four-and-one-half hours. (Usually each side is limited to one-half hour.)

In part, the expanded time was needed because of problems over the defense of the legislation. Whereas the legislation's opponents were united in their stance, its defenders were not. The Justice Department had made it clear that it believed the appointment process was an unconstitutional usurpation of executive power. Thus, the Federal Election Commission had had to hire outside counsel to defend the appointment process. Then, just a week before the case was to be argued at the D.C. Circuit Court of Appeals, the Election Commission learned that the Justice Department of President Ford (who had supported the legislation) was considering filing an *amicus curiae* (friend of the court) brief at the Supreme Court which would set out *both* sides of the constitutional issues. Apparently, Attorney General Edward Levi and Solicitor General Robert Bork believed that the spending limitations violated the First Amendment. So, while the government would argue the case for the law, it would also file a separate brief giving the other side of the argument. It was because of the government's lukewarm position that Senators Edward Kennedy, Democrat, and Hugh Scott, Republican, decided to file their

---

*Francis Valeo was the secretary of the Senate, an ex officio member of the Federal Election Commission.

own *amicus* brief at the Supreme Court to defend the law. They were also allowed argument time, an unusual gesture by the Court. Their counsel was Archibald Cox, a Harvard Law School professor and the former Watergate Special Prosecutor.*

As a result of the Justice Department's reluctance to wholeheartedly defend the legislation, much of the burden was left to Cox and a consortium of the League of Women Voters, Common Cause, and the Center for Public Financing, who joined in filing a single brief defending the statute on all fronts.

In the patchwork defense, it was argued that contribution limits did not violate the First Amendment, as had been contended by the other side. According to Deputy Solicitor General Daniel M. Friedman, Congress was attempting to prevent the influence and abuse of money in the political process. Moreover, the legislation followed three-quarters of a century of study. According the Friedman, "any adverse impact on the First Amendment right is overriden by the compelling Government interests."[20]

During oral arguments Justice Potter Stewart suggested that "money is speech and speech is money, whether it be buying television or radio time or newspaper advertising, or even buying pencils and paper and microphones." Friedman disagreed, "Money affects speech, but I would not agree that money is the same thing as speech."

The Buckley contingent argued that the spending limitations violated the Fifth Amendment rights of challengers and third-party candidates. Attorney Ralph K. Winter, Jr., argued that the limits on contributions and expenditures were invidiously discriminatory. Archibald Cox disagreed. He countered that if any group was hurt by the limits, it was the incumbents. He pointed out that of the 40 successful challengers in the 1974 congressional elections, only one outspent his incumbent opponent. Cox also noted that the overall spending limit "certainly contains no kind of discrimination between different political ideas or parties or candidates." He continued, "it is quite clear . . . that the ceilings are very close to those which have governed political campaigns in the past. For example, in 1972 and 1974, lumping the whole 2,000 candidates for the House together, 97 percent spent less than the ceiling."

For the American Civil Liberties Union, Joel M. Gora argued that although disclosure requirements were not inherently invalid, the requirements imposed by Congress "by virtue of their sweep . . . go well beyond the valid area of regulation supported by government interests." In defense of the requirements, the pro-legislation side argued that the public had a right to know the identity of major contributors.

---

*It is worth noting that Cox was fired as Special Prosecutor by President Nixon in what is remembered as the "Saturday Night Massacre." The man who carried out Nixon's order was Robert Bork.

On the issue of public funding, Brice M. Claggett argued for the Buckley group that any method of public financing was unconstitutional. However, he said if the Court rejected that position, it could still be argued that the method set up by Congress was discriminatory to minor parties. Lloyd Cutler, attorney for Common Cause, took issue with that. He said that insofar as a distinction was made, it was not "constitutionally invidious discrimination," but rather "a recognition of the differences between the larger parties and the fringe parties."

The Buckley group contended that the appointment procedure of the FEC was unconstitutional because it violated the separation of powers; under the Constitution, the group argued, appointments are the domain of the executive. Ralph S. Spritzer, Special Counsel to the Federal Election Commission, countered that the Constitution does not prohibit Congress from making appointments in cases where the appointees' functions are tied to congressional responsibilities. Congress had the duty of overseeing federal elections, and the functions of the FEC were directly related to that duty.

A VERY COMPLICATED DECISION

Two-and-a-half months later, the Supreme Court issued one of the longest and most complicated decisions in its history. It took six separate opinions and 294 pages to explain the Court's decision and reasoning. The majority *per curiam* opinion was joined in all respects by only three justices—Brennan, Stewart, and Powell. The other five justices (Burger, White, Marshall, Blackmun, and Rehnquist) concurred in part and dissented in part in separate opinions. (Justice Douglas had retired in the interim; Justice John Paul Stevens, who replaced Douglas, did not participate in the decision.)

The splintered decision held that the *size of contributions by individuals* could be limited by Congress.[21] However, the Court said that it was unconstitutional for Congress to limit candidates' use of *their own money* or the *total expenditures* candidates could make from amassed contributions.[22] The Court also struck down limits on independent expenditures (i.e., expenditures by PACs) for or against a candidate.[23] Upheld by the Court were the disclosure requirements, as they aided voters in "evaluating those who seek federal office" and as they deterred violations of the spending limits.[24] The scheme for public financing of presidential campaigns and nominating conventions was also upheld. The only point on which the entire Court agreed was that the nominating process of the Federal Election Commission was an unconstitutional violation of the separation of powers.

The most difficult part of the Court's decision was the distinction between the individual's right to contribute to a political campaign and the candidate's right to spend his or her own money. The Court started from the position that the contribution and expenditure limitations "operate in an area of the most fundamental First Amendment activities. Discussion of public issues and debate on the qualifications of candidates are integral to the operation of the system of government established by our Constitution."[25] However, the Court said that contributions by individuals provide support for *someone else's* speech, and thus a contribution limitation was only a marginal restriction on the donor's First Amendment rights.

> A limitation upon the amount that any one person or group may contribute to a candidate or political committee entails only a marginal restriction upon the contributor's ability to engage in free communication. . . . While contributions may result in political expression if spent by a candidate or an association to present views to the voters, the transformation of contributions into political debate involves speech by someone other than the contributor.[26]

Under the majority's reasoning, Congress had a justifiable purpose in limiting an individual's contributions to $1,000: to insure that elected officials are not controlled by large donors.

However, the Court saw expenditure ceilings as "direct and substantial restraints on the quantity of political speech."[27] It was for this reason, then, that Congress could *not* limit the amount a candidate could spend of his or her own money, or the total amount that he or she could spend on a campaign, or the amount that an independent PAC could spend for or against a candidate.

The Court's decision may have made it impossible to achieve one of the goals that originally motivated the legislation—that is, to control the spiraling amounts of campaign spending. Indeed, in 1980, the total amount spent on American campaigns—national and state—exceeded $1 billion. (However, it did have a positive result in presidential campaigns. While Nixon and McGovern had spent $94.7 million in 1972, Reagan and Carter, who both accepted public financing, spent a total of $58.8 million in 1980.) The decision also left intact a fundamental inequality: wealthy candidates may spend as much as they want; others must attract small donations from large numbers of people.

James Buckley ran for reelection for New York senator in 1976 and lost to Daniel Patrick Moynihan. He did not take advantage of the Court's decision by spending his own money. "I felt the obligation to match what my friends were doing, so I put in my $2,000, one thousand for the primary and one thousand for the election."[28]

Although Buckley won part of his fight, he was disappointed by the Supreme Court's decision. "Now you have the worst of two worlds. You have the ability of someone who happens to be rich to spend everything he wants and you've frozen out people who don't come up the traditional political way." He says, "I would have liked the whole bill declared unconstitutional because they went half-way. . . . In a way, the other way [the 1974 law] was better. For the political health of the system that would have been better."

Many proponents of the 1974 amendments agree with Buckley that the Supreme Court decision left inequities in the system. However, they point out that on the whole the situation in 1984 is much better than it was a decade ago before the amendments. Randy Huwa of Common Cause's Campaign Financing Project says, "We felt it was a victory. While some of our ideas presented before the Court were struck down, there were more that were upheld."[29] For the most part, the legislation prevents big money from influencing candidates. In addition, the public financing of presidential elections has made it possible for candidates—at least major-party candidates—to concentrate on campaigning rather than on fund raising, and the law has reduced the cost of those campaigns.

Other observers point with dismay to the proliferation of PACs and the fact that they can spend as much as they want independent of candidates, and launch major drives to defeat candidates they dislike.

For better or for worse money talks, but the speech it buys is only partially protected by the Constitution.

A cartoon by Burris Jenkins that appeared in Hearst newspapers around the time of the *Engel* case. *CBS Reports*

Mary Harte, a member of the Herricks school board, thought students should have the right to pray in school. Lawrence Roth, the father of two of those students, thought church and state should be separate. To Roth, school was not the place to pray. Their disparate views brought the Supreme Court to balance the inherent conflict in the religious clauses of the First Amendment: free exercise vs. establishment of religion.

GOD AND THE CLASSROOM
Free Exercise of Religion
vs. Establishment of Religion

*The law of imitation operates, and non-conformity is not
an outstanding characteristic of children. The result is
an obvious pressure upon children to attend.*

Justice Felix Frankfurter,
McCollum v. *Board of Education*

It began in 1958 with a 22-word prayer composed by the New York State Board of Regents and made a daily ritual in a Long Island public school system. Each morning, along with the flag salute, the students and teachers of the Herricks school system would recite: "Almighty God, we acknowledge our dependence upon Thee, and we beg Thy blessings upon us, our parents, our teachers and our country." Four years, 1,800 pages, and six bound volumes later, the issue exploded with a Supreme Court decision, *Engel* v. *Vitale,* which declared that it was unconstitutional for children to recite prayers in that school system or in any other public school in America.

A New York congressman attacked it as "the most tragic decision in the history of the United States."[1] A congressman from Georgia complained that the Supreme Court "put the Negroes in the schools—now they put God out of the schools."[2] Virulent opposition came from the public as well. A Long Island minister was so outraged that he turned the glass-enclosed bulletin board in front of his church into a collage of protest. Across the top of the display case, he hand-lettered, "Congratulations Khrushchev," and at the bottom, "God Bless America."

Other politicians and citizens were not so outraged. The president of the United States, John F. Kennedy, offered calm advice, "It is important for us if we're going to maintain our constitutional principle, that we support the Supreme Court decisions, even when we may not agree with them. In addition, we have in this case a very easy remedy, and that is to pray ourselves."[3] Senator Philip A. Hart, a Democrat from Michigan and a devout Catholic, backed the Court: "I don't want my children in a public school classroom to be exposed to someone else's religion or formula: so that I think the Supreme Court decision was right and proper."[4]

More than two decades later, the words "school prayer" are still fighting words—on Long Island and across the nation. The debate centers not on the protections of the First Amendment against another article in the Bill of Rights, but rather on two clauses within the First Amendment itself: "Congress shall make no law respecting an establishment of religion, or prohibiting the free exercise thereof." The two sides of the debate —"establishment" and "free exercise"—were personified by two Long Island residents, Lawrence Roth and Mary A. Harte.

Mary Harte thought she was exercising her freedom of religious expression when she suggested the prayer for school district #9. Mrs. Harte, a member of the school board serving the growing towns of Albertson, New Hyde Park, Manhasset, Roslyn, Roslyn Heights, and Wiliston, believed that there was a place for a nondenominational prayer at the beginning of each school day. After all, the carefully worded prayer had been recommended by the State Board of Regents and many school districts had adopted it. Furthermore, children had been praying in American schools since colonial times. Why not in the Herricks school system?

Actually, Mrs. Harte's first attempts to get the prayer into the school district were unsuccessful. In 1956, there was a vote of 3-to-2 against the resolution to order the school prayer. A year later, Mrs. Harte tried again, and again her motion failed. In 1958, she tried for a third time, and this time the school prayer passed.

Lawrence Roth had a different view of freedom of religion. One of many "newcomers" to the middle-class suburban communities that made up the school district, Roth believed that the school board had no mandate or right to involve itself in such activities. Religion had already become a sore issue in the school. According to Roth, a nonpracticing Jew, "It all began with a teacher who kept a statue of Christ in her third grade room. If you were bad, she would say, you would be punished by Christ. This incident caused some hard feeling between the old-timers and the newcomers in the Herricks school district." Roth explained that the new residents had been active with the Committee for Better Schools. "We wanted our kids to go to better universities" and so they had pushed hard for improving the schools. The school prayer was just another issue that further polarized the members of the community. "My basic feeling," he now explains, "was that if the state could tell us what to pray and when to pray and how to pray, there was no stopping."[5]

AMERICA'S RELIGIOUS HERITAGE

The conflict between Mrs. Harte's desire to exercise her religious beliefs and Roth's desire to be free from state interference was not new; it was older than the nation itself. God and conscience have confronted this nation with a continuing chain of moral dilemmas. The roots of the conflict go back to the very founding of the American colonies, when the

Puritans first sought refuge in the New World from religious persecution in England. Although they were religious refugees, they saw religious freedom and toleration only in terms of their own beliefs. The Puritans made church attendance compulsory, and church membership—which was granted sparingly to the "visible saints"—was a requirement for political participation. "The predominant sect in one Colony was . . . often absolutely intolerant of others; and proselytizing was anathema."[6] Thus, in the Massachusetts Bay Colony, Quakers, for example, were whipped, branded, sold as servants, had their ears cropped off, or were even hanged. Anyone preaching complete separation from the Church of England or separation of church and state was in danger of being punished or deported.

It was for this reason that clergyman Roger Williams fled the Massachusetts Bay Colony in January 1636. After living with the Indians, Williams finally took refuge in Rhode Island. Before long Baptists, Quakers, and other unorthodox believers such as Anne Hutchinson flocked to the small outpost, causing "orthodox Puritans . . . to regard that colony as a veritable 'sewer of New England.' " But it was in that "sewer" that the important tenets of religious freedom began in America. In 1638 Williams established the town of Providence. The town compact provided that the majority rule would be abided by "only in civil things." Then in 1647, when the nearby towns joined Providence to create the "democratical" Plymouth Plantations, the preamble of the document establishing the new colony declared, "And otherwise than . . . what is herein forbidden, all men may walk as their consciences persuade them, every one in the name of his God." After Williams traveled frequently to England, where he authored many treatises on religious liberty, Rhode Island was finally granted a royal charter in July 1663. The charter guaranteed that "no person within the said Colony, at any time hereafter, shall be in any wise molested, punished, disquieted or called in question for any differences in opinions in matters of religion." All people were "at all times hereafter, freely and fully [to] have and enjoy . . . their own judgments and consciences, in matters of religious concernments."[7] Here, then, was the beginning of the idea that government had no place in religious matters.

With the influx of new immigrants who belonged to an increasingly wide range of sects, toleration in the colonies became more necessary. Also imported into the colonies were the ideas of thinkers such as Locke, Blackstone, Voltaire, and Montesquieu. It was a time of Reason, of Enlightenment. As the historian Henry Steele Commager has written:

> It was the age of science, it was the age of philosophy, it was the age of enlightenment. Everywhere the scientists were philosophers and most of the philosophers were scientists, while all were enlightened. They had emancipated themselves from all but the classical past . . . [from] the past of ignorance, credulity, and superstition—and now with tireless curiosity

and feverish impatience they hurled themselves upon a new world and a new universe. They were not interested in the next world; they were interested in the world about them, the world of nature, society, politics and law; they were interested in Man.[8]

This age of reason produced a spirit of liberty in both politics and religion, as well as a new generation of leaders—men such as Thomas Jefferson, James Madison, John Adams, and Benjamin Franklin. These leaders believed in a constitutional form of government—a practical framework, above the law of legislatures and the power of individual men, which would efficiently govern the nation in matters of economics and foreign affairs and at the same time provide political freedom.

Hand in hand with political freedom went religious freedom. The rigid theocracies of the Puritans were gone. Even religious toleration was no longer sufficient. The framers of the Constitution understood, as Thomas Paine wrote in the *Rights of Man,* that "Toleration is not the opposite of intolerance, but it is the counterfeit of it. Both are despotism, the one assumes to itself the right of withholding liberty of conscience, the other of granting it."[9]

Arlin Adams, a judge of the United States Court of Appeals for the Third Circuit and an authority on religious history, explains, "The intellectual climate had changed radically from the time the Puritans had arrived and the time when the Patriots were in full sway. The Patriots were not nearly so religious; indeed, to some extent they were irreligious. They were deists. . . . Jefferson didn't go to church as such. He believed in God, and that's all. . . . By and large, these leaders were not churchgoers. They occasionally went to Christ Church in Philadelphia, but it was not a very important thing in their lives."[10]

The watershed for the idea of separation of church and state came in Virginia, a colony where the Anglican church was the established religion. In 1776, Virginia adopted a "Declaration of Rights," the first document in the colonies that declared a complete guarantee of freedom of religion. Following the revolutionary war, however, Patrick Henry made an attempt to pass a bill in the Virginia legislature that would have assessed everyone a small tax to go to the Anglican church, although he did include in that bill that nonmembers could assign the money to any other church. Jefferson, Madison, and Mason, who believed that there must be "a wall of separation between church and state," sprang into action and opposed the tax; after a nine-year struggle, the bill was defeated in 1786. Judge Adams links the bill's defeat to the sentiments that led to the First Amendment:

> That was a high watermark. And when you realize that Jefferson and
> Madison had participated in an effort to defeat that bill which would have

mixed up the church and the state, you see the ingredients that went into the drafting of the First Amendment. The Constitutional Convention met one year later in 1787. There was an undercurrent of concern that if people adopted the Constitution, the federal government might then proceed to establish some sort of church or perform other acts which might interfere with religious freedom. Many of the people refused to approve of the Constitution without some assurances that there would be amendments. Madison was elected to the first Congress in 1789, and one of the first things he did was to draft the First Amendment.

It was the peculiar union of those who wanted religious freedom and those states, such as Massachusetts, which feared that the federal government would establish a national religion different from the one already established in their state, that led to the religion clauses in the First Amendment. Even after the ratification of the Bill of Rights, official state churches existed in several colonies such as Massachusetts and Connecticut well into the nineteenth century, but the federal government was barred from interfering in religious matters.

FREE EXERCISE OF RELIGION

The Fourteenth Amendment changed this balance—although not until the decisions of the mid-twentieth century. The idea that the due process clause prohibited the states from meddling in religious expression was first asserted in *Cantwell* v. *Connecticut*,[11] in 1940. That case involved Newton Cantwell, a Jehovah's Witness, and his two teenage sons, who, in an area of New Haven that was 90 percent Catholic, played a phonograph record denouncing the Catholic church as an instrument of Satan. The Cantwells were convicted of breach of peace but appealed, arguing that their free exercise of religion, guaranteed by the First and Fourteenth Amendments, had been infringed. The United States Supreme Court overturned the convictions and for the first time concluded that the free exercise clause of the First Amendment had been incorporated or absorbed by the Fourteenth Amendment.

Two weeks after the *Cantwell* decision, the Court seemed to be retreating a bit in its opinion in *Minersville School District* v. *Gobitis*.[12] In that case 12-year-old Lillian Gobitis and her 10-year-old brother, William, were expelled from a Pennsylvania public school for refusing to salute the American flag, a practice that their father, a Jehovah's Witness, claimed was a sin, because of the biblical admonition against worshipping graven images. When the financial burden of sending his children to private school became too great, Walter Gobitis sued. He claimed that the expulsion was an unjust financial penalty for the practice of his and his children's religious convictions.

The federal district court decided that the salute to the flag could not be made compulsory without violating the free exercise of religion. After that decision was affirmed by the U.S. Circuit Court of Appeals, the Minersville school board took the case to the Supreme Court.

Justice Felix Frankfurter, who wrote the opinion upholding the school board's position, saw the case as a balancing of "the conflicting claims of liberty and authority." He posed the question: "When does the constitutional guarantee compel exemption from doing what society thinks necessary for the promotion of some great common end, or from a penalty for conduct which appears dangerous to the general good?" He said that situation in the *Gobitis* case presents "the profoundest problem confronting a democracy—the problem which Lincoln cast in memorable dilemma: 'Must a government of necessity be too *strong* for the liberties of its people, or too *weak* to maintain its own existence?' "[13]

Justice Frankfurter cautioned that such questions should not be decided by "the personal notion of judges," but rather should be resolved by the legislature of each state. "To stigmatize legislative judgment in providing for this universal gesture of respect for the symbol of our national life in the setting of the common school as a lawless inroad on that freedom of conscience which the Constitution protects, would amount to no less than the pronouncement of pedagogical and psychological dogma in a field where courts possess . . . no controlling competence."[14]

Frankfurter had stood against so-called judicial activism by the Court and did not subscribe to the notion that the Court alone was "committed [to] the guardianship of deeply-cherished liberties." He felt that the issue of the flag salute was significant for national unity and national security. "What the school authorities are really asserting is the right to awaken in the child's mind consideration as to the significance of the flag contrary to those implanted by the parent."[15] That was a legitimate function of the legislature, he reasoned, and thus the Gobitis children would either have to salute the flag or attend a private school.

Justice Harlan Fiske Stone wrote the lone dissent. The expulsion of two youths—now 15 and 16 years of age—he wrote, "would be a denial of their faith as well as the teachings of most religions to say that children of their age could not have religious convictions." Stone continued, "[the law] does more than suppress freedom of speech and more than prohibit the free exercise of religion. . . . For by this law the state seeks to coerce these children to express a sentiment which, as they interpret it, they do not entertain, and which violates their deepest religious convictions."[16]

Stone dismissed Frankfurter's stand—which had been joined by Hughes, Black, and Douglas—that the compulsory pledge to the flag was beyond the judicial scrutiny of the Court. Stone felt that protecting the rights of the children, a "helpless minority,"[17] was more important than the state concern of maintaining discipline in the schools.

Stone's sentiments were on the losing side, but not for long. Three years later, the issue of the flag pledge was back in the Supreme Court. On June 14, 1943, Stone's minority became the majority, and an angry Justice Frankfurter was lecturing his brethren from a dissenting opinion. In its 177-year history, the Supreme Court has reversed its position on several key issues, but never in the course of 36 months. What made the reversal even more unusual was that seven of the same justices were still sitting on the Court. Only Hughes and McReynolds were gone; Stone had been elevated to chief justice, and Wiley Rutledge and Robert Jackson had been appointed associate justices. Rutledge and Jackson shifted the Court slightly to the left, but more importantly, Justices Black, Douglas, and Murphy now agreed with Stone.* Rather than writing the majority opinion himself, Chief Justice Stone assigned it to Justice Jackson. Jackson's opinion in *Barnette* made it clear that the compulsory school attendance was an important factor in the outcome of the case. He declared: "To sustain the compulsory flag salute we are required to say that a Bill of Rights which guards the individual's right to speak his own mind, left it open to public authorities to compel him to utter what is not in his mind."[18]

This time the case involved the seven children in the Barnette family and the West Virginia State Board of Education. In the wake of the *Gobitis* decision, the West Virginia authorities adopted a resolution ordering a special program in all public schools "teaching and fostering . . . the ideals, principles and spirit of Americanism" and requiring the morning flag salute at the cost of expulsion for those who refused to comply. Not only had the Barnette children been expelled, but their parents had been prosecuted for causing delinquency and officials had threatened to send the children to reformatories.

The majority asserted that the Fourteenth Amendment protected citizens against the states and that the board of education was not exempted from that protection. Jackson warned, "Those who begin coercive elimination of dissent soon find themselves exterminating dissenters. Compulsory unification of opinion achieves only the unanimity of the graveyard."

In striking down the West Virginia law requiring the flag salute, Jackson stated, "It seems trite but necessary to say that the First Amendment . . . was designed to avoid these ends by avoiding these beginnings." He continued, "To believe that patriotism will not flourish if patriotic

---

*Hugo Black, in one of the last interviews of his life, told Sidney Zion of the *New York Times* that a majority of the Court might have bolted from the original Frankfurter position upholding the pledge after they had read Stone's persuasive dissent in *Gobitis,* but being so moved by Frankfurter's argument, they had assured Frankfurter that they would support his draft and were loath to break their word. Of his swift switch in so brief a span of time, Black frankly admitted he had been wrong in *Gobitis.* "Life itself is a change, and one who fails to recognize this must indeed be narrow-minded."

ceremonies are voluntary and spontaneous instead of compulsory routine is to make an unflattering estimate of the appeal of our institutions to free minds."[19]

The majority opinion concluded:

> If there is any fixed star in our constitutional constellation, it is that no official, high or petty, can prescribe what shall be orthodox in politics, nationalism, religion or other matters of opinion or force citizens to confess by word or act their faith therein. . . . We think the action of the local authorities in compelling the flag salute and pledge transcends constitutional limitations on their power and invades the sphere of intellect and spirit which it is the purpose of the First Amendment to our Constitution to reserve from all official control.[20]

Frankfurter was outraged at the shift of Black, Douglas, and Murphy and lectured them, saying, "That which three years ago had seemed . . . to lie within permissible areas of legislation is now outlawed by the deciding shift of opinion of two justices." Refusing to condemn West Virginia's attempt aimed at "the promotion of good citizenship," Frankfurter told the majority that the only check on the exercise of power is the Court's own sense of judicial self-restraint. He did not believe that the Court should tell the West Virginia legislature what they could or could not compel schoolchildren to say about patriotism. He felt the due process clause did not prohibit West Virginia from promoting "the legitimate legislative end . . . of good citizenship."[21]

THE ESTABLISHMENT CLAUSE

The establishment clause of the First Amendment was first acknowledged as being applicable to the states in *Everson v. Board of Education*,[22] which involved payment to some New Jersey parents for busing their children to parochial schools. Justice Black's opinion rang with the rhetoric of separation of church and state:

> Neither a state nor the Federal Government can set up a church. Neither can pass laws which aid one religion, aid all religions, or prefer one religion over another. Neither can force or influence a person to go to or to remain away from church against his will or force him to profess a belief or disbelief in any religion. No person can be punished for entertaining or professing religious beliefs or disbeliefs, for church attendance or nonattendance. No tax in any amount, large or small, can be levied to support any religious activities or institutions. . . . In the words of Jefferson, the clause against establishment of religion by law was intended to erect "a wall of separation between church and State."[23]

Yet, despite this pronouncement, Black and the majority reasoned that the New Jersey township had not breached the wall of separation by the bus subsidies. Their conclusion was based on the fact that the money aided the children, not the church.

In 1948, only a year later, the Court was faced with another dilemma involving religion and school, in *People of State of Illinois ex rel. McCollum* v. *Board of Education of School District N. 71.* That case turned on whether the Champaign, Illinois, school board could allow religious instruction in the public schools. Under the Champaign program, religious teachers employed by private religious groups were allowed to come into the school buildings once a week during regular school hours to teach their faith for 30 minutes. Students who did not wish to attend were required to leave their classrooms and go elsewhere to study. At the religious classes roll was taken, and reports of attendance were made to the secular teachers.

Vashti McCollum, whose child attended the school, sued. She charged that the program violated the First and Fourteenth Amendments. After the Illinois Supreme Court approved the practice, she appealed to the U.S. Supreme Court.

Justice Black delivered the opinion of the high court, which declared that the Champaign practice breached "the First Amendment . . . wall between Church and State which must be kept high and impregnable." Black and Frankfurter, who disagreed on so many matters, agreed in *McCollum,* and it is Frankfurter's concurring opinion that is most quoted: "The law of imitation operates, and non-conformity is not an outstanding characteristic of children. The result is an obvious pressure upon children to attend." Frankfurter's reasoning was that the children belonging to nonparticipating sects or families would have "a feeling of separatism."[24]

Four years later the Court qualified its judgment in the New York release-time case, *Zorach* v. *Clauson.* In this instance, the students were not taught religion within the walls of the public schools, but rather were allowed to leave school once a week to go to religious centers for instruction. That distinction was enough for the Court to conclude that "we do not see how New York by this type of 'released time' program has made a law respecting an establishment of religion." Justice William O. Douglas, writing for the majority, explained that while the First Amendment requires that there be separation of church and state "so far as interference with the 'free exercise' of religion and an 'establishment' of religion are concerned," it does not require that church and state be separated in all other respects. "Otherwise the state and religion would be aliens to each other—hostile, suspicious, and even unfriendly."[25] Douglas reasoned that if the New York law were declared unconstitutional, then it would also be unconstitutional for a Catholic student to be excused for mass on a holy day or a Jewish student to be excused for Yom Kippur.

In oft-quoted dicta, Douglas declared:

> We are a religious people whose institutions presuppose a Supreme Being.
> ... [Government] respects the religious nature of our people and accommo-
> dates the public service to their spiritual needs. To hold that it may not
> would be to find in the Constitution a requirement that the government
> show a callous indifference to religious groups. That would be preferring
> those who believe in no religion over those who do believe.[26]

Thus, long before the Herricks school board decided to have prayer
in its schools, the issue of religion and school had been before the Court
several times.

HERRICKS' TURN IN COURT

William Vitale, Jr., the president of the Herricks school board,
whose name would forever be identified with the issue of school prayer,
never anticipated any trouble. "The teachers were to be instructed that
this was not necessarily a compelling thing," he explained. "If a child for
some basic reason chose to be excused, he or she would be excused."[27] But
Vitale didn't know how much the issue gnawed at Lawrence Roth.

"A friend of mine and I discussed it every day on the train to
Manhattan," Roth recalls. He was so upset that he finally "decided to try
the ACLU. And they encouraged me that it was an issue we should deal
with. So I put an ad in the local paper, advertising for people interested
in petitioning against the school board's decision for school prayer."[28] He
ran the notice at his own expense:

> Notice: To all Herrick's school district taxpayers: A taxpayers suit will
> soon be started to challenge the legality of prayers in public schools. Coun-
> sel has been appointed.
>
> All interested parties CALL:
>   Lawrence Roth
> MAYFIAR [sic]1–7652 AFTER 5 P.M. DAILY

Meanwhile, at the ACLU the planning began. "I was a board
member of the NYCLU," William Butler explains. "[W]hen the case
came up, they decided that the lawyer could not be a Jew. He must be
Catholic, that is, someone taking the attitude that he is DEFENDING
prayer and religious freedom, not attacking it. And they looked down at
the end of the table and saw a nice Irish-Catholic boy—William Butler."[29] On taking the case, Butler candidly admits, "I never wanted to be
an expert on separation of church and state. Look, I am a conservative

corporate lawyer. I am not a civil liberties lawyer. . . . I sit as counsel some, but I can't get too excited about it." But as the son-in-law of Arthur Garfield Hayes, who had defended so many unpopular causes in the thirties and forties, Butler decided to take the case. "I knew . . . that this was the first time in the history of the United States that a state had actually composed a prayer and then inserted this prayer into one of its compulsory institutions."[30]

With the advertisement, Roth was exercising his constitutional right to bring a class action suit against the state. Approximately 50 citizens answered Roth's ad, but by the second meeting the number was down to 20 or 30. By then Bill Butler had come in. He said the petitioners should be parents with kids young enough to be in the school system for the next few years. "Others were advised against participating by their ministers," Roth explains. "At the end of the selection process, two to three months later, we had five petitioners that Butler wanted. They all had young children and the moral starch that would be necessary to deal with the criticism and the crank calls." They were Stephen Engel, Monroe Lerner, Leonore Lyons, David Lichtenstein, and Lawrence Roth. (Because the petitioners were listed in alphabetical order, Engel's name is usually associated with the case.)

Two of the five parents were members of the Jewish faith, one a Unitarian, one a member of the Ethical Culture Union, and the last an atheist. Roth was the one classified as a nonbeliever. "I was born a Jew, but I believe in a Creative Process," he now explains. "And I'm not at all sure we can change anything by petitioning to a higher being. So when affiliation came up, I explained the way I felt to Butler and he said, 'You're the atheist!' Apparently you have to have an atheist in the crowd so we started from there."

Bill Vitale was at home one evening when his doorbell rang and a process server presented him, as president of the school board, with a petition from those five parents for a hearing before the New York Supreme Court. (In New York, the term "Supreme Court" can be misleading; it is actually the lowest court. The next highest court is called the appellate division, and the highest court is the New York Court of Appeals.) Vitale told the school board members about the lawsuit, and they decided to turn the matter over to the school board attorney, Bertram Daiker, a local lawyer with offices in Port Jefferson.

Public sentiment against the suit mounted. Roth recalls that his "two sons, Joseph and Daniel, were 10 and 12 or so. They had fights because of it. Unpleasant things happened. There was especially pressure on the older one. Kids would yell at him, 'Hey, you Jew bastard!' It felt strange to him to be accused of being a Jew." Roth says his wife also felt the pressure and would jokingly say, " 'You had to be the big shot, didn't you.' "

Daniel Roth remembers the initial resentment as coming not so much from his friends as from the teachers in the school. "I definitely remember an antagonism from the teachers, no question about that. There were comments made. I remember an eighth-grade teacher in particular. She would make snide remarks about what my father was doing. . . . I was certainly singled out by her for humiliation."[31]

The anger over Roth's suit was not limited to the teachers in the school system; a group of parents were also upset. "We had a very active civil group, people of school district #9,"[32] Thomas Ford, an attorney, recalls. He says the group had often been involved in other school issues. Henry Hollenberg, an Orthodox Jew, got them all together on the school prayer issue. Fifteen parents organized as "intervenors" and hired Porter Chandler, an attorney who often represented the Catholic church.

Although Ford and others are still adamant about the school prayer issue, at least one of the 15 has changed his mind. "I was a bit on the fence at the time," Thomas Delaney says, "I did feel it was a worthy cause to back. I felt that my children should have the opportunity to say the prayer. . . . I have mellowed. I'm not as radical in my opinion. I've learned to live with the evils of our day. I look to other sources for redemption." Delaney explains his present position:

> I am in favor of religion and God. I am in favor of separation of church and state. I am not in favor of politics and theology. It seems to be contrary today. We hear a lot about separation of church and state, but not separation of state and church. Sometimes the state involves itself in the religious aspects of our lives; sometimes the church involves itself in the political aspects of our lives. When you talk about the Constitution you have to recognize that our law has its foundation in Almighty God. But when it comes to separation of church and state, I'm very sympathetic to people of all religions and no religions at all. I'm not so sure I would be so violently in favor of prayer in schools as I was 20 years ago.[33]

The hearing in *Engel* v. *Vitale* took place in the Nassau County Court House before Judge Bernard S. Meyer, and six months later his 67-page opinion was handed down. The Herricks school board had won the first round. Judge Meyer in essence decided that the 22-word prayer violated no child's constitutional rights as long as it was not compulsory. He concluded that: "[T]he 'establishment' clause of the Constitution does not prohibit the non-compulsory saying of the Regents' Prayer in the public schools, but that the 'free exercise' clause requires that respondent board take affirmative steps to protect the rights of those who, for whatever reason, choose not to participate."[34]

Roth was stunned. "It seemed strange to me that a judge would render a decision saying . . . 'this prayer is legal but if you do so and so it's going to be even more legal.' "[35] To Roth and Butler, simply excusing students from the prayer was not sufficient protection, because this alternative of being isolated from the rest of the class put enormous pressure on a child.

The parents appealed Meyer's decision to the appellate division, and that Brooklyn-based court upheld Meyer's decision. They also lost in the New York State Court of Appeals, but it was a divided bench. The majority opinion, written by Chief Judge Desmond, stated: "Saying this simple prayer may be, according to the broadest possible dictionary definition, an act of 'religion', but when the Founding Fathers prohibited 'an establishment of religion' they were referring to official adoption of, or favor to, one or more sects." The two dissenters of the seven-man court, Judges Dye and Fuld, held that the regents prayer was unconstitutional because the "state had entered a field it has been thought best to leave to the church alone. . . . [The compulsory prayer] cannot help but lead to a gradual erosion of the mighty bulwark erected by the First Amendment."[36]

Actually, there were many other school prayer cases floating around at the same time as *Engel,* and there was no guarantee that *Engel* would ever reach the United States Supreme Court. "Mine was the absolute first to reach the Court," says Butler. "My case was simple. . . . My argument with the state was that it was composing its own prayer and inserting it in compulsory institutions which will act as its churches and led by teachers who act as priests. So you have all the components of the establishment of religion. My second argument relied on Felix Frankfurter's remark that 'nonconformity is not an outstanding characteristic of little children.' " Butler admits that he was never sure about winning in the Supreme Court, "but then we were also scared that we might win in the lower courts. That way we would not have had a national decision. One way to cut the bridges of a civil libertarian quickly is to render a decision in the lower court."[37]* When four justices voted to hear the school prayer case, Lawrence Roth finally got his case docketed during the 1961–1962 term.

The oral arguments, on April 3, 1962, began with the traditional call to order by the crier, "Oyez, Oyez, Oyez. God save the United States and this honorable court." The appeal to a deity in a suit involving school prayer was a point of irony not lost on the justices. In fact, Justice Douglas quickly asked Butler, "This courtroom, where we have an announcement every time we come—'God save the United States and this honorable Court,' we haven't decided whether that's constitutional or not have we?"[38] Butler admitted that this issue had been discussed in other cases but not resolved.

---

*If the losing side does not choose to appeal the lower court opinion, the case cannot go to the Supreme Court.

Douglas continued, "We have not decided whether compulsory prayer in the halls of Congress is constitutional," and then quipped, "Is that case on its way here?" Butler retorted, "If it is, Your Honor, I'm glad I'm not bringing it." He then went on to explain that the framers of the Constitution had been concerned with this issue. "I recall very vividly reading Madison's attack on chaplains in the House of Representatives and in the Senate. Madison took the position that he thought that the use of chaplains by both sides of the House was unconstitutional."*

"I want to make it absolutely clear before this Court that I come here not as an antagonist of religion," Butler told the Court, "that my clients are deeply religious people; that we come here in the firm belief that the best safety of religion in the United States, and freedom of religion, is to keep religion out of our public life and not to confound, as Roger Williams said, the civil with the religious." He explained, "My clients say that prayer is good. But what we say here is, it's the beginning of the end of religious freedom when religious activity such as this is incorporated into the public school system of the United States."

Butler's other major argument was that the prayer was really compulsory:

> Would the little child, would "Johnny," leave the classroom; or would the parent be expected to ask the school system to excuse his child, who may be singled out as a non-conformist? I must adopt Mr. Justice Frankfurter's thesis in *McCollum* that the law of imitation applies. Little children want to be with other little children. . . . The effect would be to cast upon this child's mind some indelible mark, and I think it can be sustained that, in effect, the children are coerced into saying this prayer, because of these reasons.

In countering the arguments set forth in his opponents' briefs, Butler said that the case could be distinguished from the *Zorach* case (release time for religious instruction) because it was more than an accommodation, it was a direct participation by the school system in religious matters. Further, he said that the school board's claim that the appellant parents were only a minority was irrelevant because "the very purpose of the Constitution is to protect the minority against the majority, to protect the weak against the strong in matters of keeping separate forever the functions of the civil and the religious."

Most of the rest of Butler's time was spent answering questions as to what activities he thought might be permissible. Would a moment of silent meditation be permissible? What about Bible reading? Would you

---

*This issue was addressed in 1983, when the Court affirmed the right of state legislatures to pay chaplains.

object to saying a prayer in other public places? Justice Potter Stewart questioned Butler intently on the question of the flag salute's phrase "one nation under God." Butler's response was that the purpose of the flag salute was to pledge allegiance to the United States. "It is a political affirmation. The whole tenor of the utterance is not religious, whereas the utterance in this case is solely religious."

Counsel for the school board, Bertram Daiker, agreed that if the school prayer was "compulsive" that would make it unconstitutional, but said that great care had been taken to remove that objection. "Those children who do not wish to join in the prayer or whose parents do not wish them to join in the prayer may remain seated; they may remain silent." He added that if a student or parent wished, the student could be excused from the room, but that no such requests had been made.

Daiker asserted, "Since the earliest days of this country, going back to the Mayflower Compact, the men who put the country together have publicly and repeatedly recognized the existence of a Supreme Being, a God." He continued, "When, therefore, we say here this prayer, which Mr. Justice Frankfurter characterized as an avowal of faith, an avowal which recognizes that there is some Supreme power, some Supreme Being, we are proceeding fully in accord with the tradition and heritage that has been handed down to us." Daiker then reminded the justices that the Declaration of Independence has four references to a Creator, and that the constitutions of 49 of the 50 states recognize the existence of Almighty God. To Daiker and the school board, the prayer was not teaching religion, but simply expressing the same sentiments as are found in the state constitutions. "We are not trying here in the Herricks School District to teach religion . . . any more than . . . the prayer used in this Court."

Chief Justice Earl Warren wanted to know if the prayer was a religious practice. Daiker's response was "no more so than the saying of any prayer on any public occasion is a religious practice. Any group of men who gather together for dinner commence with a prayer. This, to that extent, is a religious practice." Daiker went on, "Whenever people gather together in a group and utter a prayer, a recognition of the Almighty, as has been consistently done since the founding of the country hundreds of years ago, we don't find constitutional objections. How, then, can we say that prayer is all right on any public occasion in a state-paid-for building, with state employees, except in the school?"

The debate, although intense, was punctuated by moments of laughter. When Porter Chandler addressed the Court for the "intervenor" parents, he pointed out that "when this case started, [the parents] had 37 children in the public schools. . . . On the last count, my clients now have 41 children in the public school. [laughter.] So there is no question of mootness here."

Chandler spoke eloquently of his clients, parents who were willing to fight for their children's right to pray:

Why are my clients here at all? They are here in the name of the free exercise of religion, if you want to put it that way. They are here because they feel very strongly that it is a deprivation of their children's right to share in our national heritage, and that it is a compulsory rewriting of our history in the fashion of George Orwell's *1984* to do what these petitioners are now seeking to do, namely to eliminate all reference to God from the whole fabric of our public life and of our public educational system.

He concluded his arguments with a final swipe at Butler and the five parents who were fighting prayer in the schools. "I would ask Mr. Butler," he said, "to recite the words of the Declaration of Independence, or to say that all men are created equal and that they're endowed by their Creator with inalienable rights."

The opinion in *Engel* v. *Vitale*[39] came down late in June 1962, two months after the oral arguments. There were three opinions, one in dissent, but there were at least five solid votes that stated that the short prayer breached the First Amendment wall that separated church from state.* Justice Black began the majority opinion by reminding all "of the historical fact that governmentally established religions and religious persecutions go hand in hand." He said that "[n]either the fact that the prayer may be denominationally neutral, nor the fact that its observance on the part of the students is voluntary, can serve to free it from the limitations of the Establishment Clause."[40]

Black rejected the accusation that banning school prayer was anti-God or hostile "toward religion or toward prayer." He said, "Nothing . . . could be more wrong. [The framers of the Bill of Rights] knew that the First Amendment . . . was written to quiet well-justified fears which nearly all of them felt arising out of an awareness that governments of the past had shackled men's tongues to make them speak only the religious thoughts that government wanted them to speak and to pray only to the God that government wanted them to pray to." He said it was "neither sacrilegious nor antireligious to say that . . . government . . . should stay out of the business of writing or sanctioning official prayers and leave that purely religious function to the people themselves."[41]

The majority opinion of Justice Black concluded with the warning of James Madison:

> Who does not see that the same authority which can establish Christianity, in exclusion of all other Religions, may establish with the same ease any particular sect of Christians, in exclusion of all other Sects? That the same authority which can force a citizen to contribute three pence only of his property for the support of any one establishment, may force him to conform to any other establishment in all cases whatsoever?[42]

---

*Justice Frankfurter had suffered a stroke and retired, and Justice White did not participate in the decision because he had not been present for the oral arguments.

Justice Douglas concurred on the ban in public schools, but went even further. He didn't want persons on the public payroll to conduct prayers, no matter how brief, "to a captive audience." That restriction would have included chaplains in Congress, criers in the Supreme Court, and teachers. "For me the principle is the same," he wrote, "no matter how briefly the prayer is said."[43]

There was one dissent to the ban on school prayer, and that came from Justice Stewart, whose views on most First Amendment issues are on the liberal side. Stewart argued that a voluntary prayer did not establish an official religion. He said the Court had "misapplied a great constitutional principle." He could not see "how an 'official religion' is established by letting those who want to say a prayer say it." In fact, he felt that "to deny the wish of these school children to join in reciting this prayer is to deny them the opportunity of sharing in the spiritual heritage of our Nation." Stewart's position was that almost every president, from Washington to Lincoln to Kennedy, then the incumbent, had in his inaugural address "asked the protection and help of God," and that "metaphors like the 'wall of separation'" are "nowhere to be found in the Constitution."[44]

The uproar over the school prayer ban was deafening. A six-column banner headline in the *New York Herald Tribune* shouted, "School Prayer Unconstitutional." Other newspapers ran similar headlines. The *New York Mirror*'s headline read "Ban Prayer in Public Schools." The *New York Times* declared, "Supreme Court Outlaws School Prayers in Regents Case Decision," and the New York *Daily News* announced, "School Prayer Held Illegal." A cartoon in the Hearst newspapers depicted a judicial chisel removing the word "God" from "In God We Trust" on a Lincoln penny.

As indicated at the beginning of this chapter, certain politicians contributed to this uproar. Governor Herman Talmadge of Georgia accused the Supreme Court of having "dealt a blow to all believers in a Supreme Being."[45] Senator James Eastland, an arch foe of the Warren Court, termed the school prayer ban a victory for "atheistic communism" and a big step toward "the destruction of the religious and spiritual life of this country."[46] Eastland threatened to introduce a bill to amend the Constitution, making it impossible for the Supreme Court to ban prayer or the reading of the Bible in schools. Over twenty years later that suggestion still lingers before the Congress. Indeed, President Ronald Reagan has said that he will push for a constitutional amendment to allow prayers in school.

Lawrence Roth and his family experienced repercussions almost immediately. Roth first heard the results of his case while at work in his manufacturing business on Broadway in Manhattan. A local newsman "called me up and said, 'You won in the Supreme Court. What do you think?' I heaved a heavy sigh of gratitude. Thank God. And that was the beginning of the trouble: 3000 letters both for and against—mostly against—the beginning of threats, pressures, and stares in the subway, and FBI surveillance."

"We got calls, 'Don't start your car; it'll blow up.' Once, kids with gas-soaked rags laid out a cross on our lawn, lit it, and left. Our neighbor put it out. There were a lot of threats and picketing. Right after the decision came out, people marched with signs, 'ROTH—GODLESS ATHEIST.'"

Daniel Roth, then 17, remembers that columnist George Sokolsky called his father "the author of the troubles that produced the outrageous Black Decision." Afterwards, "the phone didn't stop ringing, literally around the clock. They [the phone calls] were really horrible." Roth recalls one call in particular: "Somebody called up and said it was the Brooklyn Protective Association and we took a vote and decided to kill you. . . . And then the hate mail started. . . . We got about 700 pieces of mail a week, and we used to try to guess by the envelope whether it was pro or anti." But he adds, "I remember being very proud of my father. I am. I admire him for what he did."

Mary Harte, who had originally pushed for the prayer, took the defeat stoically. "Of course, we would have to abide by the Supreme Court decision."[47] Thomas Ford, one of the intervenor parents, was also resigned to follow the decision: "Well, life just goes on. We've had tragedies and triumphs and joys and sorrows and life just goes on." But at the same time he was angry: "The enormous task of overruling a Supreme Court decision, of legally opposing that mandate is really impossible. We had to have a civil war to outlaw slavery. What are we going to do to abolish abortion or get prayer back in the schools? Our founding fathers never intended to place in them [the Court] such power. That power has gone unchecked."[48]

The debate over school prayer goes on. In 1983, New Jersey's moment of silence was being tested in the courts. William Butler sees it as "an attempt to pervert trickily the constitution." He quips, "I had a law professor once who would ask, 'If you call a cow's tail a leg, how many legs does it have?' And someone would always answer, 'Five.' But, of course, it's four, because a tail is not a leg, no matter what you call it. That's what's going on here. It's still a prayer."[49]

Butler is especially concerned about the idea to amend the First Amendment to allow school prayer: "I don't think it's possible to tinker around with the First Amendment nowadays. If the First Amendment came up today, it wouldn't pass. Thank God we are stuck with it."[50]

Lawrence Roth sees the moment of silence as "an opening wedge." But his son Daniel, now a publisher, is more analytical. "The Constitution of the United States is a difficult instrument. It's a blueprint. It's a blueprint for our country the same way there's a blueprint for a house. It's not meant to be hysterically analyzed." He goes on, "People see these rulings as a prohibition, as an inhibitor, as a suppression of religion.

... I see it as a further refinement of the Constitution. ... I think the issue becomes very volatile when that distinction is lost sight of."[51]

In October 1983 the Supreme Court heard arguments in a Pawtucket, Rhode Island, case involving another question of free exercise vs. establishment. But this time the issue was not the public school but the public square. The question was whether a municipality could constitutionally display a crèche or nativity scene during the Christmas season.

In March 1984 the Court decided that Pawtucket's display of the crèche did not violate the establishment clause. For the majority, Chief Justice Burger wrote:

> To forbid the use of this creche—at the very time people are taking note of the season with Christmas hymns and carols in public schools and other public places and while the Congress and Legislatures open sessions with prayers by paid Chaplains, would be a stilted over-reaction contrary to our history and to our holdings. If the presence of the creche in this display violates the Establishment Clause, a host of other forms of taking official note of Christmas and our religious heritage are equally offensive to the Constitution.[52]

So the debate Roger Williams began continues in the very state to which he fled. Although Pastor Williams never lived to read the First Amendment, one wonders whether he would think that the "wall of separation" between church and state had been breached in the controversy over a crèche in Pawtucket.

A police photo of Dollree Mapp, May 27, 1957. *AP/Wide World Photos*

The house in Cleveland where Dollree Mapp lived in 1957. *Courtesy of Carl Delau.*

Sergeant Carl Delau was looking for a bombing suspect; instead he found some obscene books in Dollree Mapp's home. She was convicted for "possession" of obscenity under an Ohio statute and took her case to the Supreme Court. The result was not a ruling on obscenity, but on the exclusionary rule and the Fourth Amendment.

A KNOCK AT THE DOOR
How the Supreme Court Created a Rule to Enforce the Fourth Amendment

There has been no blinking the consequences. The criminal is to go free because the constable has blundered.

Judge Benjamin Cardozo, dissenting,
in *People* v. *Defore*

[O]ur holding that the exclusionary rule is an essential part of both the Fourth and Fourteenth Amendments is not only the logical dictate of prior cases, but it also makes very good sense. There is no war between the Constitution and common sense.

Justice Tom Clark, *Mapp* v. *Ohio*

It was an unseasonably raw May morning in Cleveland. Police Sergeant Carl Delau, home from a party and "a little drunk," had just fallen asleep when the phone rang at 2:30 A.M. Don King, an alleged numbers racketeer, who would later become the prominent promoter of championship boxing bouts, was on the other end of the line. "Sergeant, they just bombed my house," King excitedly reported.

"Donald, how do you know?" Delau asked in a sleepy daze.

"Well," King said, "I can look out and I don't have a front porch; I don't have a front wall."

When in response to Delau's next question, King said he had not yet called the police, Delau phoned in the report. In a few minutes, his phone rang again. This time a police dispatcher told him to "get your pants on. There is a big bomb in there."[1]

That call was the beginning of the Cleveland police's investigation of the bombing of King's house. It was also the beginning of a Supreme Court case that would have constitutional repercussions in every police station in America. For *Mapp* v. *Ohio,* as the case would be known, would establish throughout the land the Fourth Amendment right against un-reasonable search and seizure. Yet the case began as a test of obscenity law.

THE SEARCH AND SEIZURE

Three days later, on May 23, 1957, Sergeant Delau received a phone tip that a person connected with the bombing was hiding out at 14705 Milverton Road. He and his two partners drove over to the two-family house; it happened to be the home of Dollree Mapp.

Miss Mapp, as she likes to be called, still bristles with hostility when she talks about the Cleveland cops; Delau, who was a vice squad officer, himself borders on the obscene when he describes her as "a foxy girl" with "a swagger about her that was just as calm as can be and just as jibe as can be and just as flippant as can be."[2] Now in her fifties, Dollree Mapp is still a handsome, verbal woman, who has all the charisma and body English of a knockout. Married for a short time to boxer Jimmy Bivans, who during World War II briefly held the light heavyweight boxing championship, Miss Mapp had been, according to columnist Walter Winchell, the fiancée of light heavyweight champion Archie Moore.[3]

When the three plainclothesmen arrived at the Mapp house about 1:30 that afternoon, they noted the bombing suspect's car parked outside, "so we sat there and waited for a long time," remembers Delau. "And he was not leaving. . . . I said, well, how would it look if we made an inquiry. They might just say 'Hiya, come right in.' But I knew Dollree Mapp, and I figured it would be a little different than that."[4] He was right.

More than two decades after the ensuing search and arrest, Dollree Mapp and the now-retired Sergeant Delau give surprisingly similar versions of the episode. Delau and the patrolmen, Michael Haney and Thomas Devers, knocked on the side door of the house. Miss Mapp poked her head out of the upstairs window and asked what they wanted. The police responded that they wanted to make a search, but the visibly annoyed Miss Mapp said she would not open the door before calling her lawyer. A few minutes later she was back, refusing to admit them and insisting that they first obtain a search warrant.

Delau and company returned to their car to radio in, asking that another officer get a search warrant while they watched the house. At about 4:30 they returned to the side door, this time accompanied by a half-dozen uniformed colleagues. Once again they asked Miss Mapp to consent to the search, claiming to have a warrant, and once again she leaned out the window and defiantly shouted, "Nooo."

This time the police broke a pane of glass, unlatched the door, and barreled into the stairwell that led up to Miss Mapp's apartment. Observing all this from her second-floor perch, she marched downstairs and met the officers on the landing between floors.

"I said, 'Hold it. Where's the warrant?' " Miss Mapp recalls. "And he [Delau] held up the piece of paper. Now I'm just a few steps up, so I reached over and grabbed the piece of paper and put it in my bosom."[5]

This is where the two accounts part company, not so much in terms of facts—no one disputes that Delau retrieved the paper from Miss Mapp's bosom or that she was eventually handcuffed—as in the way each party remembers the attitude and conduct of the other. Miss Mapp asserts that the officers were brutal and cavalier during the search; Delau declares that Miss Mapp was continually defiant. Thus Miss Mapp says that after the paper had disappeared beneath her turtleneck sweater,

> He [Delau] said, and I heard him clearly, "What are we going to do now?" And one said, "Go after it." And I said, "Oh, no. You're not going in." . . . They handcuffed me behind my back and went into my bosom. . . . They took the paper and then I said, "I'm going to call my lawyer." . . . They searched the drawers, the kitchen cabinets, the closets, in the pills—I had some diet pills. I guess they were looking there for some man in the pill package. They went all over.[6]

Delau, who describes their relationship as that of "arch enemies" because of a previous arrest with no conviction,* disagrees vehemently with Miss Mapp's recollection of the incident:

> We didn't stampede like animals or a bunch of berserk people. . . . And I said, "Here's a search warrant." . . . And before the person could even read it to her, she grabbed it and put it down her bosom. . . . It was partially sticking up . . . and, of course, I did take the search warrant from her almost immediately. . . . But she did tussle and fight later on. And I said, "Dollree, don't do that. You come with me while we search." "No, I won't," she said . . . and she was belligerent. . . . Once we were in, she was going to be hostile to us. All the time she was playing games with us and talking cute, defying us, and threatening us. . . . And she was gonna be real nasty. And I think she took a swing at one of the uniformed men if I'm not mistaken. . . . She was, in a sense, resisting, so she was handcuffed . . . to one of the uniformed men.[7]

In Miss Mapp's bedroom, the police confiscated some "obscene" materials: "pictures of both male and female nude models with all their organs totally undressed,"[8] some pencil sketches of nudes, and four books, *London Stage Affairs, Affairs of a Troubadour, Memoirs of a Hotel Man,*

---

*According to the police report filed in this case, Miss Mapp had been arrested for possession of betting slips. However, she denies any previous arrests and in court her lawyer stipulated that she had no prior record.

and *Little Darlings.* Then the police went to the basement of the house and confiscated some policy paraphernalia (betting materials). At the time, Miss Mapp claimed that all of the contraband belonged to a former roomer, Morris Jones, whose belongings she was storing, although she now admits that the sketches were hers. Meanwhile, the bombing suspect, Virgil Ogiltree, was finally found in the first-floor apartment.* Miss Mapp was arrested and charged for possession of the betting equipment and the obscene materials.

The charge for possession of the policy paraphernalia was a misdemeanor, and she was tried and acquitted in police court. Possession of obscene material was a felony under a recently amended Ohio statute.

It was not until September 1958 that Miss Mapp went on trial for "unlawfully and knowingly having in her possession certain lewd and lascivious books, pictures, and photographs . . . being so indecent and immoral . . . that some would be offensive to the Court and improper to be placed in the records thereof."[9] By that time, the search warrant had mysteriously disappeared. Miss Mapp pleaded not guilty, and her lawyer, Alexander L. Kearns, moved to have the evidence suppressed on the grounds that the officers were required to obtain a warrant before conducting a search. It is important to note that even if the warrant could have been produced, it would not have mentioned the obscene materials. The police were empowered only to look for the bombing suspect and policy paraphernalia. However, Judge Donald F. Lybarger overruled the motion to suppress the evidence.

Regarding the question of whether the police actually had obtained a search warrant, as they testified in the Cuyahoga County Court, the official police line was and still is that the warrant was obtained but was "inexplicably" lost. (Dollree Mapp, for one, was convinced that the piece of paper momentarily nestled between her breasts was blank—although she never really had a chance to take a good look.) However, Carl Delau, after a period of silence, has recently been willing to respond to questions about the warrant. Contradicting his trial testimony, he cleared up the mystery shrouding the missing warrant:

> When the lieutenant went to get the search warrant . . . he went to the prosecutors and got a proper affidavit.† He went to the clerk's office and had it signed, went to a judge, got a judge's signature. . . . He walked out with the affidavit. . . . He only got an affidavit! He never got a warrant. And as a result, when I finally looked at it outside the scene, and I seen [sic] it was just an affidavit . . . I wasn't going to make an issue over it. . . . So, were we going to say we only had the affidavit?[10]

---

* Miss Mapp told the authors that she knew Ogiltree was downstairs.
†In order to obtain a search warrant, the officer had first to get an affidavit stating the reasons for the warrant. After getting the affidavit, he needed a judge to agree that there was probable cause as spelled out in the affidavit and to issue the warrant.

Despite the "missing" search warrant and after only 20 minutes of deliberation, the jury found Dollree Mapp guilty as charged, and she was sentenced to serve one to seven years in the Ohio State Reformatory for Women. After a friend posted her bail, Dollree Mapp appealed.

THE CONSTITUTIONAL ISSUES

Underlying Dollree Mapp's conviction were two constitutional questions, involving the First and Fourth Amendments. First, was the Ohio obscenity statute constitutional? And, second, was the search of her house an unreasonable search and seizure, and if so, was the evidence (i.e., the books, pictures, and pencil drawings) therefore not admissible in court?

The First Amendment

Although the United States Supreme Court had made it clear in *Near, DeJonge,* and other cases that the First Amendment protections for free speech and press were enforceable against the states, the Court had also asserted that those protections were not absolute. In *Near,* Chief Justice Hughes had listed some of the exceptions, including obscenity:

> No one would question but that a government might prevent actual obstruction to its recruiting service or the publication of the sailing dates of transports or the number and location of troops. *On similar grounds, the primary requirements of decency may be enforced against obscene publications.* The security of the community life may be protected against incitements to acts of violence and the overthrow by force of orderly government.[11]

In 1957, the Court had expanded its views on obscenity in *Roth* v. *United States.*[12] In that case Samuel Roth had been convicted of four counts of using the United States mails to advertise and distribute obscene materials. Speaking for the majority in upholding Roth's conviction, Justice William Brennan declared that "this Court has always assumed that obscenity is not protected by the freedoms of speech and press. . . . [T]he unconditional phrasing of the First Amendment was not intended to protect every utterance." Although "All ideas having even the slightest redeeming social importance—unorthodox ideas, controversial ideas, even ideas hateful to the prevailing climate of opinion—have the full protection of the guaranties," Brennan continued, "obscenity [is] utterly without redeeming social importance." And Brennan defined obscenity as "material which deals with sex in a manner appealing to prurient interest." He qualified that by saying the work should be considered as a whole, not just in terms of specific passages. He also said that "sex" and "obscenity" are not synonymous. The portrayal of sex "in art, literature and scientific works, is not itself sufficient reason to deny material the constitutional protection. . . . "[13]

Dollree Mapp's lawyers had never argued that the material found in her home was not obscene. The constitutional question that would eventually arise was whether the Ohio obscenity statute was overly broad. For, according to the judge's charge, even if the jury believed that the books belonged to her roomer, she was guilty of possession because she knew the obscenity was in her home. And "knowing possession" of obscene material—even holding it, packed away, for another person—was a felony.

The Fourth Amendment and the Exclusionary Rule

The other question was far more complicated. It had to do with the guarantee spelled out in the Fourth Amendment:

> The right of the people to be secure in their houses, papers and effects, against unreasonable searches and seizures, shall not be violated and no warrants shall issue, but upon probable cause, supported by oath or affirmation, and particularly describing the place to be searched, and the persons or things to be seized at the time.

In Dollree Mapp's case the matter of the warrant was at issue. Even if, as the police claimed, there had been a warrant, it did not list "obscene materials" as one of the things to be searched for.

In conjunction with the Fourth Amendment was a judge-made rule known as the "exclusionary rule," which prohibited illegally obtained evidence from being admitted in federal court. Former Supreme Court Justice Potter Stewart has described this rule as having been "jerry-built" —that is, in its development it was "a little bit like a roller coaster track constructed while the roller coaster sped along, with each new piece of track attached hastily and imperfectly to the one before it, just in time to prevent the roller coaster from crashing, but without the opportunity to measure the curves and dips preceding it or to contemplate the twists and turns that inevitably lay ahead."[14]

The development of the Fourth Amendment and the exclusionary rule traces to English and colonial history. The framers of the Bill of Rights were opposed to the use of "general warrants" by the British crown. These documents, which did not list specific persons and were issued without probable cause, were used to aid in the apprehension and prosecution of critics of the crown. Once issued, the warrants were good for the life of the monarch.

There was heightened opposition to such warrants in Britain itself at the time the American Revolution was fomenting. One of the most famous cases against those governmental abuses was *Wilkes* v. *Wood,* in

1763. John Wilkes and 49 other people were arrested for publication of pamphlet No. 45 in a series called "North Briton." Since Wilkes' name was not on the warrant, he called it "ridiculous" and "against the whole English nation." He brought civil damage suits against the government officials and won. The English Chief Justice Charles Pratt, "planting the seed for the Fourth Amendment"[15] declared that the power of governmental officials using the warrants was "totally subversive of the liberty of the subject."[16]

Another British version of the general warrant was the "writ of assistance," a legal device given to customs inspectors to search for contraband. These warrants were used to identify colonial smugglers, who were trying to avoid what they saw as tyrannical import taxes imposed by the British.

As Justice Potter Stewart points out, "What is important is the recognition that from the colonists' experience with general warrants and writs of assistance as tool of censorship and tyranny, the Fourth Amendment emerged."[17] The evolution of the meaning of the Fourth Amendment would stretch from colonial searches for smuggled tea right into Dollree Mapp's dresser drawers in Cleveland.

Almost a century elapsed between the ratification of the Constitution and the Supreme Court's justification of the exclusion of evidence on constitutional grounds, in *Boyd* v. *United States*[18] in 1886. E. A. Boyd and Sons was involved in a forfeiture proceeding for importing from Liverpool, England, 35 cases of plate glass in violation of the federal import and revenue laws. In order to prove the case, the government needed the company's invoices. Although Boyd eventually produced the records, he objected, charging that his Fourth (search and seizure) and Fifth (self-incrimination) Amendment rights had been violated. After losing the forfeiture case, Boyd appealed to the United States Supreme Court.

The high court's opinion, written by Justice Joseph Bradley and joined by six other justices, added a new dimension to the Fourth Amendment by reading it in conjunction with the Fifth. It was, Bradley said, a case in which "the Fourth and Fifth Amendments run almost into each other." The government was seeking not contraband, but private papers protected by the Fourth Amendment. Bradley concluded, "[W]e have been unable to perceive that the seizure of a man's private books and papers to be used in evidence against him is substantially different from compelling him to be a witness against himself."[19] Thus admitting the invoices into evidence was a double violation of Boyd's constitutional rights. The invoices could not be introduced, and a new trial was ordered.

The emergence of the exclusionary rule came in 1914, when a Kansas City Express Company employee, Fremont Weeks, was convicted in a federal court of using the mails to conduct an illegal lottery. The evidence used against him had been obtained when the police acquired a key to his home and took incriminating papers. Weeks then sued for return of his personal property.

In the United States Supreme Court, Justice William R. Day ruled that the property must be returned and that because of Weeks' Fifth Amendment rights the government could not enter the papers as evidence at the trial.[20] Thus, a federal rule of evidence formally was written: The federal government could not produce books and papers that it had illegally seized and could not subpoena.

After *Weeks*, the exclusionary rule began to impact upon other areas and was eventually enlarged to include contraband as well as personal papers. A few states voluntarily adopted the rule, but it was not without its critics. In 1926, Judge Benjamin Cardozo (then a member of the New York State Court of Appeals and eventually a justice on the United States Supreme Court) wrote in a dissenting opinion in *People* v. *Defore*: "There has been no blinking the consequences. The criminal is to go free because the constable has blundered."[21]

Nonetheless, until 1948, the Fourth Amendment only applied to federal searches and seizures. Then came *Wolf* v. *Colorado*.[22] In that 1948 abortion conviction case, the Court had a chance to decide whether the Fourth Amendment and its extension, the exclusionary rule, were mandated in state proceedings via the Fourteenth Amendment's due process clause.

In 1944, Julius A. Wolf, a reputable Denver physician, had been tried for conspiring to perform an illegal abortion on Mildred Cairo. He and his co-defendant had pleaded not guilty. In their trial, the district attorney attempted to introduce into evidence Dr. Wolf's appointment book, which had been obtained without a search warrant. The defense then claimed that the appointment book linking Dr. Wolf to Mildred Cairo's abortion had been obtained illegally in violation of Colorado's own version of the Fourth Amendment. The trial judge overruled the objection, and the evidence was admitted. Wolf was convicted and sentenced to 15 months to 5 years. After Wolf's sentence was confirmed by the state supreme court, the high court agreed to hear his case in March 1948.

Justice Felix Frankfurter began his eloquent opinion for the majority by insisting that a police search without a judge's specifically worded warrant was a violation of human rights:

> A knock at the door, whether by day or by night as a prelude to a search, without authority of law but solely on the authority of the police, did not need the commentary of recent history to be condemned as inconsistent with the conception of human rights enshrined in the history and the basic constitutional documents of English-speaking peoples.[23]

So, illegal searches, whether by federal, state, or city police, were now unconstitutional. Under the court's decision the Fourth Amendment protections were now enforceable upon the states because they were "implicit in the concept of ordered liberty." However, Frankfurter and five of his brethren refused to require the states to institute the exclusionary rule. It was not, they reasoned, the only remedy for disciplining the "blundering constable"; the states were free to adopt any one of a number of effective remedies to rectify wrongful searches and seizures. A suit against the offending officer or a charge of criminal trespass might be acceptable alternatives to the exclusion of tainted evidence. In their minds, the exclusionary rule was not inextricably bound to the Fourth Amendment, because the Constitution did not dictate a specific remedy. It didn't matter *how* the states enforced the Fourth Amendment—as long as they did enforce it.

The dissenters—Justices Douglas, Murphy, and Rutledge—scoffed at the idea of other remedies as unrealistic. Justice Murphy wrote, "Alternatives are deceptive. . . . there is but one alternative to the rule of exclusion. That is no sanction [against illegal searches] at all."[24]

OHIO'S RULES

Like Colorado, Ohio was one of the states that had not adopted the exclusionary rule. In fact, although an Ohio statute required warrants, they were seldom used because of a 1936 case, *State* v. *Lindway*.[25] The facts of this case were as follows.

On March 27, 1935, three plainclothes police officers, acting on a tip, arrived at the home of Mike J. Lindway, a suspected bomber. Lindway was not home and the police had no warrant. Mrs. Lindway claimed that the police barged in and then began a search in which they found bombs, rifles, revolvers, tear gas, automatic pistols, and highly explosive dynamite ostensibly being used by Lindway in nighttime bombings of homes belonging to employees of his former employer. Lindway was subsequently convicted on the strength of this illegally obtained evidence. His conviction was upheld by the Ohio Supreme Court, which ruled that the Fourth Amendment was not applicable to the states. It reasoned that an officer who searches and seizes evidence without a warrant is a trespasser and hence liable to subsequent prosecution.

As a result, this case had established for Ohio what became known as the Lindway rule: In a criminal prosecution, evidence obtained by an unlawful search was admissible if pertinent to the main issue of the case.

DOLLREE MAPP APPEALS

Such was the state of the federal and Ohio law when Dollree Mapp's obscenity conviction came up for review. The court of appeals for Cuyahoga County upheld the conviction based on the evidence and the constitutionality of the Ohio obscenity statute. When the case reached the Ohio Supreme Court, four of the seven justices believed that the statute was unconstitutional. Their reasoning was as follows: "If anyone looks at a book and finds it lewd, he is forthwith, under this legislation, guilty of a serious crime, which may involve a sentence to the penitentiary similar to the one given to this defendant. As a result, some who might otherwise read books that are not obscene may well be discouraged from doing so and their free circulation and use will be impeded."[26]

In many states that would have settled it; Miss Mapp would have won her case. However, Section 2 of Article 4 of the constitution of Ohio requires that "no law shall be held unconstitutional and void by the Supreme Court without the concurrence of at least *all but one of the judges,* except in the affirmance of the judgment of the Court of Appeals declaring a law unconstitutional and void." So she was two votes short of freedom.

It looked as if Dollree Mapp would have to go to prison; the cost of taking her case to the United States Supreme Court was beyond her means. But a friend came to her rescue and put up the money, nearly $8,000, to appeal. After granting *certiorari,** the court scheduled the argument for March 29, 1961.

Three cases were scheduled for hearing before the Court on that Wednesday in March, but the arguments in *Mapp* v. *Ohio* were unusually long—two hours—and took up most of the afternoon. As the nine justices filed in at noon, sitting in the back of the courtroom was Dollree Mapp, who had flown in from Ohio to hear her case argued. As Justice Stewart recalls, the overwhelming portion of the oral arguments that he heard that day were devoted to the issue of the constitutionality of the Ohio statute.

With all the bravado of a Clarence Darrow and the inflection of W. C. Fields, Alexander L. Kearns, Miss Mapp's lawyer, began by reciting in detail the facts in the case: the police inquiry, the breaking of glass, the retrieving of the "warrant," and the extensive search of Miss Mapp's home. Ignoring the constitutional precedents, he emphasized that the obscene material had belonged to a roomer, not to his client, and that the Ohio Supreme Court had accepted this fact and yet had upheld her conviction.

Finally, seemingly bored with the factual recitation, Justice Felix Frankfurter interrupted, asking Kearns, "May I trouble you to tell us what do you deem to be the questions that are open before this court?"[27] He explained that he couldn't tell if the question of search and seizure and the adequacy of evidence were issues to be considered.

Kearns, a bit flustered, replied that search and seizure *was* at issue and began to explain the *Lindway* case. In his mind, because the Ohio

---

*The Supreme Court is not required to review all cases appealed to it. In those cases in which it has discretionary jurisdiction, the Court must first grant a writ of certiorari. This means that four of the nine justices agree that the high court should hear the case.

legislature had enacted a statute in 1955 that required officers to obtain warrants and ensure Fourth Amendment rights, the *Lindway* case had, in effect, been overturned by the legislature. But Frankfurter, seemingly uninterested in Kearns's explanation, interrupted again, "Are you asking us to overrule the Wolf case in the court? I notice it isn't cited in your brief." Even more unsettled, Kearns shrugged off the comment by saying that he thought the state would have cited the case and that he was not asking the court to reconsider *Wolf* (the case that said the states do not have to adopt the exclusionary rule).

However, Kearns's unfamiliarity with *Wolf* did not close the question. For the first time in history, the Court had granted argument time to the Civil Liberties Union, which had become involved in the case because of the important constitutional issues. Bernard Berkman, the attorney for the Ohio Civil Liberties Union, began his presentation by referring back to Frankfurter's question and stipulating:

> The American Civil Liberties Union and its Ohio affiliate . . . [are] very clear as to the question directed toward the appellant that we are asking this court to reconsider *Wolf* v. *Colorado* and to find that evidence that is unlawfully and illegally obtained should not be permitted into a state proceeding and its production is a violation of the federal constitution's Fourth Amendment and the Fourteenth Amendment. We have no hesitancy in asking the court to reconsider it because we think that it is a necessary part of due process.

Berkman then addressed the First Amendment issue. He explained that the principal reason for his appearance was to "urge the unconstitutionality of the Ohio obscenity law." He told the justices that inasmuch as that statute made mere possession a crime, "if a normal adult has an obscene book in his possession without any criminal intent whatsoever, he has committed a felony." He continued, "As we see it, the central issue in considering the validity of this statute is this: is this an area in which the individual has a right to be let alone to be free of government restraint?"

According to Berkman and the ACLU, even though the realm of morals was a proper area for legislative enactments, "such enactments must . . . not be arbitrary or excessive. Furthermore they must not infringe upon paramount individual rights, particularly where similar legislative result may be achieved by other, less drastic measures. We submit that interposing a policeman between a normal adult and his library is not a proper means of accomplishing what otherwise might be a valid legislative purpose." He concluded, "The statute is unconstitutional."

That question of the relationship between a person and his library was one that fascinated Justice Felix Frankfurter. Shortly after Gertrude

Bauer Mahon, assistant prosecutor for Cuyahoga County, began her argument, Frankfurter stopped to question her on that point.

> Frankfurter: Let me see if I understand—it [the law] means any book on my shelves, any of my shelves, . . . found to be obscene, constitutes a possession. He does nothing but have it on his shelf . . .
>
> Mahon: A knowing possession under this statute, a knowing possession of obscenity is prohibited by this statute. . . . I would say it extends to anybody who had . . .
>
> Frankfurter: On his book shelf, merely a part of his library. He's a bibliophile and he collects first editions, not for the content, but because they are first editions. Any book on his shelf—my shelf—which I know to be obscene in content, a matter of great indifference to me because I'm interested in the fact that it was published in 1527. That makes me . . . a violator of this statute. Is that correct?
>
> Mahon: I would say so, your Honor. Any collection of obscenity would be . . .
>
> (Laughter in courtroom.)
>
> Frankfurter: Mark Twain had one of the biggest collections, and I could tell you now where it is, but it's outside your jurisdiction.
>
> (Laughter in courtroom.)
>
> But . . . you said that the purpose of this—the aim of this statute is to prevent circulation, dissemination. Now, having it on a shelf isn't disseminating it, quite the opposite. There are no more miserly people in world than bibliophiles.

Mrs. Mahon then tried to explain that anyone who had possession would have the opportunity to circulate the material, but Frankfurter countered with the fact that there had been no charge that Dollree Mapp had attempted to circulate the books and pictures.

Later, Frankfurter returned to the same issue, asking if the state had made any examination of the libraries of the universities in Ohio. Mrs. Mahon tried to avoid the question by asserting that she would find it hard to believe that any of those libraries possessed any obscene books, but that "if any of those libraries had the obscene books and pictures and the hand-penciled drawings that are to be found to be exhibits in this case, then somebody should be arrested. [Laughter.]"

Mrs. Mahon concluded by saying the state of Ohio had a right to rely on the Court's decision in the *Wolf* case and in the *Roth* case, and that the trial court had a right to rely on the *Lindway* decision: "We feel that [the Fourth Amendment's] constitutional provision does not cancel out evidence of a criminal offense."

At the conference following the argument "a majority of the Justices agreed that the Ohio statute violated the First and Fourteenth Amendments."[28] What happened after Justice Tom Clark was assigned to write the opinion is really a matter of speculation. Justice Potter Stewart has given one explanation: "I have always suspected that the members of the soon-to-be *Mapp* majority had met in what I affectionately call a 'rump caucus' to discuss a different basis for the decision. But regardless of how they reached their decision five Justices of the Court concluded that Dollree Mapp's conviction had to be reversed because evidence seized in an illegal search had to be excluded from state trials as well as federal ones. *Wolf* v. *Colorado* was to be overruled."[29]

Dollree Mapp had gone home after the oral arguments uncertain of her fate. But, as she tells it, immediately after the hearing, she had gone up to one of the bailiffs and asked, " 'How long before I can expect a decision?' And he said, 'Oh, months, months, months.' . . . And I said, . . . 'You should call me. Really you should call me collect.' He said, 'Well, you know they only come down on Monday.' . . . And every Monday I waited and every Monday he called. That thirteenth Monday, he called and he said, 'Dollree, you don't have to go to jail. It's all over.' That's the way he said it to me. That's all I heard."[30]

Miss Mapp didn't care *why* she didn't have to go to jail, just that she didn't. She admits that she had never even heard of the exclusionary rule prior to that time. But thousands of law enforcement officials had heard of the rule, and the Court's findings would have enormous impact on every law enforcement official in the nation.

Speaking for a 5-to-4 majority, Justice Clark declared that "all evidence obtained by searches and seizures in violation of the Constitution is, by that same authority, inadmissable in a state court." He reasoned that without the exclusionary rule, the Fourth Amendment guarantees would be " 'a form of words,' valueless and undeserving of mention in perpetual character of inestimable human liberty." The conclusion that the exclusionary rule is an integral part of the Fourth Amendment, he wrote, "is not only the logical dictate of prior cases, but it also makes very good sense. There is no war between the Constitution and common sense."[31]

In his final summary of the decision, Justice Clark said that once the Court had recognized that the right to privacy was enforceable against the states, it could

> no longer permit that right to remain an empty promise. . . . to be revocable at the whim of any police officer who, in the name of law enforcement itself, chooses to suspend its enjoyment. Our decision, founded on reason and truth, gives to the individual no more than that which the Constitution guarantees him, to the police officer no less than that to which honest law enforcement is entitled, and, to the courts, that judicial integrity so necessary in the true administration of justice.[32]

The exclusionary rule is now invoked every day in courts of all sizes and jurisdictions. However, the number of cases in which it frees the criminal is slight. Less than 1 percent of federal cases are not prosecuted because the evidence is inadmissable. The limits of the rule are continually being tested and challenged in the United States Supreme Court. Some politicians, lawyers, and jurists continue to argue that it has been stretched too far, allowing the criminal to go free simply because "the constable has blundered." Others hold it up as a unique American symbol of equal justice under law. Thus the debate is far from over. Chief Justice Burger has suggested that civil suits for damages against the offending officers might be a plausible compromise.[33] Others have proposed a "good faith doctrine," which would give judges the discretion to decide whether the police's conduct was within the bounds of reasonable search and seizure. In July 1984 the Supreme Court modified the exclusionary rule. The Court decided that evidence obtained through a warrant which was later invalidated by a technicality could be introduced in court. When and where the exclusionary rule's roller-coaster ride ends is a matter which the Court may decide the next time a Dollree Mapp comes along.*

*In 1973 Dollree Mapp was convicted of drug possession in New York City. Under the state's newly enacted "Rockefeller laws," Miss Mapp was sentenced to serve 20 years to life at the Bedford Hills correctional facility. After spending 9 years, 4 months, and 17 days in prison, she was paroled and her sentence was commuted. She now works on Long Island as a legal aide for prison inmates. Miss Mapp still maintains her innocence of the drug charge and has petitioned state officials for a full pardon.

Accused murderer Erwin Charles Simants being escorted to jail by Lincoln County, Nebraska, Sheriff Gordon Gilster, October 19, 1975. *AP/Wide World Photos*

When Erwin Charles Simants killed six members of the Kellie family in Sutherland, Nebraska, he did more than send terror and disbelief throughout the community. It was with respect to his case that the Supreme Court would have to adjudicate the conflict between the First and Sixth Amendments, between the competing rights of free press and fair trial.

CRIME AND ITS AFTERSHOCK
Fair Trial vs. Free Press

We reaffirm that the guarantees of freedom of expression are not an absolute prohibition under all circumstances, but the barriers to prior restraint remain high and presumption against its use continues intact.

Chief Justice Warren Burger
Nebraska Press Association v. *Stuart*

At 8:00 on the night of October 18, 1975, KNOP, the only television station in North Platte, Nebraska, began transmitting the NBC Saturday night movie, "The Deadly Tower," a dramatization of the 1966 massacre of 16 persons and the wounding of 3 others by Charles J. Whitman, a sniper atop the University Tower in Austin, Texas. By uncanny coincidence, the movie was about to provide the electronic backdrop for another grotesque mass murder.*

At about 9:18, Don Feldman, KNOP's only full-time newsman, answered a frantic call from the sheriff's office. "Something terrible has happened in Sutherland," shouted a deputy. "Hop [Sheriff Gordon "Hop" Gilster] wants you to put the following warning on the air immediately: 'Everybody lock your doors and windows. Don't answer your door without a thorough check of the person knocking or ringing your door bells. There's a sniper loose with a shotgun, and he's killing people.' "[1]

Feldman demanded proof that the sheriff's deputy was not some crank. He arranged to return the call to the county jail to confirm that the panicky warning was coming from an official source, and he told the deputy that he would require more details than "something terrible has happened." After several phone calls, including one shortwave radio call to Hop, who was 22 miles away at the scene of the crime in Sutherland, KNOP aired an "interrupt bulletin" to report that there had been a killing and that "everyone should lock their doors and admit no one." It

---

*The original version of this chapter appeared as an article by Friendly in the *New York Times Magazine* in 1976. It has been expanded and reprinted with permission of the New York Times Company.

was 9:37, and the alarming announcement was superimposed on the image of Whitman being shot down by Texas police in the NBC movie.

For the residents of Sutherland, population 840, and North Platte, population 23,000, the announcement began a night of terror—dozens of police cars flashing their red lights, policemen setting up roadblocks and searching every backyard, a television news helicopter from Denver hovering overhead. Routine sounds suddenly became frightening alerts to many families, who sat in darkened parlors with firearms at the ready.

By morning, the television and radio audiences of Sutherland and North Platte learned that six members of the James Henry Kellie family had been murdered and that a suspect had been arrested. He was identified by the sheriff, the wire services, and broadcast stations as 29-year-old Erwin Charles Simants, who lived with his sister and brother-in-law in the basement of the house next door to the Kellies.

That might well have been the story, a small-town murder reminiscent of *In Cold Blood* in its luridness and senselessness. Yet, the case of Erwin Charles Simants was headed for greater significance from the moment of those first broadcast bulletins on the night of October 18. Chance and politics would combine to make it the focus of a major constitutional debate, one that pits the defendant's right to a fair trial, embodied in the Sixth Amendment, against the press's First Amendment right to publish the news. What follows, therefore, is not intended as a report about crime but rather as an illustration of the dilemma of balancing those two constitutional safeguards of liberty.

FROM BILLY SOL ESTES TO ERWIN SIMANTS

When a person is arrested and charged in a sensational murder and the penalty may be death or a life sentence, the media has a difficult task: it must inform the public while remaining sensitive to the rights of the defendant. The reporting prior to the trial is especially critical, as prejudicial publicity implicating the subject may make the selection of an impartial jury difficult. The influence of the media has been a source of continuing concern to both judges and journalists.

In the 1950s and 1960s, "Roman circus" trials, such as the Sam Sheppard murder case, the Billy Sol Estes scandal, and the television "convictions" of Lee Harvey Oswald and Jack Ruby, spurred harsh criticism of both the courts and the press. The development of electronic journalism may have been an important factor contributing to the problem—the rapid, often emotional portrayal of events could easily distort the facts in the minds of potential jurors, perhaps irrevocably.

It was in the Estes case, in 1965, that the Supreme Court first grappled with that growing giant. Estes was accused of selling farmers nonexistent fertilizer tanks and equipment. Massive publicity, stemming from Estes' former association with Lyndon Johnson, who was then vice president, led to live coverage of the pretrial hearings.

Indeed, at least 12 cameramen were engaged in the courtroom throughout the hearing taking motion and still pictures and televising the proceedings. Cables and wires were snaked across the courtroom floor, three microphones were on the judge's bench and others were beamed at the jury box and the counsel table. . . . [t]he activities of the television crews and news photographers led to considerable disruption of the hearings.[2]

Even though during the actual trial the press was well behaved and confined to a booth at the rear of the courtroom, the Supreme Court ruled that Estes' right to a fair trial had been violated because the pretrial hearings had been televised over his objections. Justice Clark's majority opinion specifically emphasized the need for sensitivity in the pretrial hearings. "Pretrial [publicity] can create a major problem for the defendant in a criminal case," he wrote. "Indeed, it may be more harmful than publicity during the trial for it may well set the community opinion as to guilt or innocence."

Both Clark's opinion and Chief Justice Earl Warren's concurrence concluded that television coverage of a trial was prejudicial in and of itself. Warren wrote that "television is one of the great inventions of all time and can perform a large and useful role in society. But the television camera, like other technological innovations, is not entitled to pervade the lives of everyone in disregard of constitutionally protected rights."[3]

A year later, in June 1966, the Court overturned the conviction of Dr. Sam Sheppard for the second-degree murder of his pregnant wife. It had been a bizarre and brutal murder, and the local press had almost immediately begun a campaign to get Sheppard. For example, a front-page editorial on July 30, 1954, asked: "Why Isn't Sam Sheppard in Jail?"[4] Even during the trial, questionable stories continued to appear and were not dealt with by the court.

On November 24, a story appeared under an eight-column headline: "Sam Called a 'Jekyll-Hyde' by Marilyn, Cousin to Testify." It related that Marilyn had recently told friends that Sheppard was a 'Dr. Jekyll and Mr. Hyde' character. No such testimony was ever produced at the trial. The story went on to announce "The prosecution has a 'bombshell witness' on tap who will testify to Dr. Sam's display of fiery temper—countering the defense claim that the defendent is a gentle physician with an even disposition." Defense counsel made motions for change of venue, continuance and mistrial, but they were denied. No action was taken by the court.[5]

Again, Justice Clark's opinion laid out in detail the "massive and pervasive" prejudicial material that had appeared in the local media. The opinion criticized the "carnival atmosphere" at the trial and said the "court's fundamental error is compounded by the holding that it lacked power to control the publicity about the trial." Justice Clark concluded that "[s]ince the state trial judge did not fulfill his duty to protect Sheppard from the inherently prejudicial publicity which saturated the community and to control disruptive influence in the courtroom,"[6] the state must release Sheppard or order a new trial. In the later trial Sheppard was acquitted.

Such Court decisions underscored the conclusion reached in 1964, in the Warren Commission's report on the assassination of President John F. Kennedy: "The experience in Dallas during November 22–24 [1963] is a dramatic affirmation of the need for steps to bring about a proper balance between the right of the public to be kept informed and the right of the individual to a fair and impartial trial."[7]

One result of this building concern was the American Bar Association's Reardon report of 1968, which set up guidelines for the legal profession in its dealings with the press during criminal proceedings. The goal was to insure that fair trials could peacefully coexist with a free press. Many states, including Nebraska, adopted the Reardon proposal by establishing their own voluntary guidelines. In 1970, a blue ribbon panel of Nebraska's journalists, judges, and lawyers agreed on a voluntary code that listed material that was acceptable and unacceptable in reports of pending criminal litigation. The media executives agreed that they would not reveal a suspect's prior criminal record or that he had made a confession, nor would they offer any opinions about his guilt or his character or the outcome of his trial. Nevertheless, many journalists objected to guidelines out of fear that in crisis situations, guidelines might be interpreted as the rule of law.

In many cases across the nation, however, such voluntary guidelines did not seem to have much effect, and judges began to issue gag orders and prior restraints on the press. Journalists became dismayed at the increasing willingness of judges to issue such orders. So the battle lines were drawn for what one editor has called "the war between the First and Sixth Amendments."[8]

THE SUTHERLAND MURDERS

Sutherland is a bleak prairie village which actually vibrates when long Union Pacific freight trains thunder through. Its people—primarily ranchers and railroad workers—view North Platte with the suspicion with which North Platte views Omaha and Omaha views New York. In North Platte and Sutherland "gun control" are fighting words; the issue is seldom even discussed in a community in which virtually every home has a gun.

So it was not unusual that Erwin Charles Simants, an unemployed handyman and fence builder with an IQ of 75, should have access to the .22 caliber rifle in the home of his brother-in-law, William Boggs. On the evening of October 18, 1975, Simants, who is called Herbie by members of his family, grabbed the rifle and crossed the narrow yard to the house of James Henry Kellie, where he found 10-year-old Florence Kellie. He raped her and killed her; powder burns on her forehead indicated she had been shot at point-blank range.

Other members of the Kellie family, who were not in the house, on hearing the child's screams, ran inside and were murdered as the frightened Simants attempted to eliminate all witnesses. They included James Henry, 66; Audry Marie, 57; Deanna, 7; Daniel, 5; and David, 32.

Even hardened state police investigators were shocked by the fury of the massacre and the gruesome indications, later documented in part of Simants' statement, that some of the bodies had been sexually assaulted after death.

After the shootings, Simants returned the rifle to his sister's home and told his 13-year-old nephew, Butch Boggs, "I've just killed the Kellies." At Simants' request, Butch called the home of the elder Simantses, Amos and Grace. Simants told his mother about the murders and said, "I'm coming home." His father, a railroad worker, told Herbie that he didn't believe the story, but he was going over to the Kellies' to see for himself.

When Amos Simants opened the door of the Kellie residence, he was sickened by the sight and smell. Shaken, he returned home and told his wife to call an ambulance and the police. He also told his son to turn himself in. Simants instead stopped by the Rodeo Bar, across from the Union Pacific railroad tracks, and had a beer. He then walked to the Longhorn Bar, drank another beer, and fled into the high weeds behind the Kellie and Boggs houses, where he hid through the night. Shortly before 8:00 the following morning, he walked to the back door of the Boggs' house and was immediately arrested by a state police officer and Sheriff Gilster.

Whatever had transpired in the deepest, darkest, most twisted part of this man's mind, to paraphrase Simants' defense lawyer, may never be known, but much of what had happened in the Kellie house that night was known within hours by the Sutherland community. The news spread by the kind of grapevine that exists in a town this size and by a communication network unique to this one. An employee was on duty at "the light plant," the office of the local power company, which doubles as a 24-hour-a-day message center for fire, police, and other information. He was dispensing a chatter of fact, hearsay, and short-wave jargon coming in from ambulance attendants, deputy sheriffs, and town officials.

But the reporters and cameramen, pouring in during the night from all points in western Nebraska, and by chartered planes from Omaha, Lincoln, and Denver, found it difficult to obtain any official information from the county prosecutors in charge of the case. Pressured by their night editors for more facts, they confronted law officers whose emotions were already charged by the night's gruesome events and the search for the murderer, which was at this point still in process.

The deputy county attorney, Marvin Holscher, a tough prosecutor with a record of many convictions and numerous tiffs with the Nebraska media, established a sort of imaginary police line at the hedge in front of the Kellie residence. "Goddamn it, I'm not going to try this case on the lawn of this house, or in the media," he yelled. A reporter from the *Omaha World-Herald,* according to Holscher, shouted back, "You're not telling us what happened. I'm going to make you look like an ass." (The reporter, Frank Santiago, remembers it differently: "You're going to make an ass of yourself, Holscher.") The chief prosecutor, Milton Larson, recalls shouting, "There's a TV helicopter overhead, and we haven't even gotten the six bodies out."[9] It was hardly an atmosphere to nurture the spirit of the Nebraska bar-press voluntary guidelines for pretrial reporting, and over the course of the next several days, it appeared that the guidelines were all but forgotten by lawmen as well as journalists.

At 1:43 A.M. the Associated Press was finally able to transmit a story with the names of the victims and the fact that Simants, a neighbor of the Kellies, was being sought. Sheriff Hop Gilster, so overwhelmed by the events that he had suffered a slight heart attack, revealed to some reporters that the murder weapon, a .22-caliber rifle, was in police custody. According to a 6:37 A.M. AP bulletin, he also stated that "Simants apparently told his father that he was responsible for the killings." The UPI called Simants' parents and transmitted a story reporting their statement that he had confessed.

By 9:00 that morning, Simants had been booked, stripped of his clothing and boots, which would be used as evidence, and had listened three times to the "Miranda card" warning that statements he might make could be used against him. Now he was making a confession, in which he admitted to the murders and sexual assaults and answered in the negative when asked if he had been watching television the previous night.

This confession was not officially reported to the media, but 30 minutes earlier, prosecutor Larson was quoted by an AP bulletin as saying, "Simants apparently walked to his father's home after the shooting and told his father he was responsible for the deaths." However, the AP said it erred in quoting Larson; Ed Nichols, AP bureau chief in Omaha, admitted that hearsay of the ambulance driver's husband was falsely attributed to Larson.

Later that Sunday morning, Sheriff Gilster held a news conference, attended by both print and broadcast media, at which he provided information and opinions that went far beyond the guidelines precluding "opinions concerning the guilt, the innocence or the character of the accused."

Reporter:	It didn't surprise you [when a woman called the fire station to say Simants was out in the back yard]?
Sheriff:	It didn't surprise me.

Reporter:	Why didn't it surprise you?
Sheriff:	Well, a lot of times they say they return to the scene . . . .
Reporter:	You mean—after he shot those people, he went in and got a drink in a bar?
Sheriff:	Yes.
Reporter:	Why did he kill these people?
Sheriff:	I can't say at this time.[10]

That afternoon and evening Sheriff Gilster's revelations were reported in considerable detail by radio stations as well as by the AP and UPI. However, what later seemed most irresponsible to the judges and the lawyers involved in the proceeding was a television report received by KNOP from the NBC network and broadcast on the news that night and on the "Today" show the following morning. Jim Lee, a reporter for NBC affiliate KOA-TV in Denver, had flown in by chartered helicopter the night of the crime and rushed back to Denver on Sunday after the sheriff's news conference. He told his audience that "Simants reportedly confessed to his father and then fled." A Denver-based newsman, Lee had never heard of the Nebraska guidelines.

The following day, Monday, the *Omaha World-Herald*, the dominant newspaper in the state, with a circulation of 238,000, did omit any reference to Amos Simants' statement about his son's confession and did not report any of the sheriff's incriminating remarks. However, the lead of its page one story had its own implications: "He was called a hothead, a loner, a drinker by those who know him, but Erwin Charles Simants, suspected of killing six here Saturday night, remains an enigma to many."

The Monday edition of the *North Platte Telegraph*, circulation 17,000, devoted all but six inches of its front page to the mass murder, including a report that "the elder Simants tearfully said, 'My son killed five or six people here.' "

THE TUG OF RIGHTS BEGINS

Judge Ronald Ruff was a young, unassuming Lincoln County judge, who was used to sitting on trials involving misdemeanors such as speeding violations and petty larceny. The preliminary hearing, required to establish that cause existed to hold Simants for trial, was to be in his courtroom; the trial itself would be presided over by Judge Hugh Stuart, an experienced and respected district court judge with a reputation for running a disciplined courtroom. There was little love lost between the two men. "Judge Stuart," says Judge Ruff, "once accused me of being the most immature and incompetent judge he had ever met."

Judge Ruff dreaded the inflammatory aspects of the sordid Simants case, the idea that his nemesis, Judge Stuart, would preside over the trial, and the possibility of reversal. "I kept thinking of *Sheppard* v. *Maxwell*.

. . . I didn't care what was in the paper; I just didn't want to be reversed,"[11] he says.

So Judge Ruff consulted Judge Stuart about the possibility of closing the hearing to the public and restricting press coverage, so that the details of the rape and necrophilia wouldn't be reported and broadcast over and over again before jury selection. Stuart advised Ruff that it was against Nebraska statutes to close the hearing and recalls telling him, "You can't restrain the media," and that he would be "opening a can of worms" with a restraining order.[12] (Ruff claims that Stuart was vague and noncommittal about a restraining order.)

Meanwhile, Larson, the prosecutor, was on the telephone consulting the Nebraska attorney general, Paul Douglas, in Lincoln. Douglas told Larson, "Don't do it. Don't ask the court to put that restraining order on."[13]

Despite such admonitions, the prosecution and the county defender both marched straight into Judge Ruff's courtroom and moved that the news media be gagged, and the county defender also asked that the preliminary hearing be closed. Judge Ruff refused to close that proceeding, but directed that there be no reporting of any testimony or evidence produced at the hearing. "When these two constitutional provisions come into conflict . . . the right of the free press must be subservient to the right of the accused to have due process," he declared. He cited the Supreme Court's decision in *Sheppard* v. *Maxwell:* "If publicity during the proceedings threatens the fairness of the trial, a new trial should be ordered." What Judge Ruff did not say is that the Court in *Sheppard* did not recommend prior restraints on the press; its retrial order was intended to suggest alternate remedies open to judges, such as sequestering the jury, controlling the press inside the courtroom, and controlling "the releases of leads, information, and gossip to the press by police officers, witnesses, and the counsel for both sides."[14] However, Ruff read *Sheppard* as an authority for restraining orders and proclaimed, "This judge is not going to abdicate his duty." Though he previously had known little of the Nebraska bar-press guidelines, Judge Ruff further ordered that they be mandatory.

Ironically, Judge Ruff never believed for a moment that his restraining order would be obeyed. "Me gag the powerful *Omaha World-Herald* and the *Lincoln Journal* and the *Chicago Tribune?*"[15] On the other hand, many people asked why the press did not defy what it considered an unconstitutional gag order. Executives at the *Omaha World-Herald,* the *Lincoln Journal,* and the *North Platte Telegraph,* conservative by nature, say they do not believe in civil disobedience and decided to fight it out in court.

But court battles take time. Thus the preliminary hearing took place with reporters barred from revealing any evidence or testimony produced, even though the courtroom was open to the public. Those who attended got their money's worth. The purpose of the hearing was to prove that a crime was committed and that there was probable cause to believe that the suspect had committed it. In Simants' case, these facts could have been amply demonstrated in general terms, yet his preliminary hearing took up almost a full day of court and included the testimony of nine witnesses, who spelled out many of the horrifying details. Judge Ruff permitted this anomalous situation—inadvertently letting sensational information be fed to the local rumor mills while professional communications outlets remained gagged—because he was apprehensive about cutting off whatever record the prosecution wished to establish. Yet had he chosen to limit the testimony, he could have had an adequate preliminary hearing without needing to restrain the press.

The local press continued to obey the gag order, but spokesmen for the Nebraska news organizations appealed Judge Ruff's order to Judge Stuart. Judge Stuart now faced the task of reviewing a decision he had cautioned against. "I found myself with the major decision of my career and we just backed into it."

After a hearing on October 23, he decided to terminate Judge Ruff's order and initiate his own more carefully drawn restraining order. He prohibited the press from publishing any confession or admission of guilt by Simants, the results of the pathologists's report, the identity of the victims who had been sexually assaulted and the description of those crimes. He agreed with Ruff that the Nebraska bar-press guidelines should be mandatory. He also prohibited the press from reporting the specifics of the gag order.

The judge is painfully aware that this decision to continue the gag was inconsistent with his earlier advice. "I just want those nine justices to understand the position I was in," he later said. Stuart feared that he could not lift Judge Ruff's gag without exposing himself to the threat of reversal, and the thought of having the community buzzing about the necrophilia haunted him. In addition, Judge Stuart was offended by the remarks of an attorney for the Nebraska media who had lectured the court: "Goodness gracious, we want this man to have a fair trial . . . but I'd let somebody go free who was guilty before I'd deny freedom of speech."[16]

Critics of the restraining order have suggested that a change of venue would have served the Sixth Amendment without impairing the First. But in Nebraska, a state law prescribes that if a trial is moved, it must be to an adjacent county. Lincoln County's neighbors are all exposed to the same media.

THE NATIONAL PRESS GETS INVOLVED

For the national press, meanwhile, Simants' name was hardly mentioned, but the Nebraska gag order was emerging as an important story. On October 29, the Nebraska publishers contacted the Reporters' Committee for Freedom of the Press, a Washington-based legal defense fund. Larry Simms, a Boston University law graduate who had recently clerked for Supreme Court Justice Byron White, was sent to Omaha to advise the Nebraska media.

If, in those first 10 days, the judges had acted precipitously, it was now the news media's turn. Stung by a dozen prior restraints against publication in a period of a year, national media organizations decided that the Nebraska gag was the case they had been waiting for.

On the last Thursday in October, the Reporters' Committee urged the Nebraska Press Association to appeal Judge Stuart's restraining order to the highest court in the land if the Nebraska Supreme Court did not act by the following Tuesday. When the Nebraska Supreme Court delayed in considering the case, the anxious Nebraska Press Association asked Justice Harry Blackmun to expedite, under a provision by which an urgent constitutional issue can proceed to a single justice of the Supreme Court for immediate relief after state court appeals have been exhausted. Blackmun felt that with the Nebraska Supreme Court procrastinating he had to intervene, because "any First Amendment infringement that occurs with each passing day is irreparable . . . and delay itself is a final decision."[17]

On November 20, he held that the Nebraska bar-press guidelines could not be made mandatory in a restraining order because they were "riddled with vague and indefinite admonitions," and he said the press could report on the pathologist's tests and details of sexual assaults. However, he left standing the prohibition on publishing confessions or admissions of guilt or other items "strongly implicative of the accused." Blackmun reasoned that prior restraints on pretrial publicity may delay media coverage until the actual trial, but "at least they do no more than that." When the Nebraska Supreme Court finally caught up with Justice Blackmun, on December 1, it agreed both that the voluntary guidelines could not be part of the restraining order and that the gag on confessions and other information "implicative of the accused" should be sustained.

Now the goal of the Nebraska Press Association and its grand alliance was to persuade the full Supreme Court to overturn immediately the part of the original gag that Blackmun and the Nebraska high court had allowed. "We were fighting for principle," said Joe R. Seacrest, who owns the *Lincoln Journal* and the *North Platte Telegraph*. "We had no intention of publishing confessions or violating the spirit of the guidelines, which I had helped to write. But we wanted to do it voluntarily, not have some judge order us what not to print."[18] Judge Ruff, now completely out of the case, couldn't believe that his original gag was reaching such Olympian heights. "I just wanted the record to show that I wanted restraint." And, added the county judge rather plaintively, "just on this one case."[19] Those on the other side viewed this one case as "sweeping precedent" that would sanction prior restraint if permitted to stand.

THE COURT AGREES TO TAKE THE CASE

The decision of the publishers to make an issue of gag orders apparently coincided with the belief of some Supreme Court justices that there is a genuine conflict between the First and the Sixth Amendments and that the time had come to resolve it. This belief is a relatively recent one.

For most of our history, restraints on the press were argued in the state courts. (The first gag order was issued in 1893 by W. G. Lorigan, a California judge who decided that the *San Jose Mercury* could not report a divorce case because the evidence was of "a filthy nature." This ruling was struck down by the California Supreme Court.) Because the First Amendment was long considered to apply only to actions of the federal government, it was not relevant to these state proceedings. Not until 1925, in *Gitlow* v. *New York,* did the Supreme Court declare that First Amendment freedoms were so fundamental to the Anglo-American legal tradition that no state could abridge them.

For several decades, however, the Court resisted having to rule on a confrontation between the First and the Sixth Amendments. In a 1941 contempt case, *Bridges* v. *California,* [20] Justice Hugo Black articulated this reluctance: "Free speech and fair trial are two of the most cherished policies of our civilization, and it would be a trying task to choose between them."

But in December 1975 the Supreme Court seemed to have concluded that the time had come to confront the conflict directly, and on December 12, it decided to take the Nebraska case, though it denied the request to quash the parts of the prior restraint that remained. (Justices Brennan, Stewart, and Marshall voted to lift the gag; Justice White would have voided the gag insofar as it prohibited publication of what was disclosed at the open preliminary hearing.)

SIMANTS' TRIAL

Almost as an anticlimax to all the constitutional maneuvering, Erwin Charles Simants on January 5 went to trial in Judge Stuart's courtroom. After the first day, the jury selection was opened to the public, but when Judge Stuart required that the reporters each sign an agreement restricting the use of certain material that might come up, the press, on advice of counsel, refused to attend.

Of the 130 citizens called for jury duty, 72 were examined in voir dire. More than a third of those screened told the judge they had already formed an opinion on the murders. Of that group, less than half identified the media as the source of their prejudice. A larger proportion of those who had an opinion did not specifically identify the basis for their prejudgments. Friendship with the Kellies or with witnesses, discussions at work, and other word-of-mouth sources were among the factors. Ironically, in view of the gag orders, four who said they had an opinion were accepted as jurors because they said they could still view the evidence with an open mind. Once the jury was sequestered and told not to read or listen to news reports, the gag was lifted.

Simants, on the recommendation of the public defender, pleaded innocent by reason of insanity. There were seven days of extremely conclusive testimony, including the playing of Simants' painfully explicit statement before a courtroom packed mostly with high school civics students bused in from Sutherland and other communities.

On January 17, Simants was found guilty of six counts of murder in the first degree, and 12 days later Judge Stuart sentenced him to death in the electric chair. Under Nebraska law, Simants had an automatic right of appeal. At the time Simants believed he got a fair trial; so did members of the jury.

After they delivered their verdict, the members of the jury were asked by Judge Stuart whether they could have viewed the case objectively had they known of Simants' admission to his family or read in the newspapers of his confession to the police. (It is perhaps worth noting that this formal confession was not read at the pretrial hearing, so it could not have been reported in the media even if there had been no gag.) Only the foreman, Richard Anderson, answered "Yes."

Anderson said that his first impressions about Simants came from watching Sheriff Gilster on television the day of the arrest. However, because of his occupational training as an insurance adjuster, he said, "I don't believe anything to be a fact until it is documented and proven."[21]

Mrs. Beulah Loostrom, who, with her husband, John, runs a 13,000-acre farm in nearby Brady, says she knew most of the details of the sexual assaults, knew about the father's statement concerning Simants' admission, saw Gilster on television, yet thought she was able to be an impartial juror. "I've raised a family. I know you have to hear both sides," this grandmother says. "When one child comes with a story, I say, 'Well, wait, I have to hear the other side.' "[22]

Eugene Seaton, another juror, works on the county road crew and runs his own small farm. He believes in the wisdom of the judge's gag order. "Yes," he says, weighing his words very carefully, "it would be very hard to put anything I heard before the trial out of my mind." His wife heard about the murders while watching "The Deadly Tower" on television and knew something about the sexual aspects and Simants' admission to his father. But Mr. Seaton is sure that "she never discussed it with me. I'm out of doors most all the time; don't have time for much talk."[23]

Juror Robert Gerrard, a superintendent at the North Platte Gas Company, says he knew most of the details about the murders and sexual assaults "from hearsay and some from newspapers and radio."[24] His wife, Elsie, remembers hearing all the gruesome facts of the murders the Wednesday after the crime, when she went to the beauty parlor in North Platte. "My hairdresser's husband is a cousin of the Kellies, and she told me about how the little girl had been raped and then killed, and Mr. Kellie had been dragged into the bedroom." Gerrard says he had known "the Simants boys were a bunch of hoodlums. My son went to school with one and they were always beating up people." But Gerrard feels that he was able to separate these preconceived notions from the evidence in the trial.

THE SUPREME COURT DECISION

On April 18, 1976, the Supreme Court heard oral arguments in the case. Two months later, on June 30, the Court unanimously overturned the gag order. Chief Justice Burger wrote for the majority, and there were concurring opinions by Justice White, Justice Powell, and by Justice Brennan, with whom Justices Stewart and Marshall joined.

Chief Justice Burger commented that "[t]he problems presented by this case are almost as old as the Republic."[25] He acknowledged that the "speed of communication and the pervasiveness of the modern news media have exacerbated these problems." However, he concluded that "pretrial publicity—even pervasive, adverse publicity—does not inevitably lead to an unfair trial."[26]

Citing *Near* and the Pentagon Papers case,* the Chief Justice wrote, "[t]he thread running through all these cases is that prior restraints on speech and publication are the most serious and the least tolerable infringement on First Amendment rights."

Burger suggested that other less drastic measures—change of trial venue, postponement of the trial, thorough questioning of prospective jurors, and sequestration—were always available to the trial judge. "There is no finding that alternative measures would not have protected Simants's rights." And, he concluded, "We reaffirm that the guarantees of freedom of expression are not an absolute prohibition under all circumstances, but the barriers to prior restraint remain high and presumption against its use continues intact."[27]

The Court was saying that even though there may someday be a case where prior restraint of the press was constitutional, the grisly murder case in Nebraska was not it. Judge Ruff's gag—tempered by Judge Stuart and even further watered down by Justice Blackmun and the Nebraska Supreme Court—was unconstitutional.

EPILOGUE

There is a bizarre unimaginable twist to this tale of well-intended efforts to ensure a fair trial. In April 1979, the Supreme Court of Nebraska ruled that Simants had, in fact, been denied a fair trial. The villain, it

*See Chapters 3 and 4.

turns out, was not the press, but rather, local law enforcement: Sheriff
Gilster had visited the jurors three times while they were sequestered at
a Howard Johnson motel. The Nebraska high court decided that "the
fraternization of Sheriff Gilster . . . during the course of the trial presents
problems of constitutional dimensions. The sheriff was an important lay
witness on the issue of the sanity of the defendant," which, said the court,
"was the only real issue in the murder trial." The court concluded that
a "fair and impartial jury is a basic requirement of constitutional due
process" and that Sheriff Gilster's conduct violated Simants' right to a fair
trial. It vacated the conviction and sentence and ordered a new trial. At
that trial, Simants was found innocent by reason of insanity; he is now
a patient at the Lincoln Regional Center.*

The moral of this parable for our time is that well-intentioned
judges failed to identify the biggest threat to Simants' fair trial. The
weakest link was Sheriff Gilster. The judges controlled the press for a
while, but could not control their own law-enforcement officers. (Incidentally, the local community became angry at the Nebraska Supreme Court
and the public defender for overturning the conviction rather than their
sheriff, whom they reelected. Later Gilster was convicted of irregularities
pertaining to mileage and retired in ill-health.)

So the Simants case, marred by overkill and misunderstanding
from the moment the sheriff's deputy placed the first hysterical phone call
to KNOP, raises questions and teaches lessons. They do not deal with
abstractions of the law so much as the behavior of the police, reporters,
and judges in a crisis. Guidelines, Miranda cards, and copies of the Constitution mean nothing if the people who hold them have not stopped to
consider what they mean when transposed from abstract concepts to
real-life situations. Events such as the Sutherland murders come crashing
down without warning. Those involved in such an event have little time
to reflect—and never a second chance. Yet, it is in those frenzied minutes
that most constitutional dramas begin.

---

*Simants will be held at the mental institution until such time as he is judged no longer dangerous.
That determination must be made during a court proceeding in which the state and defendant
present testimony of expert witnesses.

Convicted murderer Willie Francis standing before a handwritten confession inside his Louisiana prison cell, 1947. *AP/Wide World Photos*

Willie Francis was a 17-year-old convicted murderer who was sentenced to die in the electric chair in 1946. But the "chair" didn't work. His case made the Supreme Court look at the whole concept of cruel and unusual punishment. Forty years later the Court still wrestles with the death penalty.

WILLIE FRANCIS' TWO TRIPS TO THE CHAIR
Punishment and the Death Penalty

The [cruel and unusual punishment] clause seems to express a great deal of humanity, on which account I have no objection to it; but, as it seems to have no meaning in it, I do not think it necessary. . . . Who are to be the judges? . . . No cruel and unusual punishment is to be inflicted; it is sometimes necessary to hang a man, villains often deserve whipping, and perhaps having their ears cut off; but are we in the future, to be prevented from inflicting these punishments because they are cruel?

Rep. Samuel Livermore, opposing
adoption of the Eighth Amendment[1]

If the state officials deliberately and intentionally had placed the relator in the electric chair five times and . . . had applied electric current to his body in a manner not sufficient, until the final time, to kill him, such a form of torture would rival that of burning at the stake. . . . How many deliberate and intentional reapplications of electric current does it take to produce a cruel and unusual punishment?

Justice Harold H. Burton,
dissenting in *Francis* v. *Resweber*

On January 6, 1885, Governor David B. Hill of New York stood before the state legislature for the first time as the chief executive. Only days before he had been elevated from lieutenant governor to replace Grover Cleveland, who was about to become the 22nd president of the United States. Thus Hill had been given the opportunity to escape from the sort of lackluster position in which one's accomplishments often fade from memory long before they become history. Wanting his State of the State message to have an identity of its own, the new governor addressed what he considered a vital issue—the death penalty: "The present mode of executing criminals by hanging has come to us from the dark ages, and it may well be questioned whether the science of the present day cannot provide a means for taking life of such as one condemned to die in a less barbarous manner. I commend this suggestion to the consideration of the legislature."[2]

Few remember Governor Hill's speech or even his name, but his "suggestion" to the legislature touched off a debate that has lasted a century. Within a year, a three-man commission had been appointed to investigate "the most humane and practical method known to modern science of carrying into effect the sentence of death in capital cases."[3]

Commission member Dr. Alfred P. Southwick, a dentist, had been fascinated with the possibility of using electricity for executions. Almost as an avocation, Southwick began conducting simple experiments with electrocuting animals, and he subsequently recommended electrocution as the most humane method for capital punishment.

Physicians were split on the idea. Some felt that the death would be quick and painless. Others had doubts. "There was . . . the question of the wide variations of electrical resistance in human bodies—variations that would make it almost impossible to establish what value of voltage would always produce death."[4] It was pointed out that many people had survived being struck by lightning.

After surveying Europe's various modes of execution—hanging, garroting, and beheading either by axe or guillotine (named after its inventor Dr. J. I. Guillotin)—the commission offered a bill which became chapter 489 of the laws of 1888. The bill provided that electrocution be used for all convictions for crimes punishable by death committed after January 1, 1889.

Ironically, the new legislation touched off another debate between Thomas Edison and George Westinghouse, who were already at war over whether the power industry should use direct or alternating current. In the power industry debate, Edison, who had developed the direct current system, opposed Westinghouse's alternating current as being too dangerous. However, when the issue was changed to electrocution, the positions were reversed. Edison was in favor of using alternating current, to insure a swift death. But Westinghouse was adamantly opposed to anyone using his generators for execution; he felt it would hurt the image of his alternating current. Despite Westinghouse's objections in this war within a war and his attempts to prevent the purchase of one of his generators for such use, the first electric chair installed in New York's Auburn State Prison was powered by Westinghouse generators.

William Kemmler (alias John Hort), an inmate at Auburn, had the dubious distinction of being the first person in history scheduled to die in the newly installed electric chair. He had been convicted of the axe murder of Matilda Zeigler (also called Matilda Hort) on March 29, 1889, and was scheduled to die "some day within the week commencing on Monday, the 24th day of June."

Kemmler and his lawyers, Charles H. Hatch and Bourke Cockran, argued that the sentence was "a cruel and unusual punishment within the meaning of the constitution."[5] The Cayuga County judge saw the dilemma quite clearly: "Paradoxical as it may seem, both of these positions are professedly based on grounds of mercy and humanity."[6] The state of New York advocated electrocution to avoid cruel and unusual punishment; Kemmler opposed it on the same grounds.

Ultimately, the New York State courts rejected Kemmler's argument. "We have examined this testimony and can find but little in it to warrant the belief that this new mode of execution is cruel, though it is certainly unusual," wrote Judge O'Brien of the New York Court of Appeals. "On the contrary, we agree with the court below that it removes every reasonable doubt that the application of electricity to the vital parts of the human body under such conditions and in the manner contemplated by the statute must result in instantaneous and consequently in painless death."[7]

Kemmler appealed to the United States Supreme Court. In an opinion by Chief Justice Fuller, the Court rejected the notion that the Fourteenth Amendment was designed to change the relationship of the state and federal governments. He said the amendment did not give the federal government the power to interfere with the actions of the states. Thus, the Supreme Court could not interfere with New York State's "legitimate" exercise of legislative power in designating electricity as the form of execution. However, in dictum, Fuller did define cruel and unusual punishment. "Punishments are cruel when they involve torture or a lingering death," he wrote. "It implies there is something inhumane and barbarous, something more than the mere extinguishment of life."[8]

Despite the assertions of all the experts, the execution was not as "instantaneous" and "painless" as had been predicted. It took two jolts to kill Kemmler. Reaction to the execution varied from Dr. Southwick, who saw it as "the grandest success of the age," to Dr. E. C. Spitzka, one of two physicians in charge of the electrocution, who said: "today's performance has satisfied me that the electrical system of execution can in no way be regarded as a step in civilization. The guillotine is better than the gallows, the gallows is better than electrical execution."[9]

However, despite the flaws in the first attempt, electrocution was quick to catch on—before long, 20 states had electric chairs. Those chairs would soon claim hundreds of lives.

WILLIE FRANCIS

Seventeen-year-old Willie Francis had never heard of William Kemmler's ordeal, and wasn't even sure what was actually going to happen to him on May 3, 1946, when Sheriff Gilbert Ozeene handcuffed him and put him into the police sedan that would transport him the eight miles from New Iberia, Louisiana, where he was imprisoned, to St. Martinville, where he was to die in the electric chair.

Willie Francis had been convicted of the November 1944 murder of Andrew Thomas, a St. Martinville druggist for whom Francis had worked as a delivery boy. For a long time the murder-robbery (a watch and a wallet with $4 in it were missing from the body) went unsolved. Terror permeated the small bayou town; everyone had a different suspect in mind.[10] Nine months later, in August 1945, Willie was picked up in neighboring Port Arthur, Texas. Local police had been chasing a narcotics suspect and noticed Francis, a lanky, black 16-year-old, sitting under a tree near the train station; they picked him up as a possible accomplice. The murdered druggist's wallet was found in Francis' pocket, and he apparently confessed to shooting Thomas. His written statements, made later at the station house, show that Francis was barely literate.

Willie Francis also named several other people in connection with the killing, but the police were never able to locate anyone with those names. After showing the police where he had thrown the holster of the murder weapon, Francis was formally arrested. One of 15 children, Francis could not have afforded his own counsel; his father earned $9 a week as a farm laborer. So the court appointed two local attorneys to represent him. As a recent law review article by Arthur S. Miller and Jeffrey Bowman on the Francis trial points out: "The case . . . is a dark reminder of our recent legal past. . . . At th[e] arraignment, one month after his arrest and less than a week before the start of the trial Willie first received legal counsel from two court-appointed attorneys. . . . Counsel for the defense would prove to be of little value for, in the next eight days, Willie would be tried, convicted and sentenced to death."[11] No witnesses or evidence were offered in Francis' behalf, and despite his two confessions, he pleaded "not guilty."

The trial lasted three days; the all-white, all-male jury found Francis guilty of murder in the first degree, and on September 14 he was sentenced to die in the electric chair (a mandatory sentence for first-degree murder at that time).

THE EXECUTION

The electric chair had arrived the night before. (Louisiana had no death row, but rather a portable, "circuit riding" chair, which was taken to the parish where the crime had been committed. A fellow inmate shaved Francis' head, wrists, and legs, as Captain E. Foster of the Angola State Penitentiary staff and Vincent Vanezia, an inmate "trustee," finished the final preparations for the execution. The chair had been placed in a bare anteroom near the cells which was described by an Associated Press report as "a smokey, brick-walled room little larger than an indoor tennis table."

When Francis was ushered into the makeshift death chamber, the official witnesses had already been assembled; others were milling around outside. Among them was Francis' father, who had come with a coffin.

Sydney Dupois, a local barber who died only recently,* had been asked by Sheriff Resweber to be a witness to the execution. "I was more frightened than Willie," Dupois remembered. Although some describe Francis as being in "a daze," Dupois, who was standing right next to the chair, "just like it was the barber chair," says Francis seemed calm. "Willie asked me what I was doing there. I said, 'I just came to be with you, Willie.' I was right next to him. . . . I said, 'How do you feel?' And Willie said, 'How's little Sid (Dupois' 9-year-old son)?' And I said, 'Fine, just fine, Willie.' I felt bad to see him goin' that way—I knew him so well. . . . I never did tell my wife I was a witness."[12]

Dupois watched as Francis' arms and legs were strapped to the massive, hardwood chair, which had already claimed 23 lives. Then the electrodes were attached to his body, and Captain Foster placed the hood over Francis' head. Dupois recounted the event: "Willie said, 'It hurts me the way you're doing it.' The mask was over his lips. . . . Then he [Captain Foster] said, 'It'll hurt more after a while, Willie.' "

A few moments later the generator was whirring; Foster turned on the switch. As Sheriff Resweber recalled, "When he did Willie Francis' lips puffed out [through the hood] and he groaned and jumped so that the chair came off the floor. Apparently, the switch was turned on twice and then the condemned man yelled, 'Take it off—Let me breathe.' "[13]† Dupois says, "I heard the one in charge yell to the man outside for more juice, when he saw that Willie Francis was not dying and the one on the outside yelled back he was giving all he had."

"I'd rather be hung than electrocuted," Dupois shuddered. "That's the worst thing I ever seen. . . . I was more scared than Willie was. . . . I was holding the chair. He stretched. He pushed the chair with his feet. I was moving more than Willie. . . . I thought I'd be a witness and then forget. I didn't know that I wouldn't forget."

When it was clear that Francis wouldn't die, Sheriff Resweber signaled to Foster to stop. The electrocution had somehow been botched. Francis was unstrapped and taken back to the waiting cell. The coroner

---

*Dupois was interviewed by Friendly on June 6, 1983, and died just as the manuscript was being completed.
†Later testimony confirmed that the switch was turned on twice.

took out his stethoscope, but not for the purpose he had intended. Francis' heart was still beating—"a little fast," the coroner said—but other than that there were no apparent symptoms.

The governor of Louisiana had to be phoned. Through the years there have been many communications between death row chambers and governors. Usually the response was prompt—that the execution should proceed or occasionally that a last-minute reprieve should be granted. After recovering from his initial astonishment, Governor Jimmie Davis[14] (who happened to be being entertained at the home of the warden of the Angola prison) agreed with Captain Foster that a second attempt with that generator and equipment made no sense. Willie was to be sent back to New Iberia, and another execution was scheduled for May 10.

A PLEA FOR MERCY

The execution "happening" and the deafening noise of the electric generator had aroused the curiosity of many. Bertrand de Blanc, whose law office and home were directly across from the courthouse, wandered over when he heard the whirring machine. The 35-year-old lawyer had been asked by the sheriff to be a witness but had declined. "I said, 'No, I like that guy,' and I got to liking him more."[15]

De Blanc, who had been a boyhood friend of the murder victim, Andrew Thomas, remembers that there were "about 200 people milling around. . . . The generator was making a terrible noise. Then, all of a sudden, here comes Willie walking out with the deputies. . . . Everything had been ready, with the hearse and casket and everything. . . . And everyone said, 'Hey, what happened?' So I walked over home and my wife was in the house and I said, 'Listen, the guy walked away from the chair.' "

The electric chair has always had a fascination, however ghoulish, for the American public. The bizarre quality of Willie Francis' "act of God," as some called it, made it a front-page story in cities that didn't know that St. Martinville existed. Suddenly Francis' cell was inundated with letters from sympathetic supporters all over America.

The very next day de Blanc received a call from another attorney, Jerome Broussaud. "He said, 'You know what happened?' And I said, 'Yes, I was there.' . . . So he said, 'I know you liked him. How'd you like to take the case? But they don't have any money.' " De Blanc, who had just hung out his shingle after returning from the war, shrugged and said, "I don't need it." In the end his only payment was a sack of onions from the condemned man's father.

De Blanc told Francis' father that it was "the most unusual case I've ever seen," but that "I think it's the kind of case we can win." Now, 35 years later, de Blanc explains why he took the case. "The question of guilt or innocence was beside the point. I didn't give a damn if he got a fair trial. The question was whether the man goes to the chair twice for the same offense. . . . They's done everything they were supposed to do. The whole thing about capital punishment in my opinion is the anticipation. For the two weeks, three weeks, a month, you know you're going to die the moment they pull the switch. . . . You die. You blow that, you blow the whole thing."

De Blanc had two routes to take, the judicial or the executive branch. After obtaining a 30-day stay of execution, he first attempted to have the state courts commute Francis' sentence to life, but was turned down. De Blanc then requested a hearing before the state board of pardons, which consisted of the lieutenant governor, the state attorney general, and the presiding judge of the trial court. At the same time he contacted a young lawyer in Washington whom he had heard about from a law book salesman. De Blanc had not been admitted to the District of Columbia bar and needed help to get the case through the federal courts. J. Skelly Wright had just left the United States attorneys' office and begun private practice in Washington. Then unknown, but destined to become a dominant, if lonely, federal district judge, handling many of the civil rights litigations of the late fifties and sixties, Wright signed on as Francis' unpaid advocate.

Wright had many of the same sentiments as de Blanc about the case. "Getting ready to die is part of the punishment that every person who is condemned has to suffer. But most don't have to suffer it twice, and this was the case with Willie Francis," Wright now explains. "From the day the sentence was imposed Willie began to suffer because he was under sentence to die . . . and then the preparation for death, the shaving . . . and the last supper. . . . Then they come and get you and march you to the place where you're going to be executed. That's all part of it. As a matter of fact, we argued it was the most important part of it because the only thing that was not imposed in that form of punishment was one split moment when life was eliminated."[16]

At the state board of pardons, the focus was on the issue of whether electricity had actually passed through Francis' body. Foster claimed that a loose wire had prevented it completely; de Blanc, through affidavits, tried to prove that some electricity had passed through the body.

The same district attorney who had prosecuted Willie now asked the board of pardons: "How can we expect juries to convict men to pay their debts to society when afterward what they have done is undone by another authority of law having the power to do so?" He also suggested to the board that "lynchings had gone on in the past" and that the safest way to avoid such events would be to "bring to justice and punish . . . the guilty party."[17]

In addition to submitting several written pleas for Francis' life, de Blanc made a moving speech to the board. To him it was simply a matter of justice and decency: "He died mentally; his body still exists, but through no fault of his. . . . No man should go to the chair twice. The voice of humanity and justice cries out against such an outrage."[18]

What really impressed the board was when de Blanc pulled out a picture of Francis strapped in the chair. "When they saw it they shook," de Blanc remembers. With all the theatrics of a Clarence Darrow, de Blanc asked, "Look at him, gentlemen, a beaten animal; do you think there was any hope within that brown boy on the threshold of eternity? Supposing that the chair doesn't work a second time . . . the third time . . . is this an experiment in modern forms of torture? . . . Is the state of Louisiana trying to outdo the caesars, the Nazis?"[19]

"But I guess the picture didn't have the results it should have," de Blanc now ruminates. Three days after the hearing, he sent a message to Skelly Wright in Washington: "Board refused to commute sentence. File petition and wire me." There were only three days remaining until Francis' new execution date. Governor Davis ordered a reprieve until the nation's high court could decide whether it should consider Willie's case.

The next Monday Wright received bad news from the Supreme Court clerk. Wright wired de Blanc: "Supreme Court denied writ Francis case today." But the next day there was another unbelievable twist. A clerk in the court called Wright to explain that a mistake had been made. The appeal had been "granted," not "denied."

It was autumn before Skelly Wright would argue the case before the Supreme Court of the United States. In the meantime, mail continued to pour in. Francis was a quasi-celebrity. There was even a ballad written and published about him, "De Lord Fool'd Around Wid Dat Chair."

In November de Blanc flew to Washington—one of three trips that he paid for out of his own pocket—to hear Wright argue that the Fourteenth Amendment made the Fifth and Eighth Amendments binding on the states. Wright insisted that the state of Louisiana could not put Francis' life in jeopardy twice for the same crime. To do so would be cruel and unusual punishment and unconstitutional. "How many times does the state get before the due process clause of the Fourteenth Amendment can be used to protect the petitioner from torture?" he asked.[20] Wright also contended that the second electrocution would violate the equal protection clause of the Fourteenth Amendment, because Willie's punishment would be greater than any other person's convicted of the same crime.

"The Justices seemed unusually subdued, perhaps under the impact of the terrible events which had already befallen Willie and the possibility that those events would be repeated if the Court failed to intervene," wrote Barrett Prettyman, Jr., in *Death and the Supreme Court,* the first serious work on the Willie Francis case. "The spirit of the Court was almost sullen, and the Justices . . . looked like brooding Rodin figures, black-robed and black of mood, almost resentful that this insoluble problem had been put before them."[21]

Eight Mondays after the oral arguments and two years after the murder of Andrew Thomas, it was not a united court—not even a majority, but a plurality decision—that spelled out Francis' fate. Each Monday, Skelly Wright had called the Court's clerk to see whether or not the Court had issued an opinion. "The day the opinion actually did come down, I called, and I asked the clerk which way had it come down, and he said it was reversed which meant that Willie Francis had won," Wright recalls. "But when I got to the courthouse after a much excited ride in a taxi, I called to a friend that I saw in the hallway, 'I won my case.' I said it twice, and he kind of looked at me like I was crazy because he knew the truth. He had been there, and when I got to the clerk's office I got the bad news myself. . . . I had actually lost."

Justice Stanley Reed, joined by Chief Justice Fred Vinson and Justices Hugo Black and Robert Jackson, wrote the plurality opinion. Although the four accepted for purposes of argument the proposition that violation of "the principles of the Fifth and Eighth Amendments, as to double jeopardy and cruel and unusual punishment, would be violative of the due process clause of the Fourteenth Amendment,"[22] they did not feel that these standards would be breached by sending Francis back to the electric chair.

Reed dismissed the double jeopardy claim by comparing the second death sentence to a new trial granted because of an error of law by the state that "results in a death sentence instead of imprisonment for life." With respect to cruel and unusual punishment, he stated that "the cruelty against which the Constitution protects a convicted man is cruelty inherent in the method of punishment, not the necessary suffering involved in any method employed to extinguish life humanely."[23]

The Court also rejected Wright's equal protection argument that the punishment for Willie would be *more* severe than that meted out to others guilty of the same offense. "So long as the law applies to all alike, the requirements of equal protection are met."[24]

Justice Felix Frankfurter was the swing vote, the fifth required to send Francis back to the electric chair. However, he wrote his own concurring opinion. He could not accept the notion that the Fourteenth Amendment had made the Fifth and the Eighth applicable to the states. "The Fourteenth Amendment placed no specific restraints upon the States in the formulation or the administration of their criminal law." He felt that the amendment only restricted the states "generally." The Fourteenth Amendment, he explained, "did not mean to imprison the States into the limited experience of the eighteenth century. It did mean to withdraw from the States the right to act in ways that are offensive to a decent respect for the dignity of man, and heedless of his freedom." Frankfurter felt that the due process clause only required the states to follow standards that "have been found to be implicit in the concept of ordered liberty."[25]

The federal government, according to Frankfurter, could not impose standards of fairness on the states "unless, as it was put for the Court by Mr. Justice Cardozo, [the state action] 'offends some principle of justice so rooted in the traditions and conscience of our people as to be ranked as fundamental.'" Although Frankfurter was a lifelong foe of capital punishment, he held that sending Willie Francis back to the electric chair did not offend one of those fundamental principles. Therefore, the Supreme Court had to "abstain from interference . . . no matter how strong one's personal feelings of revulsion against a State's insistence on its pound of flesh." Frankfurter reasoned that by telling Louisiana not to execute Francis he "would be enforcing [his] private view rather than the consensus of society's opinion."[26] As Miller and Bowman point out in their article, "Slow Dance on the Killing Ground," Frankfurter thought *Francis* had failed to meet the test of "Justice Oliver Wendell Holmes, who used to express [the relationship between the Supreme Court and the states] by saying that he would not strike down state action unless the action of the state made him puke."[27]

What is most curious about Frankfurter's position, as the article reveals, is that he did not think that the governor of Louisiana should let Francis go through the ordeal again and began writing high-placed friends in the state, such as attorney Monte Lemann, to try to persuade the pardons board or the governor to commute the sentence. He was the prisoner of a self-imposed dilemma—refraining from what he thought was a misuse of the Fourteenth Amendment and an imposition of national standards of decency, yet wanting to save Willie's life at the same time.

It is fascinating to note that five years later, in *Rochin* v. *California*,[28] Frankfurter felt that the use of a stomach pump to obtain evidence in a narcotics case did violate fundamental standards of decency. In fact, he compared that police action to the use of the "rack and screw."

Surprisingly, the minority opinion in the *Francis* case was written by Justice Harold H. Burton of Ohio, whose opinions were not always identified with defendants' rights. Burton was joined by Justices William O. Douglas, Wiley B. Rutledge, and Frank Murphy. The four believed that the "unusual facts" required that the case be sent back to the state in order to determine whether any current had actually passed through Willie Francis' body. "When life is to be taken," Burton wrote, "there must be no avoidable error of law or uncertainty of fact."[29]

To the four dissenters, the case presented a "violation of constitutional due process that is more clear than would be presented by many lesser punishments prohibited by the Eighth Amendment." Contrary to Frankfurter, Burton contended that "taking life by unnecessary cruel means shocks the most fundamental instincts of civilized man." Citing the *Kemmler* case of 1890, Burton said that the "all-important consideration is that the execution shall be so instantaneous and substantially painless that the punishment shall be reduced, as nearly as possible, to no more than that of death itself. Electrocution has been approved only in a form that eliminates suffering. [The Constitution] does not provide for electrocution by interrupted or repeated applications of electric current at intervals of several days or even minutes."[30]

Burton quoted the definition of cruel punishment in *Kemmler:* "Punishments are cruel when they involve torture or a lingering death."[31] To the minority, that meant no second attempt; the plurality had cited the case to support the opposite view. Burton likened the idea of repeated attempts to a form of torture that would "rival that of burning at the stake." He asked, "How many deliberate and intentional reapplications of electric current does it take to produce a cruel, unusual and unconstitutional punishment? . . . If five attempts would be 'cruel and unusual,' it would be difficult to draw the line between two, three, four and five."[32]

Thus, in a bizarre turn of events, although at least five justices thought it wrong for Francis to have to go through the ordeal again, that was to be his fate. What most shocked Skelly Wright was Justice Black's vote. "I was totally surprised," he laments. "If I had had to pick one sure vote, I would have picked him." In later years the two Southern liberal judges became intimate friends and colleagues, but Wright never discussed the case with Black. It is especially difficult to understand Black's vote in light of his dissent one year later in *Adamson* v. *California,*[33] in which he first articulated his lifelong position that the Fourteenth Amendment incorporates the entire Bill of Rights.

One gains some insight into Black's reasoning in a draft of a concurring opinion in *Francis* which he later discarded. "Our courts move, I think, in forbidden territory, when they prescribe their 'standards of decency' as the supreme rule of the people." To Black a valid sentence that was botched in the execution could not be considered to be cruel and unusual punishment—not according to his copy of the Constitution, which said nothing about such errors in execution. Despite his soon-to-be written theory of incorporation, he wrote, "I cannot agree . . . that any provision of the Federal Constitution authorizes us to rule that any accidental failure fairly to carry out a valid sentence of death on the first attempt bars execution of that sentence."[34]

Thus Willie Francis was to die, to go through the ordeal of execution twice, not because a majority of the Supreme Court thought he should, but because two justices felt that since the Constitution did not explicitly prohibit that practice, they must exert judicial self-restraint.

THE LEGAL FIGHT ENDS

Skelly Wright and Bertrand de Blanc continued their fight for Francis' life. Wright asked the Supreme Court for a rehearing because the state law had been changed in the wake of the bungled electrocution; now an experienced electrician would be required to be in charge and no convicts would be allowed to assist. The Supreme Court turned Wright down. Back in Louisiana, de Blanc tried to get a stay of execution because new evidence indicated that the executioners had been intoxicated and had been abusive to Francis. His motion was also denied.

With only days to go, Wright and de Blanc then filed a petition for habeas corpus with the United States Supreme Court, but were turned down "without prejudice." (This means they were not barred from reinstigating the litigation.) The Supreme Court was telling them that the new evidence was significant, but that they must go through the federal courts before coming to the Supreme Court.

De Blanc flew back to Louisiana to tell Francis about the Court's decision. As he recalls, Francis just looked out the cell window and said, "Leave it alone, Mr. Bert."

"I said, 'The Supreme Court said I can go back and stop this execution.'

"He said, 'No, leave it alone.' I guess he was just tired. We also had Father Hannigan, who had convinced Willie that on the day of the second execution that the minute the switch was turned on that he would see the Lord. . . . I guess he was ready to die."

Three hundred seventy-one days after the original "execution day" the generator was again parked next to the St. Martinville courthouse. This time when the switch was thrown, it worked. The coffin and grave that Francis' father had prepared were used.

Willie Francis' name is not recorded on his overgrown concrete tomb, resting under a pecan tree in the Baptist graveyard in St. Martinville. The only inscription on the small family crypt is the name of Willie's brother Adam, who was a veteran. Bertrand de Blanc, now in his seventies, but still lively and spry, looks at Willie's grave, brushes away a tear, and speculates that "if Willie's appeal was today we'd win." Judge Skelly Wright feels that today the Supreme Court would take Justice Burton's suggestion and send the "case back to the state court for a finding of fact. . . . I rather suspect that the Court today would find some way to alleviate the situation."

THE EXECUTION OF JOHN LOUIS EVANS III

It is tempting to say it couldn't happen again, but in a macabre sort of way, history repeated itself in the spring of 1983. In the neighboring state of Alabama, at Holman Prison in Atmore, John Louis Evans III was strapped into "big yellow mama," as that state's electric chair built in the 1920s is familiarly called, as a thunderstorm raged outside.[35] At 8:26 P.M. the guard who had remained in the execution chamber picked up a 3-foot-long pole with a yellow disk attached to the top; on it were written the letters R-E-A-D-Y. The switch was pulled and for 30 seconds 1,900 volts of electricity flowed through Evans' body, which slammed against the back of the chair and then pulsated in a rhythmic motion. Sparks arched around his head and left leg; a muffled sizzle could be heard as the electricity was absorbed. Soon smoke emanated from the hood over his head and wafted about the execution chamber. There was a smell of burned flesh.

Two doctors present entered the chamber to examine the body. They nodded in a way that the reporters who were there as witnesses and Evans' lawyer interpreted as meaning that Evans was dead. But then his chest gave a heave "and saliva ran from under the mask and down his smock. [Warden] White threw the switch again and this time small flames licked around Evans's head, his body straining, smoke streamed from his leg and the leather cap holding the electrodes to his skull."[36]

There was confusion. Lawyer Russell Canan began to ask for clemency. "I ask you to communicate this to the governor. This is cruel and unusual punishment. There are Supreme Court precedents for this." But Governor George Wallace, whose press secretary had been on the phone with the state's head of corrections the entire time, "would not intervene." Yet, even after the second jolt of 1,900 volts, Evans was not dead. Another application of 1,900 volts was administered, and 14 minutes after it had begun, the execution of John Louis Evans, convicted of murdering a pawnbroker, was completed.

"As it turns out, it is routine to do it two or three times," says Stan Bailey, reporter for the *Birmingham News,* who witnessed the Evans execution. "That odor stayed with me for hours. . . . It killed my appetite even though I had not eaten anything since three o'clock the previous afternoon. I didn't eat again until about that time the next day. . . . I didn't realize it had been as much of a drain on me emotionally as it had been."[37]

"John Evans was burned alive by the state of Alabama," cried his lawyer. "He was tortured tonight in the name of vengeance, disguised as justice."

Almost immediately after Evans was executed, people on both sides of the death penalty issue spoke out against the messy electrocution. The Alabama legislature began discussing lethal injections and even prison officials mused publicly about the possibility that the electric chair at Holman was cruel and unusual punishment.

John Carroll, a lawyer for the Southern Poverty Law Center, who had previously represented Evans, sued in the state courts to have Alabama's electric chair declared unconstitutional as cruel and unusual punishment, but lost. The Alabama court ruled that even though Alabama's chair may take 15 minutes and several jolts of electricity to kill someone, it was not cruel and unusual. Carroll is appealing the decision to the United States Court of Appeals for the 11th Circuit, and says he will take it to the Supreme Court if he has to.

WHAT IS CRUEL AND UNUSUAL PUNISHMENT?

"What constitute [sic] a cruel and unusual punishment has not been exactly decided," wrote Justice Joseph McKenna in 1910 in the *Weems* case. "It has been said that ordinarily the terms imply something barbarous—torture and the like."[38]

In *Weems,* the petitioner had been convicted of defrauding the United States government by falsifying a government account book. His minimum sentence was 12 years at hard labor, constantly bound in chains. In addition, he was stripped of all property rights and, upon release, would be subjected to lifetime surveillance. In overturning the sentence, Justice McKenna explained that the framers of the Bill of Rights distrusted power, power that might be tempted to cruelty. That was, he said, the motive of the Eighth Amendment. He said the amendment was not confined to the "form of evils" that the framers had experienced. Thus, he expressed the need for a living constitution that could adapt to the times:

> Time works changes, brings into existence new conditions and purposes. Therefore a principle to be vital, must be capable of wider application than the mischief which gave it birth. This is peculiarly true of constitutions. They are not ephemeral enactments, designed to meet passing occasions. They are, to use the words of Chief Justice Marshall, "designed to approach immortality as nearly as human institutions can approach it." . . . The future is their care and provision for events of good and bad tendencies of which no prophecy can be made. In the application of a constitution, therefore, our contemplation cannot be only of what has been, but of what may be.[39]

The nation has come far from the original notion of what was cruel and unusual. At the time of the drafting of the Bill of Rights, brandings and corporal punishments were common. Up until the 1830s, mutilations, dismemberments, and even sawing a person in half as an execution were considered acceptable punishments.

Beginning in 1957 and continuing for more than two decades, the Court "skillfully refused to sanction a death sentence while avoiding the ultimate decision."[40] The Court did this by finding procedural flaws in the sentencing processes. It continually skirted the issue of whether capital punishment per se was unconstitutional under the Eighth Amendment. (Many people mistakenly believe that the Court outlawed capital punishment during those years. Actually, the justices only ruled on the constitutionality of specific sentences in specific instances. A majority of the Court has never declared capital punishment unconstitutional.)

Even the 1972 *Furman* decision[41] left that question of the constitutionality of the death penalty unanswered, although five justices (Douglas, Brennan, Stewart, White, and Marshall) indicated that the death sentences of William Henry Furman, Lucius Jackson, Jr., and Elmer Branch (two for rape and one for murder) were violations of the Eighth and Fourteenth Amendments. It took 136 pages and nine separate opinions to explain the Court's decision. The reasoning of the justices who felt the sentences were cruel and unusual ranged from that of Justice Marshall, who concluded that the death penalty was morally unacceptable to the people of the United States, to that of Justice Douglas, who felt that death sentences discriminated against minorities, to that of Justice Stewart, who decided that the sentences, which had been left to the discretion of juries, were wantonly and "freakishly" imposed.

To many Court observers, especially those who opposed the death penalty, it seemed that the Court was on the threshold of declaring capital punishment unconstitutional.* However, that notion was quashed four years later in *Gregg* v. *Georgia*, [42] when seven members of the Court agreed that "the punishment of death does not invariably violate the Constitution." Writing for the majority, Justice Potter Stewart concluded that "the death sentence is not a form of punishment that may never be imposed." Stewart also said that it was constitutionally permissible for punishment to be inflicted for retribution as well as deterrence.

From 1965 to 1977, there were no executions in the United States. As of April, 1984, 16 men have been executed; hundreds more await their fate as their cases trickle up to the high court for final scrutiny.

The Supreme Court still wrestles with the definition of what is cruel and unusual and with the question of how much of that definition should be left to the states. Soon the Court may rule on whether electrocution or any particular "form" of execution is unconstitutional. That may be the legacy of Willie Francis.

---

*What actually happened was that most state legislatures rewrote their death penalty statutes to meet the procedural objections of the Supreme Court.

Daniel M'Naghten, 1843. *Illustrated London News*

When John Hinckley, Jr., shot President Reagan, the insanity defense went on trial. America was forced to examine this defense and the reasons we have it. To find its modern roots, one must look to the trial of Daniel M'Naghten in England in 1843.

THE DEFENSE
OF LAST RESORT
The Insanity Plea

What do you mean "not guilty"? I saw him do it!

Queen Victoria, in reaction to a
verdict on an assassination attempt[1]

*Ever since our ancestral common law emerged out of the
darkness of its early barbaric days, it has been a postu-
late of Western civilization that the taking of life by the
hand of an insane person is not murder. But the nature
and operation of the mind are so elusive to the grasp of
the understanding that the basis for formulating standards of criminal responsibility and the means for determining whether those standards are satisfied in a particular case have greatly troubled law and medicine for
more than a century.*

Justice Felix Frankfurter,
dissenting in *Smith* v. *Baldi*[2]

He was on his way to Yale, not to begin classes, but to make a
dramatic statement that would accomplish his life's goal: to win the
affections of actress Jodie Foster. Before deciding on this plan, he had
contemplated many scenarios: committing a mass slaughter, hijacking a
plane, or kidnapping Foster for ransom. But now his bus stopped in Washington, and he came across a newspaper listing of President Reagan's
schedule for the next day. Suddenly John Hinckley, Jr., changed his
plans; he would assassinate the President.

Hinckley had no hopes of surviving the attack. In fact, his fantasy
was to die in the act. In his final love letter to Foster, written before
leaving his Washington hotel room, he says: "I will admit to you that the
reason I'm going ahead with this attempt now is because I cannot wait any
longer to impress you. I've got to do something now to make you understand."

It was March 30, 1981—coincidentally, the day that his parents and psychiatrist had set for breaking off relations with Hinckley in a "get tough" plan. (He had either to conform to their standards or stay away.) To his parents and psychiatrist, Hinckley was not a dangerous criminal, but a maladjusted youth who needed a kick in the pants. But the confused young man had not returned home penitent; he had become even more obsessed with fulfilling his mission to win Foster's admiration. He loaded one of the many guns that he had been collecting and went to the Washington Hilton, a stop on the president's agenda. As the President left the hotel, waving to the crowd gathered outside, Hinckley began firing. He wounded President Reagan, Press Secretary James Brady, a secret service man, and a policeman. There was no doubt that he had committed the crime, as videotape cameras had recorded the event. In less than an hour, tens of millions of Americans had seen the videotape of the shooting; by the end of the day tens of millions of people had watched the utterly senseless spectacle. The only doubts that would linger for a jury to decide would be whether Hinckley was sane and whether he should be held responsible for his crime.

Over the next few days, Hinckley's troubled background became front-page news and the subject of editorial analysis. He was a lonely, friendless youth, who had slowly drifted into his own fantasy world. This world revolved around the characters in the movie "Taxi Driver," in which Jodie Foster had played a 12-year-old prostitute. In the five-year period from 1976 to 1981, Hinckley had seen the movie more than 15 times, identifying more and more with the film's central character, Travis Bickle, a disturbed loner who goes on a bloody shooting spree to rescue Foster from her plight. Both Bickle and Hinckley's tragic stories climax in assassination attempts. The fictional movie ends there, but Hinckley's real-life drama was just beginning. It would be played out in the court of justice during his trial and in the court of public opinion in heated discussions of the insanity defense.

When Hinckley's lawyers, Vincent Fuller and Gregory B. Craig, filed notice with the federal district court in Washington that he was pleading not guilty by reason of insanity, the country's examination of the insanity defense began. It was debated on national television, in the Congress, in state legislatures, and even in local bars and barbershops.

Nine months later, when a jury of seven men and five women found Hinckley "not guilty by reason of insanity," the public reaction was shock and dismay. Apparently, trial judge Barrington Parker had been so sure of a guilty verdict that he had scheduled a sentencing date. Hinckley himself had written a "sentencing statement." Speaker of the House Thomas P. O'Neill, Jr., commented, "In other countries Hinckley would be dead and buried in eight days." Senator Larry Pressler of South Dakota warned, "I think you are going to see a revolt across the country." The debate over the plea intensified as predictions circulated that Hinckley, who was sent to Saint Elizabeth's Hospital, could be out in a matter of days—despite assertions by his lawyers and parents that they would not press for early release.

WHERE DID THE INSANITY DEFENSE COME FROM?

Those who looked to the Constitution and the Supreme Court for better understanding of the insanity rules found little help. There is nothing in the Constitution about the insanity plea, and the Supreme Court has had little to say about it. In fact, as late as 1968, in *Powell* v. *Texas*,[3] the Court had refused to set a standard. In 1966 Leroy Powell had been arrested and convicted of being found in a state of intoxication in a public place. At his trial, a psychiatrist had testified that he was unable to control his behavior and drinking problem because of a psychological dependence. When Powell's case had finally come before the United States Supreme Court, his lawyers argued that his behavior lacked the critical element of *mens rea,* criminal intent. They argued that he could not be punished because his drunkenness was involuntary and stemmed from an uncontrollable compulsion. Writing for the majority, which upheld Powell's conviction, Justice Thurgood Marshall cautioned, "Nothing could be less fruitful than for this Court to be impelled into defining some sort of insanity test in constitutional terms." He continued that "formulating a constitutional rule would ... freeze the developing productive dialogue between law and psychiatry into a rigid constitutional mold. It is simply not yet the time to write into the Constitution formulas cast in terms whose meaning, let alone relevance, is not yet clear either to doctors or to lawyers."[4]

THE CASE OF DANIEL M'NAGHTEN

So where, then, does the insanity defense come from, if not from our own constitutional doctrine? Its roots are in fact thousands of years old. One can find a specific reference to the principle in the Talmud. "It is an ill thing to knock against a deaf mute, an imbecile or a minor; he that wounds them is culpable but if they wound others they are not culpable."[5] This same notion appears also in the sixth-century codes of Emperor Justinian and in the canon law of the Middle Ages. In its various manifestations, the principle states that children and insane persons cannot be held responsible for a crime because they lack malicious intent.

The most concrete source of the insanity defense, as it exists on many state lawbooks, is English law of the eighteenth century and the case of Daniel M'Naghten.* On January 20, 1843, M'Naghten, a wood-

---

*The spelling of M'Naghten is a matter of controversy. The legal records use "M'Naghten," but scholars now believe he actually spelled his name McNaughton.

turner from Glasgow in his early 30s, shot and mortally wounded Edmund Drummond, who was the private secretary of Prime Minister Sir Robert Peel and a popular civil servant. M'Naghten had been hanging around the government offices at Whitehall near Downing Street stalking Drummond, whom he thought to be Peel himself. He was "suffering from . . . delusions of persecution by what he called 'the Tories' "[6] and was convinced that only Sir Robert could help him. For some reason, this delusion led him to think that he must kill Peel.

Drummond was walking from Trafalgar Square past the station of the Royal Horse Guards, when M'Naghten took aim and fired. As Drummond staggered from this shot, which struck him in the back, M'Naghten took aim with a second pistol. But as the deranged gunman cocked his weapon and aimed, he was wrestled to the ground by Constable James Silver and, after a violent struggle, was arrested. Drummond managed to stagger to the home of his brother near Charing Cross, where the bullet was removed from his lower abdomen. Five days later, however, Drummond died of excessive bleeding.

M'Naghten's trial was originally set for 13 days after the shooting, but through the efforts of his counsels a one-month postponement was granted and the trial was set for March 3 before Lord Chief Justice Tindal, Mr. Justice Williams, Mr. Justice Coleridge, and a jury. M'Naghten was represented by four distinguished counsels, headed by Alexander Cockburn. One wonders how a woodturner happened to have such prestigious representation in the Old Bailey. Donald J. West and Alexander Walk's book on the subject sheds some light on that question: "All the circumstances of the McNaughton case suggest that this most ably conducted defense was organized by what today would be called a 'pressure group' of people, seriously concerned to bring about a much-needed reform of the law on insanity in criminal cases."[7]

Most of what little is known about M'Naghten came out at his trial. The illegitimate son of a Scottish woodturner and a poor farmer's daughter, M'Naghten was apprenticed to his natural father at the age of 15 or 16. He then became a journeyman and suffered a great disappointment when his father did not take him on as a partner. Later, he set up an independent business, which thrived for about five years. In 1834 he contracted typhus and as a result began suffering from chronic insomnia. In 1837 he was asked to leave his boarding house and moved into his workshop. His disorder became greater until, according to the trial records, he suffered from racking pains in the head and would "run out to the running Clyde and bathe his burning brow and even plunge into the river to obtain relief from the burning pain." In 1841 he sold his business because of a growing feeling of persecution. He believed that he was being continually tormented by a consortium of the Catholic church, the Jesuits, and the Tories, who followed him wherever he went, calling him "murderer." He could not sleep; he could not escape them. He went to the local constable but was put off. He fled to France but found no relief from his fantasy persecutors. In desperation, he went to his father's house, but his father simply advised him to banish such thoughts and take up the study of arithmetic. His unsettled mind led him to believe that only Sir Robert Peel could free him from his persecutors, and that belief led him to London and eventually to the court, known as the Old Bailey.

After his arrest, M'Naghten made a statement to the authorities:

> The Tories in my native city have compelled me to do this. They follow and persecute me wherever I go, and have entirely destroyed my peace of mind. . . . I cannot get no rest for them night or day. . . . I believe they have driven me into a consumption. I am sure I shall never be the man I formerly was. . . . They have accused me of crimes of which I am not guilty; they do everything in their power to harass and persecute me; in fact, they wish to murder me. It can be proved by evidence. That's all I have to say.[8]

The trial was a cause célèbre. Even the Consort Prince Albert was in the audience. Sir William Webb Follett, the solicitor general, who prosecuted the case, told the judges and jury that the only question was whether M'Naghten was capable of distinguishing between right and wrong. In his opening remarks, he told the jury, "If you believe that he was under the influence and control of some disease of the mind which prevented him from being conscious that he was committing a crime, if you believe that he did not know he was violating the law of both God and man; then, undoubtedly, he is entitled to your acquittal."[9] But Follett qualified his statement by saying that partial insanity was not enough. "[I]f he had that degree of intellect which enabled him to know and distinguish between right and wrong, if he knew what could be the effects of the crime, and consciously committed it, and if with that consciousness he willfully committed it," there would not be sufficient reason to acquit the accused.

To support this contention, Sir William quoted Sir Matthew Hale, Lord Chief Justice of England from 1609 to 1676, who recognized that "the moon hath great influence on all diseases of the brain . . . [and that] such persons commonly in the full of the moon . . . are usually at the height of their distemper. But such persons have their lucid moments . . . in such intervals have competent use of reason." Lord Chief Justice Hale had thus insisted that only total insanity provided relief from criminal liability.

The prosecution's case relied on a number of witnesses who had seen M'Naghten loitering around Whitehall prior to the shooting, in an effort to show that the crime was a premeditated, well-planned act. The prosecution also called acquaintances of the accused, who testified that they had never noticed any peculiar behavior on his part. A physician and lecturer whose classes in anatomy M'Naghten had attended testified that the accused was "shrewd and intelligent."

For the defense, barrister Alexander Cockburn began by asserting that "[t]here is no doubt . . . that, according to the laws of England, insanity absolves a man from responsibility and from the legal consequences which would otherwise attach to the violation of the law. And in this respect, indeed, the law of England goes no further than the law of every other civilized community on the face of the earth." After portraying his client as one of those unfortunates who suffered the "most appalling of all calamities . . . the deprivation of that reason, which is man's only light and guide in the intricate and slippery paths of life," Cockburn asserted:

> The question is not here, as my learned friend would have you think, whether this individual knew that he was killing another when he raised his hand to destroy him, although he might be under a delusion, but whether under that delusion of mind he did an act which he would not have done under any other circumstances, save under the impulse of delusion which he could not control, and out of which delusion alone the act itself arose.

The defense introduced witnesses who told of M'Naghten's bizarre behavior and how he had complained of his persecutions. Physicians who had observed him in prison testified that M'Naghten labored under a morbid delusion that deprived him of all restraint and control of his actions. "It was a grinding of the mind. He was tossed like a cork on the sea."

In a surprising move, the defense called Forbes Winslow, a surgeon and the author of the "Plea of Insanity in Criminal Cases." Dr. Winslow was not a defense witness and had not examined M'Naghten, but he had been present during the entire trial. Asked his opinion as to the prisoner's state of mind, he answered that he had "not the slightest hesitation in saying he is insane, and that he committed the offence in question whilst afflicted with a delusion, under which he appears to have been labouring for a considerable length of time."

At that point, Chief Justice Tindal asked the solicitor general if he was prepared to combat any of the medical evidence. When Follett replied, "No, my Lord," the chief justice stopped the case. In his charge to the jury, he stated:

> [T]he point I shall have to submit to you is whether on the whole of the evidence you have heard, you are satisfied that at the time the act was committed, . . . he had that competent use of his understanding as that he knew that he was doing, by the very act itself, a wicked and a wrong thing. If he was not sensible at the time he committed that act, that it was a violation of the law of God or of man, undoubtedly he was not responsible for that act, or liable to any punishment whatever flowing from that act.

. . . I cannot help remarking in common with my learned brethren, that the whole of the medical evidence is on the one side, and there is no part of it which leaves any doubt on the mind. . . . but if on balancing the evidence in your minds you think the prisoner capable of distinguishing between right and wrong, then he was a responsible agent and liable to all the penalties the law imposes. If not so, . . . then you will probably not take upon yourselves to find the prisoner guilty.

The jury's reply was immediate: not guilty by reason of insanity. The clerk then directed the jailer to keep the prisoner in safe custody "till Her Majesty's pleasure be known." Her Majesty, Queen Victoria, was infuriated by the verdict and "her pleasure" was to keep M'Naghten in Bethlehem Hospital, a criminal lunatic asylum, for the rest of his life.

The trial of M'Naghten had ended, but the issue was far from concluded. Queen Victoria, who had herself been the target of an assassination attempt, carried out by a man named Oxford,* immediately wrote to Sir Robert Peel. "We have seen the trials of Oxford and M'Naughton conducted by the ablest lawyers of the day—and they *allow* and *advise* the jury to pronounce the verdict of *Not Guilty* on account of *Insanity* when everybody is morally convinced that both malefactors were perfectly conscious and aware of what they did."[10] She asked Parliament to pass legislation that would require a stricter rule for insanity defenses.

Public opinion was overwhelmingly with the Queen. A letter to the *Times* reflected the public's uneasiness: "If the result of McNaughton's trial satisfies the end of justice, by proving the moral irresponsibility of the murderer, it undoubtedly leaves the security of Her Majesty's subjects from similar murderous attacks in a very unsatisfactory state."[11]

Another distressed subject wrote his scathing analysis in verse:

Ye people of England exult and be glad
For ye're now at the will of the merciless mad
Why say ye that but three authorities reign
Crown, Commons and Lord?—You omit the insane.
They're a privileged class whom no statute
    controls,
And their murderous charter exists in their
    souls.
Do they wish to spill blood—they have only to
    play
A few pranks—get aslym'd a month and a day
Then Heigh! to escape from the mad doctor's keys
And to pistol or stab whomsoever they please.

---

*In 1840 Oxford shot at and missed Queen Victoria while she was driving up Constitution hill. He was charged with treason but found not guilty by reason of his insanity.

> Now the dog has a human-like wit in creation
> He resembles most nearly our own generation
> Then if madmen for murder escape with impunity
> Why deny a poor dog the same noble immunity
> So if a dog or man bite you beware being nettled
> For crime is no crime—when the mind is
>   unsettled.[12]

The issue was raised immediately in the House of Lords, at which time the lord chancellor, Lord Lyndhurst, suggested that the opinion of the Law Lords, the prestigious committee of the House of Lords which is the closest thing to our Supreme Court, be asked as to the status of the law. Five questions were put to the Law Lords and three months later they gave their answers, which have since come to be known as the M'Naghten Rules. It is interesting to note that Chief Justice Tindal, who presided over M'Naghten's trial, also headed the committee.

Although some of the answers dealt with rules of evidence, such as whether an observer like Dr. Winslow could properly be called as a witness, the most important answers concerned criminal responsibility and charge to the jury. The judges concluded that:

> A person labouring under partial delusions only, and not otherwise insane, who did the act charged with the view, under the influence of insane delusion, of redressing or revenging some supposed grievance or wrong, or of producing some public benefit, . . . is nevertheless punishable, . . . if he knew at the time that he was acting contrary to the law of the land.
>   . . . To establish a defence on the ground of insanity it must be clearly proved that, at the time of committing the act, the party accused was labouring under such a defect of reason from disease of the mind, as not to know the nature and quality of the act he was doing, or if he did know it, that he did not know that what he was doing was wrong.[13]

It is worth noting that under these new criteria, M'Naghten himself would have been unable to meet the test and would have been convicted and hanged.

THE M'NAGHTEN RULE IN THE UNITED STATES

The M'Naghten rule, which established a stricter criterion for the insanity plea than that expressed in the M'Naghten acquittal, was quickly adopted in most jurisdictions in the United States. Many state statutes incorporated an additional element following an Alabama case, *Parsons* v. *State*, [14] in 1886. This "irresistible impulse" rule, as it is called, stipulates that: "if there be either incapacity to distinguish between right or wrong as to the particular act, or delusions as to the act, or inability to refrain from doing the act, there is no responsibility. . . . There can not be . . . a law punishing for what they cannot avoid."[15]

Although some version of the M'Naghten rule still exists in most states, the basic concept of the insanity defense has itself been called into question in the wake of the *Hinckley* verdict. The same public outrage that led to the Law Lords' ruling has caused Congress and state legislatures to suggest new standards. Some states, such as Idaho, have completely eliminated the plea, while others have substituted pleas of "guilty but insane" or "guilty but mentally ill." These new defenses attempt to appease public sentiment by attaching "guilt" to the criminal, and in some cases require that the criminal serve a minimum length of time. For instance, in the state of Alaska, if a person is judged guilty but mentally ill, he will be sentenced by a judge and then sent to a state hospital for the criminally insane. If at some time prior to the expiration of his sentence he is judged to be cured, he will serve out the remainder in a state penitentiary.

It is virtually impossible to make sweeping generalizations about the insanity defense, because the rules of evidence and sentencing vary so greatly from state to state as well as within the federal courts. What is clear is that following the *Hinckley* verdict—just as occurred following *M'Naghten*—the whole concept of the insanity defense is being questioned across the nation. This soul searching is rooted both in facts and in misconceptions. Its result may be legislation less responsive to the criminally insane than the rule set almost a century-and-a-half ago.

Two important considerations have been continually cited. First, the insanity defense is a defense of last resort. It is seldom raised and even more seldom successful. In less than one-tenth of one percent of all criminal cases is the verdict reached. On the other side of the coin, critics point out that those accused who are successful spend very little time in confinement and that they are often repeat offenders. What's more, psychiatrists have no sure way of predicting future behavior.

At one extreme are those who assert that we must protect society from violent criminals at all costs, at the other those who contend we must protect the rights of the mentally ill at all costs. Those critical of the defense see the elimination or narrowing of the plea as a necessary message to all that we're going to get tough on crime. Those who support the defense say that in a civilized society we must differentiate between those who have criminal intent and those who are incapable of controlling their actions.

At the center of the conflict is the unhappy marriage between the law and psychiatry. Lawyers, judges, and many psychiatrists are loath to turn a trial into a debate among an assembly of expert psychiatric witnesses. As one Hinckley juror lamented, "If the expert psychiatrists could not decide whether the man was sane, then how are we supposed to decide?"[16] Yet without expert testimony, it would be difficult for the judge or jury to reach any conclusions as to sanity or insanity. As Professor Alan Stone wrote, "The marriage between law and psychiatry is . . . just like many other marriages in which one hears it said at time of crisis, 'I don't know what to do. I can't live with her, and I can't live without her.' "[17]

So the balance between law and psychiatry, between the rights of the community and the rights of the mentally ill, continues to be adjusted and readjusted on a state-by-state, court-by-court, jury-by-jury basis. One can only wonder what might have happened had Hinckley been convicted and his appeal reached the Supreme Court. Unfortunately, it may take another tragedy to learn if the experimentation has run its course, or if the question is still not ripe for a constitutional formula. Until the high court is willing to weigh that balance, we must lean on the ghost of Daniel M'Naghten and the rules established in the reign of Queen Victoria.

Estelle Griswold, 1961. *AP/Wide World Photos*

Norma McCorvey a.k.a. "Jane Roe," 1984. *Gerard Murrell*

Estelle Griswold and Jane Roe never knew each other and have only one thing in common: their names are attached to two landmark Supreme Court decisions. A well-to-do Connecticut matron, Griswold believed that a Connecticut law prohibiting the use of birth control was wrong. Roe's situation was more personal; unmarried and pregnant, she wanted an abortion but couldn't obtain one in her home state of Texas. Both women fought their battles all the way to the Supreme Court and won. As a result, not only were the laws they were fighting struck down, but the Supreme Court also established a whole new concept of constitutional liberty—the right of privacy.

UMPIRING "HARMLESS, EMPTY SHADOWS" The Right of Privacy

What are these people—doctor and patients—to do? Flout the law and go to prison? Violate the law surreptitiously and hope they will not get caught? . . . It is not a choice they need have under . . . our constitutional system.

Justice William O. Douglas,
dissenting in *Poe* v. *Ullman*

It was a put-up job, a test case in which the players knew exactly what roles they were to play and were willing to take the risk to fight for what they believed in. For Estelle T. Griswold, executive director of the Connecticut Planned Parenthood League, it was an overt act of civil disobedience. When, on November 1, 1961, she opened the doors of a birth control clinic at 79 Trumbull Street in New Haven, she was begging to be arrested. It would not take long for the police to comply. Mrs. Griswold and her codefendant Dr. Charles Lee Buxton, medical director of the clinic, would soon be arrested and convicted.

Although Justice Felix Frankfurter once observed that "the safeguards of liberty have frequently been forged in controversies involving not very nice people,"[1] Mrs. Griswold and Dr. Buxton prove there are exceptions to that generalization. Griswold was a well-educated Connecticut matron, slight, handsome, and cultured. She has been described as "a Connecticut Yankee who scrounged around for furniture for the clinic and scrubbed its floors."[2] Catherine Roraback, one of the attorneys who would represent the pair, remembers Griswold as a "very dynamic woman, and I mean woman, with a capital W. . . . She felt very strongly that there should be birth control service for women in Connecticut. And she was quite willing to push it as far as she could."[3] She fought the battle for birth control despite the fact that she had not been able to have children of her own.

Griswold's dedication came from her grasp of the problems of world overpopulation. She had worked in Europe after World War II helping to relocate displaced people. After touring some of the countries where she had placed people, she later reflected:

I saw poor, hungry people in the slums of Favola in Rio de Janeiro, in the La Perla area of Puerto Rico and Algiers.

You think of people as civilized. . . . each human being living in comfort and wealth feels he is a dignified individual. A look at the slums of the world, at the chaos of a war-scorched earth, and you realize that life at the point of survival, where food, water and shelter are unobtainable is close to reversion to an animal order. Survival is first; civilization is second.[4]

It was this perspective which led Griswold to join Connecticut's Planned Parenthood League in 1954 and to become its executive director a few years later.

Whereas Griswold was global in her view, her codefendant, Dr. Buxton, was more concerned for the poor women of Connecticut who could not afford private doctors. Roraback remembers Buxton constantly reminding her that "the problem is that women who have private doctors can get all the information they want and get prescriptions [for birth control]. . . . The real problem in Connecticut is that poor women who do not have private doctors cannot get that kind of care." White-haired and bespectacled, the 60-year-old physician was described as "a gentle crusader"[5] who shunned publicity. A Princeton undergraduate and a Columbia Medical School graduate, Buxton was the head of Yale's obstetrics and gynecology department. Although research oriented, he always had time for patients and spent hours trying to set up classes for teenagers in "human physiology"—sex education.

The lifelong dedication of those two people would lead to a case that would have a revolutionary effect on the rights of Americans. When it was over, the United States Supreme Court would not only declare Connecticut's ancient anti-birth-control law unconstitutional, as Griswold and Buxton had hoped, but would also add a new gloss to the Constitution, the right of privacy. That right was not specifically written into any of the provisions of the Bill of Rights, but a majority of the Court would find "penumbras" and combinations of explicit rights that they felt guaranteed a natural or fundamental right of privacy. This new reading of the Constitution would have emanations and repercussions that would lead to a whole body of case law on civil liberties.

FROM COMSTOCK TO TRUMBULL STREET

Anthony Comstock and Margaret Sanger had one thing in common, birth control legislation. Comstock devoted himself to getting it passed; Sanger devoted herself to getting it repealed. Comstock, a "lifelong crusader for God, Country, motherhood [in wedlock] and clean living,"[6] was special legislative agent for the Y.M.C.A.'s Committee for the Suppression of Vice. Through his lobbying efforts, the Congress passed on March 3, 1873 (the eve of Ulysses S. Grant's inauguration) the Comstock

Act, which barred a long list of "obscene" and "immoral" materials from the United States mails.* Among the banned items were "every article, instrument, substance, drug, medicine, or thing which is advertised or described in a manner calculated to lead another to use or apply it for preventing conception or producing abortion."[7]

In 1879, six years later, Connecticut, Comstock's home state, followed suit and enacted its own legislation. The Connecticut law went even further than the federal legislation: it banned the "use" of any birth control device. It is interesting to note that Comstock had never intended for the legislation to limit what doctors could prescribe to patients, which is exactly what the Connecticut law was interpreted to mean.[8]

In 1912 Margaret Sanger was a nurse in New York City when she heard a doctor warn Sadie Sachs, a poor working mother, that one more pregnancy would kill her. Under the New York State law, as in many other states at the time, the only birth control the physician could prescribe was to recommend to Sadie that her husband "sleep on the roof."[9] Not long after, Sanger attended Sadie at her deathbed following a botched abortion. That event turned Sanger into a crusader. She became devoted to ending the injustice inflicted on lower-class women, who could not afford proper medical help and "whose miseries were as vast as the sky."[10] Sanger traveled throughout the country and became the mother of the nation's birth control movement as she tried to undo all the "wrong" that had been done by earlier crusaders such as Comstock. An ardent feminist and Marxist, who saw all anti-birth-control legislation as a capitalist plot "which compels a woman to serve as a sex implement for man's use,"[11] Sanger founded the Planned Parenthood Federation of America. She also opened the first birth control clinic in New York, for which act she was jailed in 1916.

Sanger was instrumental in starting Connecticut's birth control movement. In 1921 she traveled from New York to nearby Connecticut to state her case before the state legislature in Hartford, shouting her familiar cry of "Feminists, come out from under the cover of morbid respectability and let's get a look at you."[12] Three prominent Connecticut women—Mrs. Katharine Houghton Hepburn, Mrs. Katharine Beech Day, and Mrs. Josephine Bennett—didn't have to be convinced. They formed her welcoming committee, as well as the core of what would become the Connecticut Birth Control League (later the Connecticut Planned Parenthood League).

The legislature lent a deaf ear to Sanger, but her trip had sparked a deep-seated commitment in the Hartford trio of Hepburn, Day, and Bennett. The three had been active in the suffrage movement, and as Hepburn's daughter explains, "This was the next logical step. Mother felt

---

*Congress does not have direct power to ban such materials but can regulate interstate commerce and the federal mails.

the first thing that women had to have was the vote and then some control over their reproductive processes. . . . It was a process of female empowerment."[13] On February 11, 1923, they organized the first public meeting on birth control to be held in the state. To their surprise and delight, the turnout was so large that the gallery of the Parsons Theater in Hartford had to be opened.

The group grew larger and more active, perhaps in part because many women realized that Connecticut was the only state in the nation that placed an absolute ban on the *use* of birth control. Each year they lobbied for repeal of Connecticut's rigid law, and each year the effort was unfruitful. Occasionally the Connecticut House of Representatives, which largely consisted of Protestants from rural areas, would pass a repeal; however, the Senate, in which Connecticut's urban, Catholic population was better represented, invariably voted the measure down.

None of these defeats stopped the determined advocates of the birth control movement. By the 1930s, Hepburn had become so involved in the fight that she was sometimes referred to in newspapers as the "Anti-Stork Chief." Her family laughs at the label. "Mother wasn't anti-stork, or anti-baby. She had six children of her own,"* says Marian Hepburn Grant, her daughter. "She used to argue against a very nice lady who was the mother of three children. And mother would say, 'I have six children and I use birth control. If I didn't, I would have 25 children. . . . You have to be sympathetic to the ones of us who are more fertile.' "

Hepburn traveled around Connecticut and the rest of the country, making speeches for birth control. A powerful speaker, whose voice could reach the back row of any assemblage, Hepburn successfully countered the arguments of her debating opponents. In one debate, arguing against the position that birth control interfered with nature, she stated:

> [Birth control] is unnatural only in the way every other bit of our civilization is unnatural—the lighting of this room, the riding in automobiles and airplanes instead of walking barefoot.
>
> The use of the human brain is natural, be it ever so hard to make some people do it. Birth Control is the use of human intelligence that God gave us to control the forces of nature.[14]

During another debate, she countered her opponent: "To say that God wills children to be born into the world who have no chance to grow up to be normal, healthy human beings is an insult to God."[15]

In arguing against the Connecticut law, Hepburn emphasized its unfairness. Upper-class women could get birth control information from their private doctors, but the very people who needed it most—those who were poor or on relief—could not. That was the unequal justice of the

---

*Her six children were Thomas, Katharine, Richard, Robert, Marian, and Margaret. (Katharine would become a famous actress.)

Connecticut law. No legal authorities dared interfere with private physicians offering advice to affluent women; in fact, there were only a few instances where drugstores were raided for dispensing birth control prescriptions. Yet the poor were without help.

The Connecticut Birth Control League decided to do something concrete about this injustice. In 1935 it opened up the first birth control clinic in Hartford, just a few blocks from the state legislature. Within the next four years, clinics were established in Stamford, Danbury, Westport, New Britain, Greenwich, Norwalk, Bridgeport, and Waterbury. At these clinics patients were seen only if they were married and already had at least one child.

The Waterbury clinic was one of the last to open but the first to be closed. Just six months after it began operation, on June 12, 1939, police raided the clinic, located in Chase Memorial Dispensary, and arrested doctors Roger B. Nelson and William A. Goodrich and nurse Clara L. McTernan. As evidence, the officers confiscated all the clinic's contraceptive supplies. The Waterbury raid may have been triggered by the pressure from a Jesuit priest, who admonished his congregation for permitting the law of God to be violated and who accused State Attorney William B. Fitzgerald of shirking his duty to uphold the law.

Although a trial date was set for the three Waterbury staffers, their lawyer, J. Warren Upson, filed a demurrer—a pleading which acknowledges that the facts are true but argues that the defendants are not guilty because the law was unconstitutional. Upson argued that the Connecticut law was an "unconstitutional interference with the individual liberty of the citizens of Connecticut." He stipulated:

> It is respectfully submitted that the decision as to whether or not a married couple shall have children is a decision peculiarly their own and that it is a natural right which is inherent in citizens of the State of Connecticut and has been preserved to them through the centuries. If the people of Connecticut have any natural rights whatsoever, one of them certainly is the right to decide whether or not they shall have children, and to this natural right, the right to use contraceptive devices is a natural concomitant. With the powers of the State ever encroaching upon the rights of its citizens, it is surely time for the Courts to fix a point beyond which the State cannot go.[16]

What is important about Upson's argument is that it was the first statement of a natural right associated with marriage and childbearing. Although he did not specifically mention a right to privacy, his position would be echoed in the decision in Estelle Griswold's case 26 years later.

In a move that surprised almost everyone, Judge Wynne sustained the demurrer in *State* v. *Nelson,* not on the grounds of a natural right, but on the grounds of a doctor's right to prescribe medicine. After noting that the state's objective "of morality and chastity" is "laudable," he asked, "Is a doctor to be prosecuted as a criminal for doing something that is sound and right in the best tenets and traditions of a high calling dedicated and devoted to health?" He answered his question in the negative and concluded that the "statute is defective on the broad constitutional grounds."[17]

The state of Connecticut appealed the ruling, and three of the five judges on the State Supreme Court of Errors rejected Judge Wynne's ruling. To them the question of birth control was "to be addressed to the General Assembly rather than to the Court."[18] Citing a previous Massachusetts case in which the United States Supreme Court had found no constitutional problem with an anti-birth-control statute, the Connecticut court decided that the law was constitutional.

The decision was unappealable because the Connecticut high court had merely overturned Wynne's sustaining of the demurrer and ordered a trial. The state later withdrew the charges and the three defendants were never prosecuted, leaving *State* v. *Nelson* on the books. That meant that when another case came before the Connecticut courts the controlling decision would be the Connecticut Supreme Court's decision that the birth-control law was constitutional.

In the meantime, the other clinics shut down. Planned Parenthood groups were relegated to their annual fight before the Connecticut legislature and to "border runs," in which poor women were transported to clinics in New York and Rhode Island where dispensing birth control was now permitted.

Then, in the late 1950s, the birth control advocates began to look for another legal route. The law firm they hired to come up with a strategy decided that what they needed were women whose lives would be threatened by a pregnancy. Attorney Catherine Roraback explains the climate in Connecticut in the late 1950s: "It was felt quite literally that the best we would probably accomplish in any form of litigation was an exception . . . written into the law that a doctor could prescribe contraceptives for a patient . . . where pregnancy would be a life-threatening situation."

Eventually two women showed up at the Yale offices of Dr. Buxton, a dedicated member of Connecticut Planned Parenthood, who wanted the law changed. One, 26 years old, had had three congenitally abnormal children who had died shortly after birth. Dr. Buxton felt that another pregnancy would be disturbing to her physical and mental health. To the courts, she would be known as Jane Poe. The case of the second woman, known as Jane Doe, was even stronger. Twenty-five years old, she had come near death after her last pregnancy. She had remained unconscious for two weeks and was left with partial paralysis and impaired speech. Dr. Buxton felt another pregnancy would kill her. Both women trusted Dr. Buxton completely and were willing to challenge the law.

The two cases were joined along with a separate complaint by Dr. Buxton arguing that the Connecticut law deprived him of his Fourteenth

Amendment due process rights. As expected, citing the *Nelson* precedent, the Connecticut courts ruled against them.

Roraback handled the case up through the Connecticut courts, but when the time came to argue it before the Supreme Court, Planned Parenthood began looking for another lawyer. As Roraback comments, "It was not considered that a woman could argue the case in front of the Supreme Court, so you had to find a man." The man they found was Fowler Harper, a law professor at Yale who specialized in the First Amendment; he based his argument on the doctor's First Amendment freedom of expression—to candidly advise his patients.

But the United States Supreme Court ultimately dismissed the case on the grounds that it did not present a real controversy. Justice Felix Frankfurter called it a dead letter issue and wrote that the high court "cannot be umpire to debates concerning harmless, empty shadows."[19] He reasoned that the "fear of enforcement" was "chimerical," or imaginary, because the provisions of the law had gone unenforced for so many years.

Justice William O. Douglas blasted his brethren with a fiery dissent, pointing out that owners of Connecticut drugstores selling contraceptives had been prosecuted and that for several years no public or private birth control clinic had dared operate in the state.* He wrote:

> What are these people—doctor and patients—to do? Flout the law and go to prison? Violate the law surreptitiously and hope they will not get caught? By today's decision we leave them no other alternatives. It is not the choice they need have under . . . our constitutional system. It is not the choice worthy of a civilized society. A sick wife, a concerned husband, a conscientious doctor seek a dignified, discreet, orderly answer to the critical problem confronting them. We should not turn them away and make them flout the law and get arrested to have their constitutional rights determined. . . . They are entitled to an answer to their predicament here and now.[20]

In a concurring opinion, Justice William Brennan, a Roman Catholic, pointed out the crux of the legal problem in Connecticut and, in doing so, virtually invited the next Supreme Court case. "The true controversy in this case," he concluded, "is over the opening of birth-control clinics on a large scale; it is that which the State has prevented in the past, not the use of contraceptives by isolated and individual married couples." He wrote that the constitutional questions could be decided "when, if ever, that real controversy flares up again."[21]

---

*Douglas' dissent in many ways also echoed the brief of ACLU attorney Melvin Wulf. Many constitutional scholars point to Wulf's brief as the first articulation of a right of privacy. However, as we have seen, this position had been spelled out earlier in Upson's demurrer in *State* v. *Nelson*.

Estelle Griswold and Lee Buxton were about to give the Court that chance; they were about to turn those "empty shadows" into a real controversy. On the same day that the Court announced the decision against Poe and Doe—June 20, 1961—Planned Parenthood announced that it would soon be opening a clinic on Trumbull Street in New Haven.

THE ARREST

Four-and-a-half months later, Justice Brennan's "flare up" was about to ignite. One man from West Haven who was more than willing to add fuel to that fire was James G. Morris, a night manager of a car rental agency near the building in which the clinic was to open. A devout Roman Catholic, Morris believed that "a Planned Parenthood Center is like a house of prostitution. . . . It is against the natural law which says marital relations are for procreation and not entertainment. It is against the state law. I think the state law is a good law and it should be enforced."[22] After he heard that the center was about to open, Morris wrote a letter to the county prosecutor and called the state police and the New Haven mayor. When nothing happened, he went to the local media. Whether the police and prosecutor would have done anything about the clinic without Morris's complaint is unclear,* but his vocal assault did bring the controversy into the public view. As one Planned Parenthood official bragged, Morris "fell right into our laps."[23]

Just three days after the clinic opened, detectives John Blazi and Harold Berg were knocking on the second-floor door of the Trumbull Street building. Estelle Griswold had an almost "Doctor Livingstone, I presume" greeting for the officers. She knew exactly who the two men were and what they wanted; just three years earlier, she had presented Blazi with an award on behalf of the New Haven Human Relations Council.

"It was one of the easiest types of investigations you could get involved in," Detective Berg remembers. Mrs. Griswold and Dr. Buxton gave the detectives a guided tour of the clinic, pointing out the condoms and vaginal foam they were dispensing. "It wasn't one of those investigations where you had to dig out the information. . . . It was sort of 'Here it is; Here we are; Take us in; We want to test this.' "[24]

While the "raid" was going on, several patients were receiving counsel about contraception. When they realized what was going on, one woman said, "We're going on a sit down strike until we get what we came for."[25] But the investigation was amicable and, having all the information they needed, the detectives left without making any arrests or confiscating any files.

---

*The detective who investigated suggests the police might have ignored the clinic. However, the assistant prosecutor insists that Morris had nothing to do with the case.

Morris was outraged that everyone hadn't been arrested right off the bat. He kept up his tirade as the local press over the next few days repeatedly asked the question, "Will the state uphold the law?" New Haven Circuit Court Prosecutor Julius Maretz and Sixth Circuit Court Judge J. Robert Lacey soon answered that question when they issued a warrant for the arrest of Griswold and Buxton. A deal was worked out whereby the two defendants appeared voluntarily at the police court on November 10 and were booked and charged under the law that made the use of any contraceptives illegal and under another provision of the Connecticut code which made it a crime to aid and abet anyone in the commission of a crime. Griswold and Buxton, who were not handcuffed or fingerprinted, were released on $100 bail each.

Planned Parenthood voluntarily closed the clinic. During the few days it had been open, 42 women had been examined and given contraceptives. More than 75 others had set up appointments. This, according to Morris, "did an awful lot of damage."[26]

Prior to the arrests, Roraback, who was once again involved and was concerned about the privacy of the patients, had struck a deal with the prosecutor. "We made an agreement that if he would agree not to just go and grab all the clinic's records," Planned Parenthood would provide him with the records of a few consenting patients. Roraback found three women who were willing to risk arrest: Joan B. Forsberg, the wife of a minister, later to become one herself; Marie Tindall, executive director of the Dixwell Community House, which served low-income families; and Rosemary Ann Stevens, a graduate student in the Yale School of Public Health.

Forsberg, who had participated in "border runs" for the league, had come to the clinic in its first days and obtained a prescription for birth control pills. As she left, she ran into Griswold and offered her help in any way. A couple of days later, she was, as a result of the agreement with the prosecutor, being asked to turn state's evidence against the center. Forsberg was perfectly willing. However, when the police officer interviewed her, he took the birth control pills as evidence. She immediately called Griswold and said, "Now, I don't mind going to jail for this case, but getting pregnant would be something else."[27] Griswold got Forsberg another prescription.

GIVING LIFE TO DEAD WORDS

The trial was set for November 24. Roraback had waived her clients' right to a jury trial because she feared that a jury might be sympathetic; she wanted to make sure that there was a conviction. On the opening day she filed a demurrer based on the First and Fourteenth Amendment rights of freedom of expression of the doctors and social workers in the clinic. But Judge Lacey rejected the plea. When the trial was resumed on January 2, it went swiftly, with the three women testifying against Griswold and Buxton and two obstetricians testifying for them. It didn't take Lacey long to conclude that "the evidence was clear" and that the two defendants were guilty. They were each fined $100.

"This time," Griswold said after the trial, "I don't see how Mr. Justice Frankfurter can call the law dead words."[28] (Curiously enough, by the time that the Supreme Court heard the case, March 1965, Justice Frankfurter had retired in ill health and had been replaced by Byron White.)

Attorneys Roraback and Harper immediately began the long process of appeal; not surprisingly, the Connecticut courts upheld the convictions. As the lawyers prepared their briefs for the Supreme Court, they relied on the First and Fourteenth Amendments. They argued that the Connecticut statute deprived doctors, such as Buxton, and clinic operators, such as Griswold, of the right to life, liberty, and property without due process of law. In addition, they said, under the due process clause, laws cannot be "arbitrary and capricious"; they must have a reasonable relationship to the legislative purpose. The purpose of this law was for "public morality" and to discourage extramarital relations. Prohibiting the use of birth control by married couples, in Roraback and Harper's view, was not directly tied to public morality and was therefore arbitrary, capricious, and unconstitutional. It also violated a doctor's and counselor's First Amendment right of free speech—their right to counsel their patients.

While the legal strategy was being worked out, Harper called Roraback, pointing out a *New York University Law Review* article on the Ninth and Tenth Amendments and the right of privacy. "I said," Roraback remembers, "I really didn't think it was relevant. . . . But Fowler said, 'I think we ought to have it in there.'" So they included in the brief a section which argued that the Connecticut law was an unwarranted invasion of privacy.

> In our constitutional system, the principle of safeguarding the private sector of the citizen's life has always been a vital element. The Constitution nowhere refers to a right of privacy in express terms. But various provisions of the Constitution embody separate aspects of it. And the demands of modern life require that the composite of these specific protections be accorded the status of a recognized constitutional right.[29]

Planned Parenthood was arguing that although there was no *specific* mention of privacy in the Constitution, there *ought* to be. Furthermore, it argued that one could look at the First Amendment (freedom of expression and association), the Third Amendment (no quartering of soldiers in times of peace), the Fourth Amendment (no unreasonable search and seizure), and the Ninth Amendment ("the enumeration in the Constitution, of certain rights, shall not be construed to deny or disparage others retained by the people")—together with the "liberty" guaranteed by the Fourteenth Amendment—and come up with a right of privacy.

The privacy issue came to play a larger role in the legal strategy, to be emphasized over the argument based on the First Amendment. Part of the reason may be that when Fowler Harper died in 1963, Professor Thomas I. Emerson of Yale helped finish the briefs and then argued the case before the Supreme Court. As Emerson recalls, "Fowler Harper was more sanguine about the progress under the First Amendment than I was." He said he did not think the Court would decide the case on a doctor's right to give medical advice. He adds, "[What is involved] really is a right to keep the government out of a certain zone of activity, particularly dealing with sexual matters and intimacy of the home."[30]

Roraback stresses that the idea was not to "establish a right of privacy" but to "knock out the Connecticut birth control statute. . . . It was a bad statute." In working through litigation strategy, she explains, "you have a very concrete case with people and concerns, and what you're trying to do is to accomplish an immediate goal for those people. . . . You're not thinking of the long-term strategy of trying to establish the right of people to live their lives."

The brief for the state of Connecticut argued that the "decision of the General Assembly of Connecticut that the use of contraceptives should be banned is a proper exercise of the police power of the state."[31] In other words, it was one of those decisions properly left to the state, not to a court. The state also argued that the law did not infringe upon Buxton's right to practice medicine, because the practice of medicine is the "treatment, cure, and/or prevention of disease" and the women who testified were in perfect health. In the state's view, Planned Parenthood was not practicing medicine; it was dispensing contraceptives. Reasoning along these same lines, the state said that Buxton and Griswold's free speech had not been violated, because dispensing birth control was not speech but action.

As to the privacy issue, the state flatly denied that anyone's privacy had been violated, inasmuch as the three women who testified had done so voluntarily.

THE COURT DECIDES

On June 7, 1965, Justice William O. Douglas, who had written the angry dissent in *Poe,* had the privilege of turning his minority opinion into a majority when the Court, in a 7-to-2 vote, decided that the Connecticut law was unconstitutional.

Beginning with the disclaimer that the Supreme Court does "not sit as a super-legislature," Douglas went on to say that the marital relations of husband and wife were basic rights, not mentioned in the Constitution but nevertheless protected by it. Accepting the Planned Parenthood arguments, Douglas pointed to specific amendments that imply a right to privacy. He said that the "First Amendment has a penumbra where privacy is protected from governmental intrusion."[32] He reasoned that other sections of the Bill of Rights "have penumbras, formed by emanations from those guarantees that help give them life and substance. . . . Various guarantees create zones of privacy. . . . The present case . . . concerns a relationship lying within the zone of privacy created by several fundamental constitutional guarantees."[33]

It is important to note that the zone of privacy was only mentioned in terms of *married* people. As Douglas concluded:

> We deal with a right of privacy older than the Bill of Rights—older than our political parties, older than our school system. Marriage is a coming together for better or worse, hopefully enduring, and intimate to the degree of being sacred. It is an association that promotes a way of life, not causes; a harmony in living, not political faiths; a bilateral loyalty, not commercial or social projects. Yet it is an association for as noble a purpose as any involved in our prior decisions.[34]

Justice Goldberg wrote a concurring opinion in which he was joined by Chief Justice Warren and Justice Brennan. He began by asserting that he rejected the idea that the Fourteenth Amendment incorporates the Bill of Rights but believed that the "concept of liberty" protects certain fundamental rights, which are not restricted to the rights spelled out in the Bill of Rights. To Goldberg, marital privacy, though not mentioned in the Constitution, was one of those fundamental rights. He based his judgment on the fact that "the language and history of the Ninth Amendment reveal that the Framers of the Constitution believed that there are additional fundamental rights, protected from governmental infringement, which exist alongside those fundamental rights specifically mentioned in the first eight constitutional amendments."[35]

Justice Goldberg noted that the Court, in a long series of cases, had insisted that where fundamental liberties are at stake, the state must have a compelling reason for abridging those liberties. In his view the Connecticut justification of discouraging extramarital relations did not meet that test.

Justice Harlan also wrote a separate concurrence, in which he relied on the due process clause of the Fourteenth Amendment. He said that the question was whether the law "violates basic values 'implicit in the concept of ordered liberty.' " Differing from Douglas, Harlan added that the decision need not depend on "radiations" from the Bill of Rights. "The Due Process Clause of the Fourteenth Amendment stands, in my opinion, on its own bottom."[36]

Although he agreed with the majority, Justice White also wrote his own concurring opinion, in which he relied on earlier decisions of the court which "affirm that there is a 'realm of family life which the state cannot enter' without substantial justification. . . . Surely the right invoked in this case, to be free of regulation of the intimacies of the marriage relationship" came within that realm. He said that the rationale of discouraging illicit sexual relations was not sufficient state justification for the "sweeping scope of the statute," and concluded that the statute "deprives [married] persons of liberty without due process of law."[37]

Justices Stewart and Black were the lone dissenters in the case. Each wrote a separate dissenting opinion in which the other joined. Justice Black admitted that the "law is every bit as offensive to me as it is to my Brethren," but reasoned that its "evil qualities" did not make it "unconstitutional." He continued: "I like my privacy as well as the next one, but I am nevertheless compelled to admit that government has a right to invade it unless prohibited by some specific constitutional provision." He said that it was not up to judges to decide what laws are unwise or unnecessary; that was the job of the legislatures.

Black chided his colleagues for reverting to the "substantive due process" rationale which had been used by the Court to strike down economic legislation in the late nineteenth and early twentieth century (see Chapters 2 and 3). "That formula . . . is no less dangerous when used to enforce this Court's view about personal rights than those about economic rights."[38] Thus, finding no constitutional justification to do otherwise, Black said he would uphold the law.

Justice Stewart began by declaring the Connecticut statute "an uncommonly silly law," but added that the Court was not asked whether the law was "unwise, or even asinine. We are asked to hold that it violates the United States Constitution." He said he could find no general rights of privacy in the Bill of Rights or in any other part of the Constitution. "[T]o say that the Ninth Amendment," he wrote "has anything to do with this case is to turn somersaults with history." He concluded that it was the Court's duty to "subordinate our own personal views, our own ideas of what legislation is wise and what is not." If the people of Connecticut thought the law unwise, they should persuade the legislature "to take this law off the books."[39]

Two days later, the *New York Times* published an editorial rebuke to Justices Black and Stewart:

> A reasonable and convincing argument can be made—and was made by the dissenters—that this infringement on personal freedom represented in the laws of Connecticut and many other states should have been corrected by the legislatures. But the fact is that it was not corrected. To what forum but the Supreme Court could the people then repair, after years of frustration, for relief from bigotry and enslavement?[40]

Three months later, on September 20, 1965, Estelle Griswold and Lee Buxton reopened their birth control clinic in New Haven.

GRISWOLD'S LEGACY: JANE ROE

The decision in *Griswold* meant much more than the reopening of the clinic in Hartford. It established a right of privacy for married couples. Seven years later, in *Eisenstadt* v. *Baird*, the Court extended that right to single persons. William Baird was a 40-year-old former medical student who traveled around the Northeast giving birth control advice to the poor. He was convicted in Massachusetts for displaying contraceptives at a lecture at Boston University and for giving a female student some vaginal foam. His case reached the Supreme Court in 1972, and Justice Brennan wrote the opinion for the majority:

> The marital couple is not an independent entity with a mind and heart of its own, but an association of two individuals each with separate intellectual and emotional makeup. If the right of privacy means anything, it is the right of the *individual,* married or single, to be free from unwarranted governmental intrusion into matters so fundamentally affecting a person as the decision whether to bear or beget a child.[41]

But *Griswold*'s major impact came the following year in *Roe* v. *Wade.* Norma McCorvey was a 25-year-old unmarried woman who had no intention of changing the Constitution; all she wanted was a legal abortion in Texas. In August 1969, McCorvey had been working in a small town in Georgia as a ticket seller for a freak-animal side show in a traveling circus. She describes herself as "an army brat" with only a ninth-grade education who was down on her luck and trying to make ends meet. She tells the graphic story of how one night on her way back to her motel room, three men and two women attacked and raped her, leaving her lying on a country road. She finally made it back to her motel room and collapsed, but she says she was afraid to report the attack to the police. "I just thought, this is it. I'm going home back to Texas. I pawned a portable radio and an electric shaver to buy a ticket. I had no money even to eat. I walked to the bus station. . . . I finally got back to Texas and called a friend who nursed me back to the point where I could get a job."[42]

But a short time after McCorvey got back, she began feeling ill. Since she had had a child by a previous marriage, she suspected that she was pregnant and confirmed her suspicion with a visit to a clinic. She then went to the doctor who had delivered her daughter and said she wanted to have an abortion. "He said that it was against the law in Texas and that I'd have to go to New York or California or carry the baby to term." McCorvey remembers she was outraged. She said she would have the baby "but I won't keep it. I would hate it." She told the doctor she would give the baby up for adoption.

Her doctor gave her the name of an attorney who handled adoptions, but when she went to see him he asked her a number of insinuating questions about the rape. McCorvey walked out of his office. She then decided to look for a doctor who would perform an abortion; she finally found one who told her the price was $650. When she told him she didn't have that much money, he said he couldn't help her.

"I don't know if I was really touchy at the time, but it seemed that everybody I went to for help didn't have the time. . . . I felt that life had dealt me a dirty deal. I wasn't getting any aces," she now puts it. About that time, her luck changed; she met an attorney named Linda Coffee. Coffee sent her to another lawyer, Henry McCloskey, Jr., who specialized in arranging adoptions. Coffee also introduced her to Sarah Weddington, a 25-year-old graduate of the University of Texas Law School, who wanted to help McCorvey fight the Texas abortion law.

McCorvey, Coffee, and Weddington first met together at Columbo's Pizza on Mockingbird Lane in Dallas. After a few beers, Weddington turned to McCorvey and said, "Well don't you think its aggravating that you cannot have total control of your body?" McCorvey answered, "Yea, I think it's damn rude." According to McCorvey, Weddington then said, "Let's take it to the Supreme Court." "And I said, 'Why don't we?' Little did I know that she was terribly serious. I never realized. When she said Supreme Court, the only supreme court I'd ever heard of was the Federal Building in Dallas. I thought, well, she's going to go up there and argue with those people."

McCorvey says that in that first and in several subsequent conversations, Weddington questioned her closely to make sure that she was willing to go all the way with a suit. "I said, 'Damn right. It's time women should have the right to do whatever they want with their bodies.'" McCorvey only had one stipulation: she wanted to be anonymous. She now explains, "My child was very young at the time, and I didn't want her to be subject to public ridicule. I did not want my name to be exploited all over the newspapers." She also didn't want her family to know. (Her mother was a Roman Catholic and her father a Jehovah's Witness, but she says it wasn't their religious affiliations that made her want anonymity. She just knew that they would never understand.) As a result, for the purposes of the lawsuit, she was known as Jane Roe. For more than a decade no one but her lawyers knew that Jane Roe was Norma McCorvey.

Weddington and Coffee (who later dropped out of the suit) first filed a complaint against Dallas District Attorney Henry Wade, whose job it was to enforce the abortion laws.* The suit specifically named McCorvey (as Roe) but was also a class action suit for all other women—past, pres-

*Henry Wade is also remembered for his role as prosecutor of Lee Harvey Oswald for the assassination of President Kennedy.

ent, and future—in the state of Texas seeking an abortion. Norma McCorvey's complaint charged that the Texas law violated a woman's right to decide whether or not to bear children and invaded the right of privacy (protected by the First, Fourth, Fifth, Ninth, and Fourteenth Amendments) in the doctor-patient relationship. For the next few months, while the case was making its way through the courts, McCorvey "went underground," staying in "flophouses for hippies" and with friends. From time to time she would contact Weddington to find out what was happening with the case.

The gestation period of a baby is shorter than that of a constitutional issue. In June 1970 McCorvey gave birth to a daughter. She explains that the hospital made a mistake and initially brought the baby to her. Another nurse then came in and took the baby away from her. "I just got out of that bed like you wouldn't believe, and I grabbed her and I said 'Hey, wait a minute, that's my kid.' " McCorvey says she was then sedated and never saw the child again. Perhaps it was this experience which made her question the suit at one point. "I got to thinking, is it true what people are saying that abortion is killing babies? Is it true? Then I thought about all these poor children who I had personally seen parked in front of just dives—hungry, dirty, neglected, and abused. Their families were inside boozing it up. Why should these children be subject to this kind of abuse? If these people don't want these children why do they have them? And I thought I did the right thing. Because there for a long time I had my doubts. . . . If it hadn't been for Sarah's support, I don't know where I would have been."

Since McCorvey never went to any of the court proceedings, she only knew of the case through Weddington and the newspapers. Finally one day, Weddington came to her to explain that she was going to Washington to argue the case before the Supreme Court. "I said, 'What's there to argue about? It happened.' And she explained to me in minute detail exactly how it would happen and I said, 'God, the Supreme Court of the United States. My God, all those people are so important. They don't have time to listen to some little old Texas girl who got in trouble.' And she said, 'You are not understanding what I'm telling you. I have a good feeling that we're going to win this case.' "

ORAL ARGUMENTS

On December 13, 1971, Sarah Weddington, only four years out of law school, made her first appearance before the Supreme Court. The Texas abortion law was defended by Jay Floyd, an assistant attorney general.

Weddington told the Court that "pregnancy to a woman can completely disrupt her life." She pointed out that in the state of Texas many schools and colleges required a woman to quit if she was pregnant; women were often forced to leave their jobs in the early part of their pregnancies, and the state provided no unemployment compensation or welfare for them. She asserted:

> So, a pregnancy to a woman is perhaps one of the most determinative aspects of her life. It disrupts her education. It disrupts her employment. And it often disrupts her family life. And we feel that, because of the impact on women, this certainly—in as far as there are any rights which are fundamental—is a matter which is of such fundamental and basic concern to the woman involved that she should be allowed to make the choice as to whether to continue or terminate her pregnancy.[43]

As to the rights of the unborn child, Weddington said, "The Constitution, as I read it . . . attaches protection to the person at the time of birth. These persons born are citizens. . . . The Constitution, as I see it, gives protection to people after birth."

Jay Floyd argued that the case was moot (no longer a controversy) because Roe was no longer pregnant. She had had the child. However, one of the justices reminded him that it was a class-action suit: "Surely, you would—I suppose we could almost take judicial notice of the fact that there are, at any given time, unmarried pregnant females in the State of Texas."

Floyd then moved on to the crux of the case. He asserted that "there is life from the moment of impregnation." Countering Weddington's argument that women should have control of their bodies, Floyd said, "As far as freedom over one's body is concerned, this is not absolute." He cited as examples laws that prohibit the use of illicit drugs, indecent exposure, and adultery.

In his summation Floyd said, "We think these matters are matters of policy which can be properly addressed by the State legislature. We think that considerations should be given to the unborn, and in some instances, a consideration should be given to the father, if he would be objective to abortion."

Because of the heightened emotions surrounding this case (48 *amicus curiae* briefs were filed), the Court called for reargument in October 1972. One significant issue for the Court was the purpose of the 1854 Texas statute prohibiting abortion. During the second oral argument, Weddington contended that the Texas statute—like the anti-abortion laws of many other states—had been enacted to protect women from crude and life-threatening back-street abortions. During the nineteenth century, an abortion meant death for at least 50 percent of the women who underwent them. The position of the abortion rights advocates was that the anti-abortion statutes were *not* passed to protect the fetus. One fact that supported this contention was that it was not a crime in Texas for a woman to perform an abortion on herself. In addition, doctors prosecuted for performing abortions were only charged with murder if the *woman* died. Weddington's briefs and arguments pointed out that since the 1850s abortion had become safer even than childbearing. Thus the purpose of the Texas statute was no longer valid. Weddington said:

> We are not here to advocate abortion. We do not ask the Court to rule that abortion is good, or desirable in any particular situation. We are here to advocate that the decision as to whether or not a particular woman will continue to carry or will terminate her pregnancy is a decision that should be made by that individual; that, in fact, she has a constitutional right to make that decision for herself; and that the State has shown no [compelling] interest in interfering with that decision.

For the state of Texas Assistant Attorney General Robert C. Flowers asserted again that a fetus was a person from the moment of conception. Flowers said, "If we declare, as the appellees in this case have asked the Court to declare, that an embryo or a fetus is a mass of protoplasm similar to a tumor, then of course the State has no compelling interest whatsoever." However, Flowers argued that the unborn child was a person and was therefore entitled to constitutional protection: the state had a compelling interest to protect that life.

Underlying these two divergent views was the Fourteenth Amendment, which defined a citizen as a person *born* in the United States. So the Supreme Court would have to decide whether an unborn fetus was a person, entitled to constitutional protection, and whether the state of Texas could legislate to protect it.

THE COURT DECIDES

The Supreme Court's decision in *Roe* came down on January 22, 1973, the same day that former President Lyndon Johnson died. Writing for the 7-to-2 majority, Justice Harry Blackmun ruled first on the mootness issue: the case was not moot. "[T]he normal 266-day human gestation period is so short that the pregnancy will come to term before the usual appellate process is complete. If that termination makes a case moot, pregnancy litigation seldom will survive much beyond the trial state, and appellate review will be effectively denied."[44] Blackmun then ruled that the Texas statute "sweeps too broadly" and was unconstitutional.* The

---

*Justice Stewart, who dissented in *Griswold,* voted with the majority in *Roe.* He explained to a class at Columbia University in 1983 that he was a firm believer in stare decisis, the principle of adhering to settled cases. Thus, as a right of privacy had been established by a majority of the Court, it was an established legal principle which he would follow.

Court had decided that "the word 'person' as used in the Fourteenth Amendment, does not include the unborn." Although there was no mention of "penumbras" of amendments, the Court did root its decision in the right of privacy established in *Griswold:*

> The Constitution does not explicitly mention any right of privacy. In a line of decisions, however . . . the Court has recognized that a right of personal privacy, or a guarantee of certain areas or zones of privacy, does exist under the Constitution. . . . This right of privacy, whether it be founded in the Fourteenth Amendment's concept of personal liberty and restrictions upon state action, as we feel it is, or . . . in the Ninth Amendment's reservation of rights to the people, is broad enough to encompass a woman's decision whether or not to terminate her pregnancy.[45]

However, Blackmun said the right of privacy was not absolute and added a restriction: "[T]his right is not unqualified and must be considered against important state interests in regulation."[46] Thus all abortions are not legal. The Court came up with a formula based on a division of pregnancy into trimesters. In the first three months of pregnancy, the right of privacy prevails and the abortion decision is up to the woman and her doctor. However, in the second trimester states could regulate abortions in ways related to maternal health. In other words, they could require that abortions be performed under certain conditions. During the last stage of pregnancy, when the fetus was viable (could live on its own outside the mother's womb), state laws could prohibit abortion—except under circumstances in which the life or health of the mother was in danger.

Norma McCorvey first heard of the Court's decision when her roommate pointed it out in the newspaper. She had never told her friend of her involvement in the case. But when McCorvey began crying, her roommate looked at the paper and said, "Don't tell me you knew LBJ?" McCorvey said, "No, I'm Jane Roe." Two days later Sarah Weddington called. She said, "How does it make you feel to know that women are going to be able to go to a clinic and get a legal abortion?" McCorvey answered, "It makes me feel like I'm on the top of Mount Everest."

Reaction to the decision was intense. There was jubilation among women's rights and birth-control organizations. Catholic organizations assailed the decision. John Cardinal Krol of Philadelphia called the decision "an unspeakable tragedy for this nation."[47]

How far this right of privacy may extend has not yet been determined by the Court. There was a time when the Court refused to rule on the birth control issue because it was not considered a real controversy and a time when the Court would not have interfered with a state's right to ban abortions. So far the Supreme Court has not tackled other issues associated with the right of privacy—such as the right to die. Does privacy mean that the state cannot interfere with a doctor and a family's decision to turn off a respirator? Whose privacy is involved when a severely deformed infant is kept alive by extraordinary or so-called heroic medicine? the baby's? the parents? Should the state have an interest in preserving that life? What about suicide? So far these excruciating questions have not been considered by the high court. Perhaps they are not yet "ripe" for judicial decision. Whatever a future Court may decide, modern technology and "medical miracles" will undoubtedly make its deliberations over the right to live and the right to die even more agonizing.

Allan Bakke being award the degree of Doctor of Medicine, 1981. *AP/Wide World Photos*

Allan Bakke wanted to be a doctor more than anything else. But, despite his exemplary credentials, he was turned down everywhere he applied. In the instance of the University of California at Davis, Bakke felt he had been discriminated against because he was white. Davis held 16 spaces for minority candidates. When Bakke's case reached the Supreme Court, the complicated opinion established that colleges could consider race in applications but that quotas were unconstitutional.

BAKKE AND THE EQUAL PROTECTION CLAUSE
Affirmative Action vs. Reverse Discrimination

> *Our Constitution is color-blind, and neither knows nor tolerates classes among citizens. In respect of civil rights, all citizens are equal before the law. The humblest is the peer of the most powerful. The law regards man as man, and takes no account of his surroundings or of his color when his civil rights as guaranteed by the supreme law of the land are involved.*
>
> **Justice John Marshall Harlan,**
> dissenting in *Plessy* v. *Fergusson*[1]

> *I believe that admissions quotas based on race are illegal. For this reason I am inquiring of friends ... about the possibility of formally challenging these quotas through the courts. My main reason ... would be to secure admission for myself—I consider the goal worth fighting for in every legal and ethical way.*
>
> **Allan Bakke** to University of California, Davis, Dean of Admissions George Lowrey

John Tupper had an almost impossible dream that became a constitutional nightmare. A medical professor at the University of Michigan, he had been recruited in 1965 by the University of California to build a medical school at the Davis campus in 4 years. "The standard lead time to build a medical school is 6 to 10 years. We did it in 32 months,"[2] he recalls with a mixture of pride and disbelief. Davis's first class of 48 students was admitted for the fall of 1968.

But the pressures on Dr. Tupper did not end with the school's opening. Despite the University of California's initial assurances that there would be no money problems, there were. Moreover, admissions presented several problems. "The national outcry was for more manpower. . . . We were also concerned with minorities." The minority enrollment in the first two classes at the Davis medical school was low—only 14 Asian-Americans, 2 blacks, and 1 Chicano, or about 3 percent of each class. In 1969, the admissions committee set up a framework to include more minority students. The goal was that 8 out of 50 new students be drawn from minority groups. Later, in the spring of 1971, Dr. Tupper met with minority community leaders at Mr. D's (now Paradise Lounge), a black restaurant on Stockton Boulevard in Sacramento. The only white customers in the restaurant, Dr. Tupper and the other representatives of the medical school listened as one by one spokesmen for minorities challenged the school's record of low Hispanic and black representation.

Tupper rose to the challenge. "I make all of you this promise—next fall we'll have 100 [new] students in the medical school, and I guarantee you that we'll have 16 places for the disadvantaged." According to Tupper, he wasn't instituting "a quota, but a guarantee." It seemed a logical step to double the number of places held for minorities when the class size as a whole was being doubled. Yet that impulsive, well-intentioned promise would trigger one of the most explosive constitutional confrontations since *Brown* v. *Board of Education of Topeka*.[3] "Nobody in their wildest dreams," Dr. Tupper reflects, "thought little old U. C. Davis would be the site of that Supreme Court battle."

ALLAN BAKKE

No one ever doubted that Allan Paul Bakke, 32, would make a fine physician. A mechanical engineer, who had graduated from the University of Minnesota with honors, Bakke had first become interested in medicine during his stint as a marine in Vietnam, where he commanded an antiaircraft missile unit. That determination grew stronger after his discharge in September 1967. He began working at NASA's Ames Research Center in Moffet Field, California, where he had the opportunity to talk with medical teams researching the effects of space and radiation on astronauts.

Bakke had always been dedicated to hard work. Since his mother was a teacher and his father a mailman, he had had to put himself through college by serving in the Naval Reserve Officers Training Corps. Now, while working full-time with NASA, Bakke completed his master's degree in engineering at Stanford and then began taking the biology and chemistry courses that were prerequisites for medical school. At the same time, he worked nights as a volunteer in the emergency room of the El Camino Hospital in Mountain View, California. Bakke's determination to be a doctor became almost an obsession. As one admissions official at Davis later described him: "Bakke was a man who felt as strongly as anyone I've ever known about his potential as a healer of the sick and as a benefactor of the community. . . . He struck me as a character out of a Bergman film—somewhat humorless, perfectly straightforward, zealous in his approach. . . . He was an extremely impressive man."[4]

By the fall of 1972 Bakke had completed the necessary requirements for admission, and he began applying to 11 medical schools including his alma maters, the University of Minnesota and Stanford University, and the University of California at Davis.

THE DAVIS ADMISSIONS PROGRAM

Davis, one of the nine campuses of the excellent University of California system, is world famous for its agricultural school, which has contributed much to California's economic bounty. A visitor today is impressed with the campus's lush, manicured lawns, tree-lined bicycle paths, and picturesque canals. The sparkling-white medical building, like the new law school, signals Davis's transformation from an old "ag" school into an extensive educational plant. At the time Allan Bakke applied, however, the medical school looked more like an army encampment, with temporary buildings and construction ditches.

The class of medical students admitted to Davis in the fall of 1972 was the second class of 100. In accordance with Dr. Tupper's pledge, 16 places in that class had been reserved for "disadvantaged" students. The Davis admissions process had been in essence a two-tier system ever since the original setting aside of 8 places for minorities in 1969. Applicants could request to be considered under a special admissions process for disadvantaged students. That request was not automatically honored; applicants were screened by a special committee to determine whether they were truly disadvantaged. As Dr. George Lowrey, who was then director of admissions, later explained, a black student whose father was a physician and who had gone through college with little difficulty would not be considered under the special admissions program. Nor was the program represented as being solely for minorities. Nonetheless, the reality was that only minority students were considered for those 16 places, under the theory that they were the most "disadvantaged of the disadvantaged."

Under the regular admissions program, any applicant with a grade-point average of 2.5 (C+/B−) or below was automatically rejected. Applicants with a GPA above 2.5 were considered for an interview, a necessary step for admission at Davis. Of the 2,464 applicants for the 1973–1974 year—the year for which Bakke first applied—38 percent were interviewed. Each of these candidates was given a benchmark score, determined on the basis of grade-point average, Medical College Admissions Test (MCAT) scores, and the interview. For this particular year, a benchmark score of 470 meant the applicant was given one of the 84 seats in the regular admissions program.

Candidates for special admissions who had grade-point averages under 2.5 were not automatically rejected; those who showed promise were interviewed by members of the special committee. In the end, 16 candidates were recommended to the regular committee. Although these recommendations were not automatically accepted by the committee, they were rarely turned down. As compared to the regular admissions, those admitted under the special program had significantly lower statistics. In 1973, the former group had averaged a B+/A−, the latter group a C+/B−. The MCAT scores of the two groups were also significantly different.[5]

THE LONG ROAD TO AFFIRMATIVE ACTION

The Davis medical school was not alone in setting up a program designed to recruit or accept more minority students. Most universities across the country had established some sort of mechanism for increasing minority enrollments. These programs came out of the realization that under traditional admissions procedures, few members of minority groups would be admitted or even apply. The historical reasons for this situation were particularly evident in the case of blacks. As Archibald Cox (who represented the University of California in the *Bakke* case) wrote in a paper presented in 1979:

> The first and most obvious truth is to recall that after the Civil War and the abolition of slavery, black people suffered still another century of systematic discrimination, partly private and partly governmental. The result was two Americas. Socially and economically, black communities were isolated and disadvantaged. All but a very few extraordinary individuals were excluded from the mainstream of opportunity in American life. In 1968 only 2 percent of the medical doctors in the United States were blacks. There were only 216 black medical students who were attending schools other than the all-black Howard and Meharry. One saw scarcely a black face in the ranks of business executives. The skilled trades in the building and construction industry and in manufacturing establishments were closed to blacks.[6]

In 1896, in the case of *Plessy* v. *Ferguson,* the Supreme Court had sanctioned the standard of "separate but equal." This meant that segregation in schools, in public accommodations, and on public transportation was legally permissible as long as there were facilities for blacks. For over 50 years, the courts chose not to look very closely at the question of whether these segregated facilities were, in fact, "equal."

This situation changed with the Supreme Court's monumental 1954 ruling in *Brown* v. *Board of Education of Topeka.* The Court unanimously held that separate was *not* equal, that under the equal protection clause of the Fourteenth Amendment, it was unconstitutional to segregate schoolchildren because of race. The equal protection clause—"Nor shall any state . . . deny to any person within its jurisdiction the equal protection of the law"—had in fact been adopted after the Civil War, in 1868 to protect blacks from discrimination, but it had virtually gone unenforced for that purpose for nearly a century. Chief Justice Earl Warren, speaking for the Court, rejected the notion that as segregated schools had existed at the time the Fourteenth Amendment was passed, they were not meant to be covered by it. He wrote, "[W]e cannot turn the clock back to 1868. . . . We must consider public education in light . . . of its present place in American life." He recognized that "education is perhaps the most important function of state and local governments" and that "it is doubtful that any child may reasonably be expected to succeed in life if he is denied the opportunity of an education." Thus, he concluded, "Such an opportunity, where the state has undertaken to provide it, is a right which must be made available to all on equal terms."

The central question was this: "Does segregation of children in public schools solely on the basis of race, even though the physical facilities and other 'tangible' factors may be equal, deprive the children of the minority group of equal educational opportunities?" The Court's response: "We believe that it does."[7]

The *Brown* decision was the beginning of a growing effort to insure that blacks were not deprived of their civil rights and, especially, to curb governmentally sanctioned discrimination. A milestone in this effort came 10 years later, when President Lyndon Johnson pushed the Civil Rights Act of 1964 through the Congress. Among the many provisions of the act was Title VI, which prohibited discrimination on the basis of race, color, or national origin in the administration of "any program or activity receiving federal financial assistance."[8]

By the late 1960s, there was a recognition of the fact that "even if all further hostile discrimination were instantly ceased, the momentum of the past—the attitudes, the isolation, and the built-in facially nondiscriminatory rules—would continue to exclude blacks and other minorities from the mainstream of opportunity in American life until sometime in the distant future."[9] The result was what has been termed "affirmative action," or efforts by employers, educational institutions, and government to institute hiring and admissions programs that would help minorities and women compete. In universities, affirmative action meant actively recruiting minorities and setting up special admissions criteria which were not limited to purely numerical measures. The rationale for this was that members of minority groups, having been denied opportunities, could not be expected to be measured in the same way as others, who had not been denied these opportunities. As Secretary of Health, Education and Welfare Joseph A. Califano, Jr., posed the problem in a March 1977 interview in the *New York Times:* "How am I, as Secretary of HEW, ever going to find first-class black doctors, first-class black scientists, first-class women scientists, if these people don't have a chance to get into the best places [universities] in the country?"[10]

It was this problem that the Davis special admissions policy and other affirmative action programs attempted to address. Some programs, like Davis's, set up specific numerical goals. Others, such as the one at Harvard College, were not specific as to percentages or numbers, but merely recognized that diversity in the student body was something to be desired; just as admissions committees might give "extra points" to a star quarterback or a violinist or a person from a small town in Nebraska, they might also count minority status as a "plus."

BAKKE APPLIES TO DAVIS

Ironically, if Allan Bakke's mother-in-law had not been gravely ill in 1972, requiring Bakke and his wife to spend time in Iowa taking care of her, he might have been admitted to Davis without suing. His benchmark score of 468 was just shy of automatic admission, 470. But Bakke did not complete all the necessary paperwork until January of 1973 and was not scheduled for the mandatory interview until late March, by which time, under the Davis "rolling admissions policy," many of the places had already been filled. Professor Allan Sindler, of the University of California Law School, Berkeley, discusses the situation in his seminal volume, *Bakke, DeFunis, and Minority Admissions:*

> Had Bakke been able to complete his application and interview well before the close of 1972, as he had intended to, he might have been admitted on the basis of his benchmark score of 468, and there would have been no Bakke case or controversy. . . . Much earlier in that academic year virtually automatic admission was accorded applicants with a benchmark rating of 470 and promising candidates with somewhat lower scores had been accepted. By late March and April, though, over three-quarters of the total acceptances already had been extended, and the benchmark minimum of 470 was strictly enforced.[11]

Bakke was turned down at all 11 schools to which he applied. Some have speculated that his age, by then 33, was a large factor in the rejections. Indeed, the report by Dr. Theodore West, his interviewer at Davis, described Bakke as "a well-qualified candidate . . . whose main handicap is the unavoidable fact that he is now 33 years of age." Yet, despite the age factor, Dr. West had recommended Bakke as "a very desirable applicant to this medical school."[12]

Part of Allan Bakke's character was his relentless perseverance. After receiving his form-letter rejection from Davis, he wrote to Dr. Lowrey, the director of admissions, asking about any future possibility of becoming a medical student there. He suggested that his application be put on a standby status or that he be allowed to register for courses as a special student until a vacancy opened. "I realize there is no assurance that such a vacancy will develop, but I desperately want to take *any* path to a medical education. . . . Dr. Lowrey, thank you for taking the time to consider this letter. I feel certain that if anyone can help me, you can. I pray that you will."[13]

When a month had gone by without a response, Bakke wrote Dr. Lowrey once again. This time he took a different tack:

> I feel compelled to pursue a further course of action. . . . Applicants chosen to be our doctors should be those presenting the best qualifications, both academic and personal. . . . I am convinced a significant fraction . . . is judged by a separate criterion. I am referring to quotas, open or covert, for racial minorities. . . . I realize that the rationale for these quotas is that they attempt to atone for past discrimination. But instituting a new racial bias, in favor of minorities is not a just solution.
>
> In fact, I believe that admissions quotas based on race are illegal. For this reason I am inquiring of friends . . . about the possibility of formally challenging these quotas through the courts. My main reason . . . would be to secure admission for myself—I consider the goal worth fighting for in every legal or ethical way.[14]

One can speculate as to whether that letter helped or hurt Bakke's chances for admission. As a firm believer in the special admissions policy, Dr. Lowrey could not have been too pleased to see it attacked by an applicant. Yet that letter prompted a move that may have helped lead to Bakke's drive to the Supreme Court: Lowrey turned the letter over to a young admissions assistant, Peter Storandt. Storandt was deeply impressed when he read Bakke's file. Furthermore, he shared some of Bakke's views about the special admissions policy. Although he believed in affirmative action, he had his reservations about the program: "We had a program with a supportable aim, but . . . it had the effect of bringing hardships on other kinds of candidates."[15]

Storandt believed that Davis's policy actually put a lid on minority applicants, because those applicants were automatically turned over to the committee.* He had argued with the faculty that 4 or 5 of the best minority candidates should be turned over to regular admissions, so that the full 16 places would be opened to the disadvantaged. "I also felt we should be more honest about whom we were considering," he explained

---

*This contrasts to Dr. Lowrey's statement (see page 213). Storandt says very few minorities (usually Asians) were in fact admitted through the regular admissions process.

in a recent interview. "I occasionally met some nonminority candidates who were truly disadvantaged whom I thought should be considered." He cited the case of a white woman in her late twenties who had a child and who had been living in a car for two years eking by on public assistance while getting the necessary credits to apply to medical school. She had not been considered under the special admissions program. "I recognized that the language in the catalogue was not clear at all . . . I felt that if we were going to be discriminatory, we should say so."[16]

Storandt was also uncomfortable with another admissions policy of Davis (which has since been eliminated): the Dean could designate five admittees each year without regard to benchmark scores. To Storandt this policy was an attempt to buy goodwill in important places.

When he read Bakke's letter, Storandt had just returned from the annual meeting of the Association of American Medical Colleges. There, conversation had centered on *DeFunis*, a reverse discrimination case involving an affirmative action program which, as Storandt was aware, bore many similarities to Davis's. In a sensitive letter explaining Bakke's rejection, Storandt wrote that he was within the top 10 percent of the applicants, but had been turned down because of the lack of available places. Noting that none of the suggestions that Bakke had made were possible, Storandt suggested that he apply for early decision for the fall of 1974. But Storandt did not stop at that recommendation. Perhaps crossing over the boundaries of what is proper for an admissions official, he encouraged Bakke to pursue his research about the legality of quota-oriented admissions. He suggested that Bakke look into the ongoing *DeFunis* case, of which he enclosed a summary.

"I was disturbed that task force programs would spring up all over the country and relegate non-white applicants to another track," Storandt now explains. "I hoped that if it went to court, the court would say 'You're doing a good job, but fix up these things.' . . . I was worried about Davis's program, and I thought it worthwhile in principle to get an objective third-party determination."[17] That is exactly what he got.

DEFUNIS

Marco DeFunis, Jr., had applied for admission to the University of Washington Law School (UWLS) in 1970. That year 75,000 aspiring lawyers had applied for the 35,000 places in the nation's law schools. DeFunis was one of 1,601 people competing for the 300 spaces at UWLS. A white, Jewish male of Portuguese-Spanish extraction, DeFunis had graduated magna cum laude from the University of Washington, with an A— average for his four years. He had also been elected to Phi Beta Kappa. But his relatively low Law School Admissions Test (LSAT) scores (512 and 566 on two attempts) had led to his rejection. Although he was admitted to four other law schools, DeFunis wanted to attend the University of Washington, because he had a part-time job there and because his wife had no assurance of finding work in a new city. Advised that he should retake the LSAT, DeFunis attended graduate school for a year while working 30 hours a week. His third try at the LSAT earned him a 668, a score in the top 7 percent nationally. But for the purposes of his second application, the three scores were averaged to 582 and again DeFunis was rejected.

As a number of minority applicants with lesser credentials had been admitted, DeFunis felt he had been unfairly denied admission.* He decided to sue. His lawyer, Josef Diamond, first approached the admissions committee in an effort to have DeFunis admitted, but when the negotiations failed, DeFunis filed suit in the state court in the summer of 1971. Judge Lloyd Shorett swiftly ruled that the 1954 *Brown* decision meant that "public education must be equally available to all regardless of race." He instructed the university to admit DeFunis for the 1971–1972 academic year. The university complied by admitting DeFunis, but it appealed the ruling. In March 1973, the Washington Supreme Court reversed the lower court ruling. In a 6-to-2 vote, the court held that *Brown* only barred racial classifications that had the effect of stigma or the stamp of inferiority. The court said that UWLS's admissions program did not have a stigmatizing effect on nonminorities.

At this point, DeFunis was midway through his second year of law school, and since the university did not attempt to expel him, he was not inclined to appeal. However, his attorney persuaded him that he could be expelled at any time, so DeFunis took his case to the United States Supreme Court. In November 1973, the high court agreed to hear the case.

The case was argued on February 26, 1974. In late April, five justices ruled that the case was moot (no longer a controversy) because DeFunis was about to graduate. Justice William Brennan's dissent (which was joined by Justices Douglas, Marshall, and White) charged that the Court had bent over backward to get rid of the suit and predicted that the issue would soon come back to haunt it.

> The constitutional issues which are avoided today concern vast numbers of people, organizations and colleges and universities, as evidenced by the filing of twenty-six *amicus curiae* [friend of the court] briefs. Few constitutional questions in recent history have stirred as much debate, and they will not disappear. They must inevitably return to the federal courts and ultimately again to this Court.[18]

Bakke's case would be the one the Court could not duck.

---

*Under the UWLS program, members of minorities (not Asians) were separated from the regular admissions process and evaluated differently. Of the 37 minority acceptances that year, all but the seven Asians had lower overall ratings than DeFunis.

BAKKE REAPPLIES

In the meantime, taking Storandt's advice, Bakke applied for early admission to Davis for the fall of 1974. Although he assembled all the necessary materials by August of the preceding year, he faced one major stumbling block: this time he was interviewed by Dr. Lowrey, who found his views on minority admissions rather rigid. Storandt explains that Lowrey believed that he himself should handle this particular candidate. "I imagine that he put tougher than usual questions to him. . . . I never saw George Lowrey more exercised than after that interview. He was distressed by it."[19]

Bakke was rejected under the early admissions plan and again in the spring of 1974 after his application was turned over to the regular admission process. The latter rejection came the same month that the Supreme Court mooted the *DeFunis* case.

Even before this rejection, however, Bakke had been seriously looking for a lawyer. A name that came up repeatedly was that of Reynold Colvin, a partner in a small San Francisco firm. Colvin had successfully argued a case for a nonminority school administrator, obtaining a ruling that invalidated San Francisco's five-year targets for minority hiring. He felt strongly that special treatment for minorities could result in reverse discrimination.

Colvin's initial action on behalf of Bakke was to negotiate for his admission. When that effort failed, Bakke filed suit on June 20, 1974. In his first confrontation, before trial judge F. Leslie Manker, Bakke won on the broad question but lost on personal grounds. Manker ruled that since no whites had ever been admitted under the special plan, it was a violation of Bakke's rights under the equal protection clause of the Fourteenth Amendment and was also illegal under the Title VI of the Civil Rights Act of 1964. However, he did not order Bakke's admission to Davis because it had not been shown that Bakke would have been admitted had all 100 places been available.

Bakke fared much better when his case came before the California Supreme Court. The 6-to-1 decision, which was announced in September 1976, struck down the special admissions program as a violation of the Fourteenth Amendment: "We conclude that the program, as administered by the University, violates the constitutional rights of nonminority applicants because it affords preference on the basis of race to persons who, by the University's own standards, are not as qualified for the study of medicine as nonminority applicants denied admission."[20]

The California Supreme Court ordered the case remanded to the trial court, where the university would have to show why Bakke should not be admitted. Suddenly, the university acknowledged that it could not demonstrate that without the special admissions program Bakke would not have been admitted in 1973, because he "came so close to admission . . . even with the special admissions program being in operation." The

California high court then ordered that Davis admit Bakke. But that order was stayed pending appeal to the United States Supreme Court, which granted certiorari in February 1977. It was at this point that the University of California hired Archibald Cox, a Harvard law professor who had long been committed to affirmative action policies, to represent Davis at the Supreme Court.

THE CASE GOES TO THE SUPREME COURT

Oral arguments before the Supreme Court were held on October 12, 1977. Allan Bakke, now 37 years old, had been trying to get into medical school for five years. In a letter to Peter Storandt, who had since left Davis for Oberlin College, he quipped, "I may be the first person to retire from engineering to go into medicine."[21] For Bakke it was a personal matter; for the rest of the country it was a matter of wide potential impact. Few cases in the history of the Court had stimulated such emotion. No case had generated as many amicus briefs—57 in all. (Interestingly, one of the pro-Bakke briefs was written by a young lawyer named Marco DeFunis.) For minorities the case represented a test of the nation's commitment to civil rights and equal opportunities. For the pro-Bakke contingent the case was a matter of reverse discrimination, of sacrificing the American tradition of individual rights under the justification of making up for the sins of the past—slavery and state-sanctioned discrimination.

On that October morning, the spectator line ran down the marble steps of the Supreme Court building and around the block. Some people had been in line since the day before, camping out all night. Outside, demonstrators carried placards and shouted slogans. Inside, extra seats were put in all available places as the press and spectators crowded into the courtroom.

Oral arguments were expanded from the traditional one hour to two. Archibald Cox and Reynold Colvin would each speak for 45 minutes. Solicitor General Wade McCree was allotted a half hour to give the federal government's position. Although Cox, as a former solicitor general, and McCree had appeared many times before the high court, it was Colvin's first appearance.

Cox began with a forceful statement of the significance of the case:

> This case . . . presents a single vital question: whether a state university, which is forced by limited resources to select a relatively few number of students from a much larger number of well-qualified applicants, is free, voluntarily, to take into account the fact that the applicant is black, Chicano, Asian or native American to increase the number of those minority groups trained for the educational professions and participating in them, professions from which minorities were long excluded because of generations of pervasive racial discrimination.

The answer the Court gives will determine, perhaps for decades, whether members of those minorities are to have the kind of meaningful access to higher education in the professions which the universities have accorded them in recent years, or are to be reduced to the trivial numbers which they were prior to the adoption of minority admissions programs.[22]

As he tried to make the point that the 16-place program was not a quota, Cox was interrupted by a question from Justice Potter Stewart.

Stewart: It did put a limit on the number of white people, didn't it?

Cox: I think that it limited the number of non-minority and therefore essentially white, yes. But there are two things to be said about that: One is that this was not pointing a finger at a group which had been marked as inferior in any sense; and it was undifferentiated, it operated against a wide variety of people. So I think it was not stigmatizing—in the sense of the old quota against Jews was stigmatizing—in any way.

Cox compared the program to a hypothetical one which might be set up to get people from rural communities. Then Justice Harry Blackmun asked if it was the same thing as an athletic scholarship "since most institutions seek athletic prowess."

"Well," replied Cox with bemusement, "I come from Harvard, Sir . . . and I don't know whether it's our aim, but we don't do very well." Following that observation the intense mood of the courtroom was punctuated by a burst of laughter from the justices and the packed spectator section.

Wanting the Court to concentrate on the equal protection clause, Cox argued that the Title VI question (whether the admissions program violated Title VI of the Civil Rights Act of 1964) was not before the Court because the California Supreme Court had not ruled on that point. He stressed that the "Fourteenth Amendment does not outlaw race-conscious programs where there is no invidious purpose or intent, or where they are aimed at offsetting the consequences of our long tragic history of discrimination in achieving greater racial equality."

Solicitor General Wade McCree, himself a black, argued that race consciousness was a constitutionally permissible way to make up for decades of past discrimination.

The United States has . . . concluded that voluntary programs to increase the participation of minorities in activities throughout our society, activities previously closed to them, should be encouraged and supported. . . . This Court does not require a recital of the extent and duration of racial discrimination in America from the time it was enshrined in our very Constitution: in the three-fifths compromise, in the fugitive slave provision, and . . . it continues until the present day. . . . Indeed, many children born in 1954, when *Brown* was decided, are today, twenty-three years later, the very persons knocking on the doors of professional schools, seeking admission, about the country. They are persons who, in many instances, have been denied the fulfillment of the promise of that decision, because of resistance to this Court's decision that was such a landmark when it was handed down.

McCree argued that "it is not enough . . . to look at the visible wounds imposed by unconstitutional discrimination based upon race or ethnic status." He said that Davis "could and should properly consider race in affording a remedy to correct the denial of racial justice in this nation. We submit that the Fourteenth Amendment, instead of outlawing this, indeed should welcome it as part of its intent and purpose."

From the start, Reynold Colvin stressed, "I am Allan Bakke's lawyer and Allan Bakke is my client." He was telling the Court that his main purpose was to look at the individual case and to show that Bakke had been discriminated against. For Colvin, it did not matter whether the Court decided the issue on the Fourteenth Amendment or Title VI of the Civil Rights Act. What mattered was Allan Bakke. "The name of the game is not to represent Allan Bakke as a representative of some class," Colvin argued. "This is not an exercise in a law review argument or a bar examination question. This is a question of getting Mr. Bakke into the medical school." Thus Colvin spent the first 20 minutes of his argument speaking to the Court as if it were a trial court, going over the facts. Finally, Justice Lewis Powell had had enough: "We are here—at least I am—primarily to hear a constitutional argument. You have devoted twenty minutes to laboring a fact, if I may say so. I would like help, I really would, on the constitutional issues."

Colvin then argued that Davis's use of racial classification was unconstitutional "not because it is limited to sixteen, but because the concept of race itself as a classification becomes in our history and in our understanding an unjust and improper basis upon which to judge people. We do not believe that intelligence, that achievement, that ability are measured by skin pigmentation or by the last surname of an individual."

Then Colvin boxed himself into a corner by saying that leaving even one opening for a minority candidate would be unconstitutional. He said, "Numbers are unimportant. It is the principle of keeping a man out because of his race that is important." That statement led to a heated exchange with Justice Thurgood Marshall, the lawyer who had argued *Brown* in 1954 and the only black ever to sit on the Court.

Marshall:	You are arguing about keeping somebody out and the other side is arguing about getting somebody in.
Colvin:	That's right.
Marshall:	So it depends on which way you look at it, doesn't it?
Colvin:	It depends on which way you look at the problem.
Marshall:	It does? . . . You are talking about your client's rights. Don't those underprivileged people have some rights?
Colvin:	They certainly have the right to compete—
Marshall:	To eat cake.

Few who witnessed the occasionally testy arguments expected a swift or unanimous judgment. It was apparent that some of the justices were searching for a compromise, some formula by which such lofty aspirations as affirmative action and nondiscrimination could coexist under a color-blind constitution. Could a constitution be color-blind without first becoming color-conscious? That was the question before the justices. To decide the case, the Supreme Court would have to consider two important points.

The Equal Protection Clause

The Court's first consideration was whether the Davis program would be examined under the "rational basis" test of the equal protection clause or under "strict scrutiny." Up until the New Deal, the Court had imposed the loose rule of rational basis. If a state's law or action had some relevance to a justifiable end, then the Court would let it stand. Thus the Court had been willing to bend over backward to allow states to set up classifications, even racial ones, if there was at least some vague relationship between the means used and the ends desired. The idea was to prevent the Court from taking the role of "super legislature." The result was that judicial review almost always ended in the upholding the state statute.

Beginning in the late 1930s and then especially during the Warren Court years, the Court adopted a "strict scrutiny" test in cases where state action involved fundamental rights, such as the right to vote, or set up "inherently suspect" classifications, such as race or ethnic origin. Under this test, the Court looked very closely to make sure that there was a tight fit between the purpose of the statute and the means to achieve it. The state was given the burden of proof in demonstrating that there was "a compelling state interest" and that there were no other, less "onerous" or "restrictive" means by which to meet the same end.

Bakke posed a particular problem because the Court was looking at what could be termed a "positive" classification, one designed to help people against whom there had been discrimination. If the Court imposed the "strict scrutiny" test, designed to protect those minorities, it was highly probable that the Davis program would be held unconstitutional.

Yet, even this was not a certainty, as in the *Swann* case, which involved court-enforced desegregation of schools in Charlotte, North Carolina, Chief Justice Burger himself had written that "just as the race of students must be considered in determining whether a constitutional violation has occurred, so also must race be considered in formulating a remedy."[23] What complicated the situation for the University of California was that no one alleged that the medical school was guilty of past minority discrimination, as the Charlotte school system had been. The medical school's special admissions program was designed to correct a societal discrimination.

The Civil Rights Act

The other major consideration of the Court was whether the case could be decided on the basis of the Civil Rights Act of 1964, Title VI, which forbade discrimination in any program or activity receiving federal financial assistance, or whether it rested on the equal protection clause, or on both. As Justice Brennan pointed out during the oral arguments, "ordinarily, we [the Court] don't decide constitutional questions if we can affirm what you ask us to do on a Federal statutory ground." Deciding the case on the basis of the Civil Rights Act might shift the balance toward Bakke, because many people believed that the legislation was more restrictive than the Fourteenth Amendment—that it also barred discrimination against nonminorities.

After the Supreme Court's conference the week following the oral arguments, there was a clue that the justices were considering the possibility of grounding the decision in the Civil Rights Act. They requested that the parties and the Justice Department submit briefs within 30 days on Title VI "as it applies to this case."

As might be expected, Cox reiterated Davis's position that the case could not be decided on Title VI because that issue had not been decided by the California Supreme Court and hence was not open to the U.S. Supreme Court for review. Cox would later comment that no one who lived in Washington during the 1960s could doubt that the legislation was aimed at discrimination against minorities. "I cannot suppress the conviction that that reading [to bar affirmative action] stands the Civil Rights Act of 1964 on its head, thus turning a charter of liberty into an instrument of isolation."[24]

Cox and Colvin agreed that the Title VI question should not be remanded to the California Court, but Colvin argued that the Supreme Court could decide the case on the Title VI question because it had been part of Bakke's original complaint. The Justice Department took yet a different view, arguing that the case could be decided on the basis of Title VI but that it should first be remanded to the California courts because the issue had not been sufficiently explored there.

THE COURT DECIDES

As in all controversial, hard cases, the Court's decision did not come until the end of the term. On June 28, nine months after the arguments, the Supreme Court announced its decision amid confusion and controversy. There was no clear majority, but a three-way split of 4–1–4. The Court lined up with Justices Brennan, White, Marshall, and Blackmun on one side and Chief Justice Burger and Justices Stewart, Rehnquist, and Stevens on the other—leaving Justice Powell straddling the middle. The result was a compromise of sorts. Davis's special admissions program was held to be illegal, Bakke was to be admitted to Davis, but affirmative action programs could consider race as a "plus" factor—though not as the determining factor—in admissions. To explain the differing views, it took six separate opinions. Justice Powell wrote the controlling opinion. Justice Brennan wrote an opinion—concurring in part and dissenting in part—joined by Justices White, Marshall, and Blackmun. Justice Stevens wrote an opinion—concurring in part and dissenting in part—joined by Chief Justice Burger and Justices Stewart and Rehnquist. And Justices White, Marshall, and Blackmun each filed a separate opinion.

Sorting out the different views is like trying to sort the pieces of a jigsaw puzzle. Burger, Stewart, Rehnquist, and Stevens concluded that the special admissions program violated the Civil Rights Act and that it was unnecessary to decide whether it also violated the Constitution. Brennan, White, Marshall, and Blackmun argued that the Civil Rights Act went no further in prohibiting the use of race than did the equal protection clause. They then went on to hold the program constitutional. Powell agreed with the Brennan group that the statute went no further than the Constitution but disagreed with them that the program was constitutional. Powell's was thus the critical fifth vote for the Burger group's position that Davis's program was unconstitutional and Bakke must therefore be admitted. For purposes of analyzing this decision, we will now concentrate on the Powell opinion, with reference to how the other justices differed.

Justice Powell began his discussion of the Civil Rights Act by stating, "The concept of 'discrimination,' like the phrase 'equal protection of the laws,' is susceptible to varying interpretations, for as Mr. Justice Holmes declared, '[a] word is not a crystal transparent and unchanged, it is the skin of a living thought and may vary greatly in color and content according to the circumstances and the time in which it is used.' "[25] He then went on to examine the legislative history of the act to try to determine the meaning of the statute and concluded that "Title VI must be held to proscribe only those racial classifications that would violate the Equal Protection Clause or the Fifth Amendment." So, at least to Powell, the Civil Rights Act was no more confining than the Constitution.

As to whether the Court should apply strict scrutiny, as Bakke's attorney contended, or the rational basis test, Powell said that "the guarantee of equal protection cannot mean one thing when applied to one individual and something else when applied to a person of another color. If both are not accorded the same basis, then it is not equal." He continued, "Racial and ethnic distinctions of any sort are inherently suspect and thus call for the most exacting judicial examination."

Powell noted that while the framers of the Fourteenth Amendment conceived its primary purpose "as bridging the vast distance between members of the Negro race and the white 'majority,'" the amendment was framed in universal terms so that "all 'persons,' not merely 'citizens,' would enjoy equal rights under the law." Thus, he rejected Cox's argument that a racial classification of the white majority cannot be "suspect" and can be characterized as "benign."

Having set up a strict scrutiny standard, Powell had to decide whether the Davis program passed constitutional muster, that is, whether "'its purpose or interest is both constitutionally permissible and substantial, and . . . its use of the classification is "necessary to the accomplishment" of its purpose or the safeguarding of its interest.'" Translated to Davis, that meant that the reasons for the program (increasing the number of minorities in medical school, countering the effects of societal discrimination, increasing the number of physicians who might practice in underserved communities, and obtaining ethnic diversity in the student body) were "substantial enough to support the use of a suspect classification."

Powell concluded that the goal of increasing the number of minority doctors in medical schools was invalid because "preferring members of any one group for no reason other than race or ethnic origin is discrimination for its own sake." Where there had been no finding of previous discrimination, "it cannot be said that the government has any greater interest in helping one individual than in refraining from harming another." In other words, Davis could not use societal discrimination as a justification for its special admissions program. Furthermore, there was no proof that admitting more minorities to medical school helped achieve the goal of providing more doctors to underserved areas.

However, Powell did conclude that ethnic diversity was a permissible goal for an institution of higher education. Citing the First Amendment as the basis for the right of academic freedom, Powell said that in "arguing that its universities must be accorded the right to select those students who will contribute the most to the 'robust exchange of ideas,'" the Regents of the University of California were "seeking to achieve a goal that is of paramount importance." However, he qualified that position by stating that "ethnic diversity . . . is only one element in a range of factors a university properly may consider in attaining a goal of a heterogeneous student body." To Justice Powell, a program "focused solely on ethnic diversity would hinder rather than further attainment of genuine diversity." He cited the Harvard University program, which looks for farm boys, musicians, physicists, poets, and blacks but without set numerical goals, as one that met the constitutional requirements. In other words, race or ethnic background "may be deemed a 'plus' " but cannot be the primary determinant for admission.

In conclusion, Powell stated that "it is evident that the Davis special admissions program involves the use of an explicit racial classification never before countenanced by this Court. . . . The fatal flaw in petitioner's program is its disregard of individual rights as guaranteed by the Fourteenth Amendment." In other words, the California Supreme Court was correct in saying the Davis program was unconstitutional, but incorrect in stipulating that a state, through its universities, may not take race into account in admissions.

In their joint opinion partially concurring and partially dissenting, Justices Brennan, White, Marshall, and Blackmun (hereafter the Brennan group) took issue with Powell's conclusion that the Davis program was unconstitutional. "We cannot . . . let colorblindness become myopia which masks the reality that many 'created equal' have been treated within our lifetimes as inferior both by the law and by their fellow citizens."

The four agreed with Powell that Title VI did not extend beyond the Fourteenth Amendment. Its purpose was to prevent discrimination against blacks in federally funded programs, not to require racial neutrality, they said. But since the regulations *required* remedial affirmative action where there was proof of discrimination, the justices saw no justification for *barring* voluntary affirmative action programs.

In their analysis of the Fourteenth Amendment, the Brennan group concluded that "racial classifications are not *per se* invalid under the Fourteenth Amendment." Looking at the university's reasons for the program, they concluded "this is not a case where racial classifications are irrelevant and therefore prohibited." They said that statutes imposing disadvantages on minority groups had to be tested by the strictest standard. However, they said that affirmative actions benefiting minority groups and not stigmatizing majority groups should be governed by a middle standard of review—that is, they should be substantially related to important governmental objectives.

> Davis' articulated purpose of remedying the effects of past societal discrimination is . . . sufficiently important to justify the use of race-conscious admissions programs where there is a sound basis for concluding that minority underrepresentation is substantial and chronic, and that the handicap of past discrimination is impeding access of minorities to Medical School.

The Brennan group thus departed from Powell in asserting that it is permissible for an institution to adopt race-conscious programs to remove the disadvantage of past discrimination "whether its own or that of society at large. There is no question that Davis' program is valid under this test." In their view, the program had a justifiable goal which did not stigmatize any group and therefore passed the middle level of scrutiny.

The four justices concluded that the program, in setting aside a predetermined number of places for qualified minority candidates, did not violate the Constitution. They saw no difference between this approach and the Harvard approach of adding a "plus."

The comparatively short Stevens opinion, joined by Burger, Stewart, and Rehnquist, began by asserting that the case was not a class action suit, but a suit by an individual, Allan Bakke. Stating that the final order of the California Supreme Court did not forbid the use of any racial criteria in processing applications, Stevens wrote, "It is therefore perfectly clear that the question whether race can ever be used as a factor in admissions is not an issue in this case, and that discussion of that issue is inappropriate."

Stevens reminded his brethren that it was the Court's practice "to avoid the decision of a constitutional issue if a case can be fairly decided on a statutory ground." He concluded that the case could in fact be decided on the basis of Title VI of the Civil Rights Act.

The Stevens-four's reading of the statute and the legislative history was that color-blindness was required. "[T]he meaning of the Title VI ban on exclusion is crystal clear: Race cannot be the basis of excluding anyone from participation in a federal funded program." And he concluded, "The University's special admissions program violated Title VI of the Civil Rights Act of 1964 by excluding Bakke from the Medical School because of his race. It is therefore our duty to affirm the judgment ordering Bakke admitted to the University."

The immediate reaction to the decision was muddy confusion. Newspaper headlines contradicted each other. Minority leaders rejoiced and wailed. Few members of the public understood what the Court had actually decided or what it would mean to other admissions programs.

For Davis, the decision meant finding a place for Allan Bakke in the class entering in September 1978. This was not hard to do, as a number of minority admittees dropped out in protest. In fact, according to Dean Ernest L. Lewis, head of student affairs, "after *Bakke* minority applications dropped precipitously. They figured we were a racist school. . . . It's given us a psychological hurdle to go over. The perception of Davis has changed. Davis got into a problem because the school was racist—that became the perception of the man on the street. Davis must have had a racist policy, otherwise why would we have been ordered to do something that we would not otherwise be doing, and therefore we must have been racist."[26]

Since the decision the Davis medical school has grappled with the same problem it grappled with when it began in 1968: how can it get qualified minority applicants? However, Dean Lewis admits that the decision's effect was not all negative. "Who won? Ultimately the school of medicine because it was forced to look more closely at its process and what affirmative action is all about . . . to make the selection process more thoughtful, more honest. We've been able to say that. But the feeling of paranoia has been enormous."

For Allan Bakke it meant he would be given the opportunity of the medical career of which he had always dreamed. Amid the media attention given Bakke's first day at Davis, some members of the class, including minority students, came up to him, shook his hand and said in essence, "We're here on serious business, what's done is done, so let's move ahead together." Despite the publicity that he had always shunned, Bakke made it through his four years at Davis and at the graduation was given a standing ovation by his fellow students. He then returned to his home state of Minnesota where he is an anesthesiologist at the Mayo Clinic.

For the nation's colleges and universities it meant taking a close look at their admissions policies and wondering how the Court would split the next time an affirmative action policy came up for judicial scrutiny. Allan Bakke made his point in the highest court in the land, but history will render the final verdict in this classic test of rights under the Fourteenth Amendment.

One of the thousands of boats filled with Haitian refugees off the coast of Florida, 1979. *AP/Wide World
Photos*

Every day thousands of aliens arrive in the United States.
Some, such as Jean D'Eau, come seeking liberty and political asylum. Others sneak across the border trying to find jobs or a better
quality of life. But how do we decide who can stay? And once the
aliens are here, what protection does the Constitution provide?

"GIVE ME YOUR TIRED, YOUR POOR . . ."
Does the Fourteenth Amendment Protect Illegal Aliens?*

The stigma of illiteracy will mark [illegal alien children] for the rest of their lives. By denying these children a basic education, we deny them the ability to live within the structure of our civic institutions, and foreclose any realistic possibility that they will contribute in even the smallest way to the progress of our Nation.

Justice William Brennan,
Plyler v. *Doe*

Instead of allowing the political processes to run their course—albeit with some delay—the Court seeks to do Congress' job for it, compensating for congressional inaction. It is not unreasonable to think that this encourages the political branches to pass their problems to the judiciary.

Chief Justice Warren Burger,
dissenting in *Plyler* v. *Doe*

Jean D'Eau† didn't want to leave Haiti. A successful barber with strong family ties, he would have preferred to remain there running his small business. But an insignificant political mistake on his part made that plan impossible. As a result, D'Eau came to the United States, seeking the liberty he lacked in Haiti, and found himself in another political morass—the labyrinth of U.S. immigration law.

As a businessman in Haiti, D'Eau had resented the Haitian secret police, known as the Ton Tons Macoutes, coming into his barbershop with

---

*This chapter does not presume to cover all the issues related to immigration. It looks rather at some of the constitutional rights of aliens.
†Jean D'Eau is a pseudonym. His name has been changed to protect his identity.

no intention of paying him. Following the example of other barbers, D'Eau had finally objected and asked the police to pay. Then some of the barbers were arrested and disappeared. Fearing the same fate, D'Eau decided to leave Haiti. "I was afraid to talk and walk freely. I left because I'd rather take a risk and try to go to the land of liberty than remain in Haiti under such terrible conditions where I eventually would be killed."[1] He knew he had little time. In fact, his trip was organized in three days, and he was forced to leave his wife and five children behind.

D'Eau and 32 other Haitians left the country in mid-October of 1975. "We embarked on a sailboat from a small village, Flamant, on the southern coast of Haiti," he says. It would be a difficult voyage, 800 miles of steering according to the color of the water and the stars. After 2 days, they stopped in Cuba, where for 13 days "we were treated well. The Cubans gave us shelter, food and clothes, and water and food for the rest of the trip." Indeed, the Cubans offered to let them stay, but "we declined to stay in Cuba because we disliked communism. We thought that if we remained in a communist country, we would never be able to return to Haiti."

At the end of October, the 32 Haitians returned to their small vessel and set out for the United States. Fifteen more people, convinced that the United States meant freedom, also crowded into the boat. "The voyage was another five days, and we ran into great problems with Hurricane David. All our supplies were washed away. I was half-conscious. I did not drink or eat anything, and the others almost threw me overboard because they thought I was dead. However, as soon as I heard that we had reached Miami, I opened my eyes and sat up." He had made it to "the land of liberty" and walked to the shore "to rejoice." But the celebration was cut short; officials from the INS (Immigration and Naturalization Service) were immediately on the scene.

"Our first reaction to the officials was to try to run away, especially since police officials in Haiti are the equivalent to terror and possible death. However, we decided not to flee because many of the Haitians told those of us who were afraid that they had nothing to worry or fear with *these* immigration authorities. At the immigration office, we were given food, water, and medical care. Some people were sent to a hospital for special care."

Then the Haitians were questioned by the INS officials. "We were asked why we left Haiti. We talked about the oppression in Haiti." D'Eau explained that he believed that America was "a great country of life, liberty, and opportunity" and that he feared he would be killed if he remained in Haiti. But the interpreter at the interrogation told D'Eau that the officials already knew the answers that the Haitians were giving and that they were "required to ask such questions for procedure.... We were told we would be put into jail for a while and then we could leave soon after."

The reality was that D'Eau would spend the next 19 months in detention centers. "I had the understanding of America as a great country of life, liberty, and opportunity. I believed America was the country of law where I could be treated humanely, and I was surprised to find the exact opposite," D'Eau reflects.

D'Eau's first 6 months in the United States were spent in Immokenee, a detention center in Florida. "We were not hit or tortured, but we suffered a lot as we were humiliated and put into isolation." Then the authorities "told us we would be set free. But we were not freed, and instead sent to Texas via bus where we were held for another 13 months." Repeatedly, D'Eau asked about his request for political asylum, and repeatedly he was told that the INS was working on his claims. Finally, a Catholic group in Texas, the Sisters of Lorreto of El Paso, put up a $15,000 bond for the release of 45 Haitians. D'Eau was one of them. Since his release on May 19, 1977, D'Eau has been waiting for word on his asylum claim.

THE HAITIAN INFLUX

In some ways, Jean D'Eau was lucky. Had he arrived a few years later immigration officials might have put him on the first plane back to Haiti or even prevented him from reaching the shore. In 1977 and 1978 thousands of Haitians began arriving in Florida. Some came directly from Haiti; others came from the Bahamas, expelled by the government, which was facing a high unemployment rate. Then in April 1980 "freedom flotillas" began arriving from Cuba, presenting the INS with thousands of refugees asking for political asylum.* While the Carter administration had a policy of automatically granting the Cubans' request for asylum, it developed a different policy toward Haitians. Beginning with a series of internal memos, the administration and the immigration service began what was known as the Haitian Program. It was designed to deal with the Haitians in the most efficient manner—send them back home.

Mark Murphy, assistant director of the National Emergency Coalition for Haitian Refugees, explains that under the program Haitians received treatment different from that given other political refugees. Hearings of asylum claims were speeded up to the point that "about 150

---

*In April 1980, 2,000 Cubans came to the Peruvian Embassy in Havana seeking asylum. Although Castro initially responded by posting an armed guard around the compound, he soon lifted it. Before long 10,000 Cubans had crowded in. Responding to widespread public sympathy for their plight, President Carter ordered that 3,500 of the Cubans be admitted to the United States. Soon boats began arriving in Florida from Cuba. But only a portion of the Cubans they brought had been at the embassy. Castro had decided to take the opportunity to release prisoners and insane asylum inmates. Before Castro shut off the flow in the fall of 1980, 125,000 Cuban refugees had arrived in the United States.

asylum hearings were held each day,"[2] making it impossible for attorneys to prepare adequate claims for any of the Haitians. The hearings ended inevitably in rejection of all asylum claims.

Part of the reason for the different treatment has to do with politics. The United States government found itself in a delicate position. The Duvalier (Papa Doc and later Baby Doc) regime of Haiti is our ally. Haiti is strongly anticommunist. It is also a dictatorship. Joseph Etienne, executive director of the Haitian Center Council, explains, "As long as the State Department has good relations with Haiti, the administration won't give Haitians political asylum," because such an acknowledgment of the problems in Haiti would embarrass the Haitian government.[3] Thus, Haitians were being treated as economic rather than political refugees. Under INS regulations, economic refugees—those who come to get jobs or seek a better quality of life—are deportable. In contrast, individuals with legitimate claims as political refugees—those who would face death, imprisonment, or torture if they returned—are allowed to remain in the country.

Facing the possibility that the Haitians would simply all be deported, Ira Kurzban, an attorney for the Haitian Refugee Center, who had been running back and forth from asylum hearing to asylum hearing, decided to change strategies. On May 9, 1979, he began litigating a case known as *Haitian Refugee Center* v. *Civiletti.* The purpose of the suit was to insure the Haitians' due process and equal protection rights under the Fourteenth Amendment. The suit alleged unlawful discrimination against Haitians by the immigration service. It charged that there had been irregularities in deportation hearings and that Haitians were unable to adequately present their claims of asylum. It asked that the court look at the political situation in Haiti.

THE CONSTITUTIONAL ISSUES

In understanding this case, it is important to remember that the Fifth Amendment to the Constitution guarantees that "no *person* shall be . . . deprived of life, liberty, or property, without due process of law." The Fourteenth Amendment, too, uses the word "person," in barring states from abridging due process rights or equal protection of the laws. Ultimately, this means that one need not be a citizen to be entitled to constitutional protection, only a "person" physically within the jurisdiction of the United States. On the other hand, the Constitution gives Congress the power to "establish an uniform Rule of Naturalization." Many constitutional scholars argue that the framers were not talking about controlling immigration when they wrote this clause. In any event, the courts have found that Congress has "extra-constitutional" powers to legislate to exclude aliens.

For more than a hundred years after the signing of the Declaration of Independence, the borders of the United States were open to immigration. The one restriction was a provision of the Alien Act of 1798 which gave the president the power to deport any alien who he felt was a threat to the security of the country. During the nineteenth century, tens of thousands of aliens—especially Irish and Chinese—were imported as a cheap source of labor for the growing American industries.

Immigration soared between 1860 and 1920, as more than 28.5 million people came to the United States. Meanwhile, in the latter part of the nineteenth century, pressure groups began urging Congress to pass laws limiting the flow of aliens. In 1882 Congress passed the first restrictive law which excluded "idiots, lunatics, convicts and persons likely to become public charges."[4] In 1888 Congress passed legislation excluding all Chinese immigrants. In the *Chinese Exclusion Cases* of 1889, the Supreme Court ruled that Congress "can exclude aliens from its territory" because of the powers inherent in any independent nation. "Jurisdiction over its own territory . . . is an incident of every independent nation. It is part of its independence," the Court said. Thus, the powers that belong to independent nations, such as controlling immigration, could be invoked by Congress because they were necessary "for the maintenance of [the nation's] absolute independence and security."[5]

Between 1891 and 1917, Congress added paupers, anarchists, people who might not be able to earn a living because of mental or physical conditions, and all Asians except Japanese to the list of persons who could be excluded. Then, in the midst of the post–World War I depression, Congress passed the Quota Act of 1921 which limited the annual immigration of aliens of any particular nationality to 3 percent of the number of that nationality living in the United States in the year 1910. The effect of the law was to favor those of northern and western European background. For instance, Great Britain (with 2 percent of the world's population at the time) would be allotted 43 percent of the quota. Although there were modifications, the quota system did not end until 1970.

What the Haitians were challenging was whether the Congress, through its creation, the immigration service, could deport them without giving their claims fair consideration—despite the due process and equal protection guarantees of the Fifth and the Fourteenth Amendments.

THE COURTS ADDRESS THE HAITIAN ASYLUM PROBLEM

Haitian Refugee Center v. *Civiletti* was heard by Judge James Lawrence King of the U.S. District Court for the Southern District of Florida. In his 91-page decision in 1980, Judge King ruled that the Haitians had been denied due process and equal protection of the laws. In his initial summary of the case, King declared:

Much of the evidence is both shocking and brutal, populated by the ghosts of individual Haitians—including those who have been returned from the United States—who have been beaten, tortured and left to die in Haitian prisons. Much of the evidence is not brutal but simply callous—evidence that INS officials decided to ship all Haitians back to Haiti simply because their continued presence in the United States had become a problem. The manner in which INS treated the more than 4,000 Haitian plaintiffs violated the Constitution, the immigration statutes, international agreements, INS regulations and INS operating procedures. It must stop.[6]

While conceding that there is no area of law in which "Congress has more unreviewable power than in immigration and naturalization matters," Judge King said that "the discretion of Congress is not completely unfettered. Its classification with respect to aliens must have some rational basis. In addition, persons must be afforded fundamentally fair proceedings under the due process clause before they may be deported."[7] In other words, even Congress could not transcend an alien's Fifth and Fourteenth Amendment rights without some sound policy reasons.

On the issue of equal protection, King pointed out that asylum had been granted to all of the Cubans who had applied but to none of the 4,000 Haitians. "The plaintiffs charge that they faced a transparently discriminatory program designed to deport Haitian nationals and no one else. The uncontroverted evidence proves their claim."[8] Judge King ruled that while a hearing on political asylum "need not conform to all the punctilious requirements of a criminal trial," it nevertheless "must conform to our society's standards of fundamental fairness."[9]

What was probably most distressing to the U.S. government was that King spent 36 pages of his opinion discussing the conditions in Haiti. He said that "no asylum claim can be examined without an understanding of the conditions in the applicant's homeland."[10] After reviewing the testimony King decided that "Haitians in this class deserved something more than they received from INS. Clearly their claims were more political than recognized, and the uniform rejection of their claims demonstrates a profound ignorance, if not an intentional disregard, of the conditions in Haiti. It is beyond dispute that some Haitians will be subjected to the brutal treatment and bloody prisons of François Duvalier upon their deportation. Until INS can definitely state which Haitians will be so treated and which will not, the brutality and bloodletting is its responsibility."[11]

King concluded that Haitians "who came to the United States seeking freedom and justice did not find it." He said that high INS officials had decided "to expel Haitians, despite whatever claims to asylum individual Haitians might have. A program was set up to accomplish this goal.

The Program resulted in wholesale violations of due process, and only Haitians were affected."[12] The judge ruled that none of the Haitians could be deported and ordered the INS to devise a plan for reprocessing the asylum claims.

Although some lawyers who work with Haitians have cited King's decision as one of the most important rulings on the rights of refugees, others say not much really changed because of it. Mark Murphy says the changes have been only on the surface. The INS violations are "less blatant," because the immigration officials go through the proper procedures. "But in fact," he says, "the State Department continues to prejudge the applications. It's a rubber stamp type of decision-making process in the courts, and deportation notices are being handed down."

However, while the Haitian Refugee case was being litigated, Congress passed the Refugee Act of 1980 which sets up an open-door policy for all refugees. Prior to the act the term "refugee" had only applied to those leaving communist or Middle Eastern countries. Now it could also apply to people leaving countries friendly to the United States. Still, thus far it seems to have aided only Cubans. Many Haitian rights advocates say it is only a matter of time before people like Jean D'Eau receive their deportation papers.

EDUCATION AND ILLEGAL ALIENS

Thousands of aliens have come to this country not so much to find liberty, but to find opportunity—jobs and a better life. Some come through proper channels, others sneak in any way they can. Once illegal aliens are in the country, what rights do they have? What social services are they entitled to?

Jose Doe* is an illegal alien who has been in this country for 15 years. He had lived in Mexico all his life, farming his small piece of land and taking odd jobs on a nearby ranch. But what money he could make was not enough to feed his family and send his children to school. He had borrowed 300 pesos to try to make ends meet, but had no way of making enough to pay back his debt. So he decided "to risk my life"[13] and come to the United States, leaving behind his wife and four small children.

Together with a friend, Jose waited one night until dark and crossed the Rio Grande at one of its shallowest points. He found work first in the San Antonio area and then in a foundry in Tyler, Texas, a small city near Dallas. For several years he "commuted," working a while in the United States and returning to Mexico. Then in 1973, he decided to bring his family with him. His wife came first. He was able to get her into the country by paying "border crashers" to hide her in the back of a van. Then

---

*Jose Doe is the pseudonym used during the litigation in *Plyler* v. *Doe*.

his mother brought his two youngest children in the same manner. Finally, in 1976, he was able to bring his two oldest children.

When Jose brought his family, he had no idea that his children might be eligible for school. So initially, his two oldest children did not attend the Tyler schools. Then Michael McAndrew, coordinator of a project sponsored by the Roman Catholic church in Tyler and designed to assist Mexican Americans, came to Jose and asked him why his children were not in school. Jose explained that he thought that since they were in the country illegally his children could not attend. When he found that the Tyler school system didn't exclude illegal aliens, he enrolled his son Alfredo and his daughter Viviola.

THE TYLER SCHOOL SYSTEM CHANGES ITS POLICY

Tyler is a city in east Texas of about 70,000 which claims the title of the "rose capital of the world." More than 400 miles from the Mexican border, Tyler did not have a significant population of illegal aliens until the mid 1970s. According to James Plyler, former superintendent of the Tyler schools, Tyler had not paid much attention to the undocumented aliens because in the early 1970s there were only a handful attending the school system of 16,000 students.

In May 1975, the Texas legislature revised its education laws. According to the new statute, state funds would no longer be available for the education of children who were not "legally admitted" to the United States. In addition, the statute gave school districts the authority to deny enrollment to any such children.[14]

Despite the state law, Tyler schools continued to admit illegal alien children. In the 1975–1976 school year there were about 18 illegal aliens enrolled. Superintendent Plyler explains, "Even though the law said we couldn't get reimbursed for them, I thought that it was so few that I saw no reason to get concerned. My concern was for the youngsters." Plyler adds that in 1976 the illegal alien population began to increase in Tyler. "We were beginning to feel what the southern part of Texas had been telling us all along—that it's a real problem with undocumented aliens."[15] That year the school had about 27 or 28 undocumented aliens attending (including Jose Doe's two oldest children).

"Our concern," says Plyler, "was that there was a center here for Mexican Americans to get help. As a result, word began to spread rapidly that Tyler was the place to come. You didn't have to pay tuition, and there were jobs." He said the board felt that they would be "receiving more and more of these undocumented aliens . . . and that local taxpayers should not have the burden of paying for an education for these youngsters since they were illegal and the numbers were increasing more each year."

In July 1977, the school board finally decided to take action. It adopted a policy that illegal alien children would have to pay "full tuition fee"—$1,000, the average cost of a year's schooling in Tyler—to attend. As the state law did not define what a legally admitted alien was, the school board adopted its own definition: "A legally admitted alien is one who has documentation that he or she is legally in the United States, or a person who is in the process of securing documentation from the United States Immigration Service, and the Service will state that the person is being processed and will be admitted with proper documentation."[16]

Mike McAndrews, who was familiar with the situation as head of the church project, feels that the situation in Tyler in 1977 was not one that should have concerned the school board. He says that "aliens were not coming to Tyler to put their kids in school. They came because they had family or friends or people they could talk to. It had nothing to do with the school situation. In fact, many undocumented aliens didn't even know that their kids could go to school."[17]

When he heard that the school board had decided to exclude un-documented aliens who didn't pay tuition, McAndrews went to have a conference with the superintendent. "I asked, 'How are you going to accomplish this?'" he explains. "'Who will decide who can come?'" McAndrews said he told Plyler that he hoped "you don't leave it up to the principals because they have no idea who's undocumented and who's not." Finally, McAndrews says that Plyler assured him that in any event a letter would go out to the parents of children who would be excluded. "But no letter went out. On the first day of school, some children were refused. They were children whose parents couldn't speak English and were dressed poorly. There was no rhyme or reason as to who got in and who didn't. One family had two children in and two out just because the kids were in different schools. Things were so unequal, I couldn't bear it. I had no idea of the constitutional situation. I just looked at it on a human basis."

Not knowing what else to do, McAndrews "walked the Tyler legal beat looking for a lawyer." At first he had a hard time getting any help. "They didn't want to touch it, it was too political." But eventually he walked into the offices of Larry Daves and Roberta Rodkin, who told him there was a constitutional issue and they would help. Daves and Rodkin contacted the Mexican American Legal Defense and Educational Fund (MALDEF) in San Francisco while McAndrews talked to some of the families whose children had been denied admission to school.

"Basically the families came to me and talked to me," McAndrews says. "We discussed the possibility of a suit with a number of families, and ultimately four of them stayed with us. We explained the danger that they could be deported, but the four families said that if their children weren't in school, they'd leave anyway. They had nothing to lose and everything to gain." One of those families was Jose Doe's.

Peter Roos, head of educational litigation at MALDEF, had just returned from vacation when he got a call from Daves and Rodkin, whom he describes as the "only civil rights attorneys in east Texas."[18] He said he immediately got on a plane. He was already familiar with the Texas statute, and MALDEF had been studying the situation and devising a legal strategy. Over the Labor Day weekend (Texas schools open early) the lawyers worked together on the case, and on Tuesday morning they went to court to ask for a temporary restraining order. They wanted the judge to restrain the school from excluding the children until the issue was settled. "We didn't want anyone missing school, and they had already been out a week." Judge Wayne Justice of the United States District Court didn't give them a restraining order, but he did set the preliminary hearing for that Friday morning.

In order to prove the complaint, the parents had to take the stand to testify that they were residents of Tyler, that they paid taxes, and that their children had been excluded from school. "We had tremendous concern about the hearing and about the possibility that their names would become known," Roos says. So the families were referred to as the Does, Loes, Moes, and Boes. "One of the interesting things was the judge agreed to hold a 6 A.M. hearing . . . before the media woke up. I don't think the media were even informed or uninformed. I think everyone assumed that the hearing would be at 9:30, as it usually is. . . . We held the hearing *in camera*, behind closed doors. It was closed to the public."

Roos had also filed a motion for a protective order to shield the identities of the families. The judge was willing to sign it, but he was not willing to bind the United States government to it. (As soon as the complaint was filed, Judge Justice had notified the Justice Department because of the national implications of the case.) According to Roos, the judge felt that since the United States is charged with enforcement of the immigration laws, he could not in any way inhibit its ability to enforce them. "We finally had to go to our clients after an hour of horsing around with this and tell them what the situation was, and they informed us that they wanted to go ahead, and if there was any jeopardy, so be it. They didn't want their kids out of school."

Alfredo and Viviola Doe were in first and second grade at the time and barely spoke English. They remember very little about the hearing except that their father took the stand and was asked questions by an interpreter. "We were scared because we didn't understand what was happening," says Viviola.[19]

The result of the hearing was that Judge Justice issued a preliminary injunction against the school district. The children were allowed back in school until the matter was settled. In December 1977, the judge held a full hearing on a permanent injunction. At the hearing the school board argued that it was obeying the state law and that the increase of illegal aliens in the state would put special hardships on the schools. The state of Texas argued that the state law was within the constitutional authority of the state because it was enacted with the legitimate purpose of discouraging or keeping out illegal aliens. The attorneys for the aliens argued that the alien children had been discriminated against. They said that the children were entitled to the protection of the Fourteenth Amendment's equal protection clause.

Judge Justice made the injunction permanent. He ruled that the state law and the school policy did not have "either the purpose or the effect of keeping illegal aliens out of the State of Texas."[20] Further, he said that there was no significant financial burden on the state. He noted that the greatest increase in enrollment of Mexicans was that of children who were legal residents. He noted that the "illegal alien of today may well be the legal alien of tomorrow" and that without an education these children "already disadvantaged as a result of poverty, lack of English-speaking ability, and undeniable racial prejudices . . . will become permanently locked into the lowest socio-economic class."[21] Illegal aliens were entitled to the protection of the Fourteenth Amendment, he ruled, and this type of exclusion was unconstitutional.

On appeal, the Court of Appeals for the Fifth Circuit upheld the injunction and affirmed Judge Justice's ruling on the equal protection clause. The next step was the Supreme Court of the United States.

THE SUPREME COURT DECISION

As might be expected, the Supreme Court decision, issued on June 15, 1982, was far from unanimous. In fact, the Court was split 5 to 4. The result of the decision was that the Texas law was declared unconstitutional and the children were allowed to stay in school. Even the majority —Brennan, Marshall, Blackmun, Powell, and Stevens—did not agree on all points; Marshall, Blackmun, and Powell filed concurring opinions.

Writing for the majority, Justice Brennan began by noting that the state of Texas and the school board's argument was that "undocumented aliens . . . are not 'persons within the jurisdiction' of the State of Texas, and that they therefore have no right to the equal protection of Texas law." He continued, "We reject this argument. Whatever his status under the immigration laws, an alien is surely a 'person' in any ordinary sense of that term. Aliens, even aliens whose presence in this country is unlawful, have long been recognized as 'persons' guaranteed due process of law by the Fifth and Fourteenth Amendments."[22] He asserted that the "Equal Protection Clause was intended to work nothing less than the abolition of all caste-based and invidious class-based legislation. That objective is fundamentally at odds with the power the State asserts here."[23]

However, Brennan added, the conclusion that illegal aliens are protected by the Fourteenth Amendment "only begins the inquiry. The more difficult question is whether the Equal Protection Clause has been violated by the refusal of the State of Texas to reimburse local school boards for the education of children who cannot demonstrate that their presence within the United States is lawful, or by the imposition by those school boards of the burden of tuition on those children."[24]

What was at issue was whether the Texas law would be looked at under a rational basis standard or under strict scrutiny (see Chapter 13). Was it enough that the law's classification bore some reasonable relationship to a legitimate public goal? Or did the law have to meet a higher standard because it discriminated against a "suspect class" or impinged upon a fundamental right?

Justice Brennan noted first that the inadequacies of our immigration laws had created a population of millions of illegal aliens. "This situation raises the specter of a permanent caste of undocumented resident aliens, encouraged by some to remain here as a source of cheap labor, but nevertheless denied the benefits that our society makes available to citizens and lawful residents. . . . The children who are plaintiffs in these cases are special members of this underclass." Brennan then pointed out that the children of illegal aliens had no control over the fact that they were in the country illegally. Thus, he said, the law "imposes its discriminatory burden on the basis of a legal characteristic over which children can have little control. It is thus difficult to conceive of a rational justification for penalizing these children for their presence within the United States."[25]

The majority conceded that aliens were not a suspect class, so the law did not have to meet the strict scrutiny standard. They also stipulated that education is not a fundamental right guaranteed by the Constitution. However, they concluded that there was more involved in the case than "abstract questions." The Texas law "imposes a lifetime hardship on a discrete class of children not accountable for their disabling status. The stigma of illiteracy will mark them for the rest of their lives. By denying these children a basic education, we deny them the ability to live within the structure of our civic institutions, and foreclose any realistic possibility that they will contribute in even the smallest way to the progress of our Nation."[26] Thus, to the majority, even under a rational basis standard, the law was unconstitutional. Brennan concluded:

> In any event, the record is clear that many of the undocumented children disabled by this classification will remain in this country indefinitely, and that some will become lawful residents or citizens of the United States. It is difficult to understand precisely what the State hopes to achieve by promoting the creation and perpetuation of a subclass of illiterates within our boundaries, surely adding to the problems and costs of unemployment, welfare, and crime. It is thus clear that whatever savings might be achieved by denying these children an education, they are wholly insubstantial in light of the costs involved to these children, the State, and the Nation.[27]

The dissenting opinion, written by Chief Justice Burger, began with a blistering attack on the majority opinion:

> Were it our business to set the Nation's social policy, I would agree without hesitation that it is senseless for an enlightened society to deprive any children—including illegal aliens—of elementary education. . . . However, the Constitution does not constitute us as 'Platonic Guardians' nor does it vest in this Court the authority to strike down laws because they do not meet our standards of desirable social policy, 'wisdom,' or 'common sense.' . . . We trespass on the assigned function of the political branches under our structure of limited and separated powers when we assume a policy-making role as the Court does today. . . . The Court employs, and in my view abuses, the Fourteenth Amendment in an effort to become an omnipotent and omniscient problem solver.[28]

Burger then conceded that "I have no quarrel with the conclusion that the Equal Protection Clause of the Fourteenth Amendment *applies* to aliens who, after their illegal entry into this country, are indeed physically 'within the jurisdiction' of a state." However, he said the issue in the case "is whether, for purposes of allocating its finite resources, a state has a legitimate reason to differentiate between persons who are lawfully within the state and those who are unlawfully there. The distinction the State of Texas has drawn—based not only upon its own legitimate interests but on classifications established by the Federal Government in its immigration laws and policies—is not unconstitutional." He said that "once it is conceded—as the Court does—that illegal aliens are not a suspect class, and that education is not a fundamental right, our inquiry should focus on and be limited to whether the legislative classification at issue bears a rational relationship to a legitimate state purpose."[29] Although he said that as a legislator, he would not deny a free education to illegal alien children, Burger said that the state's reasons for the laws were legitimate.

The Chief Justice concluded with the warning that "the Court seeks to do Congress' job for it, compensating for congressional inaction. It is not unreasonable to think that this encourages the political branches to pass their problems to the judiciary."[30]

PLYLER AND BEYOND

In a strange way, the Tyler school system lost its case but won its real battle. As the state law was declared unconstitutional, the state of Texas was required to provide funding for illegal alien children. This meant that Tyler could continue its former policy of allowing the children in the schools, but not have to pay for them. "It solved our problem as far as money was concerned," Plyler says. "I think it solves the problem that people who need help will receive it. I think that here in the future it solved the problem of youngsters getting an education in Texas. I think over the long haul, we're going to benefit from that—we being the state of Texas."

The Doe family were also winners because their children could go to school with no questions asked. They now have six children in the Tyler schools and two more who will soon reach school age. Four of their children are American citizens because they were born here.

The question still remains as to what long-term effect the decision will have on illegal aliens' rights in general. Richard Arnett, an attorney for the Texas Educational Agency who argued *Plyler* in the Supreme Court, says "my personal opinion is that it will be a tree in the desert. There probably won't be any effect from it on any other issues either within education or as to undocumented aliens." He bases his conclusion on the fact that the circumstances in the case were unique because it dealt with children and with education. "I don't think it will go anywhere." He says that he doesn't feel the decision will have a deleterious effect on the state of Texas or immigration. "It would be naive to think that anyone in Mexico would have a copy of this case and is reading it," he quipped. "The case itself will have very little significance on the whole American system."[31]

Peter Roos believes the case will have an effect. "I've always felt that . . . certain sorts of services such as emergency medical care . . . are probably more likely to be made available under . . . *Plyler* than they were before." However, he feels that such changes won't happen overnight. "This is not a court that is hell-bent on expanding the notion of what is fundamental in society. So I don't see [those changes] happening in the foreseeable future."

In the meantime, hundreds, sometimes thousands, of illegal aliens come into the country each day. Congress is still wrestling with the problem. The Senate and the House of Representatives have each passed their own version of the Simpson-Mazzoli bill, which would (1) grant amnesty to all illegal aliens who arrived in the United States before a certain date (3.5 to 6 million), (2) provide for more agents to patrol the United States–Mexican border and (3) make it illegal for anyone to knowingly hire an illegal immigrant. As of the fall of 1984, the bills were in conference committee.

While illegal aliens pay income and social security taxes, so far the only social service they are entitled to is education for their children. If the amnesty provision of the Simpson-Mazzoli bill is passed, millions of illegal aliens living in the United States will be eligible for services such as welfare, food stamps, Medicaid, and unemployment compensation.

Father Theodore Hesburgh paints a desolate picture of the possible problems that our country may face in the future:

> I'm thinking about the year 2000—it's not inconceivable that a hundred million people would start to march on this . . . country. . . . If you had, for example, a massive famine in India, and you had literally tens of millions of people dying of starvation, and the population at that point of that country was over a billion, and they knew perfectly well there was a lot of food in Venice and Vienna and Paris and Rome and other countries in Europe . . . It could happen; it's not a science fiction. Suppose things get so bad in the Caribbean that everybody who can make a boat starts heading for the U.S.? Suppose things get so bad in Central America and South America and Mexico that literally millions of people start voting with their feet and walking across the border?[32]

America is a nation of immigrants. With the exception of native Indians, we are all either immigrants or descendants of immigrants. But many feel that our country is full, that we can no longer aspire to the words of Emma Lazurus inscribed on the base of the Statue of Liberty: "Give me your tired, your poor . . ." It is a problem that has not yet found a delicate balance.

John Marshall and Thomas Jefferson. *CBS Reports*

When the Constitution was drafted, the question that pervaded every clause was that of the balance of power between the states and the federal government. The question was finally brought before Chief Justice Marshall, who declared the supremacy of the federal government, in a case involving a bank teller in Maryland named James McCulloch.

A NATION OF STATES
States' Rights
vs. National Supremacy

We must never forget that it is a constitution *we are expounding . . . intended to endure for ages to come, and consequently, to be adapted to the various* crises *of human affairs.*

John Marshall,
McCulloch v. *Maryland*

The question of the relation of the States to the federal government is the cardinal question of our constitutional system. At every turn of our national developments we have been brought face to face with it, and no definition either of statesmen or of judges has ever quieted or decided it. It cannot, indeed, be settled by one generation because it is a question of growth, and every successive stage of our political and economic development gives it a new aspect, makes it a new question.

Woodrow Wilson, *Constitutional Government in the United States*

When the delegates to the Constitutional Convention met in Philadelphia during the summer of 1787, they came as representatives of 12 sovereign states (Rhode Island refused to send delegates)—states that had developed as virtually independent entities and banded together in a loose confederation for the common goal of obtaining liberty from Great Britain. The hastily drafted Articles of Confederation had not been a sufficient framework to tie together those diverse sovereignties into a new nation. As Edmund Randolph of Virginia stated at the opening of the Constitutional Convention, "the confederation produced no security against foreign invasion." It "could not check the quarrels between states" or protect itself "against the encroachments from the states," nor was it "even paramount to the state constitutions."[1] So the framers met for more than three months, with the formidable task of writing a constitution that would not only solve the problems of the day, but also, as James Madison put it, frame "a system which we wish to last for ages."[2]

In the early days and weeks of the convention, it was not clear that the delegates would be able to accomplish their task. One problem was that some delegates came as firm representatives of their states. Others, such as Gouverneur Morris, felt they had come "as a representative of America . . . [and] to some degree as a representative of the whole human race." Benjamin Franklin commented on Thursday, June 28, "The small progress we have made after 4 or five weeks close attendance & continual reasonings with each other—our different sentiments on almost every question, several of the last producing so many noes as ays, is methinks a melancholy proof of the imperfection of the Human Understanding. We indeed seem to feel our own want of political wisdom, since we have been running about in search of it."[3] The issue that seemed to crop up at every point in the debates was that of states' rights. Would states be represented as equal entities or by population? What powers would be taken away from the states in forming the government? How could a national, supreme government be formed without completely eviscerating the power of the states?

Those favoring a strong central government argued that encroachments by the states on the federal government were far more likely than encroachments by the federal government on the states. They contended that in all successful governments "there must be one supreme power, and one only."[4] Those supporting states' rights accused the others of wanting to abolish the state governments altogether and questioned whether the convention had the power to change the nature of the confederation. Underlying all these issues was the basic question of whether the new government was to be a confederation of the states or a creation of the people themselves.

There was no area where the conflict appeared more sharply than in the question of how the states were to be represented in Congress. The Virginia Plan, put forth by Edmund Randolph, had called for election by the people and representation according to either contributions (i.e., the amount of tax paid) or population. In response, William Paterson of New Jersey had proposed a plan in which the Congress would be elected by the state legislatures and each state would be represented equally.

The oppressive Philadelphia summer heat was intensified by the passions of the debate over representation. For several months, advocates of the two plans rose to explain their respective positions, each side remaining unconverted. Realizing that all might be lost, the delegates finally reached a compromise. The lower house of the Congress (House of Representatives) would be elected by the people, and each state would send representatives according to population (each slave being counted as three-fifths of a person and Indians not being counted at all). The upper house (Senate) would be elected by the state legislatures and each state would be equally represented by two senators.

The compromise helped resolve the deadlock in Philadelphia but did not resolve the basic issue of states' rights versus national sovereignty. Indeed, as soon as delegates met in state conventions to debate and ratify the Constitution, the issue emerged. Patrick Henry, who had declined to go to the convention, shouted, "The question turns, sir, on that poor little thing—the expression, We, the people, instead of the states of America. What right had they to say, *We the people?* Who authorized them to speak the language of *We the people,* instead of, *We the states?*"[5]

At the ratifying conventions, many Antifederalists, concerned about encroachments by the federal government on personal liberties and on states' rights, called for a bill of rights. After the Constitution was ratified and the First Congress met in 1789, James Madison pushed for those guarantees, which included what was to become the Tenth Amendment: "The powers not delegated to the United States by the Constitution, nor prohibited by it to the States, are reserved to the States respectively, or to the people." In the discussion over the amendment, Representative Thomas Tudor Tucker of South Carolina moved to add the word "expressly" before the word "delegated," but Madison objected. It would be "impossible to confine a Government to the exercise of express powers; there must necessarily be admitted powers by implication unless the Constitution descended to recount every minutia." At Madison's insistence, the word was not included. The extent of the powers of the federal government thus remained ambiguous.

Even to the Antifederalists, the Tenth Amendment was a declaratory statement, a recitation of the obvious, not a special grant of power to the states. As Justice Potter Stewart recently stated, "The Tenth Amendment just confirms a truism that the federal government is a government of specific and limited powers."[6]

The first organized states' rights movements came in 1798 in a protest over the Alien and Sedition Acts, which gave the government the right to expel aliens and to punish seditious libel. In a daring move, the Virginia and Kentucky legislatures (led by Madison and Jefferson, respectively) passed resolutions declaring the acts unconstitutional. The Kentucky resolves stated that any acts in which the federal government transcended its constitutional powers could be declared void by state legislatures. Virginia asserted that a state had the right to interpose its authority between its citizens and the federal government. The legislatures called for other states to join in the protest. Although this amounted to no more than a protest, it did help to rally the Republicans to a victory in 1800, with the election of Jefferson as president.

The issue of state versus national power eventually led the country into civil war and has continued to appear intermittently up to the present time. The doctrine of states' rights has been invoked as often by liberals as by conservatives. Although the question of the extent of national power has never been completely settled, the firmest foundation of such power lies in the opinions of Chief Justice John Marshall.

THE DARTMOUTH COLLEGE CASE

On the morning of February 2, 1819, Chief Justice Marshall's first act was to read his opinion in *Dartmouth College* v. *Woodward,* a case that had been argued the previous March but left undecided. The announcement of that decision marked the beginning of what has been called "the greatest six weeks in the history of the court,"[7] a period that would be climaxed by Marshall's own treatise on states' rights versus national supremacy.

The facts of the Dartmouth case were complicated. John Wheelock, the son of Dartmouth College founder Eleazer Wheelock, had ascended to the presidency of the college in 1779. Under the charter from King George, Eleazer could name his own successor, who would serve indefinitely unless at some time his appointment was "disapproved by the trustees." Although some of the trustees had balked at the idea of naming John, who had virtually no qualifications for the office, they had gone along with Eleazer's wishes, probably because John was willing to serve without pay and the college lacked funds to hire a president.

Over the years, however, that marriage of convenience had fallen apart. Wheelock had become an increasingly stiff and rigid man, who, characteristically, "wore the old-fashioned outfit of dun-colored coat, knee breeches with buckles, white stockings, and three-cornered beaver hat."[8] He had run the college on his own terms, making all appointments to the faculty and instituting strict rules. By 1809 a new set of trustees had come in, and they challenged Wheelock's authority by vetoing his appointments to the faculty and then, as a final slap, passing a resolution that released him from his teaching duties.

But Wheelock was not about to be outdone. Several years later, in 1815, he wrote a pamphlet entitled *Sketches of the History of Darmouth College . . . with a Particular Account of Some Late Remarkable Proceedings of the Board of Trustees from the Year 1779 to the Year 1815,* in which he outlined the "abuses" of the trustees. Wheelock made sure that each member of the New Hampshire state legislature had a copy to read. The legislature, which was at this time Federalist by a slim majority, agreed to look into the matter and sent a committee to Hanover in August. Much to Wheelock's dismay, the committee's report was severely critical—not of the trustees, but of the president. With the report as ammunition, and using the disapproval provision of the college's charter, the board of trustees mustered enough courage to oust Wheelock.

But Wheelock had made some friends in Concord, the Jeffersonian Republicans. The plight of the college became a major issue in the 1816 elections, and the Republicans, crusading for the aging president, won their first majority in the legislature. They quickly passed legislation that dissolved the royal charter, returning to Wheelock control of a new institution, Dartmouth University, under a new charter. In order to get around the trustees, the legislature increased the number of board members from 12 to 21 and provided for a board of overseers, which could veto decisions of the trustees.

What resulted was a tragic farce. The college retained the students, yet the university had the buildings. The college scraped by with contributions from alumni and parents, and classes continued to meet wherever space could be found in the town of Hanover. The original board of trustees took its case to court, but, not surprisingly, lost in the New Hampshire courts.

The college was soon out of money; it couldn't even collect its meager endowment money, because the university held all the account books. In desperation, the trustees turned to a member of the class of 1801, Daniel Webster, who was at this point a congressman from Portsmouth.* Ironically, Wheelock had been trying to get Webster's support all along, but Webster had been unwilling to get involved unless it were on a "professional" basis—that is, unless Wheelock was prepared to pay his fee. When the trustees asked for help, Webster issued the same ultimatum. His fee, for himself and Baltimore lawyer Joseph Hopkinson, would be $1,000. A gift to the college made the appeal to the Supreme Court possible.

By the time the case reached the high court, John Wheelock had died and his son-in-law had taken over as head of the university. Arguments were scheduled for March 10, 1818. The courtroom that day was crowded with representatives of private colleges, who realized that their fate also hung in the balance. Webster, the first to address the Court, gave the trustees their money's worth. He spoke for four hours, deftly bringing up every argument he could lay his hands on and driving home one important constitutional argument, that the contract clause of the Constitution forbade states from impairing the obligation of contracts. He reminded the Court that in 1810, in the case of the Georgia Yazoo land fraud, the justices had decided that "a grant is a contract." In that case the Supreme Court had overturned an act of the Georgia legislature whose effect was to repeal an act of a previous legislature selling land at ridiculously low prices. Marshall's reasoning had been that as the land

---

*Webster would eventually become senator from Massachusetts and the most celebrated orator of his age.

subsequently had been sold to innocent third parties, those contracts could not be violated by the new legislature.

Making his debut as one of the most prominent attorneys in the United States, Webster struck a chord that he knew Marshall, the great defender of property rights, would hear:

> This, sir, is my case. It is the case not merely of that humble institution, it is the case of every college in our land. . . . It is more. It is, in some sense, the case of every man who has property of which he may be stripped for the question is simply this: Shall our State legislature be allowed to take that which is not their own, to turn it from its original use, and apply it to such ends or purposes as they, in their discretion, shall see fit?

Then he continued, in the words that every Dartmouth alumnus can recite, "It is, sir, as I have said, a small college, and yet *there are those that love it.*"[9] His voice quivered, his eyes filled with tears; the justices were transfixed, and Marshall was almost moved to tears. But despite this dramatic presentation, Marshall announced at the end of the oral arguments that some of the justices had not made up their minds and that the rest were divided. The next morning, he informed the parties that the case would be continued until 1819.

When the Court reconvened almost a year later, the Chief Justice "pulled an eighteen-page opinion from his sleeve"[10] and declared that a charter was a contract within the meaning of the Constitution. The New Hampshire legislation was unconstitutional. Dartmouth College would regain its charter.

First, citing the framers' sensitivity to "giving permanence and security to contracts," Marshall concluded that "the acts of the legislature of New Hampshire . . . are repugnant to the constitution of the United States." He said that the New Hampshire legislature had converted "a literary institution, moulded according to the will of its founders, and placed under the control of private literary men, into a machine entirely subservient to the will of government. This may be for the advantage of this college in particular, and may be for the advantage of literature in general; but it is not according to the will of the donors, and is subversive of that contract, on the faith of which their property was given."[11] A contract could not be violated under the Constitution—not even by a state.

As Richard N. Current comments in his essay on the case, its repercussions were diverse and important: "The Dartmouth case enhanced the prestige of John Marshall and the Supreme Court. It extended the national power at the expense of state power. It confirmed the charter rights not only of Dartmouth College but of all private colleges. It protected and encouraged business corporations as well as nonprofit corporations. And, incidentally, it brought Daniel Webster to the top of the legal profession."[12] Webster would play a role a few weeks later in Marshall's ultimate statement of national sovereignty.

THE BANK CASE: *McCULLOCH* V. *MARYLAND*

James William McCulloch was the cashier of the Baltimore branch of the Bank of the United States. It was his job to issue bank notes and take deposits. But, beginning in May 1818, each transaction he completed was illegal, because the state of Maryland had passed a law requiring banks not chartered by the state to either purchase special stamped paper or pay $15,000 a year. Neither McCulloch nor any of the bank officers had any intention of complying. They knew that the state tax was an attempt to force the Bank out of the state, and they were not about to back down without a fight. So when the state sent John James—a bounty hunter of sorts, who received half of the fines he collected—to the bank for the purpose of gathering evidence that the state law was being violated, it was the beginning of a case that would not only call into question the constitutionality of the Bank, but the powers of the federal government over the states.

The Baltimore branch was one of 18 offices of the second Bank of the United States. It had been chartered in 1816 by the Republican Congress to try to get the country out of a monetary crisis following the War of 1812. Its predecessor, Alexander Hamilton's progeny of 1791, had been allowed to expire in 1811. The idea of a national bank had been controversial from the beginning. It had created a schism in the Washington administration between Secretary of the Treasury Hamilton and Secretary of State Thomas Jefferson. Hamilton espoused the "loose construction" theory of the Constitution:

> Every power vested in a government is in its nature sovereign, and includes by the force of the term, a right to employ all the means requisite ... to the attainment of the ends of such power.... If the end [i.e., purpose of the legislation] be clearly comprehended with any of the specified powers, and if the measure have an obvious relation to that end and is not forbidden by any particular provision of the Constitution, it may safely be deemed to come within the national authority.[13]

Jefferson espoused the "strict constructionist" view that the "necessary and proper clause" did not give Congress the power to pass laws for convenience. He said that the national Bank was not strictly necessary, because state banks could be used for government funds. Madison agreed, arguing that in passing the bill establishing the Bank Congress had gone beyond its constitutional authority. But President Washington had sided with Hamilton and had signed the bank legislation.

The second Bank was as controversial as the first. Jeffersonian Republicans—the agrarian interests—hated all banks. State bankers despised the Bank because it competed with their own and was capable of destroying them by expanding and contracting credit. Underlying the whole bank issue was the matter of states' rights. The states knew that the control of the purse strings was an important power and they were not about to surrender it. They felt that the Bank was unconstitutional because the Constitution did not explicitly give Congress the power to charter corporations. To the states' rights advocates, the nation was a confederation of sovereign states, whose power must not be usurped by a greedy or overzealous Congress.

The Bank's opponents derived further ammunition from the fact that the Bank failed to resolve the country's monetary problems. By 1818, as a result of land speculation, the dumping of British goods on the American market, and a drop in the price of American products, the country was well on the road to depression. The Bank became the scapegoat. Some members of Congress had even tried to kill it—but unsuccessfully.

At this point, Maryland was determined to make the Bank pay or get out and took it to court. McCulloch and the Bank lost in the Baltimore County court and, on appeal, in the Maryland Court of Appeals. The next step was the United States Supreme Court.

But before the case reached the high court, the bank issue became still more complicated. Word got around that many of the branches were being mismanaged and that funds were being misused. The Baltimore branch was no exception. Although the charter had limited the number of shares any stockholder could vote, McCulloch and three other stockholders had devised a scheme whereby they would purchase the shares in other people's names and then vote the shares as the people's attorneys. So, rather than having only 30 votes each (for a total of 120), they were able to control 4,000 votes and appoint their own directors. To top this off, McCulloch as cashier had been able to loan himself and his partners the money to purchase the shares. In other words, they were using the Bank's own money to buy its shares, causing a great increase in the price of the stock. After Congress got wind of some of the problems in Baltimore and elsewhere, it ordered an investigation of the Bank, ousted its president, and tried to clean things up before the *McCulloch* case reached the Supreme Court. (Eventually, McCulloch and his cohorts were charged with conspiracy but were acquitted.)

THE COURT HEARS THE CASE

Arguments for *McCulloch* began on February 22, 1819, and lasted for nine days. In a rare move, the Court suspended its own rule that only two lawyers could argue for each side and allowed three each. For the Bank were Daniel Webster, William Pinkney, and United States Attor-

ney General William Wirt. For the state of Maryland were Joseph Hopkinson (who had argued with Webster in the *Dartmouth* case), Walter
Jones, and Luther Martin, Maryland's attorney general and an ardent
states' rights advocate who had been a delegate to the Constitutional
Convention.

Because the facts of the case were not disputed, there were only two
major issues for the Court to decide: Was the Bank constitutional? Did
Maryland have the power to tax the Bank?

Webster began the arguments by saying that the questions before
the Court were "deeply interesting" and could "affect the value of a vast
amount of private property." He reminded the justices that the bank had
been legislatively accepted for nearly 30 years and concluded that "it
would seem almost too late to call it in question unless its repugnancy
with the constitution were plain and manifest."[14]

Webster then went on to argue that the Bank was constitutional.
He stressed that Congress was not limited to those powers that are enumerated, but could use all suitable means in raising and disbursing revenue.
"It is not enough to say, that it does not appear that a bank was in the
contemplation of the framers of the constitution. It was not their intention, in these cases, to enumerate particulars. The true view of the subject
is, that if it be a fit instrument to an authorized purpose, it may be used,
not being specially prohibited." He told the Court that the grant to the
Congress to pass laws that were "necessary and proper" for carrying out
its powers did not mean solely those laws that were *"absolutely indispensable,"* or otherwise the "government would hardly exist." Webster continued, "A bank is a proper and suitable instrument to assist the operations of the government, in the collection and disbursement of the
revenue; . . . the only question is, whether a bank . . . is capable of being
so connected with the finances and revenues of the government, as to be
fairly within the discretion of Congress."

On the question of whether the state of Maryland could tax the
bank, Webster pointed out that in ratifying the Constitution the people
had seen fit to "divide sovereignty, and to establish a complex system."
But he asserted that the Constitution itself and the laws passed by Congress were the *"supreme law of the land."* Reminding the Court that if
the state could tax the Bank, it could tax other government operations,
including judicial proceedings, Webster warned, "If the States may tax
the bank, to what extent shall they tax it, and where shall they stop? An
unlimited power to tax involves, necessarily, a power to destroy; because
there is a limit beyond which no institution and no property can bear
taxation."

Webster concluded by insisting that the operation of the Bank
could not be impeded by state legislation. "To hold otherwise, would be
to declare that Congress can only exercise its constitutional powers subject to the controlling discretion, and under the sufferance of the State
governments."

The two sides took turns making their presentations, until all six lawyers had spoken. Attorney General Wirt and Pinkney refuted many of the specific points raised by the other side. Pinkney, who concluded the arguments for the Bank in a forceful three-day argument, asserted that the "constitution acts directly *on* the people, by means of powers communicated directly *from* the people." Because the people had ratified the Constitution, not the states, the federal government was just as sovereign as the state governments. On the issue of the Tenth Amendment, Pinkney stated: "All powers are given to the national government, as the people will. The reservation in the 10th Amendment to the constitution . . . is not confined to powers not *expressly* delegated. Such an amendment was indeed proposed but it was perceived, that it would strip the government of some of its most essential powers, and it was rejected."

Joseph Hopkinson, for the state of Maryland, began his argument by trying to show that the Bank was not constitutional. Even if the first Bank had been constitutional, he said, the circumstances had changed so that the Bank was no longer "necessary" and therefore not constitutional. His next point was that even if the Bank were found to be within the scope of the constitutional powers of Congress, it could not establish branches within the states without the permission of the states. He said that Congress had unconstitutionally delegated the power of establishing branches to the directors of the Bank. Thus, Hopkinson argued, the branches were "located at the will of the directors," who represented the stockholders. He continued, "If this is the case, can it be contended, that the State rights of territory and taxation are to yield for the gains of a money-trading corporation; to be prostrated at the will of a set of men who have no concern, and no duty, but to increase their profits? Is this the necessity required by the constitution for the creation of undefined powers?"

On the question of the tax, Hopkinson argued that the right to tax "is the highest attribute of sovereignty, the right to raise revenue; in fact, the right to exist; without which no other right can be held or enjoyed." He said that there was nothing in the Constitution which put limit on the states' right to tax, and he urged the Court to maintain this right so that the states and the federal government could remain on friendly terms.

Walter Jones argued that the Constitution had not been formed and adopted by the people at large, "but by the people of the respective States. To suppose that the mere proposition of this fundamental law threw the American people into one aggregate mass, would be to assume what the instrument itself does not profess to establish." He asserted that the Constitution was "a compact between the States, and all the powers which are not expressly relinquished by it are reserved to the States." He then argued that the Bank was an arbitrary exercise of power, not one that was "necessary and proper."

Maryland Attorney General Luther Martin made the argument that the Tenth Amendment was written to assure the people that the central government would not try to usurp power from the states. He said that if the people had been aware of what vast powers the Congress would claim, the Constitution would never have been adopted. "We insist, that the only safe rule is the plain letter of the constitution, the rule which the constitutional legislators themselves have prescribed, in the tenth amendment, . . . that the powers not delegated to the United States nor prohibited to the States, are reserved to the States respectively, or to the people." He insisted that the power to establish a corporation was one that was reserved to the states.

THE DECISION

On March 6, four days after the oral arguments had concluded, Marshall announced the decision of the Court in a ringing pronouncement of national supremacy and his own theories of federalism. Indeed, the decision was such an overwhelming victory for the Bank that parts of it sounded almost like recitations of the arguments of Webster, Wirt, and Pinkney.

On the question of the constitutionality of the Bank, Marshall began by referring to Webster's argument in the following way: "It has been truly said that this can scarcely be considered as an open question."[15] He then proceeded to answer it as if it were an open question, adding foundation to his belief that the Bank was constitutional. Accepting Pinkney's argument that the United States was a government of the people and rejecting Jones's argument that the government was a federation of states, Marshall described the process by which the Constitution was adopted by convention. "It is true, they assembled in their several States. . . . No political dreamer was ever wild enough to think of breaking down the lines which separate the states, and of compounding the American people into one common mass," he stated. "But the measures they adopt do not . . . cease to be measures of the people themselves, or become the measures of the State governments." He continued:

> The government proceeds directly from the people; is "ordained and established" in the name of the people. . . . The assent of the States in their sovereign capacity, is implied in calling a Convention, and thus submitting that instrument to the people. But the people were at perfect liberty to accept or reject it; and their act was final. It required not the affirmance, and could not be negatived, by the State governments. The constitution, when thus adopted was of complete obligation, and bound the State sovereignties.

Here Marshall was fortifying the argument made so many times by James Madison and James Wilson during the Constitutional Convention: the federal government must be a government that derives its power and purpose from the people as a whole and the only way to transcend state rivalries was to make the United States a nation of people, not of states.

The Chief Justice then moved to the question of the extent of the powers of the federal government, a question which he admitted "is perpetually arising, and will probably continue to arise, as long as our system shall exist." He said, "If any one proposition could command the universal assent of mankind, we might expect it would be this—that the government of the Union . . . is supreme within its sphere of action." He acknowledged that among the enumerated powers there was not one to establish a bank. However, he said, it would have been impossible for the framers to spell out all the powers; had they done so, the Constitution would have been more like "a legal code." Then, in the words most often quoted, Marshall asserted, "In considering this question . . . we must never forget that it is a *constitution* we are expounding." He said that the necessary and proper clause was made "in a constitution intended to endure for ages to come, and consequently, to be adapted to the various *crises* of human affairs."

The Bank was a "means" to an "end." It was up to Congress to determine if those means were necessary in carrying out the enumerated powers.

> But we think the sound construction of the constitution must allow to the national legislature that discretion, with respect to the means by which the powers it confers are to be carried into execution, which will enable that body to perform the high duties assigned to it, in the manner most beneficial to the people. Let the end be legitimate, let it be within the scope of the constitution, and all means which are appropriate, which are plainly adapted to that end, which are not prohibited, but consist with the letter and spirit of the constitution, are constitutional.

Marshall concluded his discussion of the constitutionality issue by declaring that the Court had ruled unanimously "that the act to incorporate the Bank of the United States is a law made in pursuance of the constitution, and is a part of the supreme law of the land."

The second issue to be determined was that of the tax. In his characteristic way, Marshall began by asserting the right of states to tax but then added the qualification that a state could only tax its own people and their property. The state governments had no power to tax people of other states. As the federal government was a government of all the people, the state of Maryland could not tax it. Echoing Webster's arguments, Marshall three times declared that "the power to tax involves the power to destroy." If the states could tax the Bank, they could also tax the mails or the judicial process or any other means of government. That power would change the character of the Constitution, he said. "We shall find it capable of arresting all the measures of government, and of prostrating it at the foot of the States. . . . this principle would transfer the supremacy, in fact, to the States."

In conclusion, Marshall said, "The Court has bestowed on this subject its most deliberate consideration. The result is a conviction that the States have no power, by taxation or otherwise, to retard, impede, burden, or in any manner control the operations of the constitutional laws enacted by Congress." Thus the law passed by the Maryland legislature was "unconstitutional and void."

REACTION TO THE DECISION

Many states' rights advocates reacted to the opinion with a sense of outrage. The issue of states' rights as it pertained to slavery was being debated in Congress over the Missouri question (see Chapter 2), and many believed that the Court had gone too far. Jefferson criticized the Court as a "subtle corps of sappers and miners constantly working underground to undermine the foundations of our constitutional fabric."[16]

When Marshall returned to Virginia after the Court had adjourned, he met with a hostile reception. Many found the Court's reasoning "heretical" and "damnable." The Virginia legislature passed resolutions denouncing the decision and calling for a constitutional amendment to set up an independent tribunal to settle matters between states and the federal government.

A series of articles were printed in the *Richmond Enquirer* attacking the decision. In a rare move, Marshall himself, using the pseudonym "A Friend of the Constitution," countered with a series of letters in the *Philadelphia Union* and *Alexandria Gazette,* defending the decision.

Although Marshall's decision in *McCulloch* is considered the ultimate statement of national supremacy, some historians have concluded that it had little effect until after the Civil War. During the 30 years following the decision, the issue of states' rights flared repeatedly.

In 1828 in response to tariffs passed by Congress the legislature of South Carolina, with the help of Vice President John C. Calhoun, who remained a "silent partner" in the document, passed an exposition that resurrected the theories of the Virginia and Kentucky resolves of 1798. The federal government, this document declared, was a compact among sovereign states, and each state had a right to judge when its "agent," the federal government, had gone beyond its constitutional powers. Any congressional act that was judged to constitute such a usurpation of power could be nullified by the state.

Four years later in 1832, South Carolina formally acted on this theory by declaring that the tariffs imposed by Congress were "unauthorized by the constitution of the United States, null and void."[17] South Carolina's Nullification Act forbade the collection of tariffs in South Carolina ports, and the state threatened secession if the government tried to blockade Charleston. President Jackson, a states' rights advocate himself, issued his own proclamation reiterating Marshall's affirmation that the government was of the people, not of the states. Although Jackson was ready to send troops to South Carolina, the confrontation was avoided by a lowering of the tariffs and South Carolina's repeal of the Nullification Act.

States' rights doctrines continued to be pervasive in American history—from the refusal of Ohio, Massachusetts, and Wisconsin to comply with the Fugitive Slave Act in 1850, to the secession of the South in the Civil War, to protests against Franklin D. Roosevelt's New Deal, to attempts in the South to resist integration, to President Reagan's assertion that the federal government should be less concerned with regulation of the states. Although the issue may lie dormant for periods, it continually reappears in a new form, testing the balance of powers of state and federal government, testing the Constitution "intended to endure for ages to come, and . . . to be adapted to the various crises of human affairs."

Franklin Pierce, fourteenth President of the United States.
The Bettman Archive

An obscure incident concerning the bloody nose of a diplomat during the administration of Franklin Pierce led to a Court decision asserting broad "emergency powers" of the president. It was the start of the battle between the president and Congress over the power to wage war. This competition over war powers is an illustration of the intricacies of the constitutional concepts of separation of powers and checks and balances.

THE SACKING OF GREYTOWN
The Power to Make War

We have already given in example one effectual check to the Dog of war by transferring the power of letting him loose from the Executive to the Legislative body, from those who are to spend to those who are to pay.

Thomas Jefferson[1]

There will never be another declaration of war . . . that time is gone.

Richard M. Nixon

Those of us who learned American history at the hand of a high school drillmaster whose antiquated method was to make us memorize three significant events in each president's term of office always had trouble with our fourteenth president, Franklin Pierce. To come up with any meaningful achievement of Pierce, one must search through the innermost recesses and cobwebs of the mind or the dustiest bookshelves of the library. Yet it was during Pierce's four frustrating years in the White House, in 1854, that a seemingly obscure incident exploded into what has been described as "the most significant use of Presidential power."[2] Inadvertently, Pierce became one of the fathers of "gunboat diplomacy" and an early tester of the constitutional limits of presidential war powers. His actions, which ostensibly sought revenge for the bloodied nose of an arrogant and belligerent American diplomat in an obscure town in Nicaragua, almost caused a war with Great Britain and taught the American eagle to scream.

A DANGEROUS COMBINATION OF POLICIES AND THE RACE FOR A CANAL

Franklin Pierce became President of the United States by a fluke, perhaps a monumental mistake by the Democratic party. When the 1852 nominating convention in Baltimore failed to come up with a candidate after 48 ballots, Pierce was chosen as a compromise candidate on the 49th. "The young Hickory of the Granite Hills," as he was heralded, seemed an appropriate compromise—he came from the North, but his position on slavery was acceptable to the South. Yet the sum total of his political experience was a short stint as congressman from New Hampshire. Pierce's "only qualifications were a handsome face and figure, a credible military record in the Mexican War, and an almost blank, hence blameless political record," Samuel Eliot Morrison comments. "What the presidential office then needed was backbone, and Pierce had the backbone of a jellyfish."[3] Perhaps this is why Pierce has been listed by some historians as one of the worst and weakest presidents.

Pierce's inaugural address stressed his ill-fated plan for an expansionist administration, which he hoped would match those of his predecessors, Jackson and Polk.* The address also dealt with the related issue of protection for Americans and American business abroad. Pierce expressed his desire that Americans "realize that upon every sea and in every soil where our enterprise may rightfully seek the protection of our flag American citizenship is an inviolable panoply for the security of American rights."[4] Pierce reaffirmed the Monroe Doctrine, which stated that the United States would not tolerate any outside intervention in the Americas.

Pierce's plan was to satisfy "Young America," the progressives, with the policies of expansionism, while domestically pursuing policies that would appease the Southern slavery interests and hence preserve the Union. "Pierce cherished dreams of a vigorous foreign policy," as his biographer Roy Franklin Nichols wrote. "Diplomacy offered an unhampered field for constructive achievement." Yet "unwittingly he had planned to carry out what proved to be a most dangerous and difficult combination of policies."[5]

Pierce's foreign policy was a disaster. He failed in his attempts to purchase Cuba from Spain or annex it, and he similarly failed to annex Hawaii. Perhaps part of President Pierce's ineptness in foreign policy was a result of his personality; he was "volatile and somewhat given to flamboyant utterance," a tendency that was particularly evident in his dealings with Great Britain. But this bellicosity was somewhat assuaged by his more diplomatic secretary of state, William Marcy. One result of the two working together was that Pierce appointed "a series of undiplomatic, or worse, representatives abroad," and Marcy gave them more "conservative instructions."[6]

Among Pierce's undiplomatic diplomats was Solon Borland, a former senator from Arkansas who would eventually become a Confederate

---

*Jackson, a frontiersman, had tried to encourage westward migration by reducing the cost of public lands and by building roads and canals. Polk had run on a platform of "54° 40' or Fight" (i.e., the reoccupation of Oregon) and the annexation of Texas. During his term, he was able to accomplish both as well as acquire the New Mexico Territory and California.

general in the Civil War. Borland was appointed minister to Central America and sent to Nicaragua, which in the mid-nineteenth century was one of those slices of land where politics were largely determined by geography. The 171-mile-wide strip, with a large navigable lake in the center and many rivers, was a choice site for a connection between the Atlantic and Pacific. The need for such a connection had grown. New York and California were thousands of miles closer via Nicaragua than around Cape Horn at the tip of South America. With the Gold Rush of 1849 and the admission of California into the Union, a canal across one of the narrow Central American states—Nicaragua and Panama being the most likely spots—meant commerce and power, and the United States and Great Britain were in a frenzied race for that prize.

The race had brought the two competing countries close to war. In 1848 a British warship had seized San Juan del Norte, a small town in Nicaragua, at the mouth of the San Juan River. Its location, on the Mosquito Coast of the Caribbean, was a logical one for the eastern entrance of a canal connecting the two oceans. In an effort to avert fighting, Great Britain and the United States signed the Clayton-Bulwer treaty in 1850. The treaty committed the two nations to joint control of any canal in Central America.*

After its seizure by the British, San Juan had been renamed Greytown and became a "free city," a British protectorate under a grant from the Mosquito Indians. It was a polyglot port town, with a population of some five hundred Americans, British, Jamaican blacks, and Dutch, most of whom worked the docks and railroads or were small traders. As the engineers studied the possibilities for a canal, the rising tide of commerce generated business for the Accessory Transit Company, a combination railroad-steamer company operated by Commodore Cornelius Vanderbilt. Steamships sailed into the Greytown harbor and unloaded passengers and cargo onto smaller ships, which then sailed up the San Juan River, beginning the long and tortuous haul, first by steamer and then by train, across the isthmus. On the other end, larger ships waited at San Juan del Sur to continue the rest of the route to California.

Vanderbilt's transit company was headquartered outside Greytown in the Nicaraguan city of Punta Arenas, but its operations crept into the city limits. The town officials had authorized a fueling station, but resented the continual growth of other operations of the American-owned company. As the transit company expanded, the tension mounted. Finally, the Greytown mayor and council ordered the company to stop

---

*The French were also interested in a canal. With the Americans and British concentrating their efforts in Nicaragua, the French had set their sights on the shorter, but humid and disease-ridden route across the Isthmus of Panama, then a part of the Republic of Colombia. But the French attempt in Panama in 1883 failed because of the malaria which plagued the workers. Later, in 1914, after President Theodore Roosevelt had encouraged a Panamanian revolt from Colombia and it had become possible to combat malaria, the United States finally opened a canal across Panama.

building and to destroy all facilities not directly related to the fueling operation. Two incidents pressurized the situation. First, Greytown officials interfered when transit company security men tried to apprehend an employee who had stolen a boat load of flour. Then one of the company buildings was burned. (Some reports say it was a house; others called it more of a shack.)

Managers of the transit company were not about to be intimidated by what they regarded as "pretended" authorities and called on the Pierce administration for help. To President Pierce, American citizens and American property—even though thousands of miles away—were entitled to full protection from Uncle Sam. This policy fit right into Commodore Vanderbilt's desire that the State Department be an agent for American business interests. "Pierce and Marcy may have sometimes wondered," suggested Pierce's biographer, "whether they were managers of foreign relations or errand boys of business."[7]

An American sloop-of-war, commanded by George N. Hollins, had already been dispatched to the area under the orders of President Millard Fillmore when the situation had first started to heat up. In April 1853, when the Greytown officials threatened to destroy more property, Pierce, who had just taken office, instructed Hollins to protect the transit company. Hollins sent a party of marines ashore. Outgunned, the authorities backed down. Although what ensued was not more than an uneasy truce, the violence subsided—at least until Central American Minister Solon Borland came cruising into Greytown.

FROM BLOODY NOSE TO THE BRINK OF WAR

At the end of May, 1854, Pierce had received word that the British had decided to interpret the Clayton-Bulwer treaty to mean that they had the same rights to meddle in the affairs of Central America as they had had before. In an effort to similarly exploit the situation, Pierce sent Borland down to renegotiate a treaty with the Nicaraguans. His objectives included urging Nicaragua to adjust her boundary with Costa Rica "so that no areas of doubtful ownership might be left for nations like Great Britain to encroach upon as the latter country had done at Greytown."[8] In addition, Borland was to urge the reestablishment of a confederation of Central American states and to do all he could for the Accessory Transit Company.

Apparently, Borland had literally offered the British-occupied territory to the Nicaraguans in a draft treaty, which was quickly dumped by Pierce and Marcy. Borland, disgruntled, resigned and was on his way home when he became embroiled in the Greytown hostilities.

Although reports of what happened vary somewhat from newspaper report to newspaper report and from eyewitness to eyewitness, the following account seems likely. Borland was being ferried along the San

Juan River to Greytown on the small steamer *Routh,* captained by an American named T. T. Smith. As the ship entered the harbor some black natives in a small boat or canoe came up alongside and one of them shouted insults at the captain and passengers. One account says Borland taunted Smith, exclaiming that he should have "shot the damned nigger." Angry, Captain Smith backed up the boat, picked up his rifle, and shot the boatman dead. Smith evidently realized the gravity of what he had done; he told passengers that he "never would have done it" if Borland hadn't egged him on.[9] Borland and other passengers then boarded the ocean steamer *Northern Light.* Soon an angry crowd of Greytown officials and citizens came up alongside the *Routh* ready to arrest Smith. Borland then returned to the *Routh,* and in a role that one newspaper editorial described as that of "a bully and a braggert," he "pointed his loaded rifle and drew his best Arkansas Bowie knife," threatening to shoot the first person who came on board. Borland "decried [the officials'] right to act in as much as they did not hold their post under the government of Nicaragua and he was instructed by the American government to recognize no other."[10] In other words, since the United States hadn't officially recognized the Greytown government, its officials had no authority over any United States citizen. He also argued that in any event the shooting had occurred outside of the Greytown limits and was under the jurisdiction of the Nicaraguan government. The posse and marshall finally backed down and returned to shore.

Later that night Borland went ashore to the home of the American consul. As he recounted the incident to the American official, angry citizens held a meeting at the station house and decided that Borland should be arrested. In a few minutes, men armed with muskets arrived at the consul's home, demanding Borland. Borland repeated his argument that they had no authority over him and warned them of the repercussions of arresting a United States diplomat. In the ruckus that followed, someone in the mob threw a broken bottle, which struck Borland in the face and bloodied his nose. Although Borland was not arrested, armed citizens prevented any boats from leaving shore and so Borland was detained overnight.

When Borland got back to the United States, he immediately related his account of the incident to his superiors. He admitted that the mayor had disavowed the actions of the men who had attempted to arrest him, but added that the mayor himself had presided at the meeting where the decision had been made. He neglected to report that Captain Smith had not been prosecuted and apparently told Pierce that he believed Smith to be innocent. In the interim, the mayor and council had resigned and been replaced by a new administration.

In Washington the incident was discussed at the highest levels of government. One wonders what went through President Pierce's mind as he contemplated what action to take and whether to consult Congress:

other presidents had at least gone through the motions of consulting Congress before becoming involved in war. Pierce was being pressured by Commodore Vanderbilt's agent to use force to demand an apology for the insult to his ambassador and reparations of $24,000 (some say $26,000) for damages to the transit company. Certainly, as a Mexican War veteran, Pierce was aware of President James Polk's unbridled use of the American military. Polk had sent American troops to the Texas border whose presence instigated a skirmish with the Mexicans. However, he then went to Congress with the news that the United States was in a state of war and belatedly asked it to declare war with Mexico. Two years after the troops had been sent, in 1848, Congress reluctantly complied. Pierce's other idol, Andrew Jackson, had gone to Congress in 1831 to ask for approval to use armed vessels to protect United States shipping interests against Argentine raiders. Pierce may not have remembered that President Thomas Jefferson had gone to Congress in 1801 after he had sent ships into the Mediterranean to protect the American merchant fleet against the Barbary pirates of Tripoli. In December Jefferson reported to Congress that an American naval schooner had been fired on by a Tripolian ship of war. (Some historians suggest that Jefferson had deceived Congress and that the American ship had initiated the hostilities.) Jefferson told Congress that the American navy was "unauthorized by the Constitution, without the sanction of Congress, to go beyond the line of defense." He thus asked Congress to put American forces "on equal footing" with the enemy. Congress did not see the need of declaring war, but did give the navy permission to fight as Jefferson had asked and, in effect, authorized a limited war against Tripoli. Four years later, when the Spanish were moving into the Louisiana territory the United States had just acquired from the French, Jefferson sent a message to Congress asserting that "Congress alone is constitutionally invested with the power of changing our condition from peace to war."[11] But this time Congress denied Jefferson's request.

That Pierce did not share the Jeffersonian position that presidents need authorization from Congress to use military force had already been shown by his earlier use of Commander Hollins to protect the transit company in Greytown. And now, despite the fact that Congress was in session, he didn't bother to consult that body. Instead, in a move that became a landmark in the area of presidential war powers, he did precisely what the Accessory Transit Company wanted: he sent Commander Hollins back down to Nicaragua with instructions to extract an apology from the Greytown officials and reparations of $24,000 for damages to the transit company. (Some reports of the time assert that the actual damages were far less than demanded.)[12]

Hollins' orders, dated June 10, from Secretary of the Navy J. C. Dobbin, were that "these people should be taught that the United States will not tolerate these outrages, and that they have the power and determination to check them." However, Dobbin added a qualifier: "It is, however, very much to be hoped that you can effect the purposes of your visit without a resort to violence and destruction of property and loss of life." Hollins was told to use "prudence and good sense."[13]

On July 11, Commander Hollins sailed into the harbor aboard the U.S.S. *Cyane* and made the demands known. When it became clear that no satisfaction would be forthcoming, Hollins sent a squad of marines into the town on the morning of July 12 to post a notice. His long-winded proclamation to the people asserted that certain "outrages" had been "perpetrated by the 'authorities' . . . and people of San Juan del Norte upon the persons and property of American citizens" and that "serious insult and indignity" had been inflicted upon Minister Borland for which "no satisfactory reply has been made." He then warned, "I George N. Hollins, commander of the United States Sloop of War *Cyane,* by virtue of my instruction from the United States government at Washington do hereby solemnly proclaim and declare that it be if the demands for satisfaction in matters above named [are not complied with] I shall at 9 o'clock A.M. of tomorrow the 13th . . . proceed to bombard the town of San Juan del Norte so as to the end that the rights of our country and persons may be vindicated and as a guarantee for future protection."[14]

In a "humanitarian" move, Hollins took control of the transit company steamers and offered residents refuge on board during the impending bombardment. All but about 12 or 15, however, refused his offer and instead boarded a British frigate anchored in the harbor. (The commander of the British vessel *Bermuda* had sent a plea to Hollins, asking him to reconsider his threat.) The lieutenant in command of the shore party "took possession of the muskets, three pieces of cannon, and all the ammunition,"[15] assuring that the town was totally unarmed.

No apology received, the *Cyane*'s guns commenced firing on the town at the stroke of nine the next morning. After a 45-minute barrage, there was a pause of one hour. Hollins later explained to his superiors that the respite was to give the officials the chance to "satisfactorily arrange matters." When the officials gave no sign of complying, the *Cyane* then fired another 30-minute barrage. After a second pause, this time for three hours, Hollins ordered a final 20-minute barrage. He then sent a group of marines ashore to burn whatever buildings were left standing. Hollins reported to his superiors that he felt the action necessary "to satisfy the whole world that the United States has the power and determination to enforce that reparation and respect due them . . . in whatever quarter the outrage may be committed."[16]

Two days later the *Prometheus,* a United States steamship that had been in the harbor during the Borland incident a few weeks before, sailed back into the harbor and discovered that Greytown was no more. Only "one or two small buildings at the suburbs remain to mark the spot."[17]

Glad to be rid of the pesky town, the Accessory Transit Company offered free passage to the United States to all residents and all that they could carry.

President Pierce's biographer reports that "such a feat of arms was quite a shock to Pierce and Marcy."[18] This notion is supported by Arthur Schlesinger in *The Imperial Presidency*. He reports that "no such retaliation had been specifically ordered by President Pierce."[19]

News of the bombardment reached the American public on July 25 with a report from the *Prometheus*. Two letters to the editor of the *New York Daily Times* showed conflicting initial reactions to the incident. The first, signed "An American," criticized Borland's defiance of "the officers of justice in the execution of their official duty." The writer predicted that "if a foreign official accredited to this government were to attempt to interfere with any of our officers of justice in the execution of their official duty as Mr. Borland did, he would be locked up in the 'Tombs' in less than no time." As to the sacking of Greytown, the "American" bemoaned the loss of "property of innocent citizens." He continued, "If this is to be the policy of our government, the sooner we raise the Black Flag the better, that other victims may know what to expect from the United States."[20]

The next day a letter signed "Resident" (presumably of Greytown) recounted the events and concluded, "I think now that the nest of land pirates, which were located at San Juan, is now broken up, and they will also learn that American citizens must and will be protected."[21]

By the following week, the *New York Daily Times* reported that the Greytown incident "excites much talk at Washington and indeed everywhere calls forth the most unqualified denunciation from public opinion."[22] After sorting through reports, the New York newspapers began attacking the administration. On July 29, the *New York Daily Times* questioned the constitutionality of Pierce's mode of proceeding.

> It was clearly a case for diplomatic interference and if that failed to secure redress, the country should have been appealed to through Congress to take such steps as its honor and rights might demand. . . . [But] the President had not uttered a word of negotiations, nor a syllable about the rights of the inhabitants, nor the faintest recollection apparently that there is such a body as Congress in existence. We doubt whether our history can show an instance of more glaring usurpation than that which General Pierce has here been guilty. . . . In this case so far as the principle is concerned he might just as well have ordered Liverpool, or Havre or Havana to be bombarded as Greytown. . . . The offence against the whole spirit of the law is no less flagrant and none the less deserving the attention of Congress and the Country.

The *New York Daily Times* continued its broadsides against the Pierce administration. Having reminded the administration that it had violated the provision of the Constitution that gives Congress the power to declare war, the editors wrote in the August 1 issue, "No one, we think, will doubt or deny that the burning and sacking of Greytown was an act of war and therefore this proceeding is no where to be found in the statute books." It concluded that "it is the act of the President who is mostly responsible to his constituents, the people for this apparent violation of our liberties. Whether there was a sufficient cause of war in this respect is not the question first to be considered, for if we admit there was a cause of war, the power is vested in the Congress and not in the President."

The editorial also argued that the transit company, being chartered by the Nicaraguan government, "had no right to call upon the United States for protection. . . . We humbly protest . . . its use of the Constitution of this nation and the high office of this government for any of its speculatory purposes."

The *New York Evening Post* went even further. Its editors felt that the problem was not that Pierce had violated the Constitution, but that the Constitution itself was flawed. "The American Constitution is justly thought to be a masterpiece of wisdom but after this event, let no one deny it has serious faults . . . chiefly among these is the power of evil that is conferred on a weak and wicked Executive. The ashes [of Greytown] attest that in this respect our forefathers of the Revolution committed a deplorable error."[23]

In Pierce's defense the *Washington Union* charged that the "President and his cabinet have been grossly and wickedly misrepresented by those New York Journals." The paper asserted that "the administration discharged its duty with promptness and fidelity"[24] and argued that no judgment should be made until all the facts had been laid before the public.

But prevailing sentiment was not with the *Union*. Concerned about the destruction of property, New York merchants with property in Central America petitioned the President to cease further violations of the Constitution. They reminded him that Congress alone has the power to wage war. In England, as the London papers cried for war, U.S. Minister James Buchanan, destined to be Pierce's successor, told the British government that the United States would disavow the bombardment.

The Congress, at the motion of Representative Joseph R. Chandler of Philadelphia, requested that Pierce hand over "any official information" relevant to the destruction of Greytown, including copies of the orders given to Hollins. Despite an initial silence on the issue, Pierce did furnish this information in early August. However, a cholera epidemic had broken out on the East Coast and the oppressive 99 degree heat of Washington plus the increasingly pressing domestic issue of slavery sidetracked the Congress; little was done before the session ended.

Thus Pierce had gotten what he needed—a reprieve until emotions settled down. On December 4, when Congress resumed, President Pierce presented his view of the Greytown incident. After reciting a long history of the establishment of Greytown, which was indirectly critical of the British takeover and rule, as well as a whitewashed version of the Borland incident, Pierce told Congress, "These incidents together with the known character of the population of Greytown in their excited state, introduced just apprehensions that the lives and property of our citizens at Punta Arenas would be in imminent danger." This was his justification for sending Hollins. The President told the Congress that Hollins had appealed to the commander of the British ship *Bermuda* to intercede so that hostilities could be avoided, but "that officer did nothing more than protest against the bombardment." He said that the Greytown officials' "obstinate silence" seemed "to provoke chastisement" rather "than to escape it." In an attempt to disassociate himself from all blame, Pierce said that the *Cyane* had gone to Greytown with the hope of avoiding any violence, but that the conduct of the Greytown officials had "frustrated all the possible mild measures for obtaining satisfaction. A withdrawal from the place . . . would, under the circumstances . . . have been absolute abandonment of all claims of our citizens for indemnification, and submissive acquiescence in national indignity."[25]

Pierce had managed to shift the blame from himself, his administration, and Hollins to the British government by arguing that if the British had properly ruled their protectorate, keeping it out of the control of thieves and pirates, the incident might never have taken place.

New York Congressman John Wheeler was not satisfied. On December 11, 1854, he presented a resolution to Congress asking that a committee of 13 "investigate whether the Constitution of the United States had been violated by any officer of the government in the said transaction."[26] But nothing came of it. After the three-month recess, the Congress could not be bothered. As Alexander H. Stevens recorded, "Everything is flat. Nobody cared a cent for the message or anything else. I don't believe that the tide of popular feeling or popular interest in public affairs ever ran so low as at present in this . . . country."[27] Thus, despite Pierce's lambasting by the press, the administration had managed to stumble through the crisis with Congress. However, the issues concerning Pierce's power to make war were not resolved.

CALVIN DURAND SUES

Calvin Durand was an importer-exporter of considerable means, as well as an American citizen who had lost property during the destruction of Greytown. A few years after the incident, Durand decided to put the matter before the courts. He hired lawyers William Tracy and John Manning and sued Captain Hollins in New York District Court on the grounds of trespass by naval forces under his command. He asked the court to compensate him for the damages to property. In reality, the case was challenging the constitutionality of the powers exercised by Pierce as commander in chief. In Hollins' defense District Attorney John McKeon argued that the commander was under orders from the president to protect American lives and property.

The case was heard by United States Supreme Court Justice Samuel Nelson, who was circuit riding.* Nelson's four-page opinion was the first court interpretation of presidential war power. Nelson ruled against Durand on the basis that Hollins was acting for Commander in Chief Pierce, who had the authority to protect American citizens against the "questionable" government of Greytown.

> The question whether it was the duty of the President to interpose for the protection of the citizens at Greytown against an irresponsible and marauding community that had established itself there, was a public political question, in which the Government, as well as the citizens whose interests were involved, was concerned, and which belonged to the Executive to determine; and his decision is final and conclusive, and justified the defendant in the execution of his orders given through the Secretary of the Navy.[28]

Citing Marshall's opinion in *Marbury* v. *Madison* (see Chapter 1), Nelson concluded that the president was vested with certain "important political powers, in the exercise of which he is to use his own discretion, and is accountable only to his country in his political character, and to his own conscience."[29]

Looking back on it, Arthur Schlesinger argues that Justice Nelson's opinion in the Greytown sacking has given "presidential war" special ammunition. "[T]his special, limited, privately disapproved and generally wretched episode was cited in later years by lawyers in desperate search of constitutional justification for presidential war against sovereign states."[30] Indeed, in the more than two hundred instances in which the United States has used armed forces abroad, only five of them were declared wars—the War of 1812, the Mexican War, the Spanish-American War, and the two world wars. And of those five, only one was actually debated by Congress, the War of 1812.

THE POWER TO MAKE WAR

Had Pierce exceeded his powers? Did he need Congress' sanction to send Hollins to Greytown? Had he usurped Congress' war-making powers? The Constitution (Article I, Section 8) provides that the Congress

---

*For a century, justices of the Supreme Court were required to "ride circuit" or hear cases in lower federal courts when the high court was not in session.

"shall have the power . . . to declare War, grant Letters of Marque and Reprisal, and make rules concerning Captures on Land and Water." Yet the same document in Article II makes the president commander in chief of the armed forces and also gives the president the power to receive envoys. The treaty power and the power to appoint ambassadors are given as shared powers to the president and the Senate. This joint power of war and foreign policy has been described by Edwin S. Corwin as "an invitation to struggle for the privilege of directing American foreign policy."[31]

It is clear from Madison's notes on the debates in the Constitutional Convention that the framers did not want the executive to possess the power of "peace and war" lest the office assume the "tyrannical" powers of "monarchy." Little was said about war powers until near the end of the convention, when the report of the Committee of Detail was being discussed. That discourse, one of the few records of how these joint powers were to operate, is as inconclusive as it is short. On the clause giving Congress the power "to make war" the discussion was as follows:

> M[r] PINCKNEY opposed the vesting this power in the Legislature. Its proceedings were too slow. It w[d] meet but once a year. The H[s] Of Rep[s] would be too numerous for such deliberations. The Senate would be the best depositary, being more acquainted with foreign affairs, and most capable of proper resolutions. If the States are equally represented in Senate, so as to give no advantage to large States, the power will notwithstanding be safe, as the small have their all at stake in such cases as well as the large States. It would be singular for one authority to make war, and another peace.
>
> M[r] BUTLER. The objections ag[st] the Legislature lie in great degress ag[st] the Senate. He was for vesting the power in the President, who will have all the requisite qualities, and will not make war but when the Nation will support it.
>
> M[r] MADISON and M[r] GERRY moved to insert *"declare"*, striking out *"make"* war; leaving the Executive the power to repel sudden attacks.
>
> M[r] SHARMAN thought it stood very well. The Executive sh[d] be able to repel and not to commence war. "Make" better than "declare" the latter narrowing the power too much.
>
> M[r] ELSWORTH. there is a material difference between the cases of making *war* and making *peace*. It sh[d] be more easy to get out of war, than into it. War also is a simple and overt declaration. Peace attended with intricate & secret negociations.
>
> M[r] MADISON was ag[st] giving the power of war to the Executive, because not safely to be trusted with it; or to the Senate, because not so constructed as to be entitled to it. He was for clogging rather than facilitating war; but for facilitating peace. He preferred *"declare"* to *"make."*
>
> On the motion to insert *declare*—in place of *make,* it was agreed to.
>
> N. H. no. Mas. abs[t] Con[t] no. P[a] ay. Del. ay. M[d] ay. V[a] ay. N. C. ay. S. C. ay. Geo. Ay.[32]

Butler then moved to give the legislature (i.e., Congress) the power of peace. However, this was unanimously voted down.

Historians have read and reread those words and come up with numerous interpretations of what the consensus of the convention was. Certainly, they did not want war to be entered into lightly, but wanted the president to have the power to repel sudden attack—especially when Congress was not in session.

The drafters of the Constitution almost universally shared a particular fear—that political bodies could be corrupted. This fear grew out of their basic notions about humankind, especially the notion that people were generally incapable of resisting the temptation of power. Historian Bernard Bailyn has observed of writings of the time that "Most commonly the discussion of power centered on its essential characteristic of aggressiveness: its endless propulsive tendency to expand itself beyond legitimate boundaries."[33]

Throughout the debates over the Constitution, the delegates returned to the possibility of "intrigue" by one branch of government, by individuals, by "factions" or influential groups, by the states, or even from abroad. It was their hope to develop a form of government that would prevent the new nation from falling prey to such intrigues. Madison believed that a strong central government was required. His rationale was that the larger the constituency, the less the possibility of influence by petty local squabbles and corruptive "factions."

And because of the corrupting nature of power, the new system needed internal safeguards. The framers had seen the inadequacies of the Articles of Confederation, where all the central government's power was invested in a legislature. So they came up with two revolutionary notions for constructing the national government—first, the separation of powers into three distinct branches, and second, checks and balances through which each branch could be a brake on the others. While each branch of government had a primary responsibility of either legislative, executive, or judicial action, each also had a "check" over the other branches. Thus, for practical purposes, many powers were actually shared powers. The legislature could enact laws, but the president could veto those laws— unless his veto was overridden by a two-thirds vote of the Congress. The final review of the laws lay with the Supreme Court, whose job it was to interpret the Constitution. A law that violated the Constitution would be void. Thus while Congress was vested with the power to make laws, the two other branches shared that power in their "check."

The president could be checked by the Congress, which had the power of the purse and the power of impeachment. The chief justice would preside at the trial after the president was impeached. And the president and Congress had power over the Court, in that the appointments were to be made by the executive and approved by the Senate. In addition, justices were subject to impeachment.

Thus, the Constitution was a grand scheme in which each branch of government had the power and facility to act and to protect itself from encroachments by the other branches.

The principle of separation of power with checks was inherent in the war power. The framers carefully divided up the powers, giving the Congress the right to declare war and the president the command of the armed forces and hence the power to carry out war. The result was what Justice Robert Jackson was to call a "zone of twilight," where it was not clear when the president could act without the authorization of Congress.

Arthur Schlesinger writes that "the Founding Fathers were more influenced by John Locke than by any other political philosopher."[34] Locke's view of the social contract had one exception—"prerogative." That is, government could resort to extraordinary uses of power if the law was silent and in certain emergency situations could even transcend the law. The people and the legislature would later judge whether the use of "prerogative" were justified and "for the public good." Jefferson, who had gone to Congress to request war powers, nonetheless believed in the "prerogative." In 1810, he said, "A strict observance of the written laws is doubtless one of the highest duties of a good citizen, but it is not the highest. The laws of necessity, of self-preservation, of saving our country when in danger, are of a high obligation. . . . To lose our country by a scrupulous adherence to written law, would be to lose the law itself, with life, liberty, property and all those who are enjoying them with us; thus absurdly sacrificing the end to the means."[35]

President Pierce was an early actor in the war power "twilight zone." By sending Commander Hollins to Greytown without congressional authorization he interpreted the scope of presidential power under the Constitution and created a controversial precedent. One wonders whether Jefferson would have approved of Pierce's prerogative. Certainly, if we look, as Locke suggested, to contemporary public reaction, we see that Pierce had to weather a rough storm.

Senator Jacob Javits, in his compelling work *Who Makes War?*, saw Greytown not as a failure of the Constitution—as the *New York Evening Post* had suggested in 1854—but as an "illegitimate exercise of [presidential] authority" and "a blatant example of congressional abdication of responsibility that resulted in another precedent for later Commander in Chief forays on the high seas and in foreign territory. Congress must accept the blame if only because the executive branch under Pierce was divided, weak, and would have been susceptible to the exercise of determined action by the Congress."[36]

In any event, Congress did not act, and the notion—expressed by Locke, alluded to by the framers, and reaffirmed by Justice Nelson—that the president has special power to determine that the country faces an emergency and can act has proved crucial in subsequent history. It led President Abraham Lincoln to take extraordinary measures at the beginning of the Civil War. It justified Theodore Roosevelt's use of American forces in Latin America and Woodrow Wilson's use of troops to occupy Veracruz in 1914 and Haiti in 1915. It was a justification for Truman's sending troops to Korea and for Johnson's and Nixon's escalation of the war in Vietnam. The legal justification of protecting American lives and property has been used over and over as a rationale for American intervention on foreign soil. So pervasive had this presidential use of power become that it appeared, as Richard Nixon commented before he became president, that "there will never be another declaration of war . . . that time is gone."[37]

CONGRESS ATTEMPTS A COMEBACK

It was not until the aftermath of the Vietnam war that Congress chose to reassert itself, to try to regain the war power it was given by the framers of the Constitution. In 1972 Senators Jacob Javits, Thomas Eagleton, and John Stennis introduced the war powers bill into the Senate. After Congress overrode President Nixon's veto, the bill became law November 7, 1973. According to Javits, "The doctrine of Executive war powers has been erected for nearly two hundred years. [With the War Powers Act] we are breaking that thread of our history."[38]

The act begins by stating that its purpose is "to fulfill the intent of the framers of the Constitution of the United States and insure that the collective judgment of both the Congress and the President will apply to the introduction of United States armed forces into hostilities." The legislation stipulates that the president, as commander in chief, may send troops into hostilities only when Congress has declared war or when he has "specific statutory authorization," or during "a national emergency created by attack upon the United States, its territories, or armed forces."

In such cases, when the president does send troops he has the authority to deploy them for only 60 days, and he must report such use to the Congress within 48 hours. Congress may give the president an extension of the 60-day period or may instruct him to recall the troops before the end of the 60-day period. If Congress has been silent on the matter, under the War Powers Act the president must withdraw the troops after 60 days.

Presidents Nixon, Ford, and Reagan have all asserted that the act is unconstitutional, arguing that it ties the hands of the president. Others, such as *New York Times* columnist Tom Wicker, have argued that the act gives the president more power to make war than he had before. As this book was being written, President Reagan's use of a "peacekeeping force" in Lebanon was being widely debated in Congress and the news media; Regan finally withdrew the marines in February 1984. Should the president be able to commit United States troops to hostile situations without the sanction of Congress as the War Powers Act allows him to do, if for only 60 days? That question was also asked when President Reagan sent troops to Grenada under the rationale of protecting Americans.

WHO DECIDES?

In our scheme of separation of powers there remains the question of who decides where the war powers lie. Who decides whether the president has exceeded his constitutional responsibility should he choose not to abide by the act and keep troops in action longer than 60 days or whether Congress has put an unconstitutional restraint on the president's use of emergency powers or his power as commander in chief?

The logical solution would be to put the question before the third branch of government—the Supreme Court, whose job it is to interpret the law and the Constitution. However, there is at least one obstacle to that route—the "political question" doctrine of the Court. Under this principle of judicial restraint, the Court can decide that certain controversies between the other two branches of government are "nonjusticiable," or not properly decided by a court.* In other words, the Court can refuse to take a case because of its political nature. Examples of "political questions" might be whether peace or war exists or whether a foreign country has become an independent state.

There are three basic rationales for the Court to invoke the doctrine. First, and most widely accepted, is that the Constitution does not give the Court final determination on all constitutional questions. The Constitution explicitly commits power to act in certain fields to the executive or the Congress. Another reason for the Court to turn down a political controversy is judicial competence. In other words, the Court may not have enough information available to it to make the decision. The Congress might be better suited to make decisions relating to foreign trade, or the president might be more adept at making decisions about recognizing new nations. The third rationale is that some controversies invite judicial restraint—that is, some issues are too controversial for the Court, and the Court would have no power to enforce its decision. Such cases could result in a "constitutional gridlock," in which the branches of government were involved in a three-way tug-of-war.

What adds even more confusion to this constitutional blur is that it is up to the Court to decide when to raise the political question doctrine, and the Court is unpredictable. One might have thought that the question of whether the Congress could exclude Representative Adam Clayton Powell was a "political question," either because the Congress has the

---

*There are other reasons for nonjusticiability. One is that a case is not "ripe," or ready for judicial review. Another is that the case is "moot," or no longer a valid controversy.

explicit power to judge the qualifications of its own members or because of the potentially embarrassing conflict. However, the Warren Court decided that it was a proper question for the justices. On the other hand, over the dissents of Justices Stewart and Douglas, the Court decided not to take cases rising over the legality of the draft during the Vietnam war. Another court, at another time, in another conflict might decide a similar question differently.

In controversies between Congress and the president an additional problem arises—the problem of whether one branch of government can sue another. Louis Henkin has suggested that "[t]he President cannot bring a judicial proceeding to challenge alleged usurpations by Congress, nor can Congress (or a Congressman) sue to enjoin alleged usurpations by the President."[39] If Congress cannot sue, who can? If the president exceeds the 60-day period, how else can the act be enforced? For the War Powers Act to be tested, it may take the suit of a young man about to be drafted or of a group of marines about to be shipped to foreign soil where "hostilities are imminent."

Whether the War Powers Act will have the effect that was intended remains an unanswered question. The act may ultimately be put before the Supreme Court or it may, as Corwin said of the allocation of power in the Constitution, be just another "invitation" for Congress and the president to "struggle for the privilege of directing American foreign policy." Solon Borland's bloody nose had repercussions far beyond the destruction of Greytown, as that incident was in a sense the beginning of the struggle between the president and the Congress over the power to make war.

Epilogue

When the Constitution was signed at last, Benjamin Rush of Philadelphia wrote to Thomas Jefferson, " 'Tis done. We have become a Nation." Almost two centuries later, the debate continues over exactly what that Constitution means.

"This is not powdered wigs and pewter mugs; this is street fighting," Congresswoman Barbara Mikulski of Maryland said in a debate on executive privilege and separation of powers. Those sentiments might have been uttered by John Barron when he lost his Fifth Amendment fight over his damaged wharf, or by Erna Gans when she and other residents of Skokie, Illinois, tried to stop Frank Collin and his Nazi band from parading through their streets, or by President Franklin Pierce after the sacking of Greytown in Nicaragua.

The Constitution has been described as magnificently ambiguous. Otherwise, as Chief Justice Marshall insisted, it would be no more than a prolix legal code. It is a vernacular document intended for us all, and its survival depends upon us all. *The Constitution: That Delicate Balance*, as a television project and a book, is designed to put our 200-year-old Constitution into contemporary focus. As we approach the bicentennial of the drafting of that document, we trust that the anniversary will be celebrated not just with fireworks, cannons, and twirling batons, but also with a sense of history and a sense of destiny. The men who signed the Constitution had their difficulties hammering it out; the nineteenth- and twentieth-century justices who labored to interpret its eighteenth-century concepts have struggled with no less agony. As Judge Learned Hand observed, "The spirit of liberty is the spirit which is not too sure that it is right. . . ."[1] Citizens who, as Justice Hugo Black did, carry a small copy of the Constitution in their pocket understand that its words must transcend the temples of justice. The continuing debate about its meaning is the ultimate proof of its strength and durability.

To paraphrase George Washington, that may be the real miracle of Philadelphia.

The Constitution
of the United States
# of America

WE THE PEOPLE of the United States, in Order to form a more perfect Union, establish Justice, insure domestic Tranquility, provide for the common defense, promote the general Welfare, and secure the Blessings of Liberty to ourselves and our Posterity, do ordain and establish this CONSTITUTION for the United States of America.

Article I.

SECTION 1. All legislative Powers herein granted shall be vested in a Congress of the United States, which shall consist of a Senate and House of Representatives.

SECTION 2. The House of Representatives shall be composed of Members chosen every second Year by the People of the several States, and the Electors in each State shall have the Qualifications requisite for Electors of the most numerous Branch of the State Legislature.

No Person shall be a Representative who shall not have attained to the Age of twenty-five Years, and been seven Years a Citizen of the United States, and who shall not, when elected, be an Inhabitant of that State in which he shall be chosen.

[Representatives and direct Taxes shall be apportioned among the several States which may be included within this Union, according to their respective Numbers, which shall be determined by adding to the whole Number of free Persons, including those bound to Service for a Term of Years, and excluding Indians not taxed, three fifths of all other Persons.] The actual Enumeration shall be made within three Years after the first Meeting of the Congress of the United States, and within every subsequent Term of ten Years, in such Manner as they shall by Law direct. The Number of Representatives shall not exceed one for every thirty Thousand, but each State shall have at Least one Representative; and until such enumeration shall be made, the State of New Hampshire shall be entitled to chuse three, Massachusetts eight, Rhode-Island and Providence Plantations one, Connecticut five, New-York six, New Jersey four, Pennsylvania eight, Delaware one, Maryland six, Virginia ten, North Carolina five, South Carolina five, and Georgia three.

When vacancies happen in the Representation from any State, the Executive Authority thereof shall issue Writs of Election to fill such Vacancies.

The House of Representatives shall chuse their Speaker and other Officers; and shall have the sole Power of Impeachment.

SECTION 3. The Senate of the United States shall be composed of two Senators from each State, chosen by the Legislature thereof, for six Years; and each Senator shall have one Vote.

Immediately after they shall be assembled in Consequence of the first Election, they shall be divided as equally as may be into three Classes. The Seats of the Senators of the first Class shall be vacated at the Expiration of the second Year, of the second Class at the Expiration of the fourth Year, and of the third Class at the Expiration of the sixth Year, so that one-third may be chosen every second Year; and if Vacancies happen by Resignation, or otherwise, during the Recess of the Legislature of any State, the Executive thereof may make temporary Appointments until the next Meeting of the Legislature, which shall then fill such Vacancies.

No Person shall be a Senator who shall not have attained to the Age of thirty Years, and been nine Years a Citizen of the United States, and who shall not, when elected, be an Inhabitant of that State for which he shall be chosen.

The Vice President of the United States shall be President of the Senate, but shall have no Vote, unless they be equally divided.

The Senate shall chuse their other Officers, and also a President pro tempore, in the absense of the Vice President, or when he shall exercise the Office of President of the United States.

The Senate shall have the sole Power to try all Impeachments. When sitting for that Purpose, they shall be on Oath or Affirmation. When the President of the United States is tried, the Chief Justice shall preside: And no Person shall be convicted without the Concurrence of two thirds of the Members present.

Judgment in Cases of Impeachment shall not extend further than to removal from Office, and disqualification to hold and enjoy any Office of honor, Trust or Profit under the United States: but the Party convicted shall nevertheless be liable and subject to Indictment, Trial, Judgment and Punishment, according to Law.

SECTION 4. The Times, Places and Manner of holding Elections for Senators and Representatives, shall be prescribed in each State by the Legislature thereof; but the Congress may at any time by Law make or alter such Regulations, except as to the Place of Chusing Senators.

The Congress shall assemble at least once in every Year, and such Meeting shall be on the first Monday in December, unless they shall by Law appoint a different Day.

SECTION 5. Each House shall be the Judge of the Elections, Returns and Qualifications of its own Members, and a Majority of each shall constitute a Quorum to do Business; but a smaller number may adjourn from day to day, and may be authorized to compel the Attendance of absent Members, in such Manner, and under such Penalties as each House may provide.

Each House may determine the Rules of its Proceedings, punish its Members for disorderly Behavior, and, with the Concurrence of two thirds, expel a Member.

Each House shall keep a Journal of its Proceedings, and from time to time publish the same, excepting such Parts as may in their Judgment require Secrecy; and the Yeas and Nays of the Members of either House on any question shall, at the Desire of one fifth of those Present, be entered on the Journal.

Neither House, during the Session of Congress, shall, without the Consent of the other, adjourn for more than three days, nor to any other Place than that in which the two Houses shall be sitting.

SECTION 6. The Senators and Representatives shall receive a Compensation for their Services, to be ascertained by Law, and paid out of the Treasury of the United States. They shall in all Cases, except Treason, Felony and Breach of the Peace, be privileged from Arrest during their Attendance at the Session of their respective Houses, and in going to and returning from the same; and for any Speech or Debate in either House, they shall not be questioned in any other Place.

No Senator or Representative shall, during the Time for which he was elected, be appointed to any civil Office under the Authority of the United States, which shall have been created, or the Emoluments whereof shall have been encreased during such time; and no Person holding any Office under the United States, shall be a Member of either House during his Continuance in Office.

SECTION 7. All Bills for raising Revenue shall originate in the House of Representatives; but the Senate may propose or concur with Amendments as on other Bills.

Every Bill which shall have passed the House of Representatives and the Senate, shall, before it become a Law, be presented to the President of the United States; If he approve he shall sign it, but if not he shall return it, with his Objections to that House in which it shall have originated, who shall enter the Objections at large on their Journal, and proceed to reconsider it. If after such Reconsideration two thirds of that House shall agree to pass the Bill, it shall be sent, together with the Objections, to the other House, by which it shall likewise be reconsidered, and if approved by two thirds of that House, it shall become a Law. But in all such Cases the Votes of both Houses shall be determined by Yeas and Nays, and the Names of the Persons voting for and against the Bill shall be entered on the Journal of each House respectively. If any Bill shall not be returned by the President within ten Days (Sundays excepted) after it shall have been presented to him, the Same shall be a Law, in like Manner as if he had signed it, unless the Congress by their Adjournment prevent its Return, in which Case it shall not be a Law.

Every Order, Resolution, or Vote to which the Concurrence of the Senate and House of Representatives may be necessary (except on a question of Adjournment) shall be presented to the President of the United States; and before the Same shall take Effect, shall be approved by him, or being disapproved by him, shall be repassed by two thirds of the Senate and House of Representatives, according to the Rules and Limitations prescribed in the Case of a Bill.

SECTION 8. The Congress shall have Power To lay and collect Taxes, Duties, Imposts and Excises, to pay the Debt and provide for the common Defense and general Welfare of the United States; but all Duties, Imposts and Excises shall be uniform throughout the United States;

To borrow money on the credit of the United States;

To regulate Commerce with foreign Nations, and among the several States, and with the Indian Tribes;

To establish an uniform Rule of Naturalization, and uniform Laws on the subject of Bankruptcies throughout the United States;

To coin Money, regulate the Value thereof, and of foreign Coin, and fix the Standard of Weights and Measures;

To provide for the Punishment of counterfeiting the Securities and current Coin of the United States;

To establish Post Offices and post Roads;

To promote the Progress of Science and useful Arts, by securing for limited Times to Authors and Inventors the exclusive Right to their respective Writings and Discoveries;

To constitute Tribunals inferior to the supreme Court;

To define and punish Piracies and Felonies committed on the high Seas, and Offenses against the Law of Nations;

To declare War, grant Letters of Marque and Reprisal, and make Rules concerning Captures on Land and Water;

To raise and support Armies, but no Appropriation of Money to that Use shall be for a longer Term than two Years;

To provide and maintain a Navy;

To make Rules for the Government and Regulation of the land and naval Forces;

To provide for calling forth the Militia to execute the Laws of the Union, suppress Insurrections and repel Invasions;

To provide for organizing, arming, and disciplining the Militia, and for governing such Part of them as may be employed in the Service of the United States, reserving to the States respectively, the Appointment of the Officers, and the Authority of training the Militia according to the discipline prescribed by Congress;

To exercise exclusive Legislation in all Cases whatsoever, over such District (not exceeding ten Miles square) as may, by Cession of particular States, and the acceptance of Congress, become the Seat of the Government of the United States, and to exercise like Authority over all Places purchased by the Consent of the Legislature of the State in which the Same shall be, for the Erection of Forts, Magazines, Arsenals, dock-Yards, and other needful Building;—And

To make all Laws which shall be necessary and proper for carrying into Execution the foregoing Powers, and all other Powers vested by this Constitution in the Government of the United States, or in any Department or Officer thereof.

SECTION 9. The Migration or Importation of such Persons as any of the States now existing shall think proper to admit, shall not be prohibited by the Congress prior to the Year one thousand eight hundred and eight, but a tax or duty may be imposed on such Importation, not exceeding ten dollars for each Person.

The privilege of the Writ of Habeas Corpus shall not be suspended, unless when in Cases of Rebellion or Invasion the public Safety may require it.

No Bill of Attainder or ex post facto Law shall be passed.

No capitation, or other direct, Tax shall be laid, unless in Proportion to the Census or Enumeration herein before directed to be taken.

No Tax or Duty shall be laid on Articles exported from any State.

No Preference shall be given by any Regulation of Commerce or Revenue to the Ports of one State over those of another: nor shall Vessels bound to, or from, one State, be obliged to enter, clear, or pay Duties in another.

No Money shall be drawn from the Treasury, but in Consequence of Appropriations made by Law; and a regular Statement and Account of the Receipts and Expenditures of all public Money shall be published from time to time.

No Title of Nobility shall be granted by the United States: And no Person holding any Office of Profit or Trust under them, shall, without the Consent of the Congress, accept of any present, Emolument, Office, or Title, of any kind whatever, from any King, Prince, or foreign State.

Section 10. No State shall enter into any Treaty, Alliance, or Confederation; grant Letters of Marque and Reprisal; coin Money; emit Bills of Credit; make any Thing but gold and silver Coin a Tender in Payment of Debts; pass any Bill of Attainder, ex post facto Law, or Law impairing the Obligation of Contracts, or grant any Title of Nobility.

No State shall, without the Consent of the Congress, lay any Imposts or Duties on Imports or Exports, except what may be absolutely necessary for executing it's inspection Laws: and the net Produce of all Duties and Imposts, laid by any State on Imports or Exports, shall be for the Use of the Treasury of the United States; and all such Laws shall be subject to the Revision and Controul of the Congress.

No State shall, without the Consent of Congress, lay any duty of Tonnage, keep Troops, or Ships of War in time of Peace, enter into any Agreement or Compact with another State, or with a foreign Power, or engage in War, unless actually invaded, or in such imminent Danger as will not admit of delay.

Article II.

Section 1. The executive Power shall be vested in a President of the United States of America. He shall hold his Office during the Term of four Years, and, together with the Vice-President, chosen for the same Term, be elected, as follows.

Each State shall appoint, in such Manner as the Legislature thereof may direct, a Number of Electors, equal to the whole Number of Senators and Representatives to which the State may be entitled in the Congress: but no Senator or Representative, or Person holding an Office of Trust or Profit under the United States, shall be appointed an Elector.

[The Electors shall meet in their respective States, and vote by Ballot for two persons, of whom one at least shall not be an Inhabitant of the same State with themselves. And they shall make a List of all the Persons voted for, and of the Number of Votes for each; which List they shall sign and certify, and transmit sealed to the Seat of the Government of the United States, directed to the President of the Senate. The President of the Senate shall, in the Presence of the Senate and House of Representatives, open all the Certificates, and the Votes shall then be counted. The Person having the greatest Number of Votes shall be the President, if such Number be a Majority of the whole Number of Electors appointed; and if there be more than one who have such Majority, and have an equal Number of Votes, then the House of Representatives shall immediately chuse by Ballot one of them for President; and if no Person have a Majority, then from the five highest on the List the said House shall in like Manner chuse the President. But in chusing the President, the Votes shall be taken by States, the Representation from each State having one Vote; A quorum for this Purpose shall consist of a Member or Members from two-thirds of the States, and a Majority of all the States shall be necessary to a Choice. In every Case, after the Choice of the President, the Person having the greatest Number of Votes of the Electors shall be the Vice President. But if there should remain two or more who have equal Votes, the Senate shall chuse from them by Ballot the Vice-President.]

The Congress may determine the Time of chusing the Electors, and the Day on which they shall give their Votes; which Day shall be the same throughout the United States.

No person except a natural born Citizen, or a Citizen of the United States, at the time of the Adoption of this Constitution, shall be eligible to the Office of President; neither shall any Person be eligible to that Office who shall not have attained to the Age of thirty-five Years, and been fourteen Years a Resident within the United States.

In Case of the Removal of the President from Office, or of his Death, Resignation, or Inability to discharge the Powers and Duties of the said Office, the same shall devolve on the Vice President, and the Congress may by Law provide for the Case of Removal, Death, Resignation or Inability, both of the President and Vice President, declaring what Officer shall then act as President, and such Officer shall act accordingly, until the Disability be removed, or a President shall be elected.

The President shall, at stated Times, receive for his Services, a Compensation, which shall neither be encreased nor diminished during the Period for which he shall have been elected, and he shall not receive within that Period any other Emolument from the United States, or any of them.

Before he enter on the Execution of his Office, he shall take the following Oath or Affirmation:—"I do solemnly swear (or affirm) that I will faithfully execute the Office of President of the United States, and will to the best of my Ability, preserve, protect and defend the Constitution of the United States."

SECTION 2. The President shall be Commander in Chief of the Army and Navy of the United States, and of the Militia of the several States, when called into the actual Service of the United States; he may require the Opinion in writing, of the principal Officer in each of the executive Departments, upon any subject relating to the Duties of their respective Offices, and he shall have Power to Grant Reprives and Pardons for Offenses against the United States, except in Cases of Impeachment.

He shall have Power, by and with the Advice and Consent of the Senate, to make Treaties, provided two-thirds of the Senators present concur; and he shall nominate, and by and with the Advice and Consent of the Senate, shall appoint Ambassadors, other public Ministers and Consuls, Judges of the supreme Court, and all other Officers of the United States, whose Appointments are not herein otherwise provided for, and which shall be established by Law: but the Congress may by Law vest the Appointment of such inferior Officers, as they think proper, in the President alone, in the Courts of Law, or in the Heads of Departments.

The President shall have Power to fill up all Vacancies that may happen during the Recess of the Senate, by granting Commissions which shall expire at the End of their next Session.

SECTION 3. He shall from time to time give to the Congress Information of the State of the Union, and recommend to their Consideration such Measures as he shall judge necessary and expedient; he may, on extraordinary Occasions, convene both Houses, or either of them, and in Case of Disagreement between them, with Respect to the Time of Adjournment, he may adjourn them to such Time as he shall think proper; he shall receive Ambassadors and other public

Ministers he shall take Care that the Laws be faithfully executed, and shall Commission all the Officers of the United States.

SECTION 4. The President, Vice President and all civil Officers of the United States, shall be removed from Office on Impeachment for, and Conviction of, Treason, Bribery, or other high Crimes and Misdemeanors.

Article III.

SECTION 1. The judicial Power of the United States, shall be vested in one supreme Court, and in such inferior Courts as the Congress may from time to time ordain and establish. The Judges, both of the supreme and inferior Courts, shall hold their Offices during good Behaviour, and shall, at stated Times, receive for their Services a Compensation which shall not be diminished during their Continuance in Office.

SECTION 2. The judicial Power shall extend to all Cases, in Law and Equity, arising under this Constitution, the Laws of the United States, and Treaties made, or which shall be made, under their Authority;—to all Cases affecting Ambassadors, other public Ministers and Consuls;—to all Cases of admiralty and maritime Jurisdiction;—to Controversies to which the United States shall be a Party;—to Controversies between two or more States;—between a State and Citizens of another State;—between Citizens of different States;—between Citizens of the same State claiming Lands under Grants of different States, and between a State, or the Citizens thereof, and foreign States, Citizens or Subjects.

In all Cases affecting Ambassadors, other public Ministers and Consuls, and those in which a State shall be Party, the supreme Court shall have original Jurisdiction. In all the other Cases before mentioned, the supreme Court shall have appellate Jurisdiction, both as to Law and Fact, with such Exceptions, and under such Regulations as the Congress shall make.

The trial of all Crimes, except in Cases of Impeachment, shall be by Jury; and such Trial shall be held in the State where the said Crimes shall have been committed; but when not committed within any State, the Trial shall be at such Place and Places as the Congress may by Law have directed.

SECTION 3. Treason against the United States, shall consist only in levying War against them, or in adhering to their Enemies, giving them Aid and Comfort. No Person shall be convicted of Treason unless on the Testimony of two Witnesses to the same overt Act, or on Confession in open Court.

The Congress shall have power to declare the Punishment of Treason, but no Attainder of Treason shall work Corruption of Blood, or Forfeiture except during the Life of the Person attained.

Article IV.

SECTION 1. Full Faith and Credit shall be given in each State to the public Acts, Records, and judicial Proceedings of every other State. And the Congress may by general Laws prescribe the Manner in which such Acts, Records and Proceedings shall be proved, and the Effect thereof.

SECTION 2. The Citizens of each State shall be entitled to all Privileges and Immunities of Citizens in the several States.

A Person charged in any State with Treason, Felony, or other Crime, who shall flee from Justice, and be found in another State, shall on demand of the executive Authority of the State from which he fled, be delivered up, to be removed to the State having Jurisdiction of the Crime.

No Person held to Service or Labour in one State, under the Laws thereof, escaping into another, shall, in Consequence of any Law or Regulation therein, be discharged from such Service or Labour, but shall be delivered up on Claim of the Party to whom such Service or Labour may be due.

SECTION 3. New States may be admitted by the Congress into this Union; but no new State shall be formed or erected within the Jurisdiction of any other State; nor any State be formed by the Junction of two or more States, or parts of States, without the Consent of the Legislatures of the States concerned as well as of the Congress.

The Congress shall have Power to dispose of and make all needful Rules and Regulations respecting the Territory or other Property belonging to the United States; and nothing in this Constitution shall be so construed as to Prejudice any Claims of the United States, or of any particular State.

SECTION 4. The United States shall guarantee to every State in this Union a Republican Form of Government, and shall protect each of them against Invasion; and on Application of the Legislature, or of the Executive (when the Legislature cannot be convened) against domestic Violence.

Article V.

The Congress, whenever two-thirds of both Houses shall deem it necessary, shall propose Amendments to this Constitution, or, on the Application of the Legislatures of two-thirds of the several States, shall call a Convention for proposing Amendments, which, in either Case, shall be valid to all Intents and Purposes, as part of this Constitution, when ratified by the Legislatures of three-fourths of the several States, or by Conventions in three-fourths thereof, as the one or the other Mode of Ratification may be proposed by the Congress; Provided that no Amendment which may be made prior to the Year One thousand eight hundred and eight shall in any Manner affect the first and fourth Clauses in the Ninth Section of the first Article; and that no State, without its Consent, shall be deprived of its equal Suffrage in the Senate.

Article VI.

All Debts contracted and Engagements entered into, before the Adoption of this Constitution, shall be as valid against the United States under this Constitution, as under the Confederation.

This Constitution, and the Laws of the United States which shall be made in Persuance thereof; and all Treaties made, or which shall be made, under the Authority of the United States, shall be the supreme Law of the Land; and the Judges in every State shall be bound thereby, any Thing in the Constitution or Laws of any State to the Contrary notwithstanding.

The Senators and Representatives before mentioned, and the Members of the several State Legislatures, and all executive and judicial Officers, both of the United States and of the several States, shall be bound by Oath or Affirmation, to support this Constitution; but no religious Test shall ever be required as a Qualification to any Office or public Trust under the United States.

Article VII.

The Ratification of the Conventions of nine States shall be sufficient for the Establishment of this Constitution between the States so ratifying the Same.
DONE in Convention by the Unanimous Consent of the States present the Seventeenth Day of September in the Year of our Lord one thousand seven hundred and Eighty seven and of the Independence of the United States of America the Twelth. In Witness whereof We have hereunto subscribed our Names.

G° WASHINGTON
Presidt and deputy from Virginia

New Hampshire.

JOHN LANGDAN
NICHOLAS GILMAN

Massachusetts.

NATHANIEL GORHAM
RUFUS KING

Connecticut.

WM SAML JOHNSON
ROGER SHERMAN

New York.

ALEXANDER HAMILTON

New Jersey.

WIL: LIVINGSTON
DAVID BREARLEY.
WM PATTERSON
JONA: DAYTON

Pennsylvania.

B. FRANKLIN
ROBT. MORRIS
THOS. FITZSIMONS
JAMES WILSON
THOMAS MIFFLIN
GEO. CLYMER
JARED INGERSOLL
GOUV MORRIS

Delaware.

GEO: READ
JOHN DICKINSON
JACO: BROOM
GUNNING BEDFORD jun
RICHARD BASSETT

Maryland.

JAMES MCHENRY
DANL CARROLL
DAN: of ST THOS JENIFER

Virginia.

JOHN BLAIR—
JAMES MADISON Jr.

North Carolina.

WM BLOUNT
HU WILLIAMSON
RICHD DOBBS SPAIGHT,

South Carolina.

J. RUTLEDGE
CHARLES PINCKNEY
CHARLES COTESWORTH PINCKNEY
PIERCE BUTLER

Georgia.

WILLIAM FEW
ABR BALDWIN
Attest:
WILLIAM JACKSON, *Secretary.*

ARTICLES IN ADDITION TO, AND AMENDMENT OF, THE CONSTITUTION OF THE UNITED STATES OF AMERICA, PROPOSED BY CONGRESS, AND RATIFIED BY THE LEGISLATURES OF THE SEVERAL STATES, PURSUANT TO THE FIFTH ARTICLE OF THE ORIGINAL CONSTITUTION.

Article I.

Congress shall make no law respecting an establishment of religion, or prohibiting the free exercise thereof; or abridging the freedom of speech, or of the press; or the right of the people peaceably to assemble, and to petition the Government for a redress of grievances.

Article II.

A well regulated Militia, being necessary to the security of a free State, the right of the people to keep and bear Arms, shall not be infringed.

Article III.

No Soldier shall, in time of peace be quartered in any house, without the consent of the Owner, nor in time of war, but in a manner to be prescribed by law.

Article IV.

The right of the people to be secure in their persons, houses, papers, and effects, against unreasonable searches and seizures, shall not be violated, and no Warrants shall issue, but upon probable cause, supported by Oath or affirmation, and particularly describing the place to be searched, and the persons or things to be seized.

Article V.

No person shall be held to answer for a capital, or otherwise infamous crime, unless on a presentment or indictment of a Grand Jury, except in cases arising in the land or naval forces, or in the Militia, when in actual service in time of War or public danger; nor shall any person be subject for the same offence to be twice put in jeopardy of life or limb; nor shall be compelled in any criminal case to be a witness against himself, nor be deprived of life, liberty, or property, without due process of law; nor shall private property be taken for public use, without just compensation.

Article VI.

In all criminal prosecutions, the accused shall enjoy the right to a speedy and public trial, by an impartial jury of the State and district wherein the crime shall have been committed, which district shall have been previously ascertained by law, and to be informed of the nature and cause of the accusation; to be confronted with the witnesses against him; to have compulsory process for obtaining witnesses in his favor, and to have the Assistance of Counsel for his defence.

Article VII.

In suits at common law, where the value in controversy shall exceed twenty dollars, the right of trial by jury shall be preserved, and no fact tried by a jury, shall be otherwise reexamined in any Court of the United States, than according to the rules of the common law.

Article VIII.

Excessive bail shall not be required, nor excessive fines imposed, nor cruel and unusual punishments inflicted.

Article IX.

The enumeration in the Constitution, of certain rights, shall not be construed to deny or disparage others retained by the people.

Article X.

The powers not delegated to the United States by the Constitution, nor prohibited by it to the States, are reserved to the States respectively, or to the people.

Article XI.

The Judicial power of the United States shall not be construed to extend to any suit in law or equity, commenced or prosecuted against one of the United States by Citizens of another State, or by Citizens or Subjects of any Foreign State.

Article XII.

The Electors shall meet in their respective states and vote by ballot for President and Vice-President, one of whom, at least, shall not be an inhabitant of the same state with themselves; they shall name in their ballots the person voted for as President, and in distinct ballots the person voted for as Vice-President, and they shall make distinct lists of all persons voted for as President, and of all persons voted for as Vice-President, and of the number of votes for each, which lists they shall sign and certify, and transmit sealed to the seat of the government of the United States, directed to the President of the Senate;—The President of the Senate shall, in presence of the Senate and House of Representatives, open all the certificates and the votes shall then be counted;—The person having the greatest number of votes for President, shall be the President, if such number be a majority of the whole number of Electors appointed; and if no person have such majority, then from the persons having the highest numbers not exceeding three on the list of those voted for as President, the House of Representatives shall choose immediately, by ballot, the President. But in choosing the President, the votes shall be taken by states, the representation from each state having one vote; a quorum for this purpose shall consist of a member or members from two-thirds of the states, and a majority of all the states shall be necessary to a choice. And if the House of Representatives shall not choose a President whenever the right of choice shall devolve upon them, before the fourth day of March next following, then the Vice-President shall act as President, as in the case of the death or other constitutional disability of the President.—The person having the greatest number of votes as Vice-President, shall be the Vice-President, if such number be a majority of the whole number of Electors appointed, and if no person have a majority, then from the two highest numbers on the list, the Senate shall choose the Vice-President; a quorum for the purpose shall consist of two-thirds of the whole number of Senators, and a majority of the whole number shall be necessary to a choice. But no person constitutionally ineligible to the office of President shall be eligible to that of Vice-President of the United States.

Article XIII.

SECTION 1. Neither slavery nor involuntary servitude, except as a punishment for crime whereof the party shall have been duly convicted, shall exist within the United States, or any place subject to their jurisdiction.

SECTION 2. Congress shall have power to enforce this article by appropriate legislation.

Article XIV.

SECTION 1. All persons born or naturalized in the United States, and subject to the jurisdiction thereof, are citizens of the United States and of the State wherein they reside. No State shall make or enforce any law which shall abridge the privileges or immunities of citizens of the United States; nor shall any State deprive any person of life, liberty, or property, without due process of law; nor deny to any person within its jurisdiction the equal protection of the laws.

SECTION 2. Representatives shall be apportioned among the several States according to their respective numbers, counting the whole number of persons in each State, excluding Indians not taxed. But when the right to vote at any election for the choice of electors for President and Vice-President of the United States, Representatives in Congress, the Executive and Judicial officers of a State, or the members of the Legislature thereof, is denied to any of the male inhabitants of such State, being twenty-one years of age, and citizens of the United States, or in any way abridged, except for participation in rebellion, or other crime, the basis of representation therein shall be reduced in the proportion which the number of such male citizens shall bear to the whole number of male citizens twenty-one years of age in such State.

SECTION 3. No person shall be a Senator or Representative in Congress, or elector of President and Vice-President, or hold any office, civil or military, under the United States, or under any State, who, having previously taken an oath, as a member of Congress, or as an officer of the United States, or as a member of any State legislature, or as an executive or judicial officer of any State, to support the Constitution of the United States, shall have engaged in insurrection or rebellion against the same, or given aid or comfort to the enemies thereof. But Congress may by a vote of two-thirds of each House, remove such disability.

SECTION 4. The validity of the public debt of the United States, authorized by law, including debts incurred for payment of pensions and bounties for services in suppressing insurrection or rebellion, shall not be questioned. But neither the United States nor any State shall assume or pay any debt or obligation incurred in aid of insurrection or rebellion against the United States, or any claim for the loss or emancipation of any slave; but all such debts, obligations and claims shall be held illegal and void.

SECTION 5. The Congress shall have power to enforce, by appropriate legislation, the provisions of this article.

Article XV.

SECTION 1. The right of citizens of the United States to vote shall not be denied or abridged by the United States or by any State on account of race, color, or previous condition of servitude—

SECTION 2. The Congress shall have power to enforce this article by appropriate legislation.

Article XVI.

The Congress shall have power to lay and collect taxes on incomes, from whatever source derived, without apportionment among the several States, and without regard to any census or enumeration.

Article XVII.

The Senate of the United States shall be composed of two Senators from each State, elected by the people thereof, for six years; and each Senator shall have one vote. The electors in each State shall have the qualifications requisite for electors of the most numerous branch of the State legislatures.

When vacancies happen in the representation of any State in the Senate, the executive authority of such State shall issue writs of election to fill such vacancies: *Provided,* That the legislature of any State may empower the executive thereof to make temporary appointments until the people fill the vacancies by election as the legislature may direct.

This amendment shall not be so construed as to affect the election or term of any Senator chosen before it becomes valid as part of the Constitution.

Article XVIII.

SECTION 1. After one year from the ratification of this article the manufacture, sale, or transportation of intoxicating liquors within, the importation thereof into, or the exportation thereof from the United States and all territory subject to the jurisdiction thereof for beverage purposes is hereby prohibited.

SECTION 2. The Congress and the several States shall have concurrent power to enforce this article by appropriate legislation.

SECTION 3. This article shall be inoperative unless it shall have been ratified as an amendment to the Constitution by the legislature of the several States, as provided in the Constitution, within seven years from the date of the submission hereof to the States by the Congress.

Article XIX.

The right of citizens of the United States to vote shall not be denied or abridged by the United States or by any State on account of sex.

Congress shall have power to enforce this article by appropriate legislation.

Article XX.

Section 1. The terms of the President and Vice President shall end at noon on the 20th day of January, and the terms of Senators and Representatives at noon on the 3d day of January, of the years in which such terms would have ended if this article had not been ratified; and the terms of their successors shall then begin.

Section 2. The Congress shall assemble at least once in every year, and such meeting shall begin at noon on the 3d day of January, unless they shall by law appoint a different day.

Section 3. If, at the time fixed for the beginning of the term of the President, the President elect shall have died, the Vice President elect shall become President. If a President shall not have been chosen before the time fixed for the beginning of his term, or if the President elect shall have failed to qualify, then the Vice President elect shall act as President until a President shall have qualified; and the Congress may by law provide for the case wherein neither a President elect nor a Vice President elect shall have qualified, declaring who shall then act as President, or the manner in which one who is to act shall be selected, and such person shall act accordingly until a President or Vice President shall have qualified.

Section 4. The Congress may by law provide for the case of the death of any of the persons from whom the House of Representatives may choose a President whenever the right of choice shall have devolved upon them, and for the case of the death of any of the persons from whom the Senate may choose a Vice President whenever the right of choice shall have devolved upon them.

Section 5. Sections 1 and 2 shall take effect on the 15th day of October following the ratification of this article.

Section 6. This article shall be inoperative unless it shall have been ratified as an amendment to the Constitution by the legislatures of three-fourths of the several States within seven years from the date of its submission.

Article XXI.

Section 1. The eighteenth article of amendment to the Constitution of the United States is hereby repealed.

Section 2. The transportation or importation into any State, Territory, or possession of the United States for delivery or use therein of intoxicating liquors, in violation of the laws thereof, is hereby prohibited.

Section 3. This article shall be inoperative unless it shall have been ratified as an amendment to the Constitution by conventions in the several States, as provided in the Constitution, within seven years from the date of the submission hereof to the States by the Congress.

Article XXII.

Section 1. No person shall be elected to the office of the President more than twice, and no person who has held the office of President, or acted as President, for more than two years of a term to which some other person was elected President shall be elected to the office of the President more than once. But this Article shall not apply to any person holding the office of President when this Article was proposed by the Congress, and shall not prevent any person who may be holding the office of President, or acting as President, during the term within which this Article becomes operative from holding the office of President or acting as President during the remainder of such term.

SECTION 2. This article shall be inoperative unless it shall have been ratified as an amendment to the Constitution by the legislatures of three-fourths of the several States within seven years from the date of its submission to the States by the Congress.

Article XXIII.

SECTION 1. The District constituting the seat of Government of the United States shall appoint in such manner as the Congress may direct:

A number of electors of President and Vice President equal to the whole number of Senators and Representatives in Congress to which the District would be entitled if it were a State, but in no event more than the least populous State; they shall be in addition to those appointed by the States, but they shall be considered, for the purposes of the election of President and Vice President, to be electors appointed by a State; and they shall meet in the District and perform such duties as provided by the twelfth article of amendment.

SECTION 2. The Congress shall have power to enforce this article by appropriate legislation.

Article XXIV.

SECTION 1. The right of citizens of the United States to vote in any primary or other election for President or Vice President, for electors for President or Vice President, or for Senator or Representative in Congress, shall not be denied or abridged by the United States or any State by reason of failure to pay any poll tax or other tax.

SECTION 2. The Congress shall have power to enforce this article by appropriate legislation.

Article XXV.

SECTION 1. In case of the removal of the President from office or of his death or resignation, the Vice President shall become President.

SECTION 2. Whenever there is a vacancy in the office of the Vice President, the President shall nominate a Vice President who shall take office upon confirmation by a majority vote of both Houses of Congress.

SECTION 3. Whenever the President transmits to the President pro tempore of the Senate and the Speaker of the House of Representatives his written declaration that he is unable to discharge the powers and duties of his office, and until he transmits to them a written declaration to the contrary, such powers and duties shall be discharged by the Vice President as Acting President.

SECTION 4. Whenever the Vice President and a majority of either the principal officers of the executive departments or of such other body as Congress may by law provide, transmit to the President pro tempore of the Senate and the Speaker of the House of Representatives their written declaration that the President is unable to discharge the power and duties of his office, the Vice President shall immediately assume the powers and duties of the office as Acting President.

Thereafter, when the President transmits to the President pro tempore of the Senate and the Speaker of the House of Representatives his written declaration that no inability exists, he shall resume the powers and duties of his office unless the Vice President and a majority of either the principal officers of the executive department or of such other body as Congress may by law provide, transmit within four days to the President pro tempore of the Senate and the Speaker of the House of Representatives their written declaration that the President is unable to discharge the powers and duties of his office. Thereupon Congress shall decide the issue, assembling within forty-eight hours for that purpose if not in session. If the Congress, within twenty-one days after receipt of the latter written declaration, or, if Congress is not in session, within twenty-one days after Congress is required to assemble, determines by two-thirds vote of both Houses that the President is unable to discharge the powers and duties of his office, the Vice President shall continue to discharge the same as Acting President; otherwise, the President shall resume the powers and duties of his office.

Article XXVI.

Section 1. The right of citizens of the United States, who are eighteen years of age or older, to vote shall not be denied or abridged by the United States or by any State on account of age.

Section 2. The Congress shall have power to enforce this article by appropriate legislation.

Source Notes

Epigraph

1. Howard Simons and Joseph A. Califano, Jr., eds., *The Media and the Law,* pp. 36-37.

Chapter 1: Barron's Wharf

1. Norman Rukert, *The Fell's Point Story,* p. 19.
2. Record, *John Barron* v. *The Mayor and City Council of Baltimore,* Supreme Court of U.S., No. 88, p. 15.
3. Letter of Hezekiah Waters and other wharf owners, April 2, 1817, Baltimore Historical Society.
4. Record, *Barron,* pp. 7–8.
5. *Ibid.,* p. 24.
6. *Ibid.,* p. 26.
7. Leonard Baker, *John Marshall,* p. 127.
8. *Ibid.,* p. 120.
9. *Ibid.*
10. Clinton Rossiter, ed., *The Federalist Papers,* No. 78, pp. 465ff.
11. Jay had resigned to become governor of New York. Adams tried to reappoint him after the resignation of Chief Justice Ellsworth, but Jay felt that being governor of New York was more prestigious than being chief justice of the United States.
12. Letter of John Jay to John Adams, December 18, 1800, John Adams, *Works,* vol. IX, pp. 91–92.
13. *John Marshall: Major Opinions and Other Writings,* ed. John P. Roche, p. xxxii.
14. Chief Justice William Howard Taft, who also despised dissents, spoke of this practice of one opinion as "Marshalling the Court" (William F. Swindler, *The Constitution and Chief Justice Marshall,* p. 13).
15. Baker, *John Marshall,* p. 414.
16. Francis Stiles, *John Marshall,* p. 115.
17. Letter of Thomas Jefferson to James Pleasant, December 26, 1821, *The Works of Thomas Jefferson,* ed. P. L. Ford, vol. XII, p. 216.
18. Stiles, *John Marshall,* p. 118.
19. *Bank* v. *Dandridge,* 12 Wheat. 64, 90 (1827).
20. William Crosskey, *Politics and the Constitution in the History of the United States,* vol. II, p. 1080.
21. Alpheus T. Mason and William M. Beaney, *American Constitutional Law,* 7th ed., p. 2.

22. Baker, *John Marshall,* p. 381.
23. George McKenna, *American Politics,* p. 300.
24. Marbury was joined in the case by three others: William Harper, Robert Townshend Hooe, and Dennis Ramsay.
25. It is curious that it took Marbury so long to take the case to court. Leonard Baker suggests that his motive might have been to embarrass the Jefferson administration. See Baker, *John Marshall,* p. 395.
26. The Supreme Court had ruled on the constitutionality of a carriage tax in the case of *Hylton* v. *United States,* 3 Dall. 171 (1795), but it had declared the tax constitutional.
27. *Marbury* v. *Madison,* 1 Cranch 137, 176–177 (1803).
28. *McCulloch* v. *Maryland,* 4 Wheat. 316, 407 (1819).
29. Baker, *John Marshall,* p. 414; Edwin S. Corwin, *Marshall and the Constitution,* p. 124.
30. Walker Lewis, *Without Fear or Favor,* p. 269.
31. Baker, *John Marshall,* p. 701.
32. Francis Norton Mason, *My Dearest Polly,* p. 344.
33. *Worcester* v. *Georgia,* 6 Pet. 515 (1832).
34. *Barron,* 7 Pet. 243, 246 (1833).
35. He was in Paris as a representative of his new government.
36. Letter of Thomas Jefferson to James Madison, Dumas Malone, *Thomas Jefferson and the Rights of Man,* p. 168; *Works of Jefferson,* ed. Ford, vol. IV, p. 477.
37. Rossiter, *Federalist Papers,* p. 513.
38. *Ibid.*
39. *Annals of Congress,* 1st Cong., 1st sess., August 15, 1789, p. 732.
40. *Ibid.,* June 8, 1789, p. 425.
41. *Ibid.,* June 8, 1789, p. 432.
42. *Ibid.,* June 8, 1789, p. 440.
43. *Ibid.,* June 8, 1789, p. 441.
44. *Ibid.,* August 17, 1789, p. 775.
45. There is no record of the debate on this matter, just the final outcome.
46. *Barron,* p. 247.
47. *Ibid.*
48. Of course, the Constitution does place some specific limits on the states, as in Article I, Section 10.
49. *Barron,* p. 250.
50. *Ibid.,* p. 251.

Chapter 2: Seventeen Words

1. Harold A. Hyman and William M. Wiecek, *Equal Justice Under Law,* p. 13.
2. James MacGregor Burns, *The Vineyard of Liberty,* p. 577.
3. Don E. Fehrenbacher, *The Dred Scott Case,* p. 275.
4. *Ibid.*
5. Speech of Andrew Jackson, December 7, 1836, *Messages and Papers of the Presidents,* ed. J. D. Richardson, pp. 1513–1514, 1516.
6. Burns, *Vineyard,* p. 576.
7. *Dred Scott* v. *Sandford,* 19 How. 393, 403 (1857).
8. *Ibid.,* p. 407.

9. *Ibid.*, pp. 450–451.
10. *Ibid.*, p. 452.
11. John A. Garraty, ed., *Quarrels That Have Shaped the Constitution,* pp. 88–89.
12. Robert H. Jackson, *The Struggle for Judicial Supremacy,* p. 327.
13. Hans L. Trefousse, *The Radical Republicans,* p. 321.
14. Bernard Bailyn et al. ed., *The Great Republic—A History of the American People,* 2d ed., vol. II, p. 537.
15. 14 Stat. 27 (1866).
16. *Ibid.*, Chapter 31.
17. *Adamson* v. *California,* 332 U.S. 46, 71–72 (1946) (Black, J., dissenting).
18. Raoul Berger, *Government by Judiciary,* p. 211.
19. Charles Fairman, "Does the Fourteenth Amendment Incorporate the Bill of Rights?" 2 *Stan. L. Rev.,* 5, 8 (Dec. 1949).
20. *Ibid.*, pp. 138–139.
21. March 31, 1871, *Congressional Record,* 42nd Cong., 1st sess., pp. 83, 84, 85.
22. *Slaughterhouse Cases,* 16 Wall. 36 (1873).
23. Field was joined by Chief Justice Chase and Justices Bradley and Swayne.
24. *Slaughterhouse,* pp. 89, 93, 105.
25. *Hurtado* v. *California,* 110 U.S. 516 (1884).
26. Henry J. Abraham, *Freedom and the Court,* p. 48.
27. *Lochner* v. *New York,* 198 U.S. 45 (1905).
28. *Atkins* v. *Children's Hospital,* 261 U.S. 394 (1923).
29. *Lochner,* p. 75 (Holmes, J., dissenting).
30. *Gitlow* v. *New York,* 268 U.S. 652 (1925). For more on *Gitlow,* see Chapter 5.
31. *Palko* v. *Connecticut,* 302 U.S. 314 (1937).
32. *United States* v. *Carolene Products Company,* 304 U.S. 144 (1938).
33. *Ibid.*, p. 152.

Chapter 3: Minnesota Rag

1. Lincoln Steffens, *The Shame of the Cities,* pp. 43–44.
2. Interview with Ed Ryan, April 12, 1979.
3. This and all subsequent quotes from Guilford are from Howard Guilford, *A Tale of Two Cities,* pp. 31–37.
4. Interview with Orlin Folwick, former reporter for the *Minneapolis Morning Tribune,* April 14, 1979.
5. Copies of the *Saturday Press* are on file at the Minnesota Historical Society.
6. *Saturday Press,* November 15, 1927.
7. The account of the Shapiro dry-cleaning incident and quotes are taken from an interview with Irving Shapiro, February 22, 1979 (except as noted).
8. Letter of Sam Shapiro to Judge W. C. Leary, December 5, 1930. There is some doubt that this letter was composed by Sam Shapiro, but it reflects the Shapiro family version of the events.
9. *Ibid.*
10. *Minneapolis Morning Tribune,* November 24, 1927.
11. Complaint against Near and Guilford, File No. 272132, Minnesota Fourth District Court, November 21, 1927.
12. Temporary restraining order, File No. 272132, Minnesota Fourth District Court, November 22, 1927.

13. *Minneapolis Morning Tribune,* December 2, 1927.
14. Order denying demurrer, File No. 272132, December 9, 1927.
15. *State ex. rel. Olson* v. *Guilford,* 174 Minn. 457, 219 N.W. 770 (1928).
16. *Minneapolis Evening Tribune,* July 20, 1928.
17. Joseph Gies, *The Colonel of Chicago,* p. 237.
18. Oswald Garrison Villard, *The Disappearing Daily,* p. 136.
19. Letter of Robert R. McCormick to American Newspaper Publishers Association (ANPA), September 21, 1928.
20. Letter of Weymouth Kirkland to Robert R. McCormick, September 14, 1928.
21. Letter of William Howard Taft to Horace Taft, December 1, 1929.
22. *Gitlow* v. *New York,* 268 U.S. 652 (1925).
23. Interview with Erwin Griswold, March 7, 1980.
24. Leonard Baker, *Back to Back,* p. 31.
25. Merlo J. Pusey, *Charles Evans Hughes,* vol. II, p. 688.
26. Interview with William Gossett, March 10, 1980.
27. There is no written record or transcript of the complete oral arguments; this account has been pieced together from newspaper accounts and briefs.
28. By the very nature of the justices' conference on *Near* v. *Minnesota,* the explicit evidence available for this section is limited. Elsewhere it has been possible to find direct evidence from documents or witnesses for every quotation and to respect the most demanding criteria of evidence for conclusions of fact. The account of the justices' conference on *Near* is necessarily different. There can be no direct quotations and, indeed, no contemporary evidence on the moods of individuals or the other details of such a closed debate. In much of the authors' description there are statements that are probably true. Those probabilities are as high as anyone who was not there 50 years ago can make them. We have not traced for the reader all the reasons for the inferences. We have not cluttered the account with "probably" or "surely" or "must have argued." Nonetheless, what appears is no more—though also no less—than as close as one can get, after three years of study, to how it "must have been."
29. This and the following quotes are from *Near* v. *Minnesota,* 283 U.S. 697 (1931).
30. *Chicago Tribune,* June 3, 1931.

Chapter 4: The Myth About the Bay of Pigs

1. Speech to the American Newspaper Publishers Association, April 27, 1961.
2. Harrison Salisbury, *Without Fear or Favor,* p. 158.
3. Interview with Tad Szulc, November 27, 1983.
4. James Madison, *Notes on the Debates in the Federal Convention of 1787,* ed. Adrienne Koch, pp. 433–434.
5. Arthur M. Schlesinger, Jr., *The Imperial Presidency,* p. 333.
6. *Near* v. *Minnesota,* 283, U.S. 697, 716 (1931).
7. Max Frankel, "A Washington Education," *Columbia Forum,* Winter 1973.
8. In David Brown and W. Richard Bruner, eds., *How I Got That Story.* See Szulc's chapter, "The New York Times and the Bay of Pigs," for one of the best treatments of the subject.
9. *Ibid.,* p. 328.
10. *I. F. Stone's Weekly,* a film by Jerry Bruck, Jr., 1973.

11. Interview with Szulc.
12. Peter Wyden, *The Bay of Pigs,* pp. 45–46.
13. *La Hora,* October 30, 1960, p. 1. Translated by Jack Hitt.
14. "Are We Training Cuban Guerrillas?" *Nation,* November 19, 1960.
15. "The Facts Are There," *York Gazette and Daily,* November 25, 1960.
16. *Ibid.*
17. "Alan Gould Retires to Consultant Role," *Editor and Publisher,* February 2, 1963, p. 12.
18. Interview with Howard Handleman, December 8, 1983.
19. Interview with Karl Meyer, June 7, 1983.
20. Interview with Gilbert Harrison, May 24, 1983.
21. Arthur M. Schlesinger, Jr., *A Thousand Days,* p. 261.
22. Interview with Harrison.
23. David Halberstam, *The Powers That Be,* p. 624.
24. Interview with James Reston, June 22, 1983.
25. Salisbury, *Without Fear,* p. 163.
26. Interview with David Halberstam, November 1983.
27. Clifton Daniel, "The Press and National Security," Speech delivered to the World Press Institute, June 1, 1966.
28. *Ibid.*
29. Elie Abel, *The Missile Crisis,* p. 13.
30. Salisbury, *Without Fear,* p. 161.
31. Chalmers Roberts, *The Washington Post: The First 100 Years,* p. 161.
32. Interview with Murrey Marder, December 7, 1983.
33. Roberts, *Washington Post,* p. 352.
34. *New York Times Co.* v. *United States,* 403 U.S. 713, 753 (1971) (Harlan, J., dissenting).
35. *Ibid.,* pp. 714–715, 717 (Black, J., concurring).
36. *Ibid.,* p. 750 (Burger, C.J., dissenting).
37. *Ibid.,* p. 761 (Blackmun, J., dissenting).
38. *Ibid.,* p. 731.
39. William C. Westmoreland, *A Soldier Reports,* p. 422.

Chapter 5: Protecting "The Thought That We Hate"

1. *United States* v. *Schwimmer,* 279 U.S. 644, 654–655 (1929) (Holmes, J., dissenting).
2. *Oregonian,* July 19, 1924, p. 4.
3. E. Kimball MacColl, *The Growth of the City,* p. 485.
4. *Ibid.*
5. Oliver Wendell Holmes, "Law and the Courts," Speech delivered to the Harvard Law School Association of New York, February 15, 1913.
6. MacColl, *City,* p. 467.
7. M. Paul Holsinger, "Patriotism and the Curbing of Oregon's Radicals, 1919–1937," Paper delivered at the Seventh Annual Conference of the Western History Association, October 14, 1977.
8. William W. Pilcher, *The Portland Longshoremen,* p. 42.
9. MacColl, *City,* p. 468.
10. *Ibid.,* p. 479.
11. Interview with Don Cluster, August, 1983.

12. Record, *DeJonge* v. *Oregon* (fol. 67), pp. 8, 9.
13. Oregon Code 1930, Sec. 14–3, 110.
14. Oregon Code 1930, Sec. 14–3, 112.
15. Interview with Cluster.
16. MacColl, *City,* p. 483.
17. Record, *DeJonge,* pp. 22–23.
18. *Ibid.,* p. 45.
19. *Ibid.,* p. 16.
20. *Ibid.,* p. 32.
21. *Ibid.,* p. 41.
22. Interview with Judge Gus Solomon, April 30, 1983.
23. *Annals of Congress,* 1st Cong., 1st sess., August 15, 1789, p. 731.
24. *United States* v. *Cruikshank,* 92 U.S. 542, 551 (1876).
25. Leon Whipple, *Our Ancient Liberties,* p. 102.
26. *Ibid.,* p. 104.
27. Zechariah Chafee, Jr., *Free Speech in the United States,* p. 21.
28. Leonard W. Levy, *Freedom of Speech and Press in Early American History: Legacy of Suppression,* p. xxi.
29. See generally Leonard W. Levy, *Jefferson and Civil Liberties: The Darker Side.*
30. *Schenck* v. *United States,* 249 U.S. 47, 51 (1919).
31. *Abrams* v. *United States,* 250 U.S. 616, 620 (1919).
32. *Ibid.,* p. 623.
33. *Ibid.,* p. 628.
34. *Ibid.,* p. 630.
35. *Gitlow* v. *New York,* 268 U.S. 652, 655 (1925).
36. *Ibid.,* pp. 668, 669.
37. *Ibid.,* p. 666.
38. *Ibid.,* p. 673.
39. Henry Abraham, *Freedom and the Court,* p. 52.
40. Available in *The Methodist Federation for Social Action Brochure . . . ,* Portland, Oregon, May 18, 1975, unpaginated.
41. *DeJonge* v. *Oregon,* 299 U.S. 353, 366 (1937).
42. *Ibid.,* pp. 366, 365.
43. *Cohen* v. *California,* 403 U.S. 15 (1971).
44. *Tinker* v. *Des Moines Independent Community School District,* 393 U.S. 503 (1969).
45. *Olff* v. *East Side Union High School District,* 404 U.S. 1042 (1972).
46. Aryeh Neier, *Defending My Enemy,* p. 1.
47. *Village of Skokie* v. *National Socialist Party of America,* 69 Ill. 2d 605; 373 N.E. 21 (1978).
48. Max Cohen changed his name to Max Collin in 1946.
49. "The U.S. Neo-Nazi Movement: 1978," Report of Anti-Defamation League of B'nai B'rith, vol. 24, no. 2, March 1978.
50. Neier, *Enemy,* p. 21.
51. Interview with Erna Gans, July 20, 1983.
52. Interview with Harvey Schwartz, July 2, 1983.
53. Neier, *Enemy,* p. 1.
54. Interview with David Goldberger, July 7, 1983.

55. *Smith* v. *Collin,* 436 U.S. 953 (1978).
56. *Chaplinsky* v. *New Hampshire,* 315 U.S. 568 (1942).
57. *State* v. *Chaplinsky,* 91 N.H. 310 (1941).
58. *Collin* v. *Smith,* 447 F. Supp. 676, 702 (1978).
59. *Ibid.,* pp. 685–686.
60. *Ibid.,* pp. 700, 693.
61. Interview with Schwartz.
62. *Ibid.*

Chapter 6: Does Money Talk?

1. Transcript of Supreme Court oral arguments in *Buckley* v. *Valeo,* November 10, 1975, p. 37.
2. Paul Freund in a private conversation with Anthony Lewis. See Anthony Lewis, "The Court on Politics," *New York Times,* February 5, 1976, p. 33.
3. George Thayer, *Who Shakes the Money Tree?,* p. 25.
4. There were 73 eligible electors. Four either didn't vote or abstained.
5. James Madison, *Notes on the Debates in the Federal Convention of 1787,* ed. Adrienne Koch, p. 367.
6. *Ibid.,* p. 309.
7. *Ibid.,* pp. 309, 308.
8. *Messages and Papers of the Presidents,* ed. J. D. Richarson, vol. 1, p. 42.
9. Richard Hofstadter, *The Idea of a Party System,* p. 53.
10. *Ibid.,* p. 6.
11. Thayer, *Money Tree,* p. 28.
12. *Ibid.,* Chapter 3.
13. *Congressional Record,* 92nd Cong., 1st sess., 1971, vol. 117, pt. 41,947.
14. *Congressional Record,* 92nd Cong., 1st sess., 1971, vol. 117, pt. 41,778.
15. *Washington Post,* October 16, 1974.
16. *Congressional Record,* 93rd Cong., 2nd sess., vol. 120, pt. 10,562.
17. Interview with James Buckley, January 8, 1984.
18. *Congressional Record,* 93rd Cong., 2nd sess., vol. 120, pt. 10,562.
19. Interview with Buckley.
20. All quotes from the oral arguments are taken from the official Supreme Court transcript.
21. *Buckley* v. *Valeo,* 424 U.S. 1, 23–38 (1976).
22. *Ibid.,* pp. 51–59.
23. *Ibid.,* pp. 39–51.
24. *Ibid.,* pp. 60–84.
25. *Ibid.,* p. 14.
26. *Ibid.,* pp. 20–21.
27. *Ibid.,* p. 39.
28. Interview with Buckley.
29. Interview with Randy Huwa, March 2, 1984.

Chapter 7: God and the Classroom

1. Rep. Frank J. Becker (R., N.Y.), in "CBS Reports: Storm Over the Supreme Court," March 13, 1963, transcript, p. 66.

2. Rep. George V. Andrews (D., Ga.), *ibid.*
3. *Ibid.,* pp. 67–68.
4. *Ibid.,* p. 68.
5. Interview with Lawrence Roth, October 1, 1983.
6. Leon Whipple, *Our Ancient Liberties,* p. 67.
7. Sydney Ahlstrom, *A Religious History of the American People,* pp. 154, 167, 168, 169–170.
8. Henry Steele Commager, *The Empire of Reason,* p. 1.
9. Thomas Paine, *The Rights of Man,* p. 58.
10. Interview with Judge Arlin Adams, October 10, 1983.
11. *Cantwell* v. *Connecticut,* 310 U.S. 296 (1940).
12. *Minersville School District* v. *Gobitis,* 310 U.S. 586 (1940).
13. *Ibid.,* pp. 591, 593, 596.
14. *Ibid.,* pp. 596, 597–598.
15. *Ibid.,* p. 600.
16. *Ibid.,* p. 601 (Stone, J., dissenting).
17. *Ibid.,* p. 606.
18. *Board of Education* v. *Barnette,* 319 U.S. 624, 634 (1943).
19. *Ibid.,* p. 641.
20. *Ibid.,* p. 642.
21. *Ibid.,* pp. 665, 647 (Frankfurter, J., dissenting).
22. *Everson* v. *Board of Education,* 330 U.S. 1 (1947).
23. *Ibid.,* pp. 15–16.
24. *McCollum* v. *Board of Education,* 333 U.S. 203, 212, 227 (1948).
25. *Zorach* v. *Clauson,* 343 U.S. 306, 312 (1952).
26. *Ibid.,* pp. 313–314.
27. "CBS Reports: Storm Over the Supreme Court," p. 46.
28. Interview with Lawrence Roth.
29. Interview with William Butler, September 20, 1983.
30. "CBS Reports: Storm Over the Supreme Court," p. 47.
31. Interview with Daniel Roth, October 11, 1983.
32. Interview with Thomas Ford, September 1, 1983.
33. Interview with Thomas Delany, September 30, 1983.
34. *Engel* v. *Vitale,* 10 N.Y.2d 174, 180 (1961).
35. "CBS Reports: Storm Over the Supreme Court," p. 57.
36. *Engel* v. *Vitale,* 10 N.Y.2d 174, 180 (1961).
37. Interview with Butler.
38. This and all other statements are taken from the official transcript of oral arguments.
39. *Engel* v. *Vitale,* 370 U.S. 421 (1962).
40. *Ibid.,* pp. 432, 430.
41. *Ibid.,* pp. 434–435.
42. *Ibid.,* p. 436.
43. *Ibid.,* p. 441.
44. *Ibid.,* pp. 445, 445–446.
45. "CBS Reports: Storm Over the Supreme Court," p. 67.
46. *Ibid.,* p. 44.
47. *Ibid.,* p. 65.
48. Interview with Ford.

49. Interview with Butler.
50. *Ibid.*
51. Interview with Daniel Roth.
52. 52 U.S.L.W. 4317, 4322 (U.S. Mar. 6, 1984).

Chapter 8: A Knock at the Door

1. Interview with Carl Delau, June 7, 1983.
2. *Ibid.*
3. *Cleveland Press,* October 5, 1954.
4. Interview with Delau.
5. Interview with Dollree Mapp, June 21, 1983.
6. *Ibid.*
7. Interview with Delau.
8. Interview with Mapp.
9. *State* v. *Mapp,* Case No. 68326, trial transcript, p. 108.
10. Interview with Delau.
11. *Near* v. *Minnesota,* 283 U.S. 697, 716 (1931); emphasis added.
12. *Roth* v. *United States,* 354 U.S. 476 (1957).
13. *Ibid.,* 481, 483, 484, 487.
14. Potter Stewart, "Who Freed Dollree Mapp?" Harlan Fiske Stone Memorial Lecture, April 26, 1983, p. 4.
15. *Ibid.,* p. 13.
16. *Wilkes* v. *Wood,* 98 Eng. Rep. 489 (K.B. 1763).
17. Potter Stewart, Lecture, p. 15.
18. *Boyd* v. *United States,* 116 U.S. 616 (1886).
19. *Ibid.,* pp. 630, 633.
20. *Weeks* v. *United States,* 232 U.S. 383 (1914).
21. *People* v. *Defore,* 242 N.Y. 13, 21 (1926).
22. *Wolf* v. *Colorado,* 338 U.S. 25 (1949).
23. *Ibid.,* p. 28.
24. *Ibid.,* p. 41.
25. *State* v. *Lindway,* 131 Ohio St., 166 (1936).
26. *State* v. *Mapp,* 170 Ohio St., 427, 433 (1960).
27. All oral argument quotes are from the tape-recorded transcript.
28. Potter Stewart, Lecture, p. 8.
29. *Ibid.,* pp. 8–9.
30. Interview with Dollree Mapp.
31. *Mapp* v. *Ohio,* 367 U.S. 643, 655, 657 (1961).
32. *Ibid.,* p. 660.
33. *Bivens* v. *Six Unknown Agents,* 403 U.S. 388, 411 (1971) (Burger, C.J., dissenting).

Chapter 9: Crime and Its Aftershock

1. Interview with Don Feldman, January 1976.
2. *Estes* v. *Texas,* 381 U.S. 532, 536 (1965).
3. *Ibid.,* p. 585.
4. *Sheppard* v. *Maxwell,* 348 U.S. 333, 341 (1966).

5. *Ibid.,* p. 348.
6. *Ibid.,* pp. 357, 363.
7. *Warren Report,* p. 99.
8. Brief for Appellant, *Nebraska Press Association* v. *Stuart,* 427 U.S. 539.
9. Interview with Milton Larson, January 1976.
10. Tape recording of press conference of Sheriff Gordon Gilster, October 19, 1975.
11. Interview with Judge Ronald Ruff, January 1976.
12. Interview with Judge Hugh Stuart, January 1976.
13. Interview with Larson.
14. *Sheppard* v. *Maxwell,* 348 U.S. 333, 359.
15. Interview with Ruff.
16. Interview with Stuart.
17. In Chambers Order, *Nebraska Press Association* v. *Stuart,* 423 U.S. 1319 (Blackmun, Circuit Justice 1976).
18. Interview with Joe R. Seacrest, January 1976.
19. Interview with Ruff.
20. *Bridges* v. *California,* 314 U.S. 252 (1941).
21. Interview with Richard Anderson, January 1976.
22. Interview with Beulah Loostrom, January 1976.
23. Interview with Eugene Seaton, January 1976.
24. Interview with Mr. and Mrs. Robert Gerard, January 1976.
25. *Nebraska Press Association* v. *Stuart,* 427 U.S. 539, 547 (1976).
26. *Ibid.,* p. 548.
27. *Ibid.,* pp. 565, 570.

Chapter 10: Willie Francis' Two Trips to the Chair

1. *Annals of Congress,* 1st Cong., 1st sess., August 17, 1789, p. 754.
2. *In re Kemmler,* 136 U.S. 436, 444 (1890).
3. *Ibid.,* p. 444.
4. Theodore Bernstein, "A Great Success," *Spectrum,* February 1973, p. 55.
5. *In re Kemmler,* p. 441.
6. *In re Kemmler,* 7 N.Y.S. 145, 158 (1889).
7. *In re Kemmler,* 24 N.E. 6 (1889).
8. *In re Kemmler,* 136 U.S. 436, 447 (1890).
9. Bernstein, "Success," p. 57.
10. Interview with Sydney Dupois, June 6, 1983; interview with Jenny Durand, June 6, 1983.
11. Arthur S. Miller and Jeffrey Bowman, "Slow Dance on the Killing Ground: The Willie Francis Case Revisited," 32 *De Paul L. Rev.* 1, 6 (1983).
12. Interview with Dupois.
13. *Louisiana ex rel. Francis* v. *Resweber,* 329 U.S. 459, 480 n. 2.
14. Governor Davis is also known as a country-western singer and the composer of "Ain't She Sweet."
15. Interview with Bertrand de Blanc, June 6, 1983.
16. Interview with Judge Skelly Wright, June 12, 1983.
17. Barrett Prettyman, Jr., *Death and the Supreme Court,* p. 105.

18. *Ibid.,* p. 106.
19. *Ibid.*
20. Miller and Bowman, "Slow Dance," p. 12.
21. Prettyman, *Death,* pp. 115–116.
22. *Francis,* p. 462.
23. *Ibid.,* pp. 463–464.
24. *Ibid.,* p. 465.
25. *Ibid.,* pp. 466, 468, 469 (quoting *Palko* v. *Connecticut,* 302 U.S. 319 (1937)).
26. *Ibid.,* p. 469.
27. Miller and Bowman, "Slow Dance," p. 18.
28. *Rochin* v. *California,* 342 U.S. 165 (1952).
29. *Francis,* p. 472.
30. *Ibid.,* pp. 473, 474–475.
31. *Ibid.,* p. 476 (quoting *In re Kemmler,* 136 U.S. 436, 447).
32. *Ibid.*
33. *Adamson* v. *California,* 332 U.S. 46 (1947).
34. Miller and Bowman, "Slow Dance," Appendix i, pp. 68, 69.
35. The account of the execution is drawn from interviews with the reporters present and from newspaper accounts.
36. Mark Harris, AP wire story, April 22, 1983.
37. Interview with Stan Bailey, June 1983.
38. *Weems* v. *United States,* 217 U.S. 349, 368 (1910).
39. *Ibid.,* p. 373.
40. Bruce J. Meager, "Notes," 52 *Notre Dame Law.* 261, 265 (December 1976).
41. *Furman* v. *Georgia,* 408 U.S. 238 (1972).
42. *Gregg* v. *Georgia,* 428 U.S. 153 (1976).

Chapter 11: The Defense of Last Resort

1. Henry Cecil, *Just Within the Law,* p. 66.
2. *Smith* v. *Baldi,* 344 U.S. 561, 570 (1953) (Frankfurter, J., dissenting).
3. *Powell* v. *Texas,* 392 U.S. 514 (1968).
4. *Ibid.,* pp. 536–537.
5. Chapter 8, Section 4 of "Baba Kamma," pp. 342–343.
6. Donald J. West and Alexander Walk, eds., *Daniel McNaughton,* p. 6.
7. *Ibid.,* p. 8.
8. *Ibid.,* p. 25.
9. This and all other quotes are from trial transcript, *Queen against Daniel M'Naghten,* 4 St. Tr. (n. s.) 847; 8 Eng. Rep. 718 (1843).
10. West and Walk, *McNaughton,* pp. 9–10.
11. *Ibid.,* pp. 8–9.
12. *Ibid.,* p. 9.
13. *Ibid.,* p. 75.
14. *Parsons* v. *State,* 81 Ala. 577 (1886).
15. *Ibid.,* pp. 585, 586.
16. Joseph E. De Genora and Victoria Toensing, "Bringing Sanity to the Insanity Defense," *A.B.A. Magazine,* April 1983, p. 468.
17. Alan Stone, "The Insanity Defense on Trial," *Harvard Law School Bulletin,* 33, no. 1 (Fall 1982): 21.

Chapter 12: Umpiring "Harmless, Empty Shadows"

1. *United States* v. *Rabinowitz,* 339 U.S. 56, 69 (1950).
2. Gereon Zimmerman, "Contraception and Commotion in Connecticut," *Look Magazine,* January 30, 1962, pp. 83–83a.
3. Interview with Catherine Roraback, November 28, 1983.
4. "Birth Control's Mrs. Griswold: From Experience," *New Haven Register,* December 4, 1965.
5. *New York Times,* June 8, 1965, p. 34.
6. Henry J. Abraham and Leo A. Hazelwood, "Comstockery at the Bar of Justice: Birth Control Legislation in the Federal, Connecticut, and Massachusetts Courts," *Law in Transition Quarterly,* Fall 1966.
7. 17 Stat. 598 (1873); for revised statute see 180 S.C. art. 1461.
8. "History of Attempts to Legalize Birth Control in Connecticut," unpublished pamphlet prepared for Planned Parenthood in 1944; author unknown.
9. Margaret Sanger, *An Autobiography,* p. 91.
10. *Ibid.,* p. 92.
11. Videotape of presentation on the history of the birth control movement to the 60th anniversary dinner of Planned Parenthood League of Connecticut.
12. *Ibid.*
13. Interview with Marian Hepburn Grant, January 13, 1983.
14. *Hartford Courant,* April 6, 1935, p. 18.
15. *Hartford Courant,* December 11, 1935.
16. Demurrer to Information, *State* v. *Nelson,* J. Warren Upson, pp. 40–42.
17. Memorandum on Demurrer to Information, *State* v. *Nelson,* Judge Wynne, August 3, 1939.
18. *State* v. *Nelson,* 126 Conn. 412, 426 (1940).
19. *Poe* v. *Ullman,* 367 U.S. 497, 508 (1961).
20. *Ibid.,* p. 513 (Douglas, J., dissenting).
21. *Ibid.,* p. 509.
22. Zimmerman, "Contraception," pp. 80–81.
23. *Ibid.,* p. 81.
24. Interview with Detective Harold Berg, December 8, 1983.
25. Zimmerman, "Contraception," p. 80.
26. *Ibid.*
27. Interview with Joan Forsberg, December 9, 1983.
28. *Newsweek,* January 15, 1962, p. 55.
29. Brief for Appellants, *Griswold* v. *Connecticut,* Supreme Court of U.S. No. 496, p. 79.
30. Interview with Thomas I. Emerson, November 21, 1983.
31. Brief for Appellants, *Griswold* v. *Connecticut,* Supreme Court of U.S. No. 496, p. 9.
32. *Griswold* v. *Connecticut,* 381 U.S. 479, 482–483 (1965).
33. *Ibid.,* pp. 484–485.
34. *Ibid.,* p. 486.
35. *Ibid.,* p. 488.
36. *Ibid.,* p. 500.
37. *Ibid.,* pp. 502–507.
38. *Ibid.,* pp. 507, 510, 522 (Black, J., dissenting).

39. *Ibid.,* pp. 527, 529, 531 (Stewart, J., dissenting).
40. *New York Times,* June 9, 1965.
41. *Eisenstadt* v. *Baird,* 405 U.S. 438, 453 (1972).
42. This and all other quotes from Norma McCorvey are from interviews with the authors, February 26–28, 1984.
43. This and all other quotes from the oral arguments in *Roe* v. *Wade* are taken from the official transcript, in *Landmark Briefs and Arguments of the Supreme Court,* vol. 75, 1973.
44. *Roe* v. *Wade,* 410 U.S. 113, 125 (1973).
45. *Ibid.,* pp. 158, 152–153.
46. *Ibid.,* p. 154.
47. *Newsweek,* February 5, 1973, p. 27.

Chapter 13: Bakke and the Equal Protection Clause

1. *Plessy* v. *Fergusson,* 163 U.S. 537, 559 (1896) (Harlan, J., dissenting).
2. Unless otherwise noted, all quotes from Dr. Tupper are from interview, September 9, 1983.
3. *Brown* v. *Board of Education of Topeka,* 347 U.S. 483 (1954).
4. Robert Lindsey, "White/Caucasian—and Rejected," *New York Times Magazine,* April 3, 1977, p. 46.
5. Allan P. Sindler, *Bakke, DeFunis and Minority Admissions,* p. 58. Those admitted under the regular program scored on the average: science, 83rd percentile; verbal, 81st percentile; quantitative, 76th percentile; general knowledge, 69th percentile. The corresponding figures for those admitted under the special program: science, 35th percentile; verbal, 46th percentile; quantitative, 24th percentile; general knowledge, 33rd percentile.
6. Archibald Cox, "Minority Admissions After *Bakke,*" p. 80, paper presented at "Bakke, Webber, and Affirmative Action," a Rockefeller Foundation Conference, July 12–13, 1979.
7. *Brown,* pp. 492, 493.
8. 42 U.S.C. § 2000d (1964).
9. Cox, "Minority Admissions," p. 83.
10. Sindler, *Bakke,* p. 21.
11. *Ibid.,* pp. 68–69.
12. Trial record, *Bakke,* p. 245.
13. Sindler, *Bakke,* p. 69.
14. *Ibid.,* pp. 69–70.
15. *Ibid.,* p. 70.
16. Interview with Peter Storandt, November 21, 1983.
17. Interview with Storandt.
18. *DeFunis* v. *Odegaard,* 416 U.S. 312, 350 (1974) (Brennan, J., dissenting).
19. Interview with Storandt.
20. *Bakke* v. *University of California,* 18 Cal. 3d, 34, 38 (1976).
21. Interview with Storandt.
22. All quotes from the oral arguments are taken from the official court transcript.
23. *North Carolina State Board of Education* v. *Swann,* 402 U.S. 43, 46 (1971).
24. Cox, "Minority Admissions," p. 83.

25. This and all other quotes are from *University of California* v. *Bakke,* 438 U.S. 265 (1978).
26. Interview with Dean Ernest L. Lewis, September 9, 1983.

Chapter 14: "Give Me Your Tired, Your Poor . . ."

1. All quotes from Jean D'Eau are from interviews conducted in December 1983 and on February 16, 1984.
2. All quotes from Mark Murphy are from interviews in December 1983.
3. Interview with Joseph Etienne, November 1983.
4. Chinese Exclusion Act of May 6, 1882, 22 Stat. 58.
5. *Chinese Exclusion Cases,* 130 U.S. 581, 603–604 (1889).
6. *Haitian Refugee Center* v. *Civiletti,* 503 F. Supp. 442, 452 (1980).
7. *Ibid.*
8. *Ibid.,* p. 451.
9. *Ibid.,* p. 455.
10. *Ibid.,* p. 475.
11. *Ibid.,* p. 510.
12. *Ibid.,* p. 532.
13. All quotes from Jose Doe are from interviews on February 10 and 16, 1984.
14. Tex. Educ. Code Ann. § 21.031 (Vernon Supp. 1981).
15. All quotes from James Plyler are from interview on February 9, 1984.
16. *Plyler* v. *Doe,* 457 U.S. 202, 206 n. 2 (1982).
17. All quotes from Michael McAndrew are from interview on February 11, 1984.
18. All quotes from Peter Roos are from interview on February 9, 1984.
19. Interview with Viviola Doe, February 16, 1984.
20. *Doe* v. *Plyler,* 458 F. Supp. 569, 575 (1978).
21. *Ibid.,* p. 577.
22. *Plyler* v. *Doe,* 457 U.S. 202, 210 (1982).
23. *Ibid.,* p. 213.
24. *Ibid.,* pp. 215–216.
25. *Ibid.,* pp. 218–219, 220.
26. *Ibid.,* p. 223.
27. *Ibid.,* p. 230.
28. *Ibid.,* pp. 242, 243.
29. *Ibid.,* pp. 243, 244, 248.
30. *Ibid.,* p. 254.
31. Interview with Richard Arnett, February 8, 1984.
32. Television interview with Father Hesburgh, "The Constitution: That Delicate Balance."

Chapter 15: A Nation of States

1. James Madison, *Notes on the Debates in the Federal Convention of 1787,* ed. Adrienne Koch, pp. 29–30.
2. *Ibid.,* p. 194.
3. *Ibid.,* p. 209.
4. *Ibid.,* p. 35.
5. Alpheus Thomas Mason, *The States Rights Debate,* p. 70.

6. Television interview with Justice Potter Stewart, "The Constitution: That Delicate Balance."
7. Francis N. Stiles, *John Marshall,* p. 122.
8. Richard N. Current, "The Dartmouth College Case," in John A. Garraty, ed., *Quarrels That Have Shaped the Constitution,* p. 16.
9. *Ibid.,* p. 27.
10. Stiles, *Marshall,* p. 125.
11. *Dartmouth College* v. *Woodward,* 4 Wheat. 518, 654 (1819).
12. Current, "Dartmouth," p. 29.
13. Samuel Eliot Morrison, *The Oxford History of the American People,* vol. II, p. 42.
14. All quotes from the oral arguments are taken from transcript in the opinion, 4 Wheat. 316 (1819).
15. This and the following quotes are from the opinion in *McCulloch* v. *Maryland,* 4 Wheat. 316 (1819).
16. Stiles, *Marshall,* p. 134.
17. Morrison, *Oxford History,* p. 136.

Chapter 16: The Sacking of Greytown

1. Donald King and Arthur Levens, "Curbing the Dog of War," *Harv. Int'l L.J.* 18 (Winter 1977): 55.
2. Jacob Javits, *Who Makes War?,* p. 104.
3. Samuel Eliot Morrison, *The Oxford History of the American People,* vol. II, pp. 343–344.
4. J. D. Richardson, ed., *Messages and Papers of the Presidents,* vol. VI, p. 200.
5. Roy Franklin Nichols, *Franklin Pierce,* pp. 325, 533.
6. *Ibid.,* p. 330.
7. *Ibid.*
8. *Ibid.,* p. 263.
9. Javits, *War,* p. 106.
10. *New York Daily Times,* July 25, 1854, p. 4; August 1, 1854, p. 1; July 31, 1851.
11. Richardson, *Messages,* vol. I, pp. 327, 377–378.
12. Javits, *War,* p. 108.
13. *New York Evening Post,* August 4, 1854, p. 1.
14. *New York Evening Post,* August 2, 1854.
15. Letter to the editor, *New York Daily Times,* July 26, 1854.
16. *New York Evening Post,* August 2, 1854, p. 1.
17. *New York Daily Times,* July 25, 1854.
18. Nichols, *Pierce,* p. 346.
19. Arthur M. Schlesinger, Jr., *The Imperial Presidency,* p. 56.
20. Letter to the editor, *New York Daily Times,* July 25, 1854.
21. Letter to the editor, *New York Daily Times,* July 26, 1854 (letter signed July 15, 1854).
22. *New York Daily Times,* July 31, 1854, p. 4.
23. Javits, *War,* p. 111.
24. *Washington Union,* quoted in *New York Daily Times,* August 2, 1854.
25. Pierce, message to 33rd Cong., 2nd sess., House of Representatives, Ex. Doc., no. 1.

26. Javits, *War,* pp. 113–114.
27. Nichols, *Pierce,* p. 374.
28. *Durand* v. *Hollins,* 4 Blatch. 452, 455 (1860).
29. *Ibid.,* pp. 454–455.
30. Schlesinger, *Imperial Presidency,* p. 56.
31. Edwin S. Corwin, *The President,* p. 171.
32. James Madison, *Notes on the Debates in the Federal Convention of 1787,* ed. Adrienne Koch, p. 476; abbreviations and spellings used are as in the original.
33. Bernard Bailyn, *The Ideological Origins of the American Revolution,* p. 56.
34. Schlesinger, *Imperial Presidency,* p. 8.
35. Letter of Thomas Jefferson to J. B. Colvin, September 20, 1810.
36. Javits, *War,* p. 112.
37. Louis Henkin, *Foreign Affairs and the Constitution,* n. 23, p. 345.
38. Joseph Bessette and Jeffrey Tulis, eds., *The Presidency in the Constitutional Order,* p. 115.
39. Henkin, *Foreign Affairs,* p. 208.

Epilogue

1. Learned Hand, *The Spirit of Liberty,* p. 190.

Select Bibliography

Books

Abel, Elie. *The Missile Crisis.* Philadelphia: Lippincott, 1968.

Abraham, Henry J. *Freedom and the Court: Civil Rights and Liberties in the United States,* 3d ed. New York: Oxford University Press, 1977.

Ahlstrom, Sydney E. *A Religious History of the American People.* New Haven, Conn.: Yale University Press, 1972.

Allen, Richard C.; Austin, Jessie C.; and Ferster, Elyce Zenoff, eds. *Readings in Law and Psychiatry.* Baltimore: Johns Hopkins University Press, 1968, 1975.

Bailyn, Bernard. *The Ideological Origins of the American Revolution.* Cambridge, Mass.: Belknap, 1967.

Bailyn, Bernard, and Hench, John B., eds. *The Press and the American Revolution.* Boston: Northeastern University Press, 1981.

Bailyn, Bernard; Davis, David Brian; Donald, David Herbert; Thomas, John L.; Wiebe, Robert H.; and Woods, Gordon S. *The Great Republic—A History of the American People,* vol. II, 2d ed. Lexington, Mass.: Heath, 1981.

Baker, Leonard. *Back to Back.* New York: Macmillan, 1967.

———. *John Marshall: A Life in Law.* New York: Collier, 1974.

Banning, Margaret Culkin. *Mesabi.* New York: Harper & Row, 1969.

Barber, James David, ed. *Race for the Presidency.* Englewood Cliffs, N.J.: Prentice-Hall, 1978.

Bennett, Walter Hartwell. *American Theories of Federation.* University: University of Alabama Press, 1964.

Berger, Raoul. *Government by Judiciary.* Cambridge, Mass.: Harvard University Press, 1977.

Bessette, Joseph M., and Tulis, Jeffrey, eds. *The Presidency in the Constitutional Order.* Baton Rouge: Louisiana State University Press, 1981.

Beveridge, Albert J. *The Life of John Marshall.* Boston, 1916–1919.

Bickel, Alexander M. *The Least Dangerous Branch.* Indianapolis, Ind.: Bobbs-Merrill, 1962.

———. *The Morality of Consent.* New Haven, Conn.: Yale University Press, 1975.

———. *The Supreme Court and the Idea of Progress.* New York: Harper & Row, 1970.

Blackstone, William. *Commentaries on the Laws of England,* vol. IV. Chicago: University of Chicago Press, 1979.

Blum, Carolyn Patty, ed. *Immigration Law and Defense.* New York: Boardman, 1980.

Bowen, Catherine Drinker. *Yankee from Olympus.* Boston: Little, Brown, 1944.

Brown, David, and Bruner, W. Richard, eds. *How I Got That Story.* New York: Dutton, 1967.

Burns, James MacGregor. *The Vineyard of Liberty.* New York: Knopf, 1982.

Butterfield, Roger. *The American Past.* New York: Simon & Schuster, 1947.

Califano, Joseph A., Jr. *Governing America.* New York: Simon & Schuster, 1981.

Cappon, Lester J., ed. *The Adams-Jefferson Letters,* vols. I and II. Chapel Hill: University of North Carolina Press, 1959.

Catton, Bruce. *The Coming Fury,* vol. I. New York: Washington Square Press, 1966.

Cecil, Henry. *Just Within the Law.* London: Hutchinson, 1975.

Chafee, Zechariah, Jr. *Free Speech in the United States.* New York: Atheneum, 1969.

Chicago Tribune. *A Century of Tribune Editorials.* Chicago: Tribune Company Archives, 1847–1947.

Christie, I. R. *Crisis of Empire.* New York: Norton, 1966.

Commager, Henry Steele. *The Empire of Reason.* New York: Oxford University Press, 1977.

Congressional Quarterly. *Guide to U.S. Elections.* Washington, D.C.: Congressional Quarterly, 1975.

Corwin, Edward S. *The President.* New York: New York University Press, 1940, 1941, 1948, 1957.

———. *Presidential Power and the Constitution, Essays.* Edited by Richard Loss. Ithaca, N.Y.: Cornell University Press, 1976.

Cox, Archibald. *The Role of the Supreme Court in American Government.* New York: Oxford University Press, 1976.

Cronin, Thomas E. *The State of the Presidency,* 2d ed. Boston: Little, Brown, 1980, 1975.

Crosskey, William Winston. *Politics and the Constitution in the History of the United States,* vol. II. Chicago: University of Chicago Press, 1953.

Danelski, David J. *A Supreme Court Justice Is Appointed.* New York: Random House, 1964.

Danelski, David J., and Tulchin, Joseph S., eds. *The Autobiographical Notes of Charles Evans Hughes.* Cambridge, Mass.: Harvard University Press, 1973.

De Tocqueville, Alexis. *Democracy in America.* Edited by J.P. Mayer. Garden City, N.Y.: Anchor Books, Doubleday, 1969.

Dillon, John M., ed. *John Marshall, Complete Constitutional Decisions.* Chicago: Callagher, 1903.

Dolce, Philip C., and Skau, George H. *Power and the Presidency.* New York: Scribner, 1976.

Drew, Elizabeth. *Politics and Money: The New Road to Corruption.* New York: Macmillan, 1983.

Dunham, Allison, and Kurland, Philip B., eds. *Mr. Justice.* Chicago: University of Chicago Press, 1956.

Eagleton, Thomas. *War and Presidential Power.* New York: Liveright, 1974.

Fehrenbacher, Dan E. *The Dred Scott Case: Its Significance in American Law and Politics.* New York: Oxford University Press, 1978.

Folwell, William Watts. *A History of Minnesota,* vol. IV. St. Paul: Minnesota Historical Society, 1969.

Ford, P. L. *The Works of Thomas Jefferson,* vol XII. New York: Putnam, 1905.

Frankfurter, Felix, ed. *Mr. Justice Holmes.* New York: Coward McCann, 1931.

Frankfurter, Felix, and Landis, James M. *The Business of the Supreme Court.* New York: Macmillan, 1927.

Friedman, Lawrence M. *A History of American Law.* New York: Simon & Schuster, 1973.

Friedman, Lawrence M., and Scheiber, Harry N., eds. *American Law and the Constitutional Order.* Cambridge, Mass.: Harvard University Press, 1979.

Friendly, Fred W. *Minnesota Rag.* New York: Random House, 1981.

Garraty, John A., ed. *Quarrels That Have Shaped the Constitution.* New York: Harper & Row, 1962, 1963, 1964.

Gies, Joseph. *The Colonel of Chicago: A Biography of the Chicago Tribune's Legendary Publisher, Colonel Robert McCormick.* New York: Dutton, 1979.

Goetzman, William H. *When the Eagle Screamed.* New York: Wiley, 1966.

Green, Jack P., ed. *Colonies to Nation, 1763–1789.* New York; Norton, 1975.

Guilford, Howard A. *A Tale of Two Cities: Memoirs of Sixteen Years Behind a Pencil.* Robbinsdale, Minn., 1929.

Halberstam, David. *The Powers That Be.* New York: Dell, 1979.

Hamlin, David. *The Nazi/Skokie Conflict.* Boston: Beacon Press, 1980.

Hand, Learned. *The Spirit of Liberty,* 3d ed. Collected by Irving Dilliard. Chicago: University of Chicago Press, 1960.

Heard, Alexander. *The Costs of Democracy.* Chapel Hill: University of North Carolina Press, 1960.

Henkin, Louis. *Foreign Affairs and the Constitution.* New York: Norton, 1972.

Hermann, Donald H. J., and Thomas, Charles C. *The Insanity Defense: Philosophical, Historical and Legal Perspectives.* Springfield, Ill.. Charles C Thomas, 1983.

Hershkowitz, Leo. *Tweed's New York: Another Look.* Garden City, N.Y.: Doubleday, 1977.

Hobbes, Thomas. *Leviathan.* New York: Penguin, 1981.

Hofstadter, Richard. *The Idea of a Party System.* Berkeley and Los Angeles: University of California Press, 1969.

Hughes, Charles Evans. *The Supreme Court of the United States.* New York: Columbia University Press, 1928.

Hyman, Harold M., and Wiecek, William M. *Equal Justice Under Law: Constitutional Development 1835–1875.* New York: Harper & Row, 1982.

Jackson, Robert H. *The Struggle for Judicial Supremacy.* New York: Knopf, 1941.

Javits, Jacob, with Kellerman, Dan. *Who Makes War?* New York: Morrow, 1973.

Katz, Jay; Goldstein, Joseph; and Dershowitz, Alan M. *Psychoanalysis, Psychiatry and the Law.* New York: Free Press, 1967.

Kennedy, Robert F. *Thirteen Days.* New York: Signet, 1969.

Kent, Frank R. *The Great Game of Politics.* Garden City, N.Y.: Doubleday, 1959.

Kerber, Linda K. *Women of the Republic.* Chapel Hill: University of North Carolina Press, 1980, 1981.

King, Frank A. *The Missabe Road: The Duluth, Missabe and Iron Range Railway.* San Marino, Calif.: Golden West Books, 1972.

Kluger, Richard. *Simple Justice.* New York: Vintage, 1976.

Konefsky, Samuel J. *John Marshall and Alexander Hamilton: Architects of the American Court.* New York: Macmillan, 1969.

————. *The Legacy of Holmes and Brandeis.* New York: Macmillan, 1956.

Kurland, Philip B., and Casper, Gerald, eds. *Landmark Briefs and Arguments of the Supreme Court of the United States: Constitutional Law.* University Publications of America, selected volumes.

Lewis, Anthony. *Gideon's Trumpet.* New York: Random House, 1964.

Lewis, Walker. *Without Fear or Favor: A Biography of Chief Justice Roger Brooke Taney.* Boston: Houghton Mifflin, 1965.

Levy, Leonard W. *Freedom of Speech and Press in Early American History: Legacy of Suppression.* New York: Harper & Row, 1963.

————. *Jefferson and Civil Liberties: The Darker Side.* New York: Quandrangle, Times Book Co., 1963.

Lippmann, Walter. *Public Opinion.* New York: Free Press, 1922, 1966.

Loth, David. *Chief Justice John Marshall and the Growth of the Republic.* New York: Greenwood Press, 1949.

Lynch, Denis Tilden. *"Boss" Tweed: The Story of a Grim Generation.* New York: Boni & Liveright, 1927.

Macdonald, Dora Mary. *This is Duluth.* Duluth, Minn., 1950.

McCormick, Robert R. *The Freedom of the Press: A History and an Argument.* New York: Appleton-Century, 1936.

McCullough, David. *The Path Between the Seas: The Creation of the Panama Canal 1870–1914.* New York: Simon & Schuster, 1977.

McDonald, Forrest. *Alexander Hamilton.* New York: Norton, 1979.

McKenna, George. *American Politics.* New York: McGraw-Hill, 1976.

McKenna, George, and Feingold, Stanley, eds. *Taking Sides: Clashing Views on Controversial Political Issues,* 3d ed. Guilford, Conn.: Dushkin Publishing Group, 1983.

Madison, James. *Notes of the Debates in the Federal Convention of 1787.* Edited by Adrienne Koch. Athens: Ohio University Press, 1966.

Magruder, Alan B. *John Marshall.* Boston: Houghton Mifflin, 1885.

Malone, Dumas. *Thomas Jefferson and the Rights of Man.* Boston: Little, Brown, 1951.

Mason, Alpheus Thomas. *Brandeis: Lawyer and Judge in the Modern State.* Princeton, N.J.: Princeton University Press, 1933.

————, ed. *The States Rights Debate: Anti-federalism and the Constitution,* 2d ed. New York: Oxford University Press, 1972.

————; Beany, William M.; and Stephenson, Donald Grier. *American Constitutional Law,* 7th ed. Englewood Cliffs, N.J.: Prentice-Hall, 1983.

Mason, Francis Norton. *My Dearest Polly, Letters of Chief Justice John Marshall to His Wife, with Their Background, Political and Domestic 1716–1831.* Richmond, Va.: Garrett, 1961.

Mayer, George H. *The Political Career of Floyd B. Olson.* Minneapolis: University of Minnesota Press, 1951.

Meyers, Marvin. *The Jacksonian Persuasion.* Stanford, Calif.: Stanford University Press, 1960.

Mill, John Stuart. *On Liberty.* Indianapolis, Ind.: Hackett, 1978.

Milton, John. *Areopagitica and Of Education.* Edited by George H. Sabine. Arlington Heights, Ill.: Harlan Davidson, 1951.

Morgan, Edmund S. *The Puritan Family.* New York: Harper & Row, 1944, 1966.

Morris, Norval. *Madness and the Criminal Law.* Chicago: University of Chicago Press, 1982.

Morrison, John L. *The Booster Book: West Duluth in 1916.* Duluth, Minn., July 1, 1916.

The New York Times Company v. United States, vols. I and II (The Pentagon Papers). New York: Arno Press, 1971.

Neier, Aryeh. *Defending My Enemy.* New York: Dutton, 1979.

Nichols, Roy Franklin. *Young Hickory of the Granite Hills.* Philadelphia: University of Pennsylvania Press, 1958.

Paine, Thomas. *Common Sense.* Edited by Isaac Kramnick. New York: Penguin, 1980.

Pilcher, William W. *The Portland Longshoremen.* New York: Holt, Rinehart and Winston, 1972.

Planned Parenthood. "History of Attempts to Legalize Birth Control in Connecticut." Unpublished pamphlet, 1944.

Prettyman, Barrett, Jr. *Death and the Supreme Court.* New York: Harcourt, Brace & World, 1961.

Pringle, Henry F. *The Life and Times of William Howard Taft,* vol II. New York: Farrar & Rinehart, 1939.

Pusey, Merlo J. *Charles Evans Hughes,* vols. I and II. New York: Columbia University Press, 1963.

Richardson, J. D., ed. *Messages and Papers of the Presidents, 1789–1897,* vols. I and V. Washington, D.C.: U.S. Government Printing Office, 1897.

Roberts, Chalmers. *The Washington Post: The First 100 Years.* Boston: Houghton Mifflin, 1977.

Roche, John P., ed. *John Marshall: Major Opinions and Other Writings.* Indianapolis, Ind.: Bobbs-Merrill, 1967.

Roseboom, Eugene H. *A History of Presidential Elections,* 3d ed. New York: Macmillan, 1970.

Rosenberg, Charles E. *The Trial of the Assassin Guiteau.* Chicago: University of Chicago Press, 1968.

Rossiter, Clinton, ed. *The Federalist Papers.* New York: New American Library, 1961.

Ruckert, Norman. *The Fell's Point Story.* Baltimore: Bodine, 1976.

Salisbury, Harrison. *Without Fear or Favor.* New York: Times Books, 1980.

Sanger, Margaret. *An Autobiography.* New York: Dover, 1971.

Schlesinger, Arthur M., Jr. *The Imperial Presidency.* Boston: Houghton Mifflin, 1973.

———. *A Thousand Days.* Boston: Houghton Mifflin, 1965.

Siebert, Frederick Seaton. *A Belated Diary.* Unpublished, 1976.

Sindler, Allan P. *Bakke, DeFunis and Minority Admissions: The Quest for Equal Opportunity.* New York: Longman, 1978.

Smith, James Morton. *Freedom's Fetters.* Ithaca, N.Y.: Cornell University Press, 1956.

Steffens, Lincoln. *The Shame of the Cities.* New York: McClure, Phillips, 1904.

Stiles, Francis N. *John Marshall: Defender of the Constitution.* Boston: Little, Brown, 1981.

Stone, Harlan Fiske. *Law and Its Administration.* New York: Columbia University Press, 1915.

Swindler, William F. *The Constitution and Chief Justice Marshall.* New York: Dodd, Mead, 1978.

Thayer, George. *Who Shakes the Money Tree?* New York: Simon & Schuster, 1973.

Thayer, James Bradley. *John Marshall.* New York: Da Capo, 1974.

Todd, A. L. *Justice on Trial: The Case of Louis D. Brandeis.* New York: McGraw-Hill, 1964.

Trefousse, Hans L. *The Radical Republicans: Lincoln's Vanguard for Racial Justice.* Baton Rouge: Louisiana State University Press, 1968.

Unger, Sanford J. *The Papers and the Papers.* New York: Dutton, 1972.

Villard, Oswald Garrison. *The Disappearing Daily.* New York: Knopf, 1944.

Waldrop, Frank C. *McCormick of Chicago.* Englewood Cliffs, N.J.: Prentice-Hall, 1966.

Warren Report. *The Official Report on the Assassination of President John F. Kennedy.* Associated Press, 1964.

Warren, Charles. *Congress, the Constitution and the Supreme Court.* Boston: Little, Brown, 1925.

Wechsler, Herbert. *The Nationalization of Civil Liberties and Civil Rights.* Austin: University of Texas Press. Supplement to *Texas Quarterly,* vol. XII (1968).

———. *Principles, Politics, and Fundamental Law.* Cambridge, Mass.: Harvard University Press, 1961.

West, Donald J., and Walk, Alexander, eds. *Daniel McNaughton: His Trial and the Aftermath.* Gaskell, 1977.

Westmoreland, William C. *A Soldier Reports.* New York: Doubleday, 1976.

Whipple, Leon. *Our Ancient Liberties.* New York: T.H. Wilson, 1927.

White, Theodore H. *The Making of the President 1960.* New York: Atheneum, 1961.

Wilkinson, J. Harvie, III. *From Brown to Bakke: The Supreme Court and School Integration: 1954–78.* New York: Oxford University Press, 1979.

Wilson, Woodrow. *Constitutional Government in the United States.* New York: Columbia University Press, 1917.

Winslade, William J., and Ross, Judith Wilson. *The Insanity Plea.* New York: Scribner, 1983.

Wyden, Peter. *The Bay of Pigs.* New York: Simon & Schuster, 1980.

Wyzanski, Charles E., Jr. *Whereas: A Judge's Premises.* Boston: Little, Brown, 1965.

Yolton, John W., ed. *The Locke Reader.* Cambridge: Cambridge University Press, 1977.

Articles

Abraham, Henry J., and Hazelwood, Les A. "Comstockery at the Bar of Justice: Birth Control Legislation in the Federal, Connecticut, and Massachusetts Courts." *Law in Transition Quarterly* (Fall 1976).

American Civil Liberties Union. Select correspondence, on file at Princeton University and the *Chicago Tribune* Archives.

American Newspaper Publishers Association. Select correspondence.

Berman, Hyman. "Political Anti-Semitism in Minnesota During the Great Depression." *Jewish Social Studies* (Summer-Fall 1976).

Bork, Robert H. "Neutral Principles and Some First Amendment Problems." *Indiana Law Journal* 47 (Fall 1971).

Brandeis, Louis D. Letters and notes, on file at Harvard University Law School, Manuscript Division.

"CBS Reports: Storm Over the Supreme Court." March 13, 1963, transcript.

Corwin, Edward S. "The 'Higher Law' Background of American Constitutional Law." *Harvard Law Review* 42 (December 1928).

Cox, Archibald. "Minority Admissions After Bakke." Paper presented at "Bakke, Webber, and Affirmative Action," a Rockefeller Foundation Conference, July 12–13, 1979.

"Criminal Law—Constitutional Law—Due Process—Equal Protection." *Tulane Law Review* 2 (1947).

Daniel, Clifton. "The Press and National Security." World Press Institute (June 1, 1966).

De Genora, Joseph E., and Toensing, Victoria. "Bringing Sanity to the Insanity Defense." *ABA Magazine* (April 1983).

Fairman, Charles. "Does the Fourteenth Amendment Incorporate the Bill of Rights?" *Stanford Law Review* 2 (December 1949).

Frankel, Max. "A Washington Education." *Columbia Forum* (Winter 1973).

Frankfurter, Felix. "Chief Justices I Have Known." *Virginia Law Review* (1953).

Guilford, Howard A. "Gill's Pocket Book—Society Number," Pamphlet. Minneapolis (September 15, 1919).

Hartman, John E. "The Minnesota Gag Law and the Fourteenth Amendment," *Minnesota History* 37 (December 1960).

Holsinger, M. Paul, "Patriotism and the Curbing of Oregon's Radicals, 1919–1937." Paper presented to the Seventh Annual Conference of the Western History Association, October 14, 1972.

Hughes, Charles Evans. Select correspondence.

Janey, John. "The Minnesota Enigma." *American Magazine* 120 (September 1935).

King, Donald, and Levens, Arthur. "Curbing the Dog of War." *Harvard International Law Journal* 18, no. 1 (Winter 1977).

Leventhal, Harold. "Courts and Political Thickets." *Columbia Law Review* 77 (April 1977).

Linde, Hans. "Courts and Censorship." *Minnesota Law Review* 66 (1981).

McCormick, Robert R. "An Address." Yale, November 18, 1930. Reprinted by the Tribune Company, 1931.

———. "The Freedom of the Press." Speech: Chicago, October, 18, 1933. Reprinted by the Tribune Company, 1933.

———. Select correspondence, *Chicago Tribune* Archives.

McElwain, Edwin. "The Business of the Supreme Court as Conducted by Chief Justice Hughes." *Harvard Law Review* 63 (1949).

Meager, Bruce J. "Capital Punishment: A Review of Recent Supreme Court Decisions." *Notre Dame Lawyer* 52 (December 1976).

———. "Notes," Notre Dame Lawyer 52 (December 1976).

Mertens, William J., and Wasserstrom, Silas. "The Good Faith Exception to the Exclusionary Rule: Deregulating the Police and Derailing the Law." *Georgetown Law Journal* 70 (1981).

Miller, Arthur S., and Bowmann, Jeffrey S. "Slow Dance on the Killing Ground: The Willie Francis Case Revisited." *De Paul Law Review* 32 (1983).

Near, Jay M. Select correspondence.

Schatz, Norman L. "Due Process of Law—Cruel and Unusual Punishment by Electrocution." *Marquette Law Review* 31 (1947).

Stewart, Potter. "Who Freed Dollree Mapp?" Harlan Fiske Stone Memorial Lecture. April 26, 1983.

Stone, Alan. "The Insanity Defense on Trial." *Harvard Law School Bulletin* 33, no. 1 (Fall 1982).

Taft, William Howard. Select correspondence, on file at Library of Congress.

Walker, Frank. "Notes and Comments," *North Carolina Law Review* 42 (1964).

Zimmerman, Gereon. "Contraception and Commotion in Connecticut." *Look Magazine,* January 30, 1962.

Newspapers and Publications

Annals of Congress

Chicago Daily News
Chicago Tribune
Cleveland Press
Congressional Record

Duluth Rip-saw

Editor and Publisher

Hartford Courant
House of Representatives. Executive Documents.

"La Hora" (courtesy of the Hoover Institution on War, Revolution and Peace, Archives Division)

Mankato Free Press
Minneapolis Evening Tribune
Minneapolis Journal
Minneapolis Morning Tribune
Minneapolis Star
Minneapolis Tribune

The Nation
New Haven Register
Newsweek
New York Daily News
New York Evening Post
New York Herald Tribune
New York Times
The New Yorker
North Platte Telegraph

Omaha World Herald
Oregonian

Saturday Press

Time Magazine
Twin City Reporter

Washington Post
Washington Union

York, Pa., *Gazette and Daily*

Interviews

Judge Arlin Adams, Third Circuit, U.S. Court of Appeals
Richard Anderson, juror in *Simants* case
Richard Arnett, attorney for Texas Education Agency in *Plyler.*

Roger Baldwin, American Civil Liberties Union founder
Edward Barrett, Professor, University of California at Davis Law School
Detective Harold Berg, arresting officer in *Griswold* case
Bernard Berkman, American Civil Liberties Union lawyer in *Mapp* case
James Buckley, former Senator from New York
Warren E. Burger, Chief Justice of the United States
Pierce Butler III, grandson of Justice Butler
William Butler, lawyer for American Civil Liberties Union in *Engel* v. *Vitale*

Isadore Cohen, newsboy for Duluth *Rip-saw* and reporter for the Duluth *News-Tribune*

Clifton Daniel, former editor of the *New York Times*
Bertrand de Blanc, Willie Francis's lawyer
Jean D'Eau, Haitian refugee
Thomas Delaney, parent who wanted school prayer in Herricks School District
Carl Delau, arresting officer in *Mapp* v. *Ohio*

Jose Doe and family, illegal aliens in *Plyler* case
Sydney Dupois, witness to first Willie Francis electrocution
Jenny Durand, resident of St. Martinville, La., at time of Willie Francis

Thomas J. Emerson, attorney for Planned Parenthood in *Griswold* case

Don Feldman, reporter for *KNOP*
Orlin Folnick, former reporter for *Minneapolis Morning Tribune*
Joan Forsberg, state's witness in *Griswold*
Osmond K. Fraenkel, civil rights advocate

Erna Gans, resident of Skokie, Ill.
Mr. and Mrs. Robert Gerard, juror in *Simants* case
David Goldberger, attorney for American Civil Liberties Union in *Skokie* case
Elizabeth Hughes Gossett, daughter of Charles Evans Hughes and president of the
    Supreme Court Historical Society
William Gossett, son-in-law and associate of Charles Evans Hughes and Detroit
    attorney
Marian Hepburn Grant, daughter of Katherine Houghton Hepburn
Erwin Griswold, former Solicitor General and former dean of Harvard Law School

David Halberstam, author
Howard Handleman, retired reporter for *U.S. News & World Report*
Gilbert Harrison, former editor of *New Republic*

Milton Larson, prosecutor in *Simants* case
Beulah Loostram, juror in *Simants* case
Dr. George Lowrey, former head of admissions, University of California at Davis
    Medical School

Dollree Mapp, defendant in *Mapp* v. *Ohio*
Michael McAndrews, former liaison with Hispanic community, Tyler, Texas
Norma McCorvey, complainant in *Roe* v. *Wade*
Karl Meyer, editorial writer, *New York Times*

James Plyler, former superintendent of Tyler, Texas, schools

James Reston, columnist, *New York Times*
Peter Roos, attorney for Jose Doe in *Plyler* case
Catherine Roraback, attorney for Estelle Griswold and Lee Buxton
Daniel Roth, son of Lawrence Roth
Lawrence Roth, parent who opposed school prayer in Herricks School District
Judge Ronald Ruff, judge in *Simants* case
Ed Ryan, former Chief of Police of Minneapolis

Harrison Salisbury, former editor of *New York Times*
Harvey Schwartz, attorney for the village of Skokie
Joe R. Seacrest, publisher of *Omaha World Herald*
Eugene Seaton, juror in *Simants* case
Irving Shapiro, son of Samuel Shapiro
Judge Gus Solomon, attorney for Dirk DeJonge
Peter Storandt, former admissions officer at University of California at Davis
Judge Hugh Stuart, judge in *Simants* case

Tad Szulc, reporter for the *New York Times*

Dr. John A. Tupper, former dean of University of California at Davis Medical School

Judge Skelly Wright, Willie Francis's lawyer in the Supreme Court

Acknowledgments

We are a teaching team that writes about constitutional law with journalists' eyes and ears. Where possible we have sought out the primary players in the personal dramas which have given birth to landmark cases and resonate with the force of constitutional law. It is to all the "original casts" who spent hours telling us their stories that we owe an immeasurable debt. Norma McCorvey, Dollree Mapp, Carl Delau, Lawrence Roth, Erwin Charles Simants, Judge Hugh Stuart, Dr. John Tupper, Tad Szulc, James Buckley, Jean D'Eau, Jose Doe, and James Plyler are the people who made this book possible. We thank them for their time, their patience, and their trust.

Of course, it was not possible to interview all the people whose names appear on the cases we've written about. However, in many instances their lawyers, families, and friends were willing to help us fill in some of the facts and human aspects that the legal briefs and decisions omit. Judge Skelly Wright and attorney Bertrand de Blanc provided us with insights into the Willie Francis case. Arthur S. Miller and Jeffrey Bowman were tremendously helpful in sharing their research on the Francis case. Bowman also read the chapter and made valuable suggestions.

Clifton Daniel and Karl Meyer made large contributions to the Bay of Pigs chapter by spending time explaining how it all happened. Daniels was also willing to read over an early draft of the chapter.

Judge Gus Solomon, who argued Dirk DeJonge's case before the Supreme Court, spent time and effort telling us about the case and opening doors for us in Oregon. E. Kimball MacColl, a historian and expert on Portland's past, provided us with background material on DeJonge and the city of Portland. Osmond K. Fraenkel, the ACLU attorney who argued DeJonge's case, assisted us with details about the Supreme Court arguments.

Erna Gans and David Goldberger were on opposite sides of the Skokie conflict, but they were both willing to spend time with us recalling painful memories. Goldberger also read over a draft of the chapter. Harvey Schwartz, the Skokie village attorney, helped by recalling a number of details that never made their way into the newspapers.

David Roth, son of Lawrence Roth, and William Butler, the appellants' attorney, spent time recalling the events surrounding the *Engel* case. Judge Arlin Adams, an expert on religious history, was our teacher on much of the background material and willingly read over our chapter.

Judge Richard M. Markus of the State Court of Appeals of Ohio was helpful in providing documents from the *Mapp* case. William Banard, assistant managing editor of the *Cleveland Plain Dealer,* opened the newspaper's files to us.

The *Near* chapter is a condensation of the book *Minnesota Rag* by Fred W.

Friendly. We could list pages of people who helped on that project. However, we would like to mention again the tremendous research of John Guthman, then a law student and now a St. Paul lawyer. We are also indebted to Russell Fridley, director of the Minnesota Historical Society, and Donald B. Shank, vice president of the St. Louis County Historical Society, who were hospitable and indispensable pathfinders during the numerous explorations of Minnesota's lore.

Catherine Roraback and Thomas Emerson, attorneys in the *Griswold* case, patiently explained the history of the *Griswold* litigation. Marian Hepburn Grant spent many hours remembering the history of the birth-control movement in Connecticut and sharing her scrapbooks of material. Dr. Joan Babbott, executive director of the Planned Parenthood League of Connecticut, and Barbara Ryden opened up the files of the League to let us examine the sixty-year history of the birth control movement that preceded *Griswold*. Ron Fiscus, a professor of history at Skidmore College, was instrumental in helping us find Norma McCorvey.

Professor Edward Barrett of the University of California Law School at Davis assisted us with an insightful critique of the *Bakke* chapter.

Norman Contu of the Mexican American Legal Defense and Education Fund pointed us in the right direction in the *Plyler* case. Larry Daves helped us get in touch with the Doe family. Peter Roos, the lawyer who argued the case at the Supreme Court, and Michael McAndrews patiently filled in much of the background material.

John Carroll of the Southern Poverty Law Center provided valuable time explaining the facts behind the John Louis Evans case.

Peter Cotes, an author and an authority on Daniel M'Naghten, Michael McKensie, the court administrator of the Old Bailey, and Norman Swallow of Granada Television were our guides through the history and sites of the *M'Naghten* case.

The research trail for this book winds its way across the country—from the sub-sub basements of the Columbia libraries in New York to Baltimore's docks to a graveyard in St. Martinsville, Louisiana, to Cleveland's police stations to the University of California at Davis's Medical School and beyond. Three former students signed on with us from the early stages of the research through the final drafts—Jack Hitt, Michael Epstein, and Julius Genachowski. Without their tireless bird-dogging, this book might never have been written. Hitt concentrated on "The Myth about the Bay of Pigs", "God and the Classroom" and "Willie Francis." Epstein provided essential research for "A Knock at the Door," "Seventeen Words," "The Sacking of Greytown," and "Give Me Your Tired, Your Poor . . ." Genachowski helped with the Skokie section of "Protecting 'The Thought That We Hate' " and with "Umpiring 'Harmless Empty Shadows.' " Hitt and Epstein also filled in wherever they were needed—whether to dig through ancient legal cites or find an obscure newspaper clip or type revisions or look for photographs.

Four other former students also helped. Michael Rosenblum spent many days going through dusty boxes and records to ferret out details about Barron's wharf and Baltimore harbor at the turn of the nineteenth century. Debbie Miller spent a semester looking into the plight of Haitian refugees and their legal battle with the Immigration Service. Ivan Zimmerman took on the awesome tasking of cite-checking the chapters. Cynthia McFadden, now finishing law school, helped us with the War Powers Act and with understanding immigration problems.

Of course, the engine for *The Constitution: That Delicate Balance* was the series of television programs and the telecourse. Benno Schmidt, Jr., dean of the Columbia Law School and for many years our teaching partner, and Arthur Miller and Charles Nesson, professors at Harvard Law School, have taught us constitutional law for many years. Joining this project as moderators were Tyrone Brown, former counsel of the FCC and now a Washington attorney, and Professor Lewis Kaden of Columbia Law School. The moderators not only taught us and others how to teach; they expanded the limits of seminars to new dimensions of learning and enjoyment. The executive editor of the Media and Society Seminars and the creator of the hypothetical case studies is Stuart Sucherman. His stamp is on every minute of all 13 seminars, which were the guideposts for this book.

Robben Fleming is in very many ways the godfather of our project. It was Dr. Fleming, former chancellor of the University of Michigan and former president of the Corporation for Public Broadcasting, who asked us whether the Media and Society Seminars could be fashioned into a series of television teaching tools on the Constitution. Fleming and Newton Minnow, as consultants to Walter Annenberg, had persuaded the publisher and former ambassador to invest $150,-000,000 over a ten-year period in a series of experiments to use television for higher education. Annenberg's faith in the potential of television as a vital teaching instrument is a continuing challenge to those of us who believe that it can be more than "lights and wires in a box."

Elizabeth McCaughey, a historian who specializes in the Constitution and its origins, accelerated the background research for the book and the course we teach. C.C.N.Y. Professor George McKenna, who wrote the the teaching guide to the series, gave us insight and assistance on many of the issues in the book. Richard Mark, a son and an attorney, and Howard Gutman, a former law clerk of Justice Stewart and now a Washington attorney, painstakingly read over chapters and made valuable suggestions.

Authors in search of historical quarry are dependent on libraries. We are particularly grateful to: Philip Oxley, Janice Greer, Sam Cohen, and Jorene Robbie of the Columbia Law School Library; Wade Dores, Steven Toth, and the staff of the Columbia Journalism School library; Roger Jacobs of the United States Supreme Court Library; Ralph Monico and Carl Christianson of the St John's University Law School Library; Sally Hand, Librarian Assistant at the United States Court House in Foley Square; and Fife Symington, Maryland Historical Society.

Natalie Foster Paine, Fred Friendly's assistant, coordinated the typing and organization of the many drafts of these chapters. As in all projects, she is the person who kept our heads above paper.

We owe a special debt to Bert Lummus of Random House, who believed in this book as much as we did, and to Jennifer Sutherland, project editor on the book, who kept us on target for deadlines, accuracy, and clarity.

Ruth Friendly took a sabbatical from teaching to work on this book. Whether trudging through St. Martinsville, Louisiana, in search of Willie Francis's grave or digging for Dirk DeJonge's story in Oregon or convincing "Jane Roe" that it was important for her to share her personal ordeal, Ruth Friendly lent her grace and vitality to the "little pictures" that shaped these cases. Always at the ready with tape recorder or word processor, she was the balance wheel of our delicate balance.

In all major writing projects, it is the authors' families who deserve the most credit. They put up with the endless hours of work and travel and provided immeasurable moral support. Since this book was written under forced draft, our families were asked to give even more. James and Hadley Cornell and Ruth Friendly lived with us during the writing of this book. They continue to make the difference.

Fred W. Friendly
Martha J. H. Elliott

Index

About the Authors

Fred W. Friendly has spent virtually all his life in journalism: practicing it, shaping it, teaching it, and writing about it. With his partner, Edward R. Murrow, Mr. Friendly was responsible for many of television's most distinguished moments, including *See It Now* and *CBS Reports*. After serving as president of CBS News from 1964 to 1966, Mr. Friendly joined the Ford Foundation and was named the Edward R. Murrow Professor of Journalism at Columbia University. As communications advisor at the Foundation, he was the originating force behind the Media and Society Seminars, which created the television project "The Constitution: That Delicate Balance." Mr. Friendly has written several books, including *Minnesota Rag* and *The Good Guys, the Bad Guys and the First Amendment*.

Martha J. H. Elliott is a television producer, a writer, and an instructor at the Columbia University Graduate School of Journalism. A graduate of Vassar College and Columbia University, Ms. Elliott has worked at NBC News, at WNET, and with Mr. Friendly on many writing and television projects. In addition, she is a wife and mother and lives with her husband James Cornell and daughter Hadley in New Canaan, Connecticut.